32.95

**Underemployed
Ph.D.'s**

Underemployed Ph.D.'s

Lewis C. Solmon
University of California, Los Angeles, and
Higher Education Research Institute, Inc.

Laura Kent
Higher Education Research Institute, Inc.

Nancy L. Ochsner
American Society of Allied Health Professions

Margo-Lea Hurwicz
University of California, Los Angeles

LexingtonBooks
D.C. Heath and Company
Lexington, Massachusetts
Toronto

331.12
U 55

Library of Congress Cataloging in Publication Data

Main entry under title:

Underemployed Ph.D.'s.

  Bibliography: p.
  Includes index.
  1. Underemployment—United States. 2. Doctor of philosophy degree—
United States. 3. College teachers—Supply and demand—United States.
I. Solmon, Lewis C.

HD5709.2.U6U52	331.12'0973	80–8951
ISBN 0–669–04482–2		AACR2

Copyright © 1981 by D.C. Heath and Company

Published simultaneously in Canada

Printed in the United States of America

International Standard Book Number: 0–669–04482–2

Library of Congress Catalog Card Number: 80–8951

Contents

List of Figures

List of Tables

Preface

In *Ph.D.'s and the Academic Labor Market* (1976) Allan M. Cartter established that, for the remainder of the twentieth century, the academy's needs for new junior faculty will fall far short of Ph.D. output. In the years between the end of World War II and 1970, at least half of the Ph.D.'s coming out of the nation's graduate schools found teaching positions in colleges and universities; according to Cartter's estimates, higher-education institutions will be able to absorb only about one in five new doctorate holders during the 1980s. Moreover, as Cartter pointed out, the effects of this academic-job shortage will vary greatly by field. Thus, any predictions about future doctoral job markets will be of little value unless individual disciplines are considered separately. Cartter concluded, "If [my] prognosis is even approximately correct, the 1980s will require the creative talents of many educators, administrators, and public policy-makers to ease the adjustment problems."

Prompted by Cartter's observations, the Higher Education Research Institute (HERI) began a series of studies, under the direction of Lewis C. Solmon, on the job market for doctorate holders in the humanities, the sciences, and engineering. This book represents the culmination of five years of research on the subject. An overview of the problem is presented in chapter 1.

The first thrust was toward the humanities. With generous funding from the Andrew W. Mellon Foundation and a supplementary grant from the Rockefeller Foundation, we surveyed and interviewed humanities graduate students, humanities departments, and doctoral-level humanists employed outside academe. The results were reported in Solmon, Ochsner, and Hurwicz, *Alternative Careers for Humanities Ph.D.'s: Perspectives of Students and Graduates* (1979).

In the course of that study, it became apparent that government agencies of various kinds offer prospects of novel job opportunities to Ph.D.'s, especially those in the humanities. Therefore, under a grant from the National Endowment for the Humanities, we undertook a study of doctorate-level humanists employed in public-sector jobs. The results of this study are reported in part I of this book.

A major purpose of our research effort was to fill information gaps by providing data from surveys conducted by the institute. But description alone is of marginal value unless it is applied to policy formulation. Hence, the senior author, while engaged in this research, reported preliminary results to various audiences in universities, federal agencies, and professional organizations. During these sessions, policy options to mitigate the Ph.D.-oversupply problem were discussed and later were catalogued and evaluated. These policy alternatives, insofar as they apply to the humanities, are summarized in part I, before the empirical findings are presented.

Although the job situation will be most severe for doctorate holders in the humanities who rely almost exclusively on colleges and universities for jobs, Ph.D.'s in the sciences and engineering also face problems. The chances are that many more will be working outside academe than has been the case in the past. This prospect poses both challenges and opportunities, not only to new Ph.D.'s but also to academic science generally.

Therefore, in 1976 the Ford Foundation awarded the Higher Education Research Institute a grant to study the mobility patterns of doctorate holders in science and engineering. The National Science Foundation subsequently provided supplemental funds for the analysis of data on Ph.D.'s working outside academe, particularly those in nontraditional jobs. The results of the studies conducted under those grants are reported in part II of this book.

Since 1980 it has become apparent that policy development with respect to doctoral-level human resources must consider more than simply ways to deal with a surplus. At the instigation of the Carter administration, the National Research Council set up a committee to address the question of whether, in the long run, enough scientists and engineers would be available to meet national needs. Dr. Solmon was asked to define policies that might ensure sufficient numbers of Ph.D.'s to meet unknown future demands and to consider how these policies could be effected during a short run during which a surplus rather than a shortage is evident in many fields. This development made us aware once again of the cyclical nature of the demand–supply interactions in the labor market for Ph.D.'s. Since what is now a surplus could be transformed into a shortage rather quickly, any adjustments to the former situation must ensure that options are preserved in case the latter situation arises.

Chapter 16, in conclusion, discusses how to deal with prospective shortages in the science and engineering labor market. Just as most of the policy options during a period of an excess Ph.D. supply in the humanities (part I) are highly relevant to the sciences, so also the policies for a shortage of scientists and engineers could apply equally to the humanities. Chapter 16 is a modified version of a paper prepared by Dr. Solmon for the National Research Committee on Education in Science and Engineering.

The contributions of the individual authors are as follows. Nancy Ochsner focused on the humanities section (chapters 2–9) and Margo-Lea Hurwicz on the science and engineering section (chapters 10–15). Laura Kent's prose and ideas are reflected throughout the book. Lewis Solmon supervised and is responsible for all the analyses, but particularly for chapters 1 through 4 and 16 and for the policy discussions throughout. Of course, the resulting book reflects the views of the authors alone and not those of any other persons or agencies that provided financial or other support.

In a research program of this magnitude, many individuals and institutions deserve our gratitude. First, the representatives from our funding agencies, who were both knowledgeable about the substance of our studies and sensitive to our research style, include Claire List and Jack Sawyer of the Andrew W. Mellon Foundation; Lydia Bronte of the Rockefeller Foundation; Peter de Janosi, Fred Crossland, and Miriam Chamberlain of the Ford Foundation; Robert Trumble,

Alan Fechter, Joel Barries, and Joe Cangialosi of the National Science Foundation; and Stanley Turesky of the National Endowment for the Humanities.

The Commission on Human Resources of the National Research Council not only supported the preparation of chapter 16 but also provided a number of tabulations and names for one of the HERI surveys. For this help we thank Dr. William C. Kelly and his staff. The data on Ph.D.'s employed in the federal civil service were collected with the help of Robert Penn. In addition, we were able to utilize the membership lists of the Institute for Electrical and Electronic Engineers, the American Psychological Association, and the American Anthropological Association. We are grateful to these groups, as well as to the professional societies of all the other fields studied, for their help.

Addresses for other doctorate-level humanists were provided by William Blackburn, Michigan Department of Civil Service; James Hicks, Colorado Department of Personnel; William Boys, Illinois Department of Personnel; Philip Hamilton, Ohio Department of Administrative Services; William Turney, Washington Department of Personnel; Ronald Becker, Smithsonian Institute; and Mary Lethbridge, Library of Congress. We thank them for their help. We are especially indebted to all those people who took the time to complete the survey questionnaires.

As usual, the staff at the Higher Education Research Institute contributed greatly to this research program. Working on the study at various times were Joanne Gordon, Nancy Mattice, Patricia Nelson, Judith Lawrence, Kevin Hopkins, Molly Landi, Kathleen Harding, Barbara Kommel, and Gerald Rudisin. Barbara Gutek of the University of California at Los Angeles (UCLA) conducted several supplementary analyses. Useful insights and comments were provided by Rita Jacobs of Montclair State College; John Shumaker of the State University of New York, Albany; and William Zumeta of UCLA.

We would like to acknowledge the financial assistance of the Ford Foundation, the National Science Foundation, the National Endowment for the Humanities, the Andrew W. Mellon Foundation, and the Rockefeller Foundation for their support of the work reported in this book. All of these foundations encouraged us to use our professional judgment in conducting this project. Points of view or opinions expressed herein do not, therefore, necessarily represent the views, official positions, or policies of any of the sponsoring agencies.

As indicated earlier, this book owes much to ideas and insights of the late Allan Cartter, who worked with the principal author in the initial research effort until his untimely death in 1976. We dedicate this book to his memory.

1

The Context of the Problem: An Overview of the Ph.D. Labor Market

As we all know from anecdotes about Ph.D.'s driving cabs and tending bar, recent recipients of doctorates are having a hard time finding jobs commensurate with their skills and training. The problem, of course, is that relatively few positions have been opening up in the nation's higher-education institutions, the traditional employers of doctorate-level manpower. Most forecasters anticipate shortages of academic jobs through the 1980s and only moderate, if any, improvements during the 1990s (Bureau of Labor Statistics 1975; Cartter 1976; Dresch 1975; Freeman 1976; National Center for Education Statistics 1977; National Science Foundation 1975). The situation is critical for humanists, who in the past have had virtually no alternatives to academic employment (Solmon, Ochsner, and Hurwicz 1979), but is serious for scientists and engineers as well.

This chapter gives an overview of the labor market, both current and projected, for Ph.D.'s. We look first at the demographic, economic, and sociopolitical factors that have contributed to the shortage of faculty jobs, considering some of the arguments of those who deny that there is a crisis in academe. We then examine trends in the Ph.D. output of the nation's graduate schools, in graduate enrollments, in undergraduate majors, in student quality, and in the employment status of Ph.D. holders; from these trends, conclusions can be drawn about prospects for the coming decades. Next, we discuss current employment patterns of Ph.D.'s, giving particular attention to comparisons between natural scientists, engineers, and social scientists, on the one hand, and humanists on the other. Finally, we address a theme that runs through the book—the question of underemployment.

The Closing University Door

For higher education, the expansionist days of the 1960s are long gone. Rapid enrollment growth (as the products of the post–World War II baby boom reached college age and as larger proportions of high-school graduates continued on to college), along with an upsurge in government-supported research activity in the university (prompted by post-Sputnik fears that the United States was falling behind in the space and arms races), led to the hiring of thousands of young faculty members during the 1960s. Since the mid-1970s, however, the nation's postsecondary institutions have faced the need to retrench or perish. Stabilizing

1

or declining enrollments, coupled with inflated costs, have led to drastic reductions in faculty hiring. This situation is not likely to improve in the near future.

Demand for faculty takes three forms: enrichment demand, replacement demand, and expansion demand. *Enrichment demand* involves the reduction of student/faculty ratios or the upgrading of faculty in terms of their degree attainments. In 1975, the National Science Foundation predicted that enrichment demand would create faculty places for new science and engineering Ph.D.'s. This prediction, however, has not yet come to pass and is unlikely to do so, given the mood of budgetary constraint that characterizes the Reagan administration. As research support and other sources of funding dry up, as faculty salaries rise (however slowly), and as other costs soar with the general rate of inflation, enrichment proposals seem little more than wishful thinking.

Replacement demand—that is, for new faculty members to take the place of those who retire or die—will be minimal, in view of the relative youthfulness of a professoriat hired mostly in the 1960s and early 1970s. Recent laws prohibiting compulsory retirement at age 65, combined with soaring inflation that erodes savings, will exacerbate the problem, causing large numbers of faculty members to stay on past the "normal" age of retirement.

Equally discouraging are the prospects for *expansion demand*. The demographics of the situation are clear and well known: The traditional college-age population is shrinking, and the proportion of high-school graduates who go on to college has probably peaked. Any hope of replacing traditional students with adults or foreigners seems slight. (This possibility is discussed in more detail later on.) If enrollments remain at a constant level, the number of faculty members required will also remain stable. Not only will newly produced Ph.D.'s have difficulty in finding academic jobs, but also junior faculty will have difficulty holding on to their jobs as they are increasingly denied tenure.

Like the patient who, informed by his doctor that he has an incurable disease, at first denies his condition, many people are trying to deny the gravity of the situation in higher education. For instance, Carol Frances, in a recently published and widely publicized monograph entitled *College Enrollment: Testing the Conventional Wisdom Against the Facts* (1980), asserts that the predicted enrollment crisis need never occur. The following is a summary of her arguments and of the main objections to them. Frances maintains that college enrollments can be increased:

> If a larger proportion of the traditional college-age population goes on to college. (But standards for high-school graduation and for college entry are already appallingly low. And, given the declining economic rate of return on a college education, it seems unlikely that a much greater proportion of high-school graduates can be persuaded to attend college.)
>
> If more adults, especially adult women, attend college. (But most adults who have any interest in a college education are probably enrolled. And

adults may also be discouraged by the declining payoff on a college education.

If more foreigners enroll. (But why should foreigners, particularly those interested in the humanities, come to the United States to study? Moreover, many third-world countries are anxious to establish their own science-education capability and may be unwilling to let their citizens pursue higher education in the United States.)

If colleges take over some of the educational functions now performed by industry. (But what if industry does a better job?)

In short, Frances's scenario seems overly optimistic and could even prove harmful insofar as it encourages an ostrich attitude on the part of the nation's higher-education institutions and reduces the market responsiveness of prospective college students.

Because the controversy over the Ph.D. employment crisis is a highly political one, people's motives in asserting that there is, or is not, a crisis may be less than disinterested. Those who argue that a crisis does exist may do so in order to get more funds for postdoctoral fellowships, which serve at least to keep recent Ph.D. recipients out of the job market for a short time. Those who, on the other hand, maintain that no crisis exists may be trying to justify their continued efforts to attract students into their programs so that faculty members will have enough warm bodies to teach. Currently enrolled graduate students, especially those in the humanities, are also inclined to ignore the gravity of the situation. Even though they should realize by now that possession of the degree does not automatically guarantee them a faculty job (Duffey 1978b), many doctoral candidates act as if no problem existed. Told that the chances of getting a college position are only about one in ten, each student is convinced that he or she will be that one. Relatively few seriously consider taking nonacademic jobs; indeed, humanities students tend to regard these jobs as "second rate" (Jacobs 1977; Solmon, Ochsner, and Hurwicz 1979). Compounding the difficulty, they may even be reluctant to take faculty positions in low-status types of institutions.

Some experts, who now maintain that the supply–demand situation will reverse itself in the near future, take quite another view of the crisis. They point out that there are already shortages in computer science and in some engineering specialties. Nonacademic salaries in these fields are so much greater than those paid to professors that many graduates are taking nonacademic jobs before they complete their doctoral work; indeed, some are terminating their studies at the baccalaureate or master's-degree level. Thus, they argue, the United States may not have enough scientists in the coming decades to enable the nation to remain competitive (or to regain superiority) in the international areas of defense and innovative technology, or to solve pressing domestic problems in the areas of energy and the environment. These experts advocate a more-activist federal policy toward science.

The merits of this argument, and some of the issues it raises, are discussed in the last chapter. Suffice it to say at this point that the demographics on the college-age population are indisputable, that the financial constraints are undeniable, and that projections of future demand for more Ph.D.'s are uncertain at best.

Reduced demand for faculty constitutes a problem only if new Ph.D.'s continue to be produced at current (or slightly lower) rates and only if these new Ph.D.'s continue to press for academic jobs. On the latter point, there is no evidence to suggest that new Ph.D.'s are losing their preference for academic jobs. The numbers who want and expect these jobs are still high. For instance, of 1979 Ph.D.'s, over half of those receiving degrees in English and American literature, modern foreign languages, philosophy, history, or mathematics said that they planned to work in an educational institution. The proportions are smaller among physical and natural scientists and engineers, suggesting that doctorate recipients in these fields may be more market responsive. (National Research Council 1980)

Trends in Ph.D. Output

The National Center for Education Statistics (1978) projects that Ph.D. production will continue to grow or will at least remain constant in virtually all fields up to 1985. More specifically, the National Science Foundation (NSF) (1975) estimates that, between 1972 and 1985, the nation's universities will produce 78,000 more science and engineering Ph.D.'s than can be absorbed into faculty jobs; for the same period, the Bureau of Labor Statistics (1975) more pessimistically predicts a surplus of 190,700. Whatever the differences between these predictions, the authorities agree that there are likely to be more Ph.D.'s than faculty openings. The most recent NSF forecast predicts that by 1987 fully 17 percent of the doctoral-level science and engineering labor force will have to take jobs outside science and engineering or remain unemployed (see table 1–1). This proportion is almost double the 1977 figure of 9 percent and exceeds the pre-1977 figure by an even larger amount.

Figures 1–1 through 1–4 show the numbers of Ph.D.'s produced each year between 1967 and 1979 in selected disciplinary areas. In most fields, Ph.D. production in 1979 represented a reduction from the peak level. In the humanities, the greatest declines occurred in English and history; foreign languages and philosophy maintained relatively flat profiles. The general trend in both the social sciences and the earth sciences has been slight growth. The number of doctorates in psychology has increased steadily and rapidly. Ph.D. production in the other physical sciences dropped substantially in the early 1970s, although the last

Table 1-1

Utilization of Full-Time Science/Engineering Doctoral Labor Force, by Field, 1977, 1982, and 1987

(thousands)

Type of Utilization	Total	Physical Sciences	Engineering	Mathematical Sciences	Life Sciences	Social Sciences
			1977			
Labor force	280	70	45	20	71	73
Science/engineering (S/E) utilization	255	63	42	19	67	64
Non-S/E utilization[a]	25	7	3	1	4	9
Non-S/E utilization as percentage of labor force	9	10	6	6	6	13
			1982 Projection			
Labor force	352	83	58	25	88	97
S/E utilization	302	77	51	21	76	79
Non-S/E utilization[a]	50	6	7	4	12	25
Non-S/E utilization as percentage of labor force	14	7	12	16	14	19
			1987 Projection			
Labor force	412	95	72	28	103	113
S/E utilization	342	86	58	22	87	91
Non-S/E utilization[a]	70	9	14	6	16	22
Non-S/E utilization as percentage of labor force	17	9	19	21	16	19

Source: National Science Foundation, *Projections of Science and Engineering Doctorate Supply and Utilization: 1982 and 1987* (Washington, D.C.: U.S. Government Printing Office, 1979).

Note: Details may not add to totals because of rounding.

[a]Includes unemployed.

several years have witnessed a turnaround. In mathematics, however, the number has declined steadily since 1972. Ph.D. production in the life sciences has been fairly stable over the period, although the health fields have been growing more than others.

Table 1-2 shows data by sex on the stock (that is, the existing supply of Ph.D.'s) in 1979 and on Ph.D. production since 1967 in four broad disciplinary areas: humanities, social sciences, natural sciences, and engineering. Despite declines in peak production rates, the proportion of doctorates awarded to women has risen in each of the four areas. Although women accounted for only 29 percent of the 1979 stock in the humanities, they were awarded 30 percent of the new doctorates in the last thirteen years and 37 percent in the most recent four years (1976–1979). In the social sciences, they accounted for 20 percent

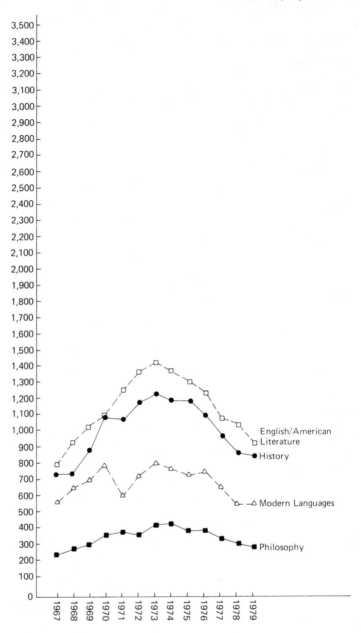

Source: National Research Council, *Summary Report 1967–1979* (separate volumes): *Doctorate Recipients from United States Universities* (Washington, D.C.: National Academy of Sciences, 1968–1980).

Figure 1–1. Number of Ph.D.'s Produced Each Year in Selected Humanities Fields

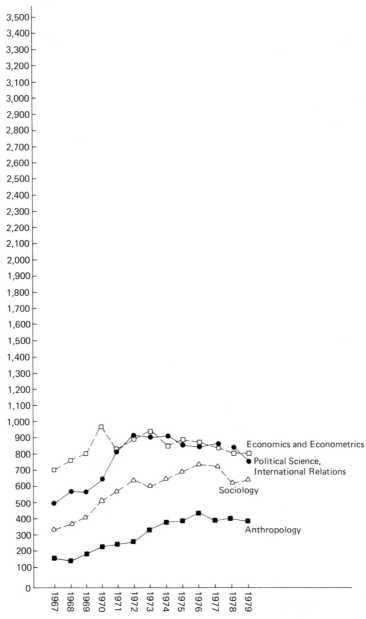

Source: National Research Council, *Summary Report 1967–1979* (separate volumes): *Doctorate Recipients from United States Universities* (Washington, D.C.: National Academy of Sciences, 1968–1980).

Figure 1–2. Number of Ph.D.'s Produced Each Year in Selected Social-Science Fields

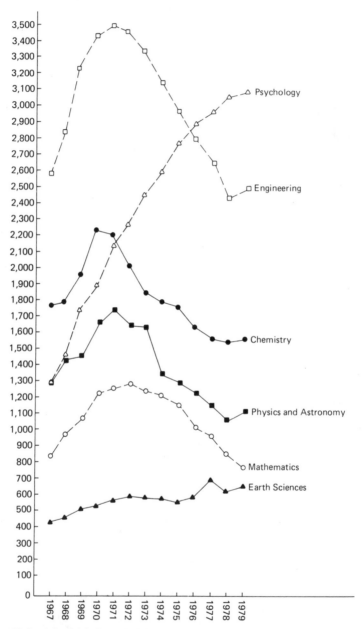

Source: National Research Council, *Summary Report 1967–1979* (separate volumes): *Doctorate Recipients from United States Universities* (Washington, D.C.: National Academy of Sciences, 1968–1980).

Figure 1–3. Number of Ph.D.'s Produced Each Year in Other Selected Science Fields

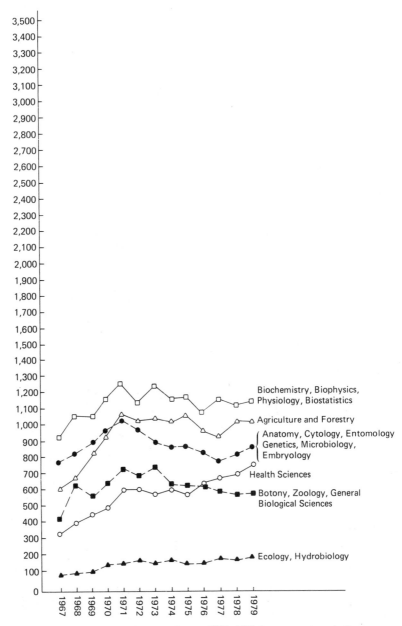

Source: National Research Council, *Summary Report 1967–1979* (separate volumes): *Doctorate Recipients from United States Universities* (Washington, D.C.: National Academy of Sciences, 1968–1980).

Figure 1–4. Number of Ph.D.'s Produced Each Year in Selected Life-Science Fields

Table 1–2
Production of Ph.D.'s, by Field and Sex, 1967–1979

Production of Ph.D.'s	Field and Sex											
	Humanities			Social Sciences			Social Fields			Engineering		
	Men	Women	Percentage of Women	Men	Women	Percentage of Women	Men	Women	Percentage of Women	Men	Women	Percentage of Women
Stock of 1979 and percentage of women overall	40,388	16,512	29	71,210	18,290	20	167,615	18,585	10	48,211	389	1
Ph.D. production												
1979	1,559	1,004	39	4,274	2,105	33	7,688	1,686	18	2,431	63	2
1978	1,666	1,037	38	4,502	1,951	30	7,558	1,522	17	2,370	53	2
1977	1,881	1,116	37	4,674	1,830	28	7,748	1,388	15	2,567	74	3
1976	2,244	1,183	34	4,850	1,733	26	8,040	1,376	15	2,738	53	2
1975	2,329	1,235	35	4,708	1,599	25	8,430	1,352	14	2,909	50	2
1974	2,571	1,160	31	4,724	1,432	23	8,548	1,238	13	3,110	34	1
1973	2,710	1,117	29	4,668	1,234	21	7,981	1,103	12	3,293	45	1
1972	2,626	982	27	4,541	1,049	19	8,208	1,002	11	3,454	21	1
1971	2,529	787	24	4,227	927	18	8,595	950	10	3,481	14	1
1970	2,533	778	23	3,492	727	17	9,273	898	9	3,418	14	0
1969	2,187	697	24	3,055	624	17	8,231	849	9	3,224	10	0
1968	1,999	569	22	2,744	550	17	7,555	738	9	2,822	11	0
1967	1,849	472	20	2,536	442	15	6,783	629	8	2,573	8	0
Total	28,683	12,137	30	52,995	16,212	23	104,638	14,731	12	38,390	450	1
Percentage of women, last 4 years			37			29			16			2

of the stock but for 23 percent of the 1967–1979 doctorates and 29 percent of the 1976–1979 doctorates; in the natural sciences, for 10 percent of the stock, 12 percent of the 1967–1979 doctorates, and 16 percent of the 1976–1979 doctorates. Women remain underrepresented in engineering, accounting for only 1 percent both of the stock and of the 1967–1979 doctorates awarded, and for only 2 percent of the 1976–1979 doctorates.

In the four major humanities fields (English, history, modern languages, and philosophy), the number of Ph.D.'s awarded grew by 65 percent between 1967 and 1973 or 1974, with English/American literature registering the largest increase (78 percent) and modern languages the smallest (42 percent). The overall decrease between 1973 and 1979 was 33 percent, with only slight variations from field to field. Since 1973 was about the time that the academic job crunch first became apparent to large numbers of people, one might argue that graduate students (or prospective graduate students) in the humanities have shown themselves to be somewhat market responsive, and that this bodes well for the future.

Any optimism should, however, be tempered by an awareness of three points. First, Ph.D. production in the four largest humanities fields still exceeds 1967 levels. Second, part of the recent decline in the number of doctoral graduates in the humanities can be attributed to the longer time that many students take to complete their studies. Seeing little immediate chance of getting regular academic faculty positions, some students are choosing to linger at their home institutions, taking whatever part-time (usually low-paying) jobs are available to them, jobs to which they will not have access once they get the doctorate. Others get the degree and then take short-term, non-tenure-track positions while waiting for more-desirable teaching jobs to open up. Thus, within the next few years, delayed degree recipients, along with those new Ph.D.'s who have temporarily settled for less-attractive faculty jobs, will swell the ranks of humanities Ph.D.'s looking for regular positions.

Third, the decrease in the number of new humanities Ph.D.'s between 1973 and 1979 was much greater among men (− 39 percent) than among women (− 7 percent). Greater numbers of women, their expectations raised by the women's movement and by affirmative-action programs, have been entering and graduating from doctoral programs in recent years. The likelihood of their curbing their aspirations is slight. The same holds true for racial and ethnic minority-group members who were previously excluded (not necessarily deliberately) from higher education beyond the baccalaureate. Indeed, women have come close to achieving parity in one leading field, English/American literature, in which they constituted 47 percent of the new doctorate recipients in 1979. In modern languages, women actually outnumber men, constituting 56 percent of the new graduates in 1979. Thus, increases (or only slight declines) in the number of women and of minority students seeking humanities doctorates will more than offset any substantial decline in the number of white men.

In the social sciences, the number of women receiving the Ph.D. degree has risen each year since 1967, whereas the number of men receiving doctorates has declined each year since 1976. Again, it seems that women have not reacted to the tight job market as men have.

In the natural sciences and engineering, women still receive only a small share of the doctorates awarded. That share has been growing, however, as women increasingly resist being "tracked out" of male-dominated fields. Thus, women could constitute an important resource for meeting any future national need for additional scientific and engineering personnel. As long as doctoral training facilities are available, however, it seems likely that any new demands will be met by additional enrollments of men as well as women.

Ph.D. production over the last few years has been too volatile to permit extrapolation. The pipeline effects that we have already described, along with changing preferences for various postbaccalaureate fields and for various oc-cupations, could result in substantially different patterns of Ph.D. production. Except for a few fields like economics, physics, and engineering (where market forces seem to operate), little is known about the extent to which labor-market conditions (both inside and outside academe) influence the individual's decision to seek a doctorate in a particular field. For additional evidence on this point, we must look at recent trends in graduate enrollments and in undergraduate majors.

Trends in Graduate Enrollments

Three problems immediately arise when we try to estimate the number of doc-torate recipients over the next few years from current graduate enrollments. First, not all graduate students receive doctorates; some aim for no more than a master's degree, and others aspire to the doctorate but drop out for various reasons before realizing their goal. Second, the length of time required to complete a doctoral program varies considerably, depending not only on the field (for example, in 1979 the "gestation period" averaged 5.2 years for chemistry and 7.9 years for history) but also on labor-market conditions (in 1967 doctoral students in history took 5.4 years to get the degree, whereas in 1979 they took an average of 7.9 years) (National Research Council 1968 and 1979). Thus, it is difficult to estimate exactly when the current crop of graduate students will actually receive their doctorates.

A third problem has to do with the measure of graduate enrollments to be used. Should one look at total (head-count) enrollments? at total full-time en-rollments? at total first-time enrollments?

We have chosen to consider data provided by the Council of Graduate Schools on total graduate enrollments and on first-time graduate enrollments for the years 1971 to 1979. These data are based on a sample, rather than on a census, of departments, and include part-time students. Hence, they must be interpreted with caution.

Table 1–3 shows that, among the departments surveyed, graduate enrollments in education increased substantially between the 1971–1972 and the 1974–1975 academic years and then declined steadily. In the humanities departments responding to the survey, enrollments grew until 1972–1973 but declined steadily from 1975–1976 on. In the social sciences, graduate enrollments tended to increase throughout the 1970s, despite a small reduction in 1975–1976

Table 1–3
Percentage Change in Total Graduate-School Enrollment, by Broad Disciplinary Area, 1971–1972 through 1978–1979 Academic Year

	Education	Humanities	Social Sciences	Physical Sciences	Engineering	Biological Sciences
1971–1972						
Percentage change	+5.7	+2.8	+3.2	−6.5	−2.0	+4.5
Response rate (%)	(75)	(77)	(80)	(80)	(59)	(80)
1972–1973						
Percentage change	+8.5	+2.8	+2.7	−1.9	No change	+9.3
Response rate (%)	(77)	(81)	(83)	(85)	(65)	(83)
1973–1974						
Percentage change	+6.3	−0.1	+9.0	−1.8	+3.6	+7.1
Response rate (%)	(77)	(82)	(83)	(83)	(64)	(84)
1974–1975						
Percentage change	+3.5	+0.6	+2.5	+1.7	+3.0	+6.1
Response rate (%)	(79)	(82)	(83)	(83)	(68)	(84)
1975–1976						
Percentage change	−5.4	−4.4	−1.8	−0.2	−1.3	+2.7
Response rate (%)	(76)	(77)	(78)	(80)	(69)	(79)
1976–1977						
Percentage change	−2.6	−4.6	+3.0	+0.1	+2.6	+3.7
Response rate (%)	(79)	(80)	(82)	(82)	(71)	(81)
1977–1978						
Percentage change	−4.2	−4.4	+1.4	−1.1	−0.5	−0.7
Response rate (%)	(92)	(94)	(95)	(94)	(84)	(96)
1978–1979						
Percentage change	−5.0	−3.5	+1.9	+1.8	+2.8	+1.7
Response rate (%)	(79)	(81)	(81)	(82)	(73)	(82)

Source: Graduate Record Examination Board, *Report on the Council of Graduate Schools, Graduate Record Examinations Board: Survey of Graduate Enrollment, 1971–1979.*

Note: Tables 1–3 and 1–4 show the percentage changes between the years in question for the discipline areas indicated. Discipline areas, as defined in the original questionnaire, include education (all fields of education); humanities (English and journalism, fine and applied arts, foreign languages and literature, library science, philosophy, and religion); social sciences (anthropology, business, economics, geography, history, political science, and sociology); physical sciences (chemistry, computer sciences, geology, mathematics, physics, and statistics); engineering (all fields of engineering); and biological sciences (agriculture, biology, health professions, home economics, psychology, and zoology).

and a slower growth rate in the years following. The physical sciences experienced losses in the early 1970s, with a slight increase in the 1974–1975 academic year and a mixed pattern since that time. The pattern of enrollments in engineering departments was similarly irregular. The biological sciences grew steadily and substantially until 1977–1978, when they suffered a slight loss in graduate enrollments; the next year witnessed a slight increase.

Judging from these graduate-enrollment trends, then, it appears that education and the humanities will continue to turn out fewer Ph.D.'s in the immediate future than they have in the past; the number of Ph.D.'s produced in the social and biological sciences will probably increase slightly; and Ph.D. output in the physical sciences and engineering will remain relatively stable. Taking these projections in conjunction with undergraduate-enrollment trends (which are discussed in the next section), we may conclude that the current oversupply of faculty in the social sciences will be exacerbated, whereas faculty shortages seem likely in engineering.

First-time graduate enrollments (table 1–4), although they generally reflect

Table 1–4
Percentage Change in First-Time Graduate-School Enrollment, by Broad Disciplinary Area, 1971–1972 through 1978–1979 Academic Year

	Education	Humanities	Social Sciences	Physical Sciences	Engineering	Biological Sciences
1971–1972						
Percentage change	+8.8	+5.7	+4.7	−8.6	—ᵃ	+7.1
Response rate (%)	(56)	(60)	(62)	(62)	—ᵃ	(62)
1972–1973						
Percentage change	+17.8	+2.8	+2.2	+5.5	+6.0	+6.0
Response rate (%)	(63)	(67)	(69)	(69)	(55)	(68)
1973–1974						
Percentage change	+5.8	−2.5	+14.2	+4.1	+12.0	+10.8
Response rate (%)	(63)	(68)	(70)	(69)	(53)	(70)
1974–1975						
Percentage change	+4.1	−2.1	−0.8	+0.3	−1.1	+5.5
Response rate (%)	(66)	(70)	(70)	(71)	(59)	(72)
1975–1976						
Percentage change	−8.8	−2.3	−7.3	−1.9	−4.5	+2.9
Response rate (%)	(64)	(65)	(67)	(68)	(60)	(67)
1976–1977						
Percentage change	−1.8	−2.9	+6.5	+5.2	+2.5	−2.5
Response rate (%)	(67)	(69)	(70)	(70)	(63)	(70)
1977–1978						
Percentage change	−9.8	−7.2	−1.8	−1.2	+2.4	−4.5
Response rate (%)	(77)	(81)	(81)	(81)	(73)	(83)
1978–1979						
Percentage change	−4.6	−2.3	−0.3	−3.8	+1.7	+0.1
Response rate (%)	(67)	(70)	(70)	(71)	(64)	(71)

Note: See notes for table 1–3.

ᵃNot included because effective response rate was lower than 50 percent.

total enrollment figures, are probably more responsive to current market conditions. During the past two years, first-time enrollments in the social sciences have declined, whereas those in engineering have risen. This finding suggests that the major imbalances implied when undergraduate enrollments are compared with total graduate enrollments may be overestimates.

Trends in Undergraduate Majors

Undergraduate enrollments in different major fields determine the maximum possible size of the next generation of practicing humanists, scientists, and engineers and—more important—the demand for faculty to teach in various fields. Table 1–5 gives data on trends in the probable major fields named by first-time, full-time freshmen entering U.S. colleges and universities between 1970 and 1980. (It should be pointed out that these choices are subject to some change; that is, a freshman naming a particular field as his or her major did not necessarily end up majoring in that field.)

Looking first at freshman choices in science (including mathematics) and engineering fields, we find that the proportions saying they will major in mathematics or statistics dropped steadily, from 3.3 percent in 1970 to 0.6 percent in 1980. The proportions naming a probable major in physical sciences peaked in the years 1973–1976 at about 2.7 percent but had declined to 2 percent in 1980. Potential engineering majors constituted 8.6 percent of the 1970 entering freshman class and (after some swings during the decade) 11.8 percent of the 1980 entering class. The biological sciences peaked in popularity at 7 percent in 1973, but then declined to 3.7 percent in 1980, close to their 1970 level of 3.5 percent. The proportions of entering freshman naming agriculture rose from 2 percent in 1970 to a high of 3.9 percent in 1975 but then declined to 2.9 percent in 1980. The proportions naming probable majors in the health-professional fields (non-M.D.) increased from 7.4 percent in 1970 to 10.6 percent in 1972 and then dropped to 7.9 percent in 1980. In short, engineering was considerably more popular, and agriculture and the health professions slightly more popular, in 1980 than in 1970; mathematics and statistics were much less popular in 1980 than in 1970; and the popularity of the physical and biological sciences was about the same.

Turning to freshman choices in the humanities, we find that virtually all fields lost ground during the 1970s. The proportions of entering freshmen naming English as their probable major dropped from 3 percent in 1970 to 0.9 percent in 1980; comparable figures for the arts and humanities were 12.7 percent and 7.4 percent; for history and political science, the figure dropped from 5.4 percent in 1970 to 2.6 percent of the incoming freshmen in 1980.

In converting these data on probable major to total undergraduate enrollments in various fields, several factors must be considered, including field switching and differential college-dropout rates in various fields. Although the rates of

Table 1-5
Probable Major Field, of All Freshmen, by All Institutions, 1970–1979

Major	1970	1971	1972	1973	1974	1975	1976	1977	1978	1979	1980
English	3.0	2.2	1.6	1.5	1.3	1.0	1.0	1.0	1.0	0.9	0.9
Arts, humanities	12.7	12.1	12.4	9.5	9.3	8.3	8.3	7.8	7.3	7.7	7.4
Education	11.6	9.9	7.3	12.2	10.5	9.9	9.3	8.8	8.0	8.4	7.7
History, political science	5.4	4.2	3.9	1.6[a]	3.7	3.5	3.1	3.0	2.8	2.6	2.6
Social sciences	8.9	8.6	7.8	9.9[b]	6.8	6.2	5.6	5.4	5.3	5.5	4.7
Business	16.2	16.4	15.5	17.7	17.9	18.9	20.9	22.2	23.9	24.3	23.9
Mathematics, statistics	3.3	2.7	2.2	1.7	1.4	1.1	1.0	0.8	0.9	0.6	0.6
Physical sciences	2.3	2.0	1.9	2.7	2.6	2.7	2.7	2.3	2.4	2.3	2.0
Engineering	8.6	7.2	6.9	6.6	6.6	7.9	8.5	9.3	10.3	10.6	11.8
Biological sciences	3.5	3.6	3.9	7.0	6.7	6.3	6.2	4.7	4.6	4.0	3.7
Agriculture (including forestry)	2.0	3.2	3.2	2.8	3.8	3.9	3.6	3.6	3.2	3.0	2.9
Health professional (non-M.D.)	7.4	8.8	10.6	10.4	7.5	7.3	6.9	9.1	8.6	7.9	7.9
Other	12.9	16.8	18.2	11.7	17.4	18.0	18.2	17.3	17.1	17.4	19.4
Undecided	2.2	2.3	4.6	4.7	4.5	5.0	4.7	4.7	4.6	4.8	4.7

[a]For 1973 only, history is combined with geography instead of political science.
[b]For 1973 only, social sciences include political science, but not geography.

change in different fields were modified somewhat when these adjustments were made (Solmon 1979), the general patterns were the same. Thus, it is clear that demand for faculty to teach undergraduates will decline in the humanities, the social sciences, and mathematics, whereas demand for business and engineering faculty may increase. It should also be pointed out that the proportions reported here must be applied to a pool of first-time, full-time freshmen that is shrinking each year. It is uncertain whether Ph.D. production will adjust to reflect these changes in undergraduate enrollments, but the trends so far seem to be in the right direction.

Trends in Student Quality

One issue important to policy formulation that has not received sufficient attention is that of changes in the quality (that is, the intelligence and creative potential) of students in different fields. A particular discipline in the sciences or humanities will not necessarily decline in vitality, whatever the overall decrease in the numbers of students enrolling in the discipline, as long as it continues to attract the same share of the nation's best minds as it has attracted in the past. If those who opt out of a particular field (perhaps to pursue careers in business, law, or orthodontics) are the drones rather than the stars, scholarship will not suffer.

Impressionistic information on this question is inconsistent and suspect. In attempting to justify their high acceptance rates or to promote the employability of their graduates, department chairmen may well exaggerate the quality of their students; in trying to garner more funds for graduate and postdoctoral fellowships, they may well emphasize a decline in student quality.

Although highly tentative, data on changes in the proportions of highly able students choosing different major fields provide a more-objective view of the question of quality. Table 1–6 shows how students with A averages in high school were distributed among major fields in 1971 and in 1978; again, the fields represent probable majors indicated by entering freshmen. Given the rampant grade inflation at the high-school level during the 1970s, these figures are more useful than are statistics on the average grade-point averages (GPAs) of students entering different fields in the two years under consideration.

Clearly, the arts and humanities were not attracting as large a share of high-quality students in 1978 (9 percent) as in 1971 (19 percent); chemistry, physics, and the other physical sciences also suffered losses (from 10 percent in 1971 to 6 percent in 1978), as did economics, psychology, and the other social sciences (from 11 percent in 1971 to 8 percent in 1978). The biological sciences were stable, attracting 6 percent of the A students in both years. The fields registering the greatest improvements with respect to student quality were engineering (from 8 percent in 1971 to 14 percent in 1979) and business (from 8 percent in 1971 to 18 percent in 1979).

Although these figures refer to anticipated undergraduate majors, they may

Table 1–6
Percentage of Those with High-School A Averages Entering
Various College Majors, 1971 and 1978

Probable Major Field	Those with an A Average in High School	
	1971	*1978*
English (language and literature)	3	1
History	2	0
Other arts and humanities	14	8
Biological science	6	6
Business	8	18
Engineering	8	14
Education	7	6
Chemistry	2	2
Physics	1	1
Other physical science	7	3
Professional	20	20
Economics	0	1
Psychology	4	2
Other social science	7	5
Other field	10	12

Sources: American Council on Education, Staff of the Office of Research, *The American College Freshman: National Norms for 1971* (Washington, D.C.: American Council on Education, 1971; A.W. Astin, M.R. King, and G.T. Richardson, *The American Freshman: National Norms for Fall 1978* (Los Angeles: American Council on Education and University of California at Los Angeles, 1979).

be taken as indicative of trends in actual majors and in graduate enrollments as well. Those who defect from science at the undergraduate level may be the least-able students—those who cannot handle difficult subject matter—or the most able—those who want to assure themselves of higher incomes by going into business, law, or medicine. Moreover, given grade inflation and shrinkage of the total pool of undergraduates, these proportions probably represent fewer truly bright people in the most recent years. Thus, although the final verdict is not yet in, it seems reasonable to agree with those observers who fear that science (as opposed to engineering) has been losing talent. It seems even more reasonable to agree with those who believe that the quality of humanities students has declined in recent years.

Trends in Employment Status

Just how much difficulty have recent Ph.D.'s experienced in finding jobs? Generally speaking, doctorate holders have very low unemployment rates compared with the population at large. Nonetheless, as table 1–7 shows, the 1979 unemployment rate for all doctorate-level humanists who got their degrees between 1936 and 1978 was 2 percent, more than twice as high as the unemployment

Table 1-7
Employment Status of Ph.D.'s, by Field and Year of Doctorate, 1979
(*percent*)

Field of Ph.D. Degree		Employment Status			Not Employed			
		Employed Full Time	Employed Part Time	Postdoctoral Appointment	Total	Seeking Employment	Not Seeking Employment	Retired
All scientists and engineers	1936–1978 graduates	88.0	3.2	3.1	5.2	0.9	1.1	3.2
	1973–1978 graduates	84.9	2.9	8.7	3.1	1.3	1.7	—a
Chemistry	1936–1978 graduates	87.3	2.8	3.1	6.4	1.0	1.1	4.4
	1973–1978 graduates	81.9	1.6	12.1	3.6	1.4	2.2	0.0
Engineering	1936–1978 graduates	94.4	2.2	0.7	2.4	0.5	0.5	1.4
	1973–1978 graduates	94.7	1.1	1.5	2.3	1.3	1.0	0.0
Psychology	1936–1978 graduates	85.6	6.6	2.1	4.9	1.1	1.6	2.2
	1973–1978 graduates	82.9	7.6	4.7	4.0	1.8	2.2	—a
Social sciences	1936–1978 graduates	89.1	3.4	0.9	5.6	1.1	0.8	3.8
	1973–1978 graduates	92.3	3.1	1.9	2.3	1.4	0.9	—a
All humanities	1936–1978 graduates	81.6	6.8	0.7	10.3	2.0	2.2	6.1
	1973–1978 graduates	81.7	9.4	0.9	7.5	3.7	3.7	0.1
History	1936–1978 graduates	82.3	6.5	0.9	10.0	1.4	1.8	6.8
	1973–1978 graduates	83.4	9.2	0.8	6.4	2.8	3.6	0.0
English/American language and literature	1936–1978 graduates	82.4	6.3	0.4	9.7	1.7	2.7	5.4
	1973–1978 graduates	81.9	8.3	0.4	8.0	3.1	4.9	0.0
Modern language and literature	1936–1978 graduates	79.0	6.4	0.8	13.5	3.1	2.5	7.9
	1973–1978 graduates	80.3	9.0	1.6	9.0	5.7	2.9	0.4

Source: National Research Council, *Science, Engineering, and Humanities Doctorates in the United States: 1979 Profile* (Washington, D.C.: National Academy of Sciences, 1980).
aLess than 0.1 percent

rate for scientists and engineers (0.9 percent). Among more-recent graduates (those who received the doctorate between 1973 and 1978), humanists were almost three times as likely (3.7 percent) as were scientists and engineers (1.3 percent) to be unemployed and seeking jobs. In addition, postdoctoral appointments were more common among recent graduates (especially those in science and engineering)—another reflection of the poor job market. Recent doctorate recipients were also more likely to be neither employed nor retired, but not to be seeking jobs either; this was particularly true for humanities Ph.D.'s. Perhaps these people, discouraged by the poor job market, simply gave up even trying to find work. Doctorate-level humanists, particularly the younger ones, were also more likely than were doctorate-level scientists and engineers to be employed part time rather than full time. The relatively high rates of part-time employment and of withdrawal from the labor force (that is, being unemployed but not seeking work) may also be attributable in part to the relatively large proportion of women in this group.

Perhaps a better measure of the employment problems confronting new Ph.D.'s is the proportion who were still seeking jobs at the time they received the doctorate. Table 1–8 indicates that in 1969 these figures averaged about 16 percent for humanists and about 15 percent for scientists and engineers (with considerable variation by field). In 1979 the figure had risen only slightly among scientists and engineers (to about 16 percent), but about one in three humanists was still looking for a job at the time he or she got the doctorate. These figures seem less startling when one realizes that they translate into fewer than 900 new humanities Ph.D.'s who did not have jobs in 1979. But if each year of a decade produces the same number of unemployed new doctorate holders, if these Ph.D.'s remain unemployed over a period of time, and if equal or greater numbers are *under*employed, then we may be talking about more than 20,000 doctorate-level humanists who are not doing what they were trained to do.

Current Employment Patterns

To what extent are Ph.D.'s from various fields working in nonacademic jobs? To what extent are their jobs related to the disciplines in which they were trained? What exactly do they do in their jobs? Table 1–9, showing the employment patterns of Ph.D.'s working full time in 1977, throws some light on these questions.

Humanists were much more likely than were scientists to be employed in colleges and universities. Only 10 percent of the humanists, compared with 44 percent of the scientists, held nonacademic jobs. On the other hand, scientists were more likely to have jobs related to their doctoral disciplines. Only 6.4 percent worked outside of science, whereas 17 percent of the humanists worked outside of the humanities.

Table 1-8
Employment Status of New Ph.D.'s, by Field, 1979 and 1969

Field of Ph.D. Degree	Percentage Seeking Employment at Time of Receipt of Doctorate (1979)	1979		Percentage Seeking Employment at Time of Receipt of Doctorate (1969)	1969		Average Annual Percentage Change in Unemployment
		Total	Seeking Employment		Total	Seeking Employment	
Foreign language and literature	38.1	704	268	14.3	655	95	16.6
English and American language and literature	33.9	911	309	14.3	935	134	13.7
History	32.2	829	267	10.3	829	85	21.3
Education	25.9	7,370	1,908	19.3	4,650	897	3.4
Psychology	24.1	3,081	741	17.0	1,756	299	4.2
Agricultural science	21.6	1,008	218	18.7	812	152	1.6
Political Science	21.3	766	163	13.4	558	75	5.9
Mathematics	20.6	768	158	17.7	1,065	188	1.6
Engineering	17.2	2,494	429	20.4	3,251	663	−1.6
Economics	14.7	802	118	10.3	706	73	4.3
Medical science	12.0	751	90	12.7	425	54	−0.6
Earth science	11.8	646	76	13.1	503	66	−1.0
Physics and astronomy	11.6	1,108	128	13.1	1,454	191	−1.2
Other bioscience	11.4	2,717	311	13.2	2,337	308	−1.4
Chemistry	9.4	1,567	148	9.5	1,962	187	−1.0

Table 1–9
Full-Time Employment of Ph.D.'s, by Field, Type of Employer, and Primary Work Activity

| | Percentages In Science/Humanities | | | | | |
| | Two- or Four-Year College | | | Other | | |
Field	Teaching/ Research	Adminis- tration	Other	Teaching/ Research	Adminis- tration	Other
All science/ engineering	44.4	5.8	2.4	18.7	14.0	8.3
Mathematics	69.6	5.8	1.9	10.0	4.7	3.2
Physics	44.2	5.4	1.0	26.1	12.9	3.8
Chemistry	29.0	2.9	0.9	31.1	22.3	6.4
Earth science	45.3	4.2	0.8	23.8	14.9	7.6
Engineering	28.1	6.4	0.9	29.4	22.3	8.6
Biological science	56.7	6.7	2.7	15.1	10.3	4.9
Psychology	38.4	5.2	5.3	6.1	11.7	27.4
Social science	59.7	7.0	2.9	6.7	5.9	4.0
All humanities	69.7	5.4	4.3	1.8	0.7	1.2
History	66.2	4.4	4.2	2.4	1.5	2.1
Philosophy	71.7	4.3	4.8			
English/American literature	75.7	4.9	4.6	1.2		0.5
Modern languages	76.9	4.8	3.7	2.6	0.4	0.9

Source: L. C. Solmon, "Ph.D.'s in Nonacademic Careers: Are There Good Jobs?" In *Current Issues in Higher Education: 1979* (Washington, D.C.: American Association for Higher Education, 1979). Reprinted with permission.

These figures varied considerably by field, especially among scientists. For example, about four in five mathematicians and social scientists, but only slightly more than one in three chemists and engineers, worked in colleges and universities. Similarly, 14 percent of the social scientists, but only 3.4 percent of the earth scientists, had jobs unrelated to their scientific discipline. As the table makes clear, there was considerable variation by field in primary work activity as well. However, this discussion will deal chiefly with the differences between the two broad groups of doctorate holders.

Primary work activities have been divided into three categories in this table. Teaching and research are combined into one category, since faculty may have either as their main activity; nonacademic jobs in this category are chiefly in research. The second category is administration; the third, labeled "other," represents a variety of primary work activities.

Teaching/research was the primary work activity of over three-fourths of the humanists but of slightly less than two-thirds of the scientists, who were almost twice as likely as humanists to be administrators (23 percent versus 12 percent). Roughly the same proportions of each group were involved in "other" primary work activities (12 percent of the scientists, 10 percent of the humanists).

| Two- or Four-Year College | | | Percentages Outside Science/Humanities Other | | | | | Part Time |
Teaching/ Research	Adminis- tration	Other	Teaching/ Research	Adminis- tration	Other	Full Time	Part Time	as Percentage of Full Time
1.8	1.6	0.1	0.4	1.5	1.0	251,584	6,366	2.53
1.2	1.6		0.4	0.7	0.9	14,178	237	1.67
1.8	1.4	0.2	0.5	1.3	1.3	22,707	384	1.69
1.2	1.1	0.1	0.6	2.9	1.8	37,488	583	1.56
1.0	0.8			0.9	0.7	8,353	121	1.45
0.9	1.2		0.1	1.6	0.5	40,792	348	.85
0.4	1.3	0.1	0.2	0.9	0.8	41,745	1,140	2.73
1.6	1.7	0.1	0.3	1.4	0.6	28,642	1,789	6.25
5.9	3.3	0.4	0.9	1.9	1.4	37,487	1,082	2.89
5.3	4.0	1.0	1.0	2.0	3.7	51,054	2,785	5.46
4.9	3.8	1.2	1.7	2.4	5.2	13,974	741	3.37
6.8	4.2	0.8	0.7	2.6	4.1	4,233	191	4.51
2.5	4.4	1.0	0.4	1.9	3.0	14,391	730	5.07
2.6	2.3	0.6	0.9	1.1	3.3	8,326	547	6.57

Looking just at those doctorate holders working in colleges and universities, we find that humanists were slightly more likely to be engaged in teaching/ research or "other" primary work activities, whereas scientists were slightly more likely to be administrators. Whatever their primary work activity, scientists more frequently had jobs related to science, whereas humanists more frequently had jobs outside the humanities; this difference, which was particularly marked among academic administrators, may mean that humanists tended to hold higher-level (universitywide) administrative positions.

Differences between the two groups of Ph.D.'s with respect to primary work activity were much more marked in nonacademic employment settings. Close to half of all humanists working outside of colleges and universities, but only one-fifth of the nonacademically employed scientists, were engaged in "other" primary work activities. Scientists were much more likely than humanists to be researchers or administrators. In addition, scientists working outside the academy can more easily find jobs in science: Only 7 percent of the group held jobs outside science. In contrast, only one-third of the nonacademically employed humanists had jobs connected with the humanities.

Two conclusions can be drawn from these data. First, manpower analysts

may be overly optimistic in assuming that scientists and engineers, because of
their long tradition of working in nonacademic employment settings, will en-
counter relatively few problems stemming from the academic job crunch. Although they may have less cause than humanists to be concerned about declining
college enrollments, they nonetheless should be aware that, if federal and other
support for nonacademic science dries up, they too may be in trouble, since they
have little experience with anything other than research, administration, and
related activities in science. Of the more than 250,000 scientists and engineers
working full time in 1977, only 7,300 had nonacademic jobs outside science.

Second, unlike scientists and engineers, humanists have no cushion of traditional nonacademic employment to fall back on when faculty jobs are unavailable; there is no humanist analog to the nonacademic science community.
Nonetheless, one-tenth of doctorate-level humanists who were employed full
time in 1977 (or approximately 5,300 individuals) were working outside academe, over half of them in research or administration. It is impossible to know
from these data whether they held what would generally be regarded as "doctorate-level" jobs.

Table 1–10
Type of Employer, by Year of Doctorate and Broad Disciplinary Area, 1978

		Type of Employer			
Field		Educational Institution	Four-Year College/ University/ Medical School	Two-Year College	Elementary/ Secondary School
All scientists	1936–1978 graduates	54.3	52.2	1.4	0.7
and engineers	1973–1978 graduates	50.8	48.2	1.6	1.1
Chemistry	1936–1978 graduates	34.5	32.2	1.8	0.4
	1973–1978 graduates	25.2	23.8	1.2	0.2
Engineering	1936–1978 graduates	35.6	35.4	0.2	*
	1973–1978 graduates	29.0	28.9	0.1	0.0
Psychology	1936–1978 graduates	51.4	46.3	1.7	3.5
	1973–1978 graduates	48.6	42.3	1.5	4.8
Social sciences	1936–1978 graduates	75.0	72.9	1.5	0.6
	1973–1978 graduates	69.3	66.6	1.7	1.0
All humanities	1936–1978 graduates	86.6	79.6	4.4	2.5
	1973–1978 graduates	82.0	72.9	5.7	3.4
History	1936–1978 graduates	81.4	72.9	5.6	2.9
	1973–1978 graduates	70.7	61.0	5.8	3.9
English/American	1936–1978 graduates	89.0	82.8	4.3	1.9
language and literature	1973–1978 graduates	85.6	76.7	7.1	1.8
Modern language	1936–1978 graduates	90.4	83.8	2.9	3.7
and literature	1973–1978 graduates	88.2	79.3	4.0	5.0

[a]Less than 0.1 percent

Underemployment

We now come to a fundamental set of questions that will be addressed in the remainder of this book: What constitutes underemployment for a doctorate holder? Is the Ph.D. who is engaging in work activities for which he or she is not trained necessarily underemployed? Is the Ph.D. who is not using the skills that he or she learned in graduate school necessarily underemployed? Does taking a nontraditional job necessarily mean being underemployed?

If we allow that a person with a doctorate in English who is teaching grammar to eleven-year-olds has an appropriate job, can we argue that his former classmate who holds part-time, non-tenure-track positions in three different colleges is underemployed? Is a doctorate holder who works in industry and earns three times the salary he would make as a professor to be considered underemployed because he neither teaches nor does research?

Tradition influences our view of "appropriate" work. As table 1–10 shows, in 1978 close to four in five of all doctorate-level humanists, compared with 52 percent of all scientists and engineers, worked in four-year colleges and uni-

				Type of Employer			

Business/ Industry	Government	Hospital/ Clinic	Nonprofit Organization	Museum/ Historical Society	Research Library, Archives	Other	No Report
27.6	10.5	3.0	3.3			0.9	0.5
28.0	11.7	4.4	3.9			1.0	0.2
54.9	6.2	1.1	2.6			0.2	0.5
65.2	5.3	1.3	3.0			0.1	0.0
50.3	9.4	0.1	3.8			0.5	0.3
57.8	8.9	*	3.6			0.4	0.4
18.7	6.0	15.6	4.0			0.6	0.7
15.4	10.0	20.8	4.3			0.5	0.3
8.0	10.1	0.2	4.2			2.1	0.5
8.6	13.9	0.3	5.5			2.4	0.1
5.6	2.6		3.4	0.5	0.3	0.2	0.9
8.6	3.8		3.4	0.8	0.4	0.1	0.9
4.7	5.3		5.2	1.1	1.1	0.1	1.0
11.2	8.8		4.7	2.3	1.3	0.4	0.5
7.4	1.8		1.1	0.0	—a	—a	0.8
10.0	2.5		0.8	0.0	0.0	—a	1.1
4.5	1.4		2.2	0.1	0.1	0.1	1.2
6.8	2.0		2.0	0.1	0.1	0.0	0.7

versities. The proportions of 1973–1978 doctorate recipients so employed were smaller, however; 73 percent of humanists and 48 percent of scientists. To some observers, including the National Research Council (1980), these figures—along with the greater proportion of recent humanities Ph.D.'s working part time— are cause for concern that doctorate-level humanists are underemployed. But surely the fact that larger proportions of recent humanities Ph.D.'s are working in business, government, and the nonprofit sector can be interpreted positively as well as negatively—as a sign that new job options are opening up for humanists.

Table 1–11 gives a more detailed view of the primary work activities of Ph.D.'s employed in 1978. Close to two-thirds of the humanists, compared with about three in ten scientists and engineers, reported that their primary work activity was the traditional one: teaching. Most of the remainder were engaged in other acceptable work activities: management/administration (13.2 percent of all humanists), writing/editing (5.4 percent), research (4.7 percent), consulting (2.6 percent), the performing arts (1.1 percent), and curatorial work (0.7 percent). Only 3.6 percent of all doctoral-level humanists, and 5.7 percent of those re-

Table 1–11
Primary Work Activity of Ph.D.'s, by Year of Doctorate and Broad Disciplinary Area, 1978

		Primary Work Activity		
		Management/Administration		
			Consulting/ Professional	
Field		Teaching	Services	Total
All scientists and engineers	1936–1978 graduates	29.9	8.4	23.8
	1973–1978 graduates	28.7	11.1	17.8
Chemistry	1936–1978 graduates	20.6	2.9	32.0
	1973–1978 graduates	15.7	1.3	23.9
Engineering	1936–1978 graduates	19.6	6.0	31.9
	1973–1978 graduates	13.2	7.6	23.1
Psychology	1936–1978 graduates	27.1	36.0	19.0
	1973–1978 graduates	24.9	41.5	15.4
Social science	1936–1978 graduates	52.1	4.0	19.6
	1973–1978 graduates	51.6	5.4	15.8
All humanities	1936–1978 graduates	65.1	2.6	13.2
	1973–1978 graduates	65.8	2.7	10.4
History	1936–1978 graduates	57.8	2.5	15.1
	1973–1978 graduates	50.9	4.9	14.9
English/American language and literature	1936–1978 graduates	71.3	2.2	11.9
	1973–1978 graduates	74.5	1.9	7.1
Modern language and literature	1936–1978 graduates	68.6	2.1	10.1
	1973–1978 graduates	71.8	1.1	9.5

[a]Less than 0.1 percent.

ceiving doctorates between 1973 and 1978 were engaged in activities other than those just specified. In addition, 1973–1978 humanities graduates were more likely to be performing artists and curators and less likely to be administrators and researchers than were all humanities graduates.

According to the National Research Council (1980), almost half of the doctorate-level humanists who work at nonacademic jobs that are unrelated to their fields (and close to 70 percent of the recent graduates so employed) say they took their current jobs because no position in their field was available. But even though these people may be disappointed that they could not find more closely related jobs, it does not follow that their skills are being underutilized.

Conclusion

In this chapter we have tried to give an overview of the current and prospective labor market for doctorate holders, with special attention to differences in the situations of—and the outlook for—scientists (including natural and social scientists and engineers) and humanists. Some of the evidence suggests that market

| | | | | Primary Work Activity | | | | |
| | | | | Management/Administration | | | | |
of Research and Development	of Educational Programs	of Other Activities	Writing/ Editing	Marketing Production/ Inspection	Curatorial	Performing Arts	Other	No Report
14.3	5.7	3.8	1.7	2.3			1.9	1.3
11.3	3.4	3.1	1.7	2.2			1.8	0.9
25.6	3.0	3.4	1.3	4.5			2.1	1.2
21.1	1.3	1.4	0.4	3.8			1.4	1.5
23.2	4.7	4.0	0.8	3.5			1.8	0.8
20.1	1.3	1.7	0.9	3.0			0.5	—a
5.5	6.9	6.5	1.6	0.6			1.0	1.3
3.6	5.1	6.7	0.9	0.7			1.0	1.2
6.1	9.5	4.0	3.3	1.1			3.0	1.7
6.4	5.8	3.6	3.4	1.9			3.4	1.4
			5.4		0.7	1.1	3.6	3.7
			5.3		1.3	1.9	5.7	2.6
			6.8		0.8	0.0	4.2	4.5
			6.8		1.9	0.0	8.4	2.3
			7.6		0.7	0.2	2.5	1.8
			7.3		1.4	0.7	4.4	1.8
			3.2		0.4	0.1	4.2	5.6
			3.4		0.7	0.0	5.3	4.0

adjustments are occurring—that is, that reduced academic demand has led to decreases in Ph.D. production and in graduate enrollments. Nonetheless, it is clear that new thinking is needed if oversupplies in some fields and shortages in others are to be avoided.

The nation faces a situation in which one-third of new humanities Ph.D.'s have not found jobs by the time they graduate, in which up to 15 percent of those with doctorates in science and engineering take jobs outside their field, in which the preferences of college freshmen for different fields vary erratically from year to year, and in which a substantial proportion of doctoral students—especially those in the humanities—still hope for and expect to get faculty jobs.

Of the various strategies that have been proposed for coping with the academic-job crisis (strategies that will be discussed in chapters 3 and 4), the only one that is not just a short-run expedient or that does not create more problems than it solves is the proposal to channel new Ph.D.'s into nonacademic jobs. As a first step in operationalizing this proposal, the other employment sectors—namely, government and the private sector—must be investigated for the purpose of identifying jobs that will prove satisfying to doctorate holders. Next, new Ph.D.'s must be encouraged to explore career options that, for many of them, will constitute nontraditional employment.

Education policymakers and planners must make the effort to convince new Ph.D.'s that good jobs exist outside academe. Otherwise, doctorate holders may be forced to take tedious, make-work jobs that give them little scope for exercising their talents and training. The inevitable result will be disillusionment and disaffection for these highly educated individuals and a waste of valuable resources for the nation.

Can the nonacademic sectors provide enough challenging and rewarding jobs to absorb an oversupply of Ph.D.'s? The answer to this question depends, among other things, on the general strength of the economy, the magnitude of government and private support for research and development, and the priority given to various issues confronting the United States. The available data can guide us only so far. Significant changes in federal policy, the international situation, and the public mood could alter the picture suddenly and drastically. Therefore, we must look at what actually is rather than what might be. Our hope is that, by identifying doctorate holders who are now productively employed outside of academe, we can encourage others to follow them.

Part I
Humanities Ph.D.'s
in the Public Sector

2

Questions of Definition and Value

College teaching has been the traditional career of humanities Ph.D's. As table 1–9 indicated, only 10 percent of all full-time-employed doctorate-level humanists in 1977 had nonacademic jobs; and of those who had academic jobs, only about 16 percent were administrators or were engaged in "other" primary work activities in colleges and universities. The vast majority were teachers/researchers.

But with the humanities claiming a decreasing share of shrinking undergraduate enrollments, and with all the other constraints on new-faculty hiring, faculty jobs for doctorate-level humanists will certainly become much scarcer in the years ahead. And even though Ph.D. output and graduate enrollments in the humanities have declined, the supply of humanities Ph.D.'s will nevertheless continue to exceed the demand in academe. Therefore, possible solutions to this oversupply must be explored and evaluated.

Before we turn our attention to the proposed solutions and present findings from our study of the nature of jobs in the public sector that might constitute viable career options for humanities Ph.D.'s, it seems appropriate for us to consider just what is meant by "the humanities" and what value they have. Certain problems of definition exist; and, according to Topf (1975), "nothing more directly reflects the crisis in the humanities than that the very attempt to define them is lost in abstractions, all of which sound equally plausible and equally grand." Traditionally, the humanities have been defined either in terms of their content or in terms of their method.

In establishing the National Foundation for the Arts and the Humanities through Public Law 89–209, the U.S. Congress defined the humanities as "language, both modern and classic; linguistics; literature; history; jurisprudence; philosophy; archeology; the history, criticism, theory, and practice of the arts; and those aspects of the social sciences which have humanistic content and employ humanistic methods." Levi (1970) criticizes this content approach in favor of distinguishing between the method of the humanities and the method of the sciences. The ultimate difference between the scientific and the humanistic treatment, according to Levi, is "the difference between the qualitative and the quantitative, the factual and the evaluative, the impartial and the objective on the one hand against the purposive and the dramatic on the other" (p. 43). The humanities study the works of man, whereas science studies nature.

Both approaches have their difficulties, especially when we look closely at specific fields. For instance, the National Foundation for the Arts and the Humanities includes linguistics among the humanities. Yet the study of linguistics ranges from the extreme of acoustical phonetics to that of literary poetics. The former deals with the "physics" of language—phonation, airstream processes, vowel formats, and so forth (Ladefoged 1971), whereas the latter deals with metrics, stylistics, and "aesthetics." Unquestionably, the structural and descriptive linguists use the scientific method in their work. Going back to Levi's distinction between studying nature and studying the works of man, to what extent is language biologically determined (see, for instance, Chomsky 1965) and to what extent is it the product of human beings? We know that language changes over time according to certain "laws" that are as systematic as the laws underlying biological evolution. Should language studies be regarded as humanistic only if they focus on the language of creative literary works? Where do studies of "ordinary language"—such as Wittgenstein (1958) carried out in his later work—fit into this scheme?

Similarly, anthropology would seem to have both scientific and humanistic elements. The National Endowment for the Humanities lists anthropology as a humanistic field; but its parent agency, the National Foundation for the Arts and the Humanities, does not. The field of history is subject to the same ambiguities. On some campuses, it is housed, both physically and conceptually, within the humanities; on others, it is part of the domain of the social sciences.

But perhaps the difficulty lies not so much with the humanities themselves as with our need to categorize, compartmentalize, and label and with our tendency to think in dichotomies. Perhaps we should think instead of a continuum, with the humanities at one end, the "hard" sciences at the other, and the social sciences somewhere in the middle. Indeed, we might do well to remember that not too many years have passed since psychology was regarded as a subdivision of philosophy. Nor should we reject the notion of a humanistic method simply because it does not follow the same rules (for example, the requirement of replicability) as the scientific method.

If it is difficult to define the humanities, how much more difficult it is to specify their value. Just how "useful" are the humanities, and in what ways? How important is it that they be "useful"? There are two schools of thought on these matters, one of which can be labeled *elitist,* the other, *utilitarian.*

According to the elitist view, best represented by Robert Maynard Hutchins (1936), and Thorstein Veblen (1918), the value of the humanities is intrinsic. They do not, and should not, serve any utilitarian purpose. Rather, they should be studied for their own sake. They require no further justification. Historically, only the aristocratic few have had the leisure to pursue humanistic studies. Of course, the technological advances wrought by science have changed this situation considerably, so that people at all socioeconomic levels find themselves with more leisure time on their hands. One could argue that, at this moment in history, humanistic study might prove itself useful by giving people something to do with their leisure time. But the more dedicated of the elitists might reject this argument on the grounds of its utilitarianism. In any event, the elitist view is a politically loaded one. Why should a democratic society value the humanities if they impart no practical good to all its citizens but instead serve the pleasure of the few? Indeed, as Levi (1970) explains, the fact that aristocracy is at the heart of the humanistic tradition presents an unconscious stumbling block to its acceptance in a democracy.

Those who take the utilitarian view believe that the humanities are "relevant" and that they serve a "function," but descriptions of this function range all the way from vague generalizations that humanistic studies help to develop the "whole person" or the "ideal citizen" to assertions that fairly specific skills and abilities derive from humanistic studies. To take an example of the former, Reagor (1978) states that, whatever the specific content, the goal of the humanities is to "put people in touch with the essentials of human life, to create a consciousness of the importance of values, and to nurture and train those aspects of being and personality that are our highest attributes: reason, imagination, and the ability to communicate." Such statements are impossible either to prove or to refute.

Most humanists would agree that value or value experience is the "unifying principle of the humanities, or, at the very least, that the humanities 'have to do with values' " (Levi 1970, p. 34). This value function is often used to justify the requirement that business and science students take courses in the humanities. Mayhew and Ford (1974) state that "the professional fields have finally begun to realize the contributions that the humanities long claimed they could make to the attitudes, values, ethics, and indeed the humaneness of professional people" (p. 31). Without the humanities, they further contend, engineering and the other professions become sterile and lose their relevance to society. Exposure to the humanities gives medical students "enlivened consciences," "increased responsiveness," and a "quickened ethical sense" (p. 47).

Some of the other claims that have been made regarding the utilitarian value of the humanities are as follows:

The humanities spur the development of the student's "analytical ability," "balanced judgment," "vigor of mind and imagination," and "understanding of men and social forces conditioning the time" (Mayhew and Ford 1974, p. 47).

The humanities, especially at the graduate level, foster the "ability to think clearly and to weigh and appraise everything" (Congressman Gerald Ford, as quoted in Levi 1970).

The humanities promote "sensitivity to uses of language and the ability to organize and write a piece of prose" (Sullivan 1977, p. 27); critical thinking, research skills, and writing ability (Solmon, Ochsner, and Hurwicz 1979);

and "the ability to analyze and then make coherent reports of such analysis" (Jacobs 1977, p. 21).

The humanities enable students to make better use of their leisure time (Scally 1976).

According to Joseph Duffey (1978a), chairman of the National Endowment for the Humanities (NEH), the humanities "secure the essential understanding of both the past and the present without which we are ill-equipped to face the future" (p. 90). The task for the NEH, then, is "to encourage those activities which promote learning in areas related to understanding our heritage as a people so that we can better realize our potential as men and women and our purpose as a nation" (Duffey 1978a, p. 91). Once again, it is hard either to prove or to refute such a statement, although that difficulty does not necessarily invalidate the statement. Generalizations about the overall purposes and goals of the sciences are equally subject to vagueness and grandiosity.

Nonetheless, whereas the public is willing to take for granted the value and usefulness of the sciences and the professions, the humanities receive no such widespread public acceptance. In a time of crisis marked by declining enrollments, reduced resources, and failing public support, the dilemma of humanists is to sell a group of disciplines that they previously insisted needed neither defense nor justification, and, moreover, to sell an aristocratic ideal to a democratic audience. Faced with this dilemma, humanists have responded in one of two ways. Some have retreated to the ivory tower, taking the attitude that any change in the humanities to accommodate the needs and demands of society represents prostitution, dilution, and compromise. Others have advanced to the barricades, proclaiming the utilitarian value of the humanities, cataloging their benefits, and specifying how humanistic training can be useful to the general (nonacademic) society.

It is not our purpose in this book to resolve questions about the value of the humanities or to come up with a comprehensive definition. Rather, we want simply to delineate some of the issues and to emphasize the need for clear, specific, and workable terms. Lacking a definition, we take the expedient approach of accepting the NEH definition of the humanities.

3 Some Proposed Solutions to the Humanities Crisis

Numerous solutions to the humanities-job crisis have been proposed. In this chapter, we will consider some of these solutions in terms of their costs, their relative practicality, their potential impact on individual freedom and choice, the possible danger they may pose of wasting talent and other resources, and the effects of short-run market disequilibrium. Ultimately, however, any policy decision will be based more on political than on economic considerations.

The proposed solutions have been divided into five categories, four of which are covered in this chapter: balancing demand and supply, financing new academic jobs, stimulating new demand for humanities courses, reorganizing academe to create new jobs, and expanding the nonacademic market for humanists. Proposals in this last category are discussed in chapter 4.

Balancing Demand and Supply

The proposed solutions in this category involved reducing (or redistributing) the supply of humanities, Ph.D.'s by means of either coercion or persuasion. An inherent problem with most of these solutions is that they also involve decreases in the numbers of undergraduate or graduate students, leaving current faculty with fewer students to teach and making the academic-job market even tighter for new Ph.D.'s.

Reduce the Supply of Graduates in Low-Demand Fields

An obvious solution—to halt or slow down the production of Ph.D.'s in low-demand fields (proposed by Breneman 1977; Jacobs 1977; Woodruff 1977)— would probably create more problems than it would alleviate. For one thing, manpower forecasting is notoriously risky. Even in the short run, labor-market predictions are often inaccurate. Ph.D. production requires four to ten years, depending on the field, with doctoral candidates in the humanities averaging more years than most. Thus, it is unlikely that the supply-and-demand balance could be fine tuned enough to ensure a balance some eight to ten years in the future.

Even if low-demand fields were identified, what mechanism could be used to reduce Ph.D. production? Enrollments would have to be limited by some national organization or collusion of universities. As with most collusion models, however, it is in the interest of most participants to violate the agreement. Institutions keeping the agreement would find that their tenured faculty lacked the students they need. Institutions violating the agreement would be able to promise their graduates less competition for existing jobs.

Even if universities abided by some agreement to reduce enrollments, the question of whom to admit and whom to exclude would remain. What criteria should be used? Reliance on grades, test scores, and ability to pay would represent a giant step backward from any progress toward affirmative-action goals made in the last decade. Many late bloomers would never be given a chance to prove themselves. Perhaps even more to the point, if students—presumably aware of the dismal academic job prospects—still choose to enroll, who has the right to deprive them of their freedom to do so?

Other suggestions for reducing doctoral-level enrollments are to cut low-quality programs (Breneman 1977; Carnegie Commission on Higher Education 1973); to block the establishment of new programs (Carnegie Commission 1973); to replace U.S.-resident degree candidates with foreign students (Hope 1977); and to limit first-year financial aid.

The first of these suggestions—eliminating low-quality programs—immediately raises the question of how to determine quality. Although the strategy of ranking all programs nationwide on the basis of quality (however defined) and closing down the ones at the bottom may appeal to faculty in elite institutions, it would work unnecessary hardship on many people. Not all graduate students can pick and choose among the nation's top institutions. They may be tied to a particular locale by their own or their spouses' jobs. Low-prestige departments may nonetheless effectively serve state or local needs, offering students (including those who attend for enjoyment or for career advancement) opportunities they would otherwise not have. We believe, therefore, that no national program of departmental "genocide" can be justified.

In those states (for example, New York, Florida, and Louisiana) that have already taken the approach of closing down certain programs altogether, it is usually the public rather than the private institutions that have been affected. This solution is not always desirable, particularly for those prospective students who cannot afford the tuition at private schools. Perhaps programs at nearby institutions should be combined, or only one of two neighboring programs be shut down.

Blocking the establishment of new doctoral programs, especially in low-demand fields, is a much easier approach, except that manpower forecasting is not sufficiently refined to guarantee that the "cobwebs" can be eliminated (Freeman 1971). By the time graduates of the so-called high-demand fields enter the labor market, they may no longer be in demand; conversely, we may face a shortage of "low-demand" Ph.D.'s a few years down the line.

Replacing prospective U.S. students with foreign students would keep tenured faculty employed and the production of U.S. Ph.D.'s at a minimum. Once again, however, the problem of inaccurate manpower forecasting arises, unless we propose to hire the foreign Ph.D.'s when an unexpected shortage occurs. And would foreign students, especially those whose command of English is limited, really be interested in studying the humanities rather than science or the professions? Would foreign governments subsidize study in these areas?

As for the last suggestion, reducing financial aid would probably have little effect on potential graduate students in the humanities because they receive comparatively little such aid in the first place.

Increase Tracking at Lower Educational Levels

If, starting in junior high school, the educational system took steps to discourage young people's interest in oversubscribed fields—either by restricting what is taught or by instilling different values (for example, giving new prestige to manual labor), the numbers seeking to enter college and, later, graduate school might be reduced, thereby obviating the need to limit graduate-school entry.

One problem with this approach is that it might inordinately affect minority youth, youth from low-status socioeconomic backgrounds, and late bloomers, depriving them of the opportunity or the motivation to attend college. Second, by the time the first wave of junior-high-school students affected by such a policy was ready for college or graduate school, the manpower situation might have changed, with serious shortages as a result. Third, junior-high- and high-school teachers would probably be unwilling to comply with such a policy. Fourth, humanities programs have relatively few entrance requirements, making it difficult to alter the precollege curriculum in ways that would disqualify students from entry. Such is not the case with the sciences, where earlier deficiencies in mathematics or basic-science courses are difficult to make up. Finally, the fewer students in college or graduate school, the fewer faculty needed and the fewer positions opening up for new Ph.D.'s.

Let the Market Work through Salary Adjustments

In a market economy, the ultimate reflection of an oversupply of labor is reduced salary. When manpower is in short supply, salaries rise; when there is a surplus of manpower, they fall. College and graduate-school enrollment patterns may eventually respond to such changes. Moreover, if academic salaries are low relative to salaries in government or the private sector, faculty in some fields may be encouraged to leave academe, although humanities faculty seem to be less market responsive than their counterparts in business and engineering.

Moreover, it is precisely in the academic sector that salary differentials are least likely to be implemented. Developing separate salary schedules for faculty of the same rank in different fields is difficult. Although new faculty can be started at different salary levels, and accelerated salary advancement can be arranged, rarely can existing salaries be reduced to reflect a softening of the job market. Threatened with such reductions, humanities faculty can band together with other faculty members to advocate unionization, less attention to merit, standardized pay scales, and so on.

Currently, in periods of rapid inflation, real purchasing power can be reduced if discretionary raises are limited or eliminated. Many colleges, however, provide automatic cost-of-living adjustments for all faculty, an arrangement that could not easily be changed.

Finally, any reduction in the real salaries of humanities faculty that might be achieved would be effective only if humanists are sensitive to salary and only if they are offered higher salaries outside of academe.

Provide Better Information to Students

Most observers agree that faculty members should help their graduate students not only to look more honestly at themselves and their abilities but also to learn about the job market, if not to find academic or nonacademic jobs (Haberly 1977). Apparently, however, many humanities faculty feel no such responsibility. An American Council on Education survey of faculty indicated that fewer than 30 percent of humanities faculty believe that preparation for employment is an important goal in teaching (Bayer 1973; Solmon, Ochsner, and Hurwicz 1979). Therefore, it is unlikely that faculty will do much to help their students learn about or find jobs.

Many people wonder why, with academic-job prospects so dismal, such a large number of graduate students continue to enroll in humanities programs. Simple ignorance seems an unlikely explanation. Since the early 1970s, professional societies in the humanities have encouraged departments to warn prospective students that they will probably have little chance of getting academic jobs; and most students are probably aware of the shortage of teaching and administrative positions in four-year colleges and universities.

But students lack information in two important areas. First, they know little or nothing about nonacademic employment. They stereotype jobs in government or the private sector as second rate, exploitative, and unchallenging; and they assume that nonacademic employers will look with disfavor on their job applications. Second, they have little sense of their own relative capabilities, tending to have unrealistically high opinions both of themselves and of the quality of their graduate programs (Solmon, Ochsner, and Hurwicz 1979).

Hence, not only must better information be made available to humanities students, but they also must be convinced to act on it rather than to assume that unemployment will always be someone else's problem. If students are fully informed and still choose to enroll in the humanities, they do so at their own risk; but it is unconscionable to lure or keep students with erroneous or incomplete data.

The primary information source for most students is graduate faculty, most of whom know little, if anything, about jobs outside academe and who, moreover, may be reluctant to provide information that will accelerate the decline in enrollments. A minimum class size is needed if faculty are to continue teaching their cherished seminars and to avoid teaching undesirable lower-level courses now handled by graduate teaching assistants, who would be in short supply if enrollments dropped.

Job information should be as accurate as possible and should be presented persuasively, with easy-to-understand statistics being used as necessary. The credibility of job information also depends on its source. It is one thing to read about the academic-job crunch in *Newsweek* and quite another to hear about it from one's faculty adviser. Convincing the faculty to inform their students is an essential aspect of this particular proposed solution.

Of course, if it is true that many faculty members believe that future job opportunities should not be a factor in a prospective student's decision to enroll in a humanities program, and if students accept the view that the humanities should be studied for their own sake rather than to develop salable skills, then no amount of job information will deflect potential students from enrolling in graduate humanities programs.

Encourage Geographic Mobility

Many people say that the academic-job crisis could be alleviated in part if new Ph.D.'s were given better information about low-demand geographical areas where faculty are needed and if they were encouraged to relocate there (by, for example, the guarantee that their moving expenses would be paid).

Aside from the all-too-pertinent question of whether such areas exist, this solution overlooks the self-imposed immobility that characterizes many Ph.D.'s. For instance, geographical preferences (including those related to climate) are often strong factors in job choice. Thus, such inducements as moving subsidies might have no effect. In any case, many institutions could not afford to pay such subsidies.

The same strictures apply to the suggestion that Ph.D.'s be encouraged to look abroad for academic jobs. Compounding the difficulty, anti–U.S. feeling runs high in some foreign countries; language could constitute a considerable barrier; and foreign universities may not welcome humanities faculty with the same enthusiasm they accord to science and engineering or professional faculty.

Develop Substitutes for Education for Upward Mobility

In a surplus job market, most of the market-response solutions involve reducing the supply of Ph.D.'s. An alternative is to reduce the desire for higher education, which would in turn reduce college enrollment, the number of college graduates, and eventually the supply of Ph.D.'s. Of course, the fallacy here is the usual one: If there were fewer students to teach, job openings for new Ph.D.'s would become even scarcer.

Because higher education has always been the best vehicle for upward social and economic mobility in this nation, more and more people have sought college and graduate training in order to improve their status. Some argue, however, that the income advantages of attending college have now diminished to the point where a college education no longer serves such a purpose (Freeman 1976).

Although some potential students may be influenced by this argument, it is difficult to identify alternative routes to improved wealth and status. Perhaps the prestige of manual labor could be upgraded. However, many craft industries, such as the construction trades, still impose entry limitations.

Most other systems for attaining status are inimical to a democracy. For example, no one would advocate a caste system or a family-background system for inferring status or wealth. The only other alternative is to eliminate status altogether. This might be possible in a perfectly egalitarian system, but even supposedly classless societies (including socialist and communist systems) have developed status hierarchies. Since open access to higher education still seems the best hope for upward mobility in this country, many students will continue to attend college and to seek advanced degrees.

Financing New Academic Positions

The proposed solutions discussed in this section all involve the direct input of new financial resources into humanities departments. Although many of the policies discussed in other sections also carry real costs, the proposals covered here make more explicit the requirement for new money.

Establish more Postdoctoral Fellowships and Related
Programs for Ph.D.'s

Many programs of postdoctoral fellowships or fixed-term assistant professorships for recent humanities Ph.D.'s already exist. For instance, the Mellon Foundation has set up such a program. Three-year postdoctoral awards to candidates who have had their degrees no longer than one year (like those offered by the National Science Foundation) are being advocated, as are subsidized teaching positions for new Ph.D.'s.

Generally, the duties and responsibilities of postdoctoral fellows include teaching courses previously handled by graduate teaching assistants (for example, freshman English and other basic courses) and carrying out nonteaching functions (for instance, serving as associates on the research projects of senior faculty).

According to proponents, postdoctoral fellowships provide a mechanism whereby young scholars can enter academe, thus benefiting both the young scholars themselves and the humanities departments, which might otherwise be denied the infusion of new blood.

Some of the disadvantages are obvious. The graduate students who would otherwise function as teaching or research assistants suffer not only because their already minimal financial support is cut but also because they are deprived of the valuable training experience involved in teaching and in working closely with senior faculty.

Gardner (1972) has pointed out that only the federal government can afford to pay the costs of any major reforms that might take place either within disciplines or within institutions as a whole. The prospect of government funding for large numbers of postdoctoral fellowships poses the threat of government interference in academic affairs. According to Topf (1975), the humanities should not look to the government to help them through hard times because the potential for politicization is too high. An artifical demand may be created where none existed before, and too much money may lead to the deterioration of intellectual standards.

Another difficulty with government funding is that it tends to be unstable or sporadic. During expansionist periods, the government may wholeheartedly support research and development activities in universities; when times are lean, however, that support may be drastically reduced or even withdrawn completely. Kidd (1974) warns that such short-run measures are inefficient.

The establishment of the National Endowment for the Humanities (NEH) and the National Endowment for the Arts (NEA) represented in part an effort to assure more-stable support of humanistic research and other projects. Neither organization, however, addresses directly (or even very indirectly) the academic employment crisis. And the stability of their funding has been uncertain—particularly in light of proposed budget cuts for the 1982 fiscal year.

The professional associations have done, and have the potential to do, much more to alleviate the problem. For instance, Booth (1977) proposes that the Modern Language Association (MLA) and other humanities-centered organizations set up a national lobby to improve both the educational and the professional fate of all humanities teachers.

Provide New Sources of Support for Current Faculty

New Ph.D.'s in the humanities are not the only ones who face an unemployment crisis. Humanists already employed as faculty members find their jobs jeopardized by declining enrollments, declining proportions of undergraduates majoring in the humanities, and the resultant reallocation of resources within the university. Junior faculty who previously would have been awarded tenure go unpromoted

and may be forced to seek new jobs. Senior faculty who might serve as synthesizers for their disciplines are denied opportunities for research.

To alleviate this situation, new support programs for current faculty are
being advocated. However, it is doubtful that substantial sources of funding for
research in the humanities can be found. The potential social value of such
research would inevitably be compared with the social value of research in
medicine or physical science, to the detriment of the former. Who would argue
that money should be spent to finance research on Shakespeare's imagery when
it could instead be spent on research that might result in a cure for cancer?

*Employ Humanities Ph.D.'s in Elementary and Secondary
Schools*

Some people have suggested the hiring of more humanities Ph.D.'s at the elementary and secondary levels. These highly trained humanists, they say, might
help to improve humanities education, the teaching of basic skills, and even
literacy at these lower levels of the education system. The California Council
for the Humanities in Public Policy recently funded a small pilot project in which
three humanists worked for three months in the San Mateo Union High School
District during the spring of 1979 (Stix 1979). The program is to be extended
to a nearby school district next year; if successful, it may become statewide.

Since only three humanists were funded, and for a very short period, plans
to implement the program on a broader scale may be overly optimistic. Such
institutionalized enrichment of elementary and secondary education is very
costly, especially if salary schedules require higher pay for those with higher
degrees. It should be borne in mind that elementary and secondary teachers are
not in short supply. Moreover, it is presumptuous to assume that Ph.D.'s can
be more effective than regular teachers or that they are more capable of teaching
basic skills than are those trained for elementary and secondary teaching.

*Employ Humanities Ph.D.'s in Community Colleges and
Continuing-Education Programs*

Despite assumptions to the contrary, the Ph.D. supply has not led community
colleges and continuing-education programs to attempt to recruit Ph.D.'s, although some observers maintain that doctorate-level faculty might enrich education in these settings. In January 1977, only 18 percent of full-time faculty
in two-year colleges had the Ph.D. degree [National Science Foundation (NSF)
1977]. In 1976–1977, only 13 percent of all new full-time faculty appointees
in the humanities had the Ph.D. degree (Atelsek and Gomberg 1978). The
apparent reason for these hiring practices is that two-year colleges have little use

for faculty with the type of research skills developed in doctoral training. Rather, they emphasize teaching ability and "practical experience acquired in industrial employment. Thus, community and junior college administrators might prefer an experienced high-school science teacher with proven instructional skills and interest in students or a mechanical engineer with several years employment in industry over a young Ph.D. just graduated from a major university" (NSF 1978, p. 3). According to the same report: "a few universities have initiated programs to train doctoral students specifically to teach in two-year institutions. Graduates of these programs have readily found employment at community and junior colleges" (NSF 1978, p. 3).

Not only are doctorate-level humanists considered less desirable than teachers with lower degrees, but also they usually cost more to hire. Moreover, two-year colleges and continuing-education programs may prefer to enrich their faculties by hiring more female and minority faculty rather than by hiring research-oriented Ph.D.'s.

Another shortcoming of this proposed solution is that the majority of doctorate recipients are reluctant to teach in such settings; this prejudice may disappear as openings in four-year colleges and universities become scarcer.

Provide Sabbaticals for All Elementary, Secondary, and
College Teachers

This proposal for dealing with surplus humanities Ph.D.'s rests on two dubious assumptions: first, that sabbaticals increase the effectiveness of teachers at all levels, and, second, that humanities Ph.D.'s will be hired to take the place of those on sabbatical. No empirical evidence exists for the first claim. As to the second, the greater likelihood is that the absent faculty member's courses will be handled by his or her currently employed colleagues. In any event, increases in sabbaticals would entail high costs; and there is no clear source of funding to cover such costs.

Expand National Lobbying Efforts to Increase Funds for the
Humanities

This proposed solution might logically be included in any of the five categories. But because the suggestions in this section all entail increased funding for the humanities, it is discussed here.

Recently the American Association for the Advancement of the Humanities (AAAH) was founded, to serve a function analogous to that of other lobbying groups such as the American Association for the Advancement of Science, the American Association of University Professors, and the National Education

Association. If it is to be effective, it must formulate a careful case for the humanities and present it well, avoiding the internal rivalries that all too often trouble such organizations.

Spokespersons must go beyond arguments that young Ph.D.'s are "needed" in academe, that the job market is bound to get better, and that the humanities have a right to a piece of the subsidy pie. They must address the nonvocational, nonacademic benefits of humanities education.

The primary justification for public subsidy of education is that benefits accrue to others besides those receiving the education. Otherwise, it makes no more sense to subsidize an individual's education than to subsidize a private citizen's trip to Hawaii. However, if benefits from one person's education spill over to benefit others (as was the case, for example, with the development of the polio vaccine), and if prospective students consider only the individual benefits of education when they decide to pursue a degree, then some subsidies will have to be provided if society's needs are to be met. By reducing costs, subsidization will induce more people to purchase more schooling than they otherwise might. Thus, public subsidy brings society as a whole into greater equilibrium.

Therefore, lobbying efforts for the humanities must be directed at establishing the social rather than the individual value of humanistic fields. It will be difficult to document the large-scale effects—or to make favorable comparisons with the benefits that accrue from other uses of public funds (for instance, for medical research).

Stimulating Demand for Humanities Education

Many of the proposed solutions to the humanities crisis involve creating more jobs but do not directly address the substance of those jobs. Thus, new professorships are advocated even though it is not clear just what is to be taught to whom. More-definite alternatives are needed.

The eight suggestions in this category describe ways to stimulate demand for humanities education in the hope that more derived demand for humanities faculty members will result. The first five suggestions propose new clienteles for humanities education. The last three propose new requirements that will compel increased utilization of humanities faculty; all three assume that lengthening Ph.D. programs, increasing requirements for the degree, and raising standards will help the humanities. These efforts will inevitably increase the costs of graduate education, discouraging many students from entering or completing programs and thus reducing labor-market competition. Another possible byproduct of these policies is that future humanities Ph.D.'s will be better trained, more productive, and generally more marketable.

Encourage Adults to Take Humanities Courses for
Enjoyment or Enrichment

This proposal, promoted by advocates of lifelong learning, rests on the notion
that, in our humanistically oriented but humanistically deprived society, citizens
should study the humanities for their own good. It should be noted that between
1890 and 1920 the Chautauqua—a kind of traveling higher-education system—
flourished in many parts of this country, fading out with the advent of radio,
which brought information and entertainment directly into the home. The success
of different kinds of extension and continuing-education programs suggests that
many adults are still interested in more-active intellectual use of their leisure
time than is involved in watching television.

Traditional course offerings in the humanities would have to be revamped
and repackaged in order to attract nontraditional (adult) students. Not only must
the curriculum be made as appealing as possible to adults who may not have
gone to college earlier or whose college education may be years in the past (and
who thus may lack a strong academic background), but also the scheduling of
classes (as to both time and place) must be more flexible to facilitate the at-
tendance of adults who may work during the day.

The main problem with this proposal is that many current faculty members
and aspirants to faculty positions are unwilling to adjust themselves to such a
wide range of content areas and working conditions. Perhaps recent Ph.D.'s
would be less rigid in these matters than are older faculty. The other major
difficulty is that the demand for such programs is probably not sufficiently
widespread to open up many new academic jobs for recent Ph.D.'s.

Encourage Adults to Take Humanities Courses for Career
Advancement

The three major purveyors of education for adult works are large corporations
(such as American Telephone and Telegraph and International Business Ma-
chines), trade unions, and traditional education institutions such as high schools
and colleges.

A Conference Board study estimated that in 1975 industry spent about $400
million on seminars, programs, and courses at colleges and universities (Lee
1979). There are currently more than forty year-round university programs serving almost all the industrial sectors of the country (Gomberg n.d.), as well as
many local or international union programs offered cooperatively through colleges or universities. Certain jobs—particularly in education and government—
have salary schedules that automatically build in raises for more education or
more degrees, but most jobs reward only work-related skills acquisition.

According to the human-capital school, employers are most willing to help finance specific (rather than general) training for their workers since such training is most likely to be useful on the current job. General training, on the other hand, may be useful in a number of jobs. Hence, the current employer will be disinclined to pay for the acquisition of general skills lest the worker change jobs or demand a higher salary. Since most humanities education is general, not specific, the likelihood that employers will subsidize their workers (either by paid educational leave or by tuition payments) to take humanities courses is slight (except, perhaps, in cases where such an educational experience would improve the worker's life satisfaction and thus alleviate job boredom).

To those who argue that business and industry in the United States should model themselves after their counterparts in some other countries by becoming more generous in their support of non-work-related education for their workers, the only reply is that the situation here is different. In the first place, workers in many other nations maintain a steadfast loyalty to their employers and thus are unlikely to change jobs as a result of acquiring more general skills. In Japan, for example, workers traditionally stay with the same firm for their entire careers. Second, workers in many other countries are much less likely than are U.S. workers to have had a college education. Sending workers back to school is an easy way to upgrade the educational attainment of the work force in some countries; for instance, Germany, France, and Great Britain provide stipends to workers who want to return to school. But employers in the United States have no incentive to adopt such a policy since a large pool of college graduates is already available to them. Thus, we must be cautious about advocating certain lifelong-learning policies simply because they have worked in other countries. In particular, it is uncertain whether most U.S. firms would be willing to subsidize humanities education for their employees.

Recruit Foreign Students

The United States has a long history of providing higher education to the citizens of other nations, particularly those from less-developed countries with poor higher-education systems. But, for the reasons specified earlier in this chapter, there is little chance that substantial numbers of foreign students can be attracted into humanities programs. Foreign students are far more interested in enrolling in such fields as mathematics, science, and engineering (National Research Council 1978) than in the humanities (where language presents a more serious barrier). Likewise, their governments are far more willing to subsidize their study in these areas than they would be to subsidize a (nonutilitarian) humanities education for their students. One additional problem was not mentioned before: In the past, many foreign students have been reluctant to return to their own countries after completing their studies in the United States; unless some mechanism is developed to force them to do so, then the problem of finding jobs for graduates will only be exacerbated.

*Develop Interdisciplinary Programs that Include the
Humanities*

This proposal and the one that follows are aimed at increasing the demand for humanities not by adding to the total number of students but by encouraging students in other fields to take humanities courses. Bowie (1977), Mayhew and Ford (1974), and Lawrence (1978) are leading proponents of interdisciplinary studies at the graduate level. Generally, interdisciplinary study is presumed to be broadening for both humanities and nonhumanities students.

However attractive interdisciplinary studies may seem in the abstract, their usefulness in a tight job market is questionable. It has not been established either that humanities courses make the graduates of interdisciplinary programs more marketable or that the graduates of interdisciplinary programs are more marketable at all.

Again, faculty inflexibility and unwillingness to teach nontraditional courses that must be tailored to the special needs of students must be taken into account. The types of humanities programs that would be of greatest utility in interdisciplinary programs—namely, those in the grammer and culture of a foreign language, rather than in the literature of a foreign country—are precisely those that traditional faculty may be most reluctant to teach.

Finally, nonhumanities disciplines are also feeling the pinch of declining enrollments. Whether faculty and administrators in political science, international relations, economics, and the like would be amenable to having their students take courses in the humanities rather than courses in their own disciplines is uncertain at best, unless a reciprocal situation exists, in which case enrollments in humanities courses would drop.

*Persuade Professional Schools to Introduce Humanities
Courses*

It has become increasingly popular to suggest that fields such as law, medicine, and business could benefit from courses in ethics (to develop a sense of social responsibility), English composition (to improve writing skills), and foreign languages (to increase ability to communicate in other languages for political and business purposes). Indeed, many professional schools have responded by adding humanities-like courses to their curricula. The question becomes whether it is more efficient to retrain some faculty members of professional schools to teach these courses or to hire humanities Ph.D.'s to teach them, hoping that the latter will modify their approach as necessary.

Humanists themselves seem somewhat divided on the issue. Goyne (1977) argues that combining humanistic values with a professional component represents not a dilution or a compromise but a valuable educational experience, whereas Topf (1975) sees a danger of the humanities becoming "applied," "productive," and politically influential—and suffering as a consequence.

It is also increasingly popular to suggest that vocational or career education incorporate humanities courses. But can the "values" of the humanities be separated from humanistic subject matter and methodology and "grafted onto technical-vocational subject matter" (Jones 1976)? Some experts would say that they cannot.

Nevertheless, the infusion of humanities into vocational or professional programs offers some hope of increasing the demand for humanities Ph.D.'s, either directly—by having the humanists teach the courses—or indirectly—by having them retrain faculty in professional and vocational fields so that these faculty can teach the courses.

Revise Curricula to Require More Humanities Courses

Over the past decade or so, higher education in the United States seems to have abandoned some of its more-rigorous academic traditions and to have become more open and flexible, as is evidenced by such developments as increased electives, more-individualized programs, grade inflation and pass–fail or non-graded systems, and the introduction of women's and ethnic studies. Some critics deplore these developments, citing the growing number of college graduates who are incapable of writing or of understanding basic scientific concepts. Others have despaired at the vocationalization of the traditional college curricula.

Thus, when Harvard University announced its new "core curriculum," one interpretation was that this leader in U.S. higher education was "toughening its standards," as part of a more-general cultural movement that "speaks to a popular yearning for a return to old values and social order" (Keller 1979, p. 3). However, the associate dean of faculty of Harvard's School of Arts and Sciences asserts that the true purpose of the core curriculum—which imposes an eight-course requirement on undergraduates—is a practical one in view of the complexity of today's society. Some comprehension of "the state of current scholarly understanding of people, nature and society should be part of the intellectual baggage of every educated man and woman" (Keller 1979, p. 3).

Considering Harvard's prestige, many institutions will probably follow its lead. If the return to the core curriculum does indeed provide useful skills for coping with today's world, then this movement should be applauded. If, on the other hand, it merely compels students to take courses that turn out to have little direct relevance to their later lives, then in the long run it will simply weaken the links between college education and the workplace. In short, the efficacy of

Harvard's new core curriculum and—more important—its replicability and value at other institutions remain to be proved.

Reinstitute Foreign-Language Requirements for the Ph.D.

In the past, when the doctorate was regarded as the badge of the true scholar, all doctoral candidates were required to demonstrate their competency in at least one foreign language. As the number of years required to get a Ph.D. increased, and as important scholarly works in other languages came to be translated quickly into English, the foreign-language requirement became less defensible. All too often, the student fulfilled that requirement by cramming just long enough to be able to translate a 500-word passage in a foreign language, and then forgot the whole thing, rather than developing the ability to write and speak a foreign language. Thus, many of the nation's doctoral programs dropped the foreign-language requirement.

The debate continues. On the one hand, some people—mostly in the social and physical sciences and engineering—argue that students might better spend their time mastering a computer language or studying some area of advanced mathematics. On the other hand, some people argue that, because an increased awareness of the world scene is essential to all college graduates and because the community of scholars has become increasingly internationalized, the foreign-language requirement should be continued, reinstituted, or even expanded.

Whatever the relative merit of these arguments, enrollments in foreign-language courses have continued to decline, with disastrous consequences for those with doctorates in these fields, who must either take part-time academic positions, work outside academe (often in unrelated jobs), or not work at all.

Any movement to impose a foreign-language requirement, either at the doctoral or the undergraduate level, must be based on something more than the desire to provide more academic jobs for foreign-language Ph.D.'s. The usefulness of foreign-language courses must be compared with the usefulness of other kinds of courses. Unfortunately, such a comparison bodes ill for foreign-language faculties, whose best hopes rest directly on the reinstitution of the language requirement.

Require Further Credentialing by Means of a Professional Entry Examination

Since the content and methodologies of different humanities fields vary considerably, some people have suggested that the equivalent of the bar examination for lawyers be instituted for doctorate-level humanists in order to ensure standardization and high quality. A related suggestion is that credentials be renewed at specified intervals.

Such requirements might increase the demand for doctorate-level humanists who could prepare people to take the examination and who might help screen out some contenders, thus reducing competition for available jobs. Nonetheless, those who did not pass the examination would still be surplus Ph.D.'s.

Such make-work proposals run counter to the creative, individual, and scholarly nature of the humanities and impugn the adequacy of peer review in ensuring quality. Moreover, it is unlikely that graduate students would be willing to make any further investment in an education whose value (at least in terms of finding employment) is increasingly in doubt. Even so, during a period of radical upheaval in the humanities, the possibility that such a requirement may be imposed cannot be taken lightly.

Reorganizing Academe

Most of the proposed solutions included in this category involve some fairly radical changes in the structure of academic employment. Thus they would probably be resisted by current faculty members and by the groups that represent them. Even if they were implemented, however, they might do little to relieve the tight academic-job market for new Ph.D.'s; or they might shift the problem upward, to senior faculty.

Reduce the Salaries of Current Faculty

No professional meeting in the humanities goes on these days without a session on the job market at which some graduate student or recent Ph.D. does not stand up and ask, "Why not cut the salaries of current faculty members to free up funds so some of us can be hired?" This solution has some theoretical appeal, especially to those who advocate the previously discussed "market solution," which would allow salaries to fall in areas of oversupply.

It is, however, totally unrealistic. Current humanities faculty, the unions, the American Association of University Professors (AAUP), and other faculty members fearing the same treatment if surpluses should ever occur in their fields would raise a monumental protest. Moreover, virtually no mechanism exists whereby contracts can be rewritten to cut nominal salaries.

Even if money were freed up in this way, why should it be spent to hire new faculty in fields where student demand is declining? Would it not make better sense to reallocate it to other disciplines where demand is still strong?

Institute Some Form of Job Sharing

Whereas the previous suggestion involved reduced salaries for the same amount of work, this proposal involves less pay for less work by one person, or the same pay for the same amount of work by more than one person.

The concept of job sharing emerged from the women's movement; it was suggested that a husband and wife split one faculty appointment and take home one full salary between them. The advantage, from the feminist point of view, is that both parents not only would have some kind of career but also could share childrearing and household responsibilities. It is extremely unlikely that such an arrangement could be extended to people not bound by family ties.

A second form of job sharing is the increased use of a part-time faculty. In this case, questions of eligibility for tenure and fringe benefits would have to be negotiated separately, whereas in the first form of job-sharing, it would be assumed that each party in the arrangement is eligible for fringe benefits, tenure, and sabbaticals (but on a prorated basis).

A third type of job sharing involves a single faculty member's working part time at two or more neighboring institutions, an arrangement being developed by Kalamazoo College. A university could thus hire more faculty members, although each would work only part-time and be paid accordingly. It should be immediately apparent, however, that if a given number of positions is available at a group of neighboring colleges and universities, the total number of people employed would not increase. To split appointments among institutions in this way makes sense only if an institution does not have sufficient funds to hire a full-time person; if several institutions in this situation pool their resources, they could between them hire a full-time person.

Yet another variant is the suggestion that professors could, while retaining tenure, work half time, at half salary, in return for free time to consult. If enough professors in a given department agreed to such an arrangement, full-time positions for recent Ph.D.'s would become available; and the department might reap the benefits of new ideas and new perspectives. But problems of existing contracts, tenure, and the like would remain. Moreover, consulting opportunities for humanists are scarce; current faculty can hardly be expected to alter their living standards to half-pay rates, even if they are only doing half the work. Finally, participants in job sharing would lose the prestige that normally accrues to a full-time appointment.

Reduce the Use of Part-Time Faculty

Whereas the previous suggestion was aimed at increasing access to the university, even on a part-time basis, this suggestion is intended to enable more humanities Ph.D.'s to get full-time faculty jobs.

From the standpoint of the institution, the use of part-time faculty has several advantages. For instance, although a regular faculty member might be paid $12,000 or more to teach about six courses per academic year, part-time faculty members can usually be hired for about $1,000 per course. Hence, in direct salary costs alone, part-time faculty cost the institution only about half as much. In addition, part timers are usually ineligible for fringe benefits and do not have to be awarded tenure after a given period of time. Part timers can be hired when course enrollments warrant and laid off when demand for a particular course drops. Finally, in some situations part-time faculty are ineligible to become members of academic unions; thus, at some institutions, the use of large proportions of part timers will sap the potential strength of the union, a situation that would cause administrators no grief.

Those advocating more full-time positions for humanities Ph.D.'s also propose that part-time faculty be made eligible for fringe benefits, tenure, union membership, and so forth. Such changes would, of course, make it more costly for universities to use part-time faculty. But, rather than hiring more full-time faculty, an institution might choose instead simply to reduce course offerings in the humanities. The extent to which either of these alternatives is chosen should be the basis for evaluating the proposal to reduce the use of part-time faculty.

Institute Early-Retirement Programs

In recent years, various efforts have been made to entice tenured faculty to retire before the mandatory retirement age. When these efforts are successful, the happy result is that regular faculty positions are opened up, thus allowing the institution to replace higher-paid senior faculty with cheaper new blood. Unfortunately, these efforts have seldom been successful, chiefly because increased longevity and rapidly rising inflation negate any possible appeal of early retirement for the senior faculty member. Many faculty members who choose early retirement do so in order to take a position at another institution (usually in a location and climate more desirable for an older person), thus taking an appointment that might otherwise have been offered to a junior faculty member or a new Ph.D.

From the institution's perspective, early-retirement programs are costly since they involve either increasing pensions or offering them at an earlier point in the faculty member's life. Finally, as a solution to the problem of the surplus in humanities Ph.D.'s, early retirement is inconsistent with recent legislation to extend the retirement age; it is likely, in fact, that mandatory retirement will be abolished completely in the 1980s.

Terminate the Appointments of Foreign Faculty Members

Arguing that U.S. colleges and universities should be obliged to employ U.S. citizens rather than foreigners, some people have urged the drastic expedient of terminating the appointment of foreign faculty members (as some Canadian colleges are now doing). This suggestion overlooks the stringency of application procedures for permanent-resident visas. The applicant must present affidavits from U.S. citizens attesting that his or her skills are unique and thus that his or her employment will not take a job away from a U.S. citizen.

The actual number of foreign scholars employed in U.S. colleges and universities is relatively small; thus, the termination of their employment would hardly be worth the disruptions that would surely result. Not only might such a policy arouse international ill will; but it also would represent a serious encroachment on civil rights.

A less-extreme alternative would be to implement an informal policy whereby new foreign faculty appointments, particularly at the junior level, are discouraged except on a case-by-case basis. Indeed, foreign governments might be more willing to subsidize the education of their students in this country if they were assured that those students would be compelled to return to the home country; in this way, enrollments could be increased without a corresponding increase in competition for scarce jobs.

Any blanket prohibition against the hiring of foreign scholars, however, runs counter to the U.S. academic tradition and would deprive our colleges and universities of some of the best minds in the world, as well as depriving many gifted scholars of the opportunity to contribute their talents.

Abolish Tenure

Originally instituted to protect and perpetuate academic freedom, the tenure system is now being held responsible for stagnancy and rigidity in U.S. higher education. Whatever the truth of these charges, the prospects for complete abolition of tenure are slight; any such efforts would be strongly resisted by current faculty (since tenure is, after all, their only form of formal job security) and by the groups that represent them. And even if tenure were eliminated entirely, the result might be only to shift the employment crisis upward to older faculty.

Nonetheless, the movement to replace tenure with some other system is strong; and some institutions are experimenting with alternatives. Gardner (1978–1979) predicts "the end of tenure and a new system of fairly short-term contracts, analogous to sports, with a limited number of long-term contracts for selected superstars" (p. 92). In a recent *Wall Street Journal* article, Cooney (1979) reports that Columbia University has recently been hiring a large proportion of temporary teachers in the humanities "since only eight tenure-track jobs were offered last year compared with 30 in 1968" (p. 1). Columbia is also extending the period that nontenured faculty can remain on campus from six to nine years. At Hampshire College in Massachusetts, all faculty are now being hired on a renewable-contract basis with no tenure provision. Calling the recipients of these temporary faculty appointments "gypsy scholars," Cooney describes some of the responses in academe to these changes: Many educators are concerned that the higher-education system will eventually suffer if potential college teachers are forced to seek employment elsewhere, and that the quality of scholarship will suffer in the scramble to make credentials appear as impressive as possible; most demoralized by the erosion of the tenure system are those faculty members in their thirties and forties who previously would have been awarded tenure (Cooney 1979).

Expand Faculty Unionization

Collective bargaining came to the campus in the 1970s. In 1965 virtually no colleges or universities were unionized (Kemerer and Baldridge 1975). According to Bennett and Johnson (1979), 480 of some 2,400 institutions are now unionized, representing about 25 percent of the nation's 540,000 faculty members. Recent statistics indicate that the union movement may be slowing down, particularly since most of the two-year colleges were unionized by 1979.

But increased faculty unionization does not imply an improvement in the job prospects of new humanities Ph.D.'s. Traditionally, unions serve the interest of their current members; any expansion in membership may threaten those vested interests. Moreover, if unionization tends to centralize power within the university and within systemwide administrations (Kemerer and Baldridge 1975), then it ultimately may have an unfavorable effect on the humanities-job crisis: As college administrators make budget decisions on a wider basis, they will probably reallocate funds away from low-demand fields like the humanities and into disciplines where enrollments are relatively high. In short, unionization either will have no effect at all on the humanities job crisis or will make it worse.

Shift Power from Faculty to Administrators

In the era of campus unrest in the 1960s, some policymaking power shifted from administrators to faculty members and students. Now, at the beginning of the 1980s, the faculty still retains much of that power, although the student voice in campus affairs rarely rises above a whisper. The situation for humanities Ph.D.'s might be improved if policymaking power were returned to the administration.

A prime example of faculty-serving policy is the current academic reward system, which values research and publication above all other activities, including teaching, community service, curriculum revision, and the placement of graduates in jobs. Unless that reward system is changed, faculty members—particularly the tenured—will have little incentive to emphasize other possible priorities.

Administrators, on the other hand, must be concerned with the long-term vitality of their institutions; this necessity makes them more aware of the problems of declining enrollments and shrinking budgets. If modifications and innovations that may eventually help to improve the academic-employment situation for humanities Ph.D.'s are to be introduced, it is the administration and not the faculty that will introduce them.

Conclusion

Most of the proposals discussed in this chapter seem to us to offer little hope of solving the job crisis currently faced by doctorate-level humanists. The high costs of implementing many of the suggestions, along with current faculty's inflexibility and unwillingness to change their ways, are major stumbling blocks in most cases.

In the next chapter we discuss what we regard as the most-promising group of proposed solutions: those that have to do with expanding the nonacademic-job market for humanists.

4 The Most-Promising Solutions

In the previous chapter we reviewed a number of proposals that have been made for solving the employment crisis currently facing new humanities Ph.D.'s. Some of these proposals (such as developing new vehicles for upward mobility or terminating the employment of foreign scholars) are too implausible to be taken seriously. Others (for example, letting the market work through salary adjustments, or employing more humanities Ph.D.'s in elementary and secondary schools, community colleges, and continuing-education programs) have a surface appeal but, on closer inspection, prove to be impractical. Still others related to stimulating demand for humanities courses and teachers (for example, encouraging adults to take humanities courses either for enjoyment and enrichment or for career advancement, or persuading professional schools and vocational education to introduce more humanities courses) are good as far as they go but would probably have little overall effect on the academic-job crisis; adults and professional students could not be attracted into humanities courses in sufficient numbers to make up for the decline in traditional-aged freshmen and thereby to open up new academic jobs for recent humanities Ph.D.'s. Still other proposed solutions, especially those connected with adjusting the supply to the demand, are essentially self-destructive; that is, if they were effectively to reduce the number of graduate students entering humanities fields, and thus to reduce the number of Ph.D.'s graduating (which, in turn, would presumably make competition for existing academic jobs less fierce), they would at the same time reduce the number of students for existing faculty to teach, making it very unlikely that new jobs would open up. Finally, many of the solutions would work only in the short run or would shift the academic-job crisis upward to current faculty; for example, keeping new humanities Ph.D.'s occupied with postdoctoral fellowships for a year or two merely postpones their entry into the turbulence of the marketplace; abolishing tenure or forcing current faculty to work half time for half pay, on the grounds that they can then take advantage of (scarce or nonexistent) consulting opportunities, merely expands the crisis.

What is needed, then, is some solution (or group of solutions) that conceivably will have fairly far-reaching and long-term effects, that will reduce the number of Ph.D.'s competing for academic jobs without also reducing the number of students available to take humanities courses, that will not be prohibitively expensive to implement, and that is compatible with the emphasis on individual freedom and choice that is the keystone of our democratic society. There is one solution that seems to fit these requirements: expanding the nonacademic-job market for doctorate-level humanists.

A respectable proportion of humanists already avail themselves of this solution. According to the National Research Council (1978), about 10 percent of all full-time employed humanities Ph.D.'s already work outside academe, about half of them as either researchers or administrators.

Many people see the current slump in the academic-job market as an opportunity for business and industry to recruit humanists and thus to make use of talents previously unavailable to them. Sullivan (1977) states that humanists have "a capacity for work, analytical skills, and adaptability. These skills are transferable: textual analysis [a humanist's tool] is not that different from credit analysis [a banker's tool]." Most of all, humanities Ph.D.'s can provide business with "something very rare and highly needed": writing ability. "The single note most frequently struck by businessmen talking on the subject is the scarcity of people in their world who can write anything at all with clarity and coherence" (Sullivan 1977). Another observer describes humanities Ph.D.'s as bright, persistent, and able to perform under pressure; as having oral-communication skills derived from their teaching experience; and as having the ability to set priorities and to raise questions about value or quality (Bowie 1977).

Of course, not all potential nonacademic employers of humanists may recognize or value these qualities. Some may believe that the skills and knowledge of the humanist have no applicability to business or technical tasks and that it would be easier and cheaper to train nonhumanists to write than to retool humanists for jobs in the business world.

For their part, humanists themselves may have reservations about taking nonacademic jobs. They may feel that such jobs lack the prestige of full-time faculty appointments. For instance, they may be prejudiced against jobs in government on the grounds that such jobs are routine, bureaucratic, and "political" (in a pejorative sense). They may be biased against jobs in the private sector on the grounds that such jobs are cutthroat and exploitative or that they demand that one become an "organization man," lacking the supposed freedom and autonomy of the faculty member. Indeed, there is ample evidence that such attitudes prevail among graduate students in the humanities (Solmon, Ochsner, and Hurwicz 1979). Humanists who do not hold these stereotypes may nonetheless believe that they stand little chance of getting employment in government or in the private sector, or they may be uncertain about how to get such jobs.

In this chapter, then, we will discuss four categories of proposals related to expanding the nonacademic-job market for humanities Ph.D.'s. The first category comprises suggestions as to how humanists can more effectively be prepared for such jobs; the second, suggestions for directly influencing nonacademic employers to hire humanists; the third, suggestions for making nonacademic jobs more attractive to humanists; and the fourth, helping humanists to find jobs in the nonacademic sector and to get the jobs they go after.

Preparing Humanists for Nonacademic Jobs

The proposals in this category have to do with ways in which graduate education in the humanities could be changed so as to make Ph.D.'s more employable in settings other than academe.

Revise the Content of Doctoral Programs

It has been suggested that the doctoral program in the humanities could be made more practical by adding courses in business, applied foreign languages, and so forth. A related suggestion is that the function of the master's degree be reformulated: Two master's degrees—one in a humanities field and the other in business administration or some other professional program—might be more useful than the Ph.D. for graduate students considering nonacademic careers. The major advantage of both suggestions is that humanities graduates with a background in applied courses presumably would emerge with more marketable skills. Moreover, this kind of preparation would do much to convince the prospective employer that the humanities graduate is not applying for a nonacademic job as a last resort after having failed to get a faculty position; the applicant would have proved that his or her intentions were serious.

Of course, such a solution presupposes that the decision to take a nonacademic job is made fairly soon after entry to graduate school. It also assumes that humanities students, many of whom have little background in mathematics or science, are capable of succeeding in technical courses outside their major field.

Introduce a Work Component into Doctoral Programs

Suggestions in this category include requiring humanities students to get and keep part-time jobs (preferably in nonacademic settings) at the same time that they are working on the doctorate. Internships for selected graduate students are another possibility. The advantages of adding such a work component are several.

1. When they graduate, students would already have some familiarity with, and experience in, nonacademic jobs.
2. They would be better prepared for such jobs than are most current doctorate recipients.
3. They would give evidence to potential employers of having anticipated alternative careers.
4. If they were effective workers, they might do much toward breaking down the negative stereotypes that some nonacademic employers have with respect to humanists.

5. Because they had paying jobs, more of them could afford the costs of graduate education.
6. Some humanists might continue with the same employer after receiving the Ph.D. degree, thus reducing competition for academic jobs.

Nonetheless, this proposal must be pursued cautiously. Some graduate students are justified in aspiring to purely academic careers; for them, a work component would be a waste of time. If entry to the graduate program were contingent on the student's having a job, then some potentially excellent people might be lost to the system; after all, the ability to get a part-time nonacademic job is not related to one's prospects of success in a graduate humanities program.

Certain organizational questions arise: Would students receive academic credit for their outside work? If so, control would have to be exercised to assure that the work experience merited such credit. Who would exercise this control? If employers must pay students, will they demand greater productivity and be less concerned about their teaching responsibilities? Are all nonacademic employers able—and willing—to provide and effective learning environment for part-time, temporary student workers?

Require that Applicants to Doctoral Programs Have Prior Work Experience

Whereas the former proposal would require the student to have a part-time job *while* in school, this proposal would stipulate that the student have work experience *before* entering graduate school. It has the same advantages as the work-component proposal just discussed.

As with the previous proposal, not all students, however highly qualified, would be able to find nonacademic jobs; barring their entry to graduate school on those grounds seems both unfair and unwise. Quite possibly, those students who want to go directly from full-time undergraduate study into full-time graduate study are the very ones who have the most to contribute to the humanities. Finally, many people who hold full-time salaried jobs may be unwilling to forego that income in order to return to graduate school.

Establish Postdoctoral Business-Orientation Programs

Several programs already in existence around the country take humanities Ph.D.'s and give them brief but intense exposure to economics, management, finance, and other business areas. One example is New York University's Careers in Business program, which has as its purpose making humanists more marketable in the business world.

Its proponents assert that this approach neither demands that the graduate student divide time, attention, and energy between the job and graduate study (a shortcoming of the work-component approach), nor requires the student to interrupt his or her normal progression directly from college into graduate study (a shortcoming of the prior-work-experience approach).

The effectiveness of such programs remains to be proved. Some firms may commit themselves beforehand to hiring program participants. If that is the case, can the programs themselves be credited with the participant's subsequent employment? Virtually no real evaluations of these programs have been conducted. Certainly we know that a relatively large proportion of participants in these programs have obtained jobs. But was this *because of* the programs? Would certain of the graduates have been desirable nonacademic employees even without the programs? Are the programs serving merely as placement rather than as training activities? This is a particularly important question if corporations agree to hire participants before they see what they have learned. And has it been established that graduates have learned relevant skills in the programs? We will not know for quite a while whether those who have been hired from these programs can establish long-term niches in either the corporate world or the public sector. Nor will we know whether their roles will be different from those of humanists who enter nonacademic careers without the benefit of the programs?

Such programs tend to be expensive. For example, in its first year, New York University's Careers in Business programs cost the foundations that support it $360,000 and has so far resulted in the placement of fewer than fifty Ph.D.'s. Might these resources be used more effectively? Careful evaluation—especially cost-benefit analysis—is necessary before these programs are deemed preferable to less costly programs of direct placement that do not involve an education component.

Convincing Nonacademic Employers to Hire Humanists

It has been suggested that "if 1,000 corporations in this country each hired two humanities PhDs per year for the next eight years, 16,000 surplus PhDs would be absorbed into productive jobs by 1985" (Solmon, Ochsner, and Hurwicz 1978, p. 189). The public sector is another fertile source of jobs for humanists, as the remainder of this book attempts to show. Simply giving humanists better preparation for nonacademic jobs will not be enough, however, to guarantee that they will be hired in such jobs. Direct efforts must be made to publicize and promote humanists as potentially productive workers outside of academe, with emphasis being given to their special competencies, such as writing ability. Many executive officers of large companies who themselves have training in the liberal arts may believe that humanists could contribute much to the company. The trouble is that most corporate hiring is not done by executive officers; the recruiters who visit university campuses seek people with specific business and technical skills, such as accounting or engineering skills.

Subsidize Nonacademic Employers for Hiring Humanists

Clearly, corporations will incur costs when they hire humanists rather than people with more-traditional backgrounds. Training will have to be more extensive, and workers will be less productive at first. Hence, subsidization by public or private funding agencies might encourage nonacademic employers to hire humanists by defraying some of these costs. Moreover, if prestigious philanthropic foundations were to subsidize appointments in industry—much as they subsidize postdoctoral academic fellowships—the prestige of such nonacademic positions might be increased, encouraging more humanities students to seek them. Although, as with many subsidization programs, there is some danger that the hiring would stop once the funds stopped flowing, the chances are that if humanists proved themselves to be valuable employees, that danger could be avoided.

The subsidization of private, profit-making organizations by private or public funding sources carries with it both political and public-relations problems. These problems could be avoided if subsidies were limited to humanities-related (usually non-profit-making) institutions such as libraries, museums, archives, and historical societies, as is now the case with grants from the National Endowment for the Humanities. These types of organizations have traditionally employed small numbers of humanists and, if they had the funds, might well be willing to employ more of them.

Several benefits would result. First, humanists could conduct research in settings that would not require them also to teach students and that did not depend on increased enrollments to support researchers. Second, public facilities such as libraries and museums would be more accessible to professionals and nonprofessionals alike; their benefits might be more widely disseminated to the general public as well. Third, the prospect of this new source of employment might encourage students to continue to enroll in humanities programs, thus easing the academic-job crisis. Finally, local facilities might eventually become self-supporting by charging users for the services offered.

Is Public Subsidy Necessary?

The question of whether public subsidy (as opposed to foundation funding) is necessary would have to be considered carefully, bearing in mind that the taxpayer's money is now going to help support graduate schools. Because libraries and museums may more immediately benefit the communities in which they are located, their subsidization may be a more defensible use of public funds. The nation's enthusiastic response to such exhibits as the Tutankhamen exhibition and historic Williamsburg suggests that citizens may prefer that their money be spent on similar projects in the future (projects that could give employment to humanists) rather than going to an enterprise that serves chiefly to produce more humanists, who then find themselves without jobs.

Making Nonacademic Jobs More Attractive to Humanists

Much has already been said about the reluctance of some humanities graduate students even to consider taking nonacademic jobs. Although this reluctance is in part due to erroneous stereotypes about jobs in government and business, much of it has a valid basis. Doctorate-level humanists fear that, by taking such jobs, they will lose the chance to do scholarly research and to publish the results of that research. Since their graduate training was aimed primarily at giving them research skills, jobs that give them no opportunity to exercise those skills may represent a considerable waste and a constant source of frustration. The two proposals that follow are intended to correct that situation.

Increase Access to Research Facilities

One of the main complaints of doctorate holders employed outside of academe, particularly those who do not do research as part of their jobs, is that research facilities are not available to them. The New York Public Library—once famous for being open twenty-four hours a day—is now rarely open beyond normal working hours. University libraries in the Washington, D.C., area usually deny outsiders access to stacks on the grounds that if all the highly educated people in the Washington area were allowed to use them, their facilities and resources would be unduly strained.

Thus, one way to increase the desirability of nonacademic employment is to ensure that the humanists so employed have access to university libraries and other research facilities; in this way, they can continue to conduct research as an avocation. Subsidization of libraries and similar facilities to support such an arrangement might be a wise expenditure of public funds.

A related proposal calls for universities to establish positions, such as research associate, that involve no duties and obligations and no pay. Their primary function is to provide qualified researchers, not otherwise connected with the university, with access to the library and other facilities. Again, small incentive grants for the establishment of these positions might encourage nonacademically employed humanists to pursue their own research interests.

Facilitate Publishing by Nonacademics

Many nonacademics, especially those who carry out research in their spare time, complain that, without an institutional affiliation, they have difficulty in getting their work published. Several solutions to this problem have been suggested. The most common is to establish a journal specifically designed to publish articles by nonacademics. If the work was of high enough quality, such a journal might sustain itself, through sales, advertising, and so forth, as well as existing journals do, although some initial subsidization might be required.

An alternative solution calls for existing journals to adopt a kind of affirmative-action policy by committing themselves to devote a certain amount of space in each issue to articles by nonacademics. Alternatively, some agency might pay a bounty to journals that publish papers by those pursuing nonacademic careers. It would be interesting to see whether the quality of research published by financially pressed journals would decline as a result of such subsidies.

The position of research associate described previously might also serve a purpose here. Those holding such positions might be able to use university letterhead in submitting articles for publication. It would be interesting to see whether an author's having an institutional affiliation affects the probability of an article's being accepted for publication.

Helping Humanists Find Nonacademic Jobs

Even when they are willing to take other than faculty jobs, doctorate-level humanists may have little notion of the best way to go about getting such jobs. The two proposals here are intended to help them in this respect.

Encourage Graduate Students to Use Counseling and
Placement Services

University counseling and placement services are used mostly by undergraduates, whereas graduate students typically rely on faculty for job information and guidance. All too often, however, humanities faculty are incapable of helping their students find nonacademic jobs and may even be unwilling to do so. When the new doctorate recipient belatedly realizes that the "old-boy" network has failed to provide an academic job, he or she may visit the university placement office; by that time, however, the damage has been done.

Students should be encouraged to visit the career-counseling center and the placement office early in their graduate programs. The counselors and other staff in these facilities are trained to advise students on job opportunities, the appropriate preparation for different jobs, and specific employer needs. They can connect students with industry and government recruiters. These services are a valuable resource that is underutilized by humanities Ph.D.'s. However, we cannot ignore the deficiencies of counseling centers with respect to knowledge of the competencies of graduate students in the humanities and experience in linking humanities Ph.D.'s with nontraditional employers. It is likely that some training of counselors needs to be supported.

Some of the professional associations—including the American Philosophical Association, the Modern Language Association, and the American Historical Association—are now concerning themselves with the employment problems of humanities graduate students and are taking steps to orient them toward nonacademic careers and to help them find jobs. The American Philosophical Association, for example, has established a committee on placement, with a subcommittee on nonacademic placement that is staffed by philosophers who have actually held nonacademic positions (Bowie 1977).

Encourage Graduate Students to Make Use of Published Guides

A number of books available on how to get a job might prove useful to humanities graduate students. For instance, Richard Bolles's *What Color Is Your Parachute?* (1972) offers some helpful advice: Stress all your competencies rather than just those that have been learned in graduate school; emphasize any previous experience that relates to the job being sought; do research on the firm with which you are seeking a job; draft a resume tailored to the needs of a specific employer.

The problem with popular how-to books is that the suggestions they offer may lose some of their initial effectiveness when they become widely known and used. The job applicant must also exercise common sense in acting on such advice.

Conclusion

If all else fails, of course, the conscription of doctorate-level humanists into nonacademic jobs may be the only answer. About the only precedent (other than the Selective Service System) for such forced service in this country is the Work Project Administration (WPA) in effect during the Great Depression of the 1930s. Such jobs would probably pay very little and would be of very low status. On the other hand, they may represent more-realistic and socially beneficial alternatives than the creation of assistant professorships or research positions at "regular" pay. It is unlikely, however, that the public would accept the reduced freedom inherent in such conscription.

A much more acceptable solution is for those humanists unable to find traditional jobs to look voluntarily for nonacademic jobs. Chapters 5 through 9 are devoted to an examination of humanists who hold such jobs in the public sector.

5 An Overview of Public-Sector Employment

As chapter 4 suggested, the most-promising solution to the academic-job crisis for doctorate-level humanists seems to be nonacademic employment, that is, employment in government or in the private sector. However, very few humanities students consider either of these alternatives. According to a 1975 survey (Solmon, Ochsner, and Hurwicz 1979), only 6 percent of the humanists surveyed said that, at the time they entered graduate school, they had seriously considered a job in government; only 4 percent had considered a job in business; and only 6 percent had considered public service such as the Peace Corps, Vista, or volunteer work. The alternatives (to entering graduate study in their particular field) that they were most likely to have entertained were teaching at the elementary or secondary level, doing graduate work in another discipline, or attending professional school. Similarly, even though most of the nonacademically employed humanities Ph.D.'s already in the labor force work in the private sector, interviews with graduate students indicate that the public sector is more attractive to them than the private sector because they feel that government jobs have "fewer invidious characteristics than jobs in the corporate world" (Solmon, Ochsner, and Hurwicz 1979, pp. 187–188).

In addition to being somewhat skeptical about employment in the private sector, humanists tend to believe that corporate employers strongly favor people with degrees in fields directly related to the job—for example, a master's degree in business administration for those in administrative positions. Conversely, they believe that the government may be more flexible and more willing to hire people from different disciplines for similar positions. This belief may have considerable validity. Since government agencies have never been constrained by the need to maximize profits, they may be more inclined than are private-sector employers to hire highly educated humanists without knowing exactly what they do. Moreover, the government sector has grown rapidly in recent years and will probably continue to do so over the long run, if not during the next couple of years. For these reasons, the remainder of this section focuses on evaluating the public sector as a potential employer of humanities Ph.D.'s. Comparisons will be made between doctorate-level humanists and nonhumanists (natural scientists, social scientists, and engineers) working in the public sector.

The Sample

In the course of several studies of alternative careers for Ph.D.'s the Higher Education Research Institute (HERI) collected data on 5,144 Ph.D.'s in both humanities and nonhumanities fields who were employed in federal, state, or local governments. Names and addresses were obtained from a variety of sources: graduate schools, professional societies, the federal civil-service employee file, the personnel records of five state civil-service departments, the National Research Council's Comprehensive Roster file, the Library of Congress, the Smithsonian Institution, and state historical societies. In addition, direct appeals to readers were made through notices in professional journals and an advertisement in *The New York Times*.

The questionnaire mailed out to government-employed humanists differed slightly from that mailed out to natural scientists, social scientists, and engineers (See appendix A for copies of both questionnaires.) The 5,144 respondents represent a response rate of about 40 percent, which is satisfactory, especially since only one questionnaire mailing was possible in most cases. Although the respondents to the HERI surveys do not necessarily constitute a representative sample of publicly employed Ph.D.'s, the group is large enough to yield considerable information. Nowhere else can such detailed data be found on such a large group of doctorate holders.

Table 5–1 compares National Research Council (NRC) estimates of the numbers of government-employed Ph.D.'s with the numbers of HERI respondents. Five broad disciplinary areas are covered: the humanities, the social sciences, the natural sciences (including mathematics), engineering, and psychology (which was considered separately from the other social sciences because of the large number of cases involved). The specific fields subsumed within each of these broad categories are also indicated in the table. For federal-government employees, federal Civil Service Commission (CSC) estimates are shown. NRC estimates are generally higher than CSC estimates because the latter include only those employees with civil-service status. The large discrepancy between NRC and CSC estimates in the social sciences and the fact that the CSC estimate for the humanities is larger than the NRC estimate indicate that the two agencies categorize different fields differently. NRC estimates of the number of humanists employed by state and local governments demonstrate the uncertainty of these data. With only five states participating, HERI got responses from 86 percent of the estimated number. Clearly, the NRC estimate is much too low.

Although it is not shown in the table, close to three-fifths of the respondents in the humanities sample have their doctorates in history; 11 percent, in English/American language and literature; 10 percent, in foreign languages; 11 percent, in philosophy; and 12 percent in other humanities fields. Of the nonhumanist sample, the greatest proportion (42 percent) have doctorates in the physical sciences (for example, chemistry or physics). Twenty-two percent are biological scientists; 15 percent are psychologists; 11 percent are engineers; and 10 percent have doctorates in other social sciences (for example, sociology or anthropology). The reader is reminded that the distribution by field of respondents to the HERI surveys may not be representative of the actual distribution of doctorate-level humanists and nonhumanists employed in the public sector.

Table 5–1
Comparison of HERI Sample with NRC Estimates of Ph.D.'s Employed in the Public Sector, by Broad Disciplinary Area

	Broad Disciplinary Area[a]				
Employer	Humanities	Social Sciences	Natural Sciences	Engineering	Psychology
Federal government					
Civil Service Commission estimates[b]	827	886	8,048	986	1,894
Total NRC estimates[c]	725[d]	2,183	10,238	3,940	2,183
Total HERI respondents	640	440	2,720	500	576
Ratio of HERI sample to NRC estimates	0.905	0.199	0.265	0.127	0.263
State and local government					
Total NRC estimates[c]	136	880	2,941	377	1,122
Total HERI respondents	117	32[e]	21[e]	7[e]	91[e]
Ratio of HERI sample to NRC estimates	0.860	0.036	0.007	0.018	0.081

[a]In the NRC estimates, the humanities include history, philosophy, English/American literature, modern languages, and other humanities. The social sciences include anthropology, archeology, communications, linguistics, sociology, economics, econometrics, social statistics, geography, area studies, political science, public administration, international relations, urban and regional planning, history and philosophy of science, general and other social sciences. The natural sciences include mathematics, computer sciences, physics/astronomy, chemistry, earth sciences, and biological sciences. In the HERI studies, the humanities include history, English/American language and literature, philosophy, foreign languages, and other humanities. Social sciences include anthropology, sociology, economics, and political science; natural sciences include physics, mathematics, geology, chemistry, biological sciences, and other sciences.

[b]Includes only those fields listed in the preceding footnote.

[c]Based on the NRC estimates in *Science, Engineering, and Humanities Doctorates in the United States, 1977* Profile Tables 1.5A and 2.5A.

[d]Includes libraries, museums, and historical societies.

[e]Although HERI explicitly sought names of government-employed humanists in five states, no such search was conducted for the other broad disciplinary areas. In all cases, the HERI state-government sample cannot be regarded as nationally representative.

Where Ph.D.'s Work in the Public Sector

The principal shortcoming of most published data on Ph.D.'s employed in the public sector is that they are aggregated to such an extent that detailed analyses are impossible. Thus, although estimates of the raw numbers of government-employed Ph.D.'s their fields, and their work activities are possible, virtually no information has heretofore been available on their specific employers in the public sector. As mentioned previously, the HERI sample may not be representative but is large enough to give us some sense of the wide dispersion of doctorate holders across government agencies. Table 5–2 shows the total number, as well as the number in each of the five disciplinary areas, employed by various departments; agencies; and other units of federal, state, and local governments. Generally, we would expect Ph.D.'s from certain disciplinary areas to be con-

Table 5–2
Specific Employers of Ph.D.'s in the Public Sector, by Broad Disciplinary Area

	Total	Broad Disciplinary Area				
		Humanities	*Social Sciences*	*Natural Sciences*	*Engineering*	*Psychology*
Federal government	4,876	640	440	2,700	500	576
Department of State	115	58	21	4	1	1
Agency for International Development		8	17	4	0	1
Department of Energy	153	7	9	115	22	0
Department of Commerce	362	2	19	41	8	1
Bureau of the Census		3	8	9	0	0
National Oceanic and Atmospheric Administration		0	5	79	12	0
National Bureau of Standards		0	2	144	22	7
Department of Interior	315	13	12	79	1	1
Bureau of Land Management		3	4	11	1	0
U.S. Geological Survey		2	2	151	9	0
Bureau of Mines		0	3	21	2	0
Department of Health, Education, and Welfare	434	22	45	69	1	23
National Institute of Mental Health		0	4	3	0	20
National Institute of Education		5	4	0	1	5
Office of Education		14	4	0	0	5
Food and Drug Administration		0	0	95	1	2
Public Health Service		0	5	65	1	3
Social Security Administration		15	10	5	0	2
Department of Agriculture	521	13	25	417	13	1
Forest Service		3	4	45	0	0
Department of Defense	85	21	8	34	19	3
Department of the Army	454	60	6	159	40	24
Corps of Engineers		10	7	24	14	0
Army research laboratories		1	2	69	10	28
Department of the Navy	459	18	9	74	38	20
Naval research laboratories		0	0	122	29	8
Naval Oceanic Systems Center		0	0	34	17	0
Naval Surface Weapons Center		0	0	61	19	0
Marine Corps		10	0	0	0	0

Air Force	144	28	5	58	37	16
Coast Guard	7	0	0	6	0	1
Department of Transportation	50	2	5	15	25	3
Department of the Treasury	49	12	17	12	0	8
Department of Labor	27	7	13	6	0	1
Department of Justice	31	0	10	11	1	9
Executive Office of the President	23	3	11	6	1	2
Agencies						
General Services Administration	14	5	6	2	1	0
National Science Foundation	25	3	4	12	3	3
National Aeronautics and Space Administration	240	5	0	157	75	3
Veterans Administration	504	28	6	135	4	331
Environmental Protection Agency	99	3	4	91	1	0
Nuclear Regulatory Commission	48	2	2	32	12	0
Trade commissions	21	0	21	0	0	0
Federal Reserve System	31	12	18	1	0	0
General Accounting Office	10	2	4	1	0	0
Federally funded laboratories	59	1	2	37	18	1
Library of Congress	48	44	3	0	0	0
Smithsonian Institution	63	26	9	28	0	0
National Archives	27	27	0	0	0	0
Other libraries and museums	30	25	1	4	0	0
National Endowment for the Humanities/Arts	17	14	3	0	0	0
U.S. government (otherwise unclassified)	411	103	61	172	40	35
State and Local Government	268	117	32	21	7	91
Department of education	15	13	0	0	0	2
Department of mental health	60	10	2	0	0	48
Department of human resources	12	8	1	0	0	3
Department of state	27	7	2	6	0	10
Historical societies	19	19	0	0	0	0
State and local government (otherwise unclassified)	137	60	27	15	7	28

Source: Based on responses to HERI survey of Highly Trained Public Sector Employees, 1978.

centrated in particular agencies (humanists in libraries, museums, and archives; natural scientists in energy, agriculture, and environmental protection; social scientists in health, education, and welfare and in other service areas); but this is not always the case. Moreover, the reader should bear in mind that, for every government-employed doctorate holder responding to the HERI surveys, several more either may not have been identified on the mailing rosters or may have decided not to return the questionnaire.

Table 5–3 shows the ranking of specific types of government employers (that is, departments, agencies, and other units) according to the total numbers of Ph.D.'s they employ. The Department of Agriculture is the leading employer of respondents to the HERI survey. Of the 521 Ph.D.'s identified as working for that department, close to 90 percent are natural scientists. All major disciplinary areas are represented, although there is only one psychologist. Ranking second is the Veterans Administration, which employs 504 of the HERI respondents; almost two-thirds of them are psychologists, and over one-fourth are natural scientists.

Table 5–3
Ranking of Specific Employer, by Total Number of Ph.D.'s Employed

Specific Employer	Total Number of Ph.D.'s Employed[a]	
1. Department of Agriculture	521	(1 psychologist)
2. Veterans Administration	504	(4 engineers)
3. Department of the Navy	459	
4. Department of the Army	454	
5. Department of Health, Education, and Welfare	434	(4 engineers)
6. Department of Commerce	362	
7. Department of the Interior	315	(1 psychologist)
8. National Aeronautics and Space Administration	240	(no social scientists, 3 psychologists)
9. Department of Energy	153	(no psychologists)
10. Air Force	144	
11. Department of State	115	(1 engineer, 2 psychologists)
12. Environmental Protection Agency	99	(3 humanists, 4 social scientists, 1 engineer, no psychologists)
13. Department of Defense	85	(3 psychologists)
14. Smithsonian Institution	63	(no engineers, no psychologists)
15. Federally funded laboratories	59	(1 humanist, 2 social scientists, 1 psychologist)
16. Department of Transportation	50	(2 humanists, 3 psychologists)
17. Department of the Treasury	49	(no engineers)
18. Nuclear Regulatory Commission	48	(2 humanists, 2 social scientists, no psychologists)
19. Library of Congress	48	(no natural scientists, no engineers, 1 psychologist)
20. Department of Justice	31	(no humanists, no engineers)

[a]Each of these departments or agencies employs at least five Ph.D.'s from each of the five broad disciplinary areas, with exceptions as noted.

The armed services give employment to substantial numbers of doctorate-holders. Indeed, if the figures for the U.S. army (454), navy (459), and air force (144) are combined, the total is 1,057, making the military rather than the Department of Agriculture the chief employer of Ph.D.'s in the public sector. All disciplinary areas are represented in each of these three services, with natural scientists predominating. Many of the doctorate holders work in army and navy research laboratories.

The Department of Health, Education, and Welfare (HEW) ranks as the fifth-most-important public-sector employer of Ph.D.'s, with 434 HERI respondents representing all the broad disciplinary areas, although there are only four engineers. Natural scientists predominate in such HEW agencies as the Food and Drug Administration and the Public Health Service, whereas humanists are most likely to be employed in the Social Security Administration and the Office of Education.

Ranking next on the list of major federal employers of Ph.D.'s are the Department of Commerce, with 362, and the Department of the Interior, with 315. Both departments are most likely to employ natural scientists, who work in agencies like the National Bureau of Standards, the National Oceanic and Atmospheric Administration, and the U.S. Geological Survey. At least five doctorate holders from each of the broad disciplinary areas have jobs with the two departments; only one psychologist, however, was identified as working for the Department of the Interior.

The National Aeronautics and Space Administration (NASA) employs 240 of the HERI respondents, most of them natural scientists or engineers. Somewhat surprisingly, more doctorate-level humanists than social scientists and psychologists were identified as working at NASA.

The next twelve agencies listed in table 5–3 employ significantly fewer Ph.D.'s than do the first eight agencies. For instance, the Department of Energy employs 153 HERI respondents, mostly natural scientists, although all disciplinary areas except psychology are represented. The Department of State employs 115 respondents, chiefly humanists and social scientists, many of whom work in the Agency for International Development. Ninety-nine HERI respondents, the great majority of them natural scientists, work for the Environmental Protection Agency. The Department of Defense employs 85 of the HERI respondents: 34 natural scientists, 21 humanists, 19 engineers, 8 social scientists, but only 3 psychologists. That such a high proportion (about 25 percent) are humanists may come as a surprise to those who view the defense department as a highly technical agency.

Although special efforts were made to survey humanists in the Smithsonian Institution, only 26 of the 63 respondents from the Smithsonian have a doctorate in the humanities; the remainder are 28 natural scientists and 9 social scientists. Federally funded research laboratories employ 59 HERI respondents, chiefly natural scientists. The Department of Transportation employs 50, mostly engineers; the Department of the Treasury employs 49, mostly social scientists; the Nuclear Regulatory Commission employs 48, most of them either natural scientists or engineers; the Library of Congress employs 48, almost all of whom are humanists; and the Department of Justice employs 31, chiefly natural scientists, social scientists, and psychologists—but no humanists.

Table 5–3 also indicates that sixteen of the twenty leading government employers provide jobs for at least five Ph.D.'s from at least three of the five broad disciplinary areas. In other words, the federal government offers a variety of job opportunities for Ph.D.'s in all fields. Although the job market in the public sector will not offset the academic-job crunch for humanists, the public sector nevertheless has potential as a major alternative employer if humanists can be persuaded to consider such careers.

Table 5–4 shows the most-promising public-sector employers for Ph.D.'s in each of the five broad disciplinary areas, as indicated by the numbers now employed that were identified by the HERI surveys. Clearly, natural scientists have the widest scope, with the Department of Agriculture being their chief employer. The Veterans Administration is the strongest federal employer for psychologists; the Department of the Navy, for engineers; and the Department of Health, Education, and Welfare, for social scientists. Looking more closely at those with doctorates in the humanities, we find that the largest number (71) work for the Department of the Army. The Department of State employs 66; the Department of Health, Education, and Welfare, 56; the Library of Congress, 44; and the Veterans Administration, 28. When all those employed by libraries, museums, and archives are considered together, however, these institutions become the most-important public-sector employers of humanists.

Two hundred sixty-eight respondents to the HERI questionnaires are employed in state or local governments. Despite special efforts to identify humanities Ph.D.'s employed in this sector, only 117 responded to the HERI questionnaire. They are fairly evenly distributed among state departments of education, of mental health, of human resources, and of state. About 16 percent (19 people) work in historical societies. The other large group identified as being employed by state governments consists of psychologists working in state mental-health departments. Thus, the data are much less helpful in informing us about the specific employers of those in state or local governments than about the specific employers of their federal counterparts. Nevertheless, we may conclude that doctorate-level humanists are rather widely distributed among state-government agencies.

Analysis, by Employer Type and Primary Work Activity

As the preceding discussion indicates, the public sector comprises a wide variety of specific employers: federal or state departments, agencies, and other such

Table 5–4
Ranking of Specific Employers, by Number of Ph.D.'s Employed from Each Broad Disciplinary Area

Humanities

1. Department of the Army	71
2. Department of State	66
3. Department of Health, Education, and Welfare	56
4. Library of Congress	44
5. Veterans Administration	28
6. National Archives	27
7. Smithsonian Institution	26
8. Other libraries and museums	25

Social Sciences

1. Department of Health, Education, and Welfare	72
2. Department of State	38
3. Department of Commerce	34
4. Department of Agriculture	29
5. Trade commissions	21
6. Department of the Interior	21
7. Federal Reserve System	18
8. Department of the Treasury	17

Natural Sciences

1. Department of Agriculture	462
2. Department of the Navy	291
3. Department of Commerce	273
4. Department of the Interior	262
5. Department of the Army	252
6. Department of Health, Education, and Welfare	237
7. National Aeronautics and Space Administration	157
8. Veterans Administration	135

Engineering

1. Department of the Navy	103
2. National Aeronautics and Space Administration	75
3. Department of Commerce	42
4. Federally funded laboratories	18
5. Department of the Interior	13
6. Nuclear Regulatory Commission	12

Psychology

1. Veterans Administration	331
2. Department of Health, Education, and Welfare	65
3. Department of the Army	52
4. Department of the Navy	28

units. For the purposes of this analysis, with its focus on humanists, all public-sector jobs have been classified as belonging to one of four *employer types*.

1. Libraries, museums, and archives (also referred to as "the library group"), which may be either federal (for example, the Library of Congress, the Smithsonian Institution, and the National Archives) or state/local.

2. Human-services organizations, which also may be either federal (for example, the Veterans Administration; the Department of Health, Education, and Welfare) or state/local (for example, state mental hospitals).
3. Federal agencies other than libraries, museums, and archives or human-services organizations (for example, the Department of State, the National Science Foundation, the armed services, and federally funded laboratories).
4. State/local agencies other than human-services organizations or libraries, museums, and archives (for example, a state department of finance or of education).

The reader should bear in mind that "federal agencies" or "state/local agencies," when referred to in the text as employer types, cover only those agencies that are not libraries, museums, and archives or human-services organizations.

In addition to classifying all government-employed Ph.D.'s according to where they work, we classified them according to what they do—that is, their *primary work activity*—as follows.

1. Research of all types.
2. Administration and management (of research and development programs, of education programs, or of other types of programs).
3. Other activities (for example, environmental protection, engineering, health services, performing or creative arts, training).

Thus, all respondents to the HERI surveys are grouped according to their employer type and their primary work activity; these classifications will be used in many of the analyses reported in the rest of this book. Table 5–5 shows the distribution of doctorate-level humanists and of natural scientists, social scientists, and engineers (the latter group being referred to, for convenience, as "nonhumanists") among the four employer types and the three primary work activities.

By far, the largest group of public-sector humanists in our sample—347 of 636, or 54 percent—work in federal agencies (that is, federal units that are not in the library group and are not human-services organizations). Slightly more than 25 percent work in libraries, museums, and archives. Twelve percent are employed in state and local agencies, and only 7 percent in human-services organizations.

Relatively few of the humanists identified by the HERI survey—only 13 percent—work primarily as researchers, with those employed by the library group being most likely to report research as their primary work activity. About one-quarter are administrators; of these, 58 administer research-and-development (R&D) programs, and 97 administer programs other than R&D or education. Those humanists employed in libraries, museums, and archives are least likely

Table 5–5

Distribution of Humanists and Nonhumanists, by Employer Type and Primary Work Activity

(percent)

Employer Type	Primary Work Activity			
	Research	*Administration*	*Other*	N
Libraries, museums, archives				
Humanists	17	8	75	168
Nonhumanists	59	16	25	44
Human-services organizations				
Humanists	9	32	58	43
Nonhumanists	21	21	58	810
Federal agencies				
Humanists	12	30	58	347
Nonhumanists	49	25	26	2,841
State and local agencies				
Humanists	13	29	58	78
Nonhumanists	23	26	51	57
Total humanists	13	24	62	636
Total nonhumanists	43	24	33	3,752

Note: These totals differ from those shown in other tables because of nonresponse to particular questionnaire items.

to say that administration is their primary work activity. The largest proportion—three-quarters of the library-group employees and 58 percent of those working in each of the other three employer types—report "other" primary work activities. For humanists, these other activities are most likely to be library, museum, and archival work (reported by 124) or writing and editing (reported by 84). Program planning and budgeting are primary work activities for 17 humanities Ph.D.'s; consulting and professional services, for 12; personnel and employee relations, for 10; public relations, for 8; and public safety, law enforcement, or community services, for 8. Eleven say that they act as historians within their agencies.

Like the humanists, the government-employed scientists and engineers are most likely to be working for federal agencies (2,841 of 3,752, or 76 percent). But unlike the humanists, the next largest proportion (22 percent) work in human-services organizations. Only a very small proportion work in the library group or in state and local agencies (less than 2 percent in both cases). As to primary work activity, scientists and engineers are far more likely than are humanists to be researchers (43 percent versus 13 percent) and far less likely to be engaged in "other" primary work activities (33 percent versus 62 percent). Of those nonhumanists who are researchers, larger-than-average proportions are employed in the library group (59 percent) and in federal agencies (49 percent). Equal proportions of humanists and of scientists and engineers are administrators; but, as the table indicates, they are distributed rather differently among the employer types.

Distribution of Humanists, by Field of Doctorate

Humanists with doctorates in English are somewhat more likely than are most others to work in human-services organizations and in state and local agencies but not in libraries, museums, and archives. As might be expected, they are the most likely of any group to say that writing and editing are primary work activities but are relatively unlikely to be researchers or to do library, museum, or archival work.

Much larger than average proportions of those with doctorates in foreign languages work in federal agencies, but relatively few work in state- or local-government agencies or in libraries, museums, and archives. Very few report their primary work activity as research or as library, museum, and archival work; a larger-than-average proportion do "other" work.

Of those whose doctoral field was philosophy, unusually large proportions work in human-services organizations, and somewhat larger-than-average proportions in state and local agencies. Only one individual was identified as working in the library group. These Ph.D.'s tend to report their primary work activity as administration of programs other than R&D or education, or as consulting and professional services.

Doctorate-level historians are far more likely than members of any other group to work in libraries, museums, and archives; but they are unlikely to be employed in human-services organizations. Relatively large proportions do library, museum, and archival work; writing and editing; and research; few administer programs other than R&D or education. Not surprisingly, they are the only group to report that their primary work is that of acting as historian.

Those with doctorates in other humanities are least likely of any group to work in federal agencies; relatively large proportions work in human-services organizations. Their patterns with respect to primary work activity are not distinctive.

Conclusion

Although the public sector has never been a major employer of Ph.D.'s, especially those with degrees in the humanities, the foregoing analyses make it clear that doctorate holders from all fields are fairly widely distributed among federal agencies and that doctorate-level humanists have found jobs in a variety of state- and local-government agencies. Thus, other humanists—faced with the academic-job crunch—might be well advised to seek employment in the public sector. Information about those who have been successful in finding satisfying and productive—although nontraditional—employment in government could do much not only to break down prejudices against humanities Ph.D.'s as potential employees in other than academic jobs but also to encourage new graduates to seek such employment. Chapters 6 and 7 provide such information.

6 Finding Public-Sector Jobs: The Whys and the Hows

As chapter 5 indicated, any Ph.D.'s—including those with degrees in the humanities—are employed in the public sector and are, moreover, rather widely distributed among a variety of federal, state, and local agencies. But, as was also pointed out in chapter 5, very few doctorate-level humanists reported that, at the time they entered graduate school, they had seriously considered any option other than the traditional one—that is, employment as academic faculty.

Thus, several questions arise: First, do those humanists identified in the Higher Education Research Institute (HERI) studies as currently employed in the public sector start out with traditional career goals; and if so, what makes them change their minds? Second, having changed their minds, how do they go about seeking jobs in the public sector; and what methods or contacts prove most effective? Third, having secured such jobs, what do they perceive to be the relationship between those jobs and their graduate training?

This chapter tries to answer these questions. Moreover, it is intended to be of some practical value to more-recent doctorate recipients who may be considering public-sector jobs. After all, one can go about looking for a job in many different ways; and for some types of jobs, one method may be more effective than others. For instance, looking through the "Help Wanted" section in a local newspaper is much more practical for a person seeking sales or secretarial work than for someone who wants a teaching position or a partnership in a law firm. Although most graduate students in the humanities know which search methods are appropriate for academic positions (the old-boy network, professional-society meetings and journals) they do not necessarily know how to go about looking for nonacademic jobs. Further, recent Ph.D.'s should be aware that the field of their doctorate may limit their opportunities to find closely related nonacademic jobs. That this lack of relationship between formal education and work does not necessarily make nonacademic jobs undesirable is, of course, a major theme of this book. Finally, those applying for nonacademic jobs should know which of their competencies to emphasize, since some skills, abilities, and areas of knowledge—acquired in graduate school and elsewhere—may be more valuable than others in certain types of nonacademic jobs. Thus, the last part of this chapter deals with various links between graduate training and the current job.

Two basic approaches are used in presenting the data. The first is based on the field of the doctorate. Humanists are compared with nonhumanists (natural scientists, social scientists, and engineers). In addition, five fields within the humanities, (English, foreign languages, history, philosophy, and other humanities) are compared with one another. The second approach involves comparisons by employer type (libraries, museums, archives; human-services organizations; federal agencies; state and local agencies) and by primary work activity (research, administration, other) within each employer type.

Reasons for Changing Career Goals

To determine, first, just what the initial career plans of humanists now working in the public sector had been, we looked at their responses to a questionnaire item that read, "Did you enter graduate school expecting to become a college or university teacher?" Overall, about four in five say they did have such expectations; about one-tenth say they did not expect to become college teachers; and the rest say they were undecided on that point when they entered graduate school. These response patterns did not differ by age group, even though one would suppose that more-recent Ph.D.'s had entered graduate school less hopeful of academic employment.

In short, the majority of publicly employed humanists have failed to fulfill their initial career expectations. Of course, some of these people may have previously worked as academic faculty and then switched to government jobs; others may hold part-time teaching positions in addition to their primary positions in government. Nonetheless, the data suggest that most of the humanities sample must, at some point, have changed their earlier career goals.

Although no such item appeared on the questionnaire for scientists and engineers, there was a somewhat comparable item that read, "If I could begin my career again, I would like to become a college professor." Slightly more than half agree (either somewhat or strongly) with this statement, and about 45 percent disagree. Thus, public employment is less likely to represent a second-choice career for nonhumanists.

Just why do some humanists who, at graduate-school entry, plan to become college teachers change their career goals? One item on the HERI questionnaire listed nine possible reasons.

1. Available teaching positions were limited or unattractive.
2. Decided I did not enjoy teaching.
3. Available job opportunities in previous field were limited or unattractive.
4. Decided I did not enjoy first-choice career.
5. Found more-attractive or challenging job opportunities elsewhere.
6. Changed career aspirations for personal or family reasons.
7. Became outdated in my first-choice field.
8. Became interested in a different area of study.
9. Was terminated in a job.

The questionnaire for scientists and engineers contained a similar item, except that the first and second of these reasons were not included. On both questionnaires, respondents were instructed to mark all reasons that applied.

Among government-employed humanists who had initially expected to become college teachers, the most-common reasons for changing career goals are limited or unattractive teaching opportunities (cited by 68 percent of the total group, but much more often by those with doctorates in English, foreign languages, and history than by those with doctorates in philosophy or other humanities); the greater attractiveness of other job opportunities (cited by 47 percent of the total group, but more frequently by those in English and other humanities than by those in the three remaining humanities areas); and personal or family reasons (cited by 24 percent of the total group, with a high of 47 percent of those with doctorates in philosophy). Least-often cited as reasons for changing career goals are becoming outdated in one's field (3 percent of the total group); not enjoying one's first-choice career (7 percent); not enjoying teaching (11 percent of the total group, with a high of 17 percent among foreign-language Ph.D.'s; and being terminated in a job (11 percent overall, with a high of 17 percent among those with degrees in English).

Analyzing the data by employer type and primary work activity, one finds that administrators in federal agencies are especially likely to mention finding more-attractive job opportunities elsewhere as their reason for changing career goals (72 percent, compared with 47 percent overall). Those employed in human-services organizations and performing work activities other than research or administration are especially likely to mention limited or unattractive teaching opportunities, job termination, and personal or family reasons, all of which can be regarded as negative reasons. Researchers in libraries, museums, and archives are especially likely to say that they simply did not enjoy teaching.

Of those scientists and engineers who indicate that they changed their career goals at least once since leaving graduate school, half say that they found more-attractive job opportunities elsewhere (with administrators being more likely than researchers and those with other primary work activities to cite this reason); two in five say that the available job opportunities in their previous field were limited or unattractive; and three in ten say they became interested in a different area of study (only half as many humanists mention this last reason). As is the case with humanists, very few scientists and engineers say that their career goals changed as a result of their becoming outdated in their field (4 percent) or being terminated in a job (9 percent).

In summary, the dominant reasons for changing career goals balance out for the two groups. Humanists most often mention limited or unattractive *teaching* opportunities (an option not included on the science and engineering questionnaire); finding more-attractive or challenging job opportunities elsewhere is the second-most-common reason among humanists. Among nonhumanists, the latter reason ranks first, and the second most frequently mentioned is limited or unattractive *job* opportunities in the first-choice field. Thus, goal change among the Ph.D.'s in our sample is motivated by both positive and negative considerations.

Job-Search Method

Once they have decided—for whatever reasons—to look for a job in the public sector, how do doctorate-level humanists go about their job search? What contacts or methods do they use? Do they try a wide variety of methods, or do they tend to concentrate on just one method? Do they get their government jobs through an active search, or are they more likely to be passive, depending on luck or hoping for an unsolicited offer? Do they rely more on formal or informal channels? And how effective are the different methods?

One item on the HERI survey read, "In securing your present job, which of the following job-search methods/contacts (a) did you use, and (b) were successful?" The eighteen options were:

1. My former professors.
2. Colleagues in my organization/institution.
3. Colleagues in other institutions.
4. College/university placement office.
5. Public/state employment service.
6. Private employment agency.
7. Civil-service application.
8. Recruiting teams from government, industry.
9. Professional contacts.
10. Direct personal application to employer.
11. Professional organizations, meetings.
12. Newspaper advertisements.
13. Professional journals, periodicals.
14. Met new employer through previous job.
15. Unsolicited offer.
16. Parents/other relatives.
17. Friends.
18. Luck/chance.

Respondents were instructed to mark all options that applied. An identically worded item appeared on the questionnaire for scientists and engineers.

Given the nature of the sample—Ph.D.'s employed in the public sector—it is hardly surprising to find that, of the wide range of job-search methods available, the most commonly used (by 53 percent of the humanists and 51 percent of the scientists and engineers) is the civil-service application. Indeed, it is somewhat surprising that the proportions are not greater (although not all public-sector jobs are civil-service positions, of course). Perhaps these highly trained people do not have to go through regular channels in applying for government jobs; or perhaps many of them had previously held government jobs, and their earlier applications were still valid. Not only is civil-service application the most-common method, but it is also the most effective: 43 percent of both samples say that they got their current jobs through this method.

The two other most frequently used methods or contacts are direct personal application to the employer (mentioned by 52 percent of the humanists and by 38 percent of the scientists and engineers) and professional contacts (mentioned by 39 percent of each sample). Both proved to be fairly effective: 37 percent of the humanists and 28 percent of the nonhumanists said that direct personal application had helped them to get their current jobs; 26 percent of both groups indicated that their professional contacts had been valuable.

Perhaps because they face a tighter job market, humanists seem to search for jobs more actively and to try a wider variety of methods. Thus, larger proportions of humanists than of scientists and engineers mention using former professors (36 percent versus 31 percent), college or university placement offices (28 percent versus 12 percent), friends (25 percent versus 14 percent), public or state employment services (13 percent versus 6 percent), and newspaper advertisements (11 percent versus 6 percent). A larger proportion of humanists (16 percent) than of nonhumanists (9 percent) report that their friends were helpful to them in their last job search. Otherwise, humanists have only slightly greater success with these methods than do nonhumanists. Finally, about one-quarter of the humanists, but only 11 percent of the scientists and engineers, say that luck or chance played a role in their securing their current jobs.

Since the effectiveness of a particular job-search method may vary with the type of job sought, the following discussion highlights our findings for humanists, by employer type and primary work activity. Those humanists in libraries, museums, and archives are somewhat less likely than are humanists in the other three employment settings to use civil-service application and also less likely to report success with this method. They are somewhat more likely to use professional contacts, former professors, and colleagues from other institutions or organizations and to report success in getting their jobs through these methods. In addition, 7 percent of the researchers and administrators in the library group say they were attracted into their government jobs by recruiting teams. The humanists working in human-services organizations tend to rely most heavily on civil-service application and direct personal application and to find these methods effective. In addition, they are more likely than others to say that friends and professional journals and periodicals had been helpful to them. Relatively few say they relied on professional contacts. As might be expected, those working for federal agencies most frequently used, and found successful, civil-service application. The humanists working for state- and local-government agencies seem to have used a wide variety of methods and contacts in getting their current jobs and are more likely than others to find public or state employment agencies, newspaper advertisements, and contacts made through their previous jobs helpful.

Generally, researchers are especially likely to attribute their success in landing a job to chance or luck; former professors also seem to be valuable contacts for this group. Administrators rarely used (and thus are less likely to report success with) college placement offices, state or public employment agencies, or civil-service application. Most helpful to them are professional contacts and their colleagues at their former institutions or organizations. Luck or chance seems to play little part in their success in securing a job, and they are more likely than others to have received an unsolicited offer. Except that civil-service application seems to have been the most-effective job-search method, no very clear pattern emerges for those engaged in "other" primary work activities.

Relationship of Current Job to Graduate Field

Having found employment in the public sector, to what extent do doctorate-level humanists perceive these jobs as compatible with their graduate training? Because in the past 90 percent of all humanities Ph.D.'s became faculty members in colleges and universities, teaching jobs in academe are probably regarded by this group as most closely related to graduate training, even though graduate study emphasizes research over teaching. Indeed, according to an earlier study (Solmon, Ochsner, and Hurwicz 1979) that included faculty members and private-sector employees as well as government employees, 83 percent of the humanists who were college professors said that their jobs were closely related to their doctoral studies; in contrast, only 17 percent of those who were administrators in the private sector considered their jobs closely related to their graduate training. Overall, regardless of employment sector, 54 percent of the humanists saw themselves as holding closely related jobs.

In the current study, both the questionnaire for humanists and that for scientists and engineers included an item that asked respondents to indicate whether their current jobs were "closely related," "somewhat related," or "not related" to their graduate training. Table 6–1 presents the results by graduate field, and table 6–2 by employer type and primary work activity, for both samples.

As table 6–1 shows, almost half the government-employed humanists say their jobs are closely related to their graduate training; 37 percent say they are somewhat related; and 15 percent say the two are not related. There is considerable variation by field: Fewer than one-third of those with doctorates in English, foreign languages, or philosophy—compared with more than half of those with doctorates in history or other humanities—see their jobs as closely related to their graduate training.

Table 6–1

Relationship of Current Job to Graduate Training, by Graduate Field

(percent)

	Closely Related	Somewhat Related	Not Related	N
Humanities				
English	23	55	22	65
Foreign languages	22	47	32	60
Philosophy	32	51	17	41
History	56	32	12	380
Other humanities	53	31	16	77
Total	48	37	15	623
Nonhumanities				
Biological sciences	67	28	5	831
Other natural sciences	50	40	9	1,640
Engineering	60	33	6	412
Psychology	70	26	3	595
Other social sciences	63	31	6	405
Total	59	34	7	3,883

Scientists and engineers are much more likely than are humanists to perceive a close relationship between their government jobs and their graduate training. Only 7 percent (less than half the proportion for humanists) believe that the two are not related. Most likely to be in closely related jobs are psychologists and biological scientists; least likely are other natural scientists.

Table 6–2 indicates that, regardless of employer type, researchers in both samples are generally the most likely to see themselves as holding closely related jobs. In addition, 70 percent of the nonhumanists performing other primary work activities in human-services organizations say their jobs are closely related to their graduate training; these are probably psychologists doing clinical work or counseling, activities that are traditional for the field. In most cases, administrators are the least likely to see a close relation between job and graduate training. Relatively large proportions of humanists working in human-services organizations or performing administrative or other tasks in federal agencies say that their jobs are not at all related to their graduate training.

The reasons that government-employed Ph.D.'s give for working in jobs less than closely related to their graduate training are shown in table 6–3. Almost twice as many humanists as scientists and engineers say that employment opportunities were scarce for people in jobs related to their doctoral study; those with degrees in English, foreign languages, or history are more likely than those with degrees in philosophy or other humanities to cite this reason. The second-most-common reason among humanists (cited by 48 percent, compared with only 23 percent of the nonhumanists) is that jobs related to their doctoral field were not available, with English and history Ph.D.'s being especially likely to

Table 6–2
Relationship of Current Job to Graduate Training, by Employer Type and Primary Work Activity
(percent)

	Closely Related	Somewhat Related	Not Related	N
Humanities				
Libraries, museums, archives:				
Research	84	10	5	19
Administration	—	—	—	9
Other	63	31	6	106
Human-services organizations:				
Research	—	—	—	4
Administration	18	54	27	11
Other	26	37	37	22
Federal agencies:				
Research	72	19	8	37
Administration	40	39	21	80
Other	38	37	26	179
State/local agencies:				
Research	—	—	—	6
Administration	38	50	12	17
Other	44	41	16	31
Science and engineering				
Libraries, museums, archives:				
Research	100	0	0	28
Administration	—	—	—	7
Other	90	10	0	11
Human-services organizations:				
Research	69	28	3	180
Administration	42	46	12	175
Other	70	26	4	495
Federal agencies:				
Research	70	27	3	180
Administration	45	45	10	734
Other	48	41	11	768
State/local agencies:				
Research	46	46	8	13
Administration	44	50	6	18
Other	44	34	22	32

Note: Percentages not shown for those cells with fewer than ten cases.

give this reason. Among nonhumanists, those with degrees in other natural sciences are more likely than those in other fields to cite these two negative reasons for taking a job that was less than closely related.

Better pay is the third-most-common reason given by humanists (45 percent, compared with 32 percent of nonhumanists) for working in a somewhat related or unrelated field; those with degrees in philosophy and English are particularly likely to be motivated by this reason. This does not necessarily mean that hu-

Table 6–3
Reasons for Working at a Job that Is Only Somewhat Related or Is Not Related to Graduate Training, by Graduate Field
(percent)

Reason	English	Foreign languages	Philos- ophy
Never planned to take a closely related job.	0	10	3
Changed field to one I prefer more.	22	29	29
Exposed to another field and became interested.	43	37	52
Prefer present work.	41	29	48
First job unrelated to doctoral study; became interested in this work.	6	12	16
Tried closely related employment, but did not like it.	7	6	3
Joined family business or firm.	0	0	0
Found job that offers better chance for career advancement.	28	43	36
Pay is better where I am.	52	43	58
No longer in closely related job due to promotion.	4	6	3
Wanted part-time work, flexible hours.	0	0	0
Wanted to work at home.	0	0	0
Jobs related to doctoral study not available where I live, and do not want to move.	13	24	13
Jobs related to my doctoral field not available.	46	37	36
Could not get a closely related job, but would prefer one.	26	31	19
Limited in job selection by situation of spouse, family responsibilities.	7	14	13
Employment opportunities scarce for people in jobs related to my doctoral study.	65	61	48
Have become technologically obsolete in field of doctoral study.	7	12	3
In the military.	0	4	0
Better quality work environment where I am.	13	18	13
N	54	51	31

manists in the public sector earn more than their nonhumanist counterparts; rather, they may simply feel that salaries in the public sector are higher than salaries for college teachers in their discipline. It is tempting to use this finding as evidence that humanists are just as (or more) interested in money than are those from other fields. But it is also possible that the salaries of humanities faculty are so low that humanities Ph.D.'s must take nonacademic jobs just to reach parity with science-faculty members. In any case, it should not be surprising that, even among humanists, salary is an important consideration when it comes to choosing a job.

Becoming interested in another field after being exposed to it is mentioned by 38 percent of the humanists as a reason for working in their current (less than closely related) jobs; those with degrees in philosophy or in other humanities are most likely to choose this response. Among scientists, this reason is cited by 45 percent, making it the top-ranked motive for this group. Finally, 34 percent of the humanists, compared with 30 percent of the nonhumanists, see their jobs as

History	Other Humanities	Total	Biological Sciences	Other Natural Sciences	Engineering	Psychology	Other Social Sciences	Total
2	8	4	4	9	9	6	7	8
13	25	20	11	20	15	10	7	15
32	47	38	44	47	42	47	37	45
19	31	28	2	5	3	5	5	4
6	6	8	8	12	10	9	14	11
4	3	4	3	4	4	10	8	4
0	0	0	0	0	0	0	0	0
35	31	34	30	29	30	32	38	30
42	42	45	33	27	29	41	48	32
6	6	6	21	16	28	20	11	18
1	3	1	0	0	0	1	1	0
1	0	0	0	0	0	0	0	0
12	6	13	8	7	10	4	4	7
57	33	48	24	27	16	13	22	23
29	22	28	18	15	14	12	22	16
9	19	11	11	8	12	9	14	9
62	33	58	30	34	20	22	26	30
3	8	6	12	15	8	7	4	12
2	0	2	3	1	1	0	3	1
11	14	13	15	10	13	12	20	12
170	36	342	272	816	157	169	147	1,561

offering a better chance for career advancement; foreign-language Ph.D.'s and social scientists other than psychologists are most apt to give this reason.

Least likely to be cited as reasons by members of either sample are wanting part-time work and flexible hours, wanting to work at home, being in the military, joining a family firm or business, and never having planned to take a closely related job, although one-tenth of the foreign-language Ph.D.'s give this last reason.

Some provocative differences between humanists and nonhumanists emerge from this comparison. For instance, 28 percent of the humanists, compared with only 4 percent of the scientists and engineers, say simply that they prefer their present work; those with doctorates in philosophy or English are especially likely to give this reason. One-fifth of the humanists and 15 percent of the nonhumanists say they changed their field to one that they prefer more, a reason most frequently mentioned by Ph.D.'s in foreign languages and philosophy. The implication would seem to be that some humanists, after receiving the doctorate, simply lose interest in their doctoral field. This loss of interest is much less common among scientists and engineers. On the other hand, 28 percent of the humanists, compared with 16 percent of the scientists and engineers, say they could not get a closely related job but would prefer one. Apparently, humanists are more likely than are nonhumanists to be unhappy about holding jobs unrelated to their graduate field; those with doctorates in philosophy are an exception, in that only 20 percent check this reason.

About one-eighth of the nonhumanists, but only 6 percent of the humanists, cite becoming technologically obsolete in their doctoral field as a reason for taking an unrelated job; biological scientists and other natural scientists are especially likely to feel that they have become outdated. Scientists and engineers are three times as likely as humanists (18 percent versus 6 percent) to say that they had been promoted out of a closely related job (presumably into administration or management, which they tend to regard as less than closely related to their graduate training); engineers in particular tend to cite this reason.

In summary, humanists are somewhat more likely than are scientists to take less than closely related jobs for negative reasons; scientists are somewhat more likely to cite positive incentives. This difference is, of course, chiefly due to the tighter academic-job market for humanists.

Even though one may work at a job that is not closely related to one's graduate training, it does not follow that doctoral study has been a complete waste; the competencies acquired during graduate school may prove to be valuable on the job. Several items on the HERI questionnaire were designed to explore further the usefulness of graduate study (as well as that of other types of training) to government-employed Ph.D.'s.

Ways in Which Graduate Training Is Useful

One item that appeared on both the humanities questionnaire and the sciences and engineering questionnaire read, "Looking back on your graduate education, please indicate the extent to which it was useful in the following ways." Six options were listed.

1. Provided a skill that enabled me to get my first job.
2. Increased my chances of finding a good job.
3. Helped me choose my life goals.
4. Gave me knowledge and skills that I use in present job.
5. Graduate degree a factor in being hired by present employer.
6. Graduate degree necessary for promotion.

Generally, scientists and engineers find their graduate training to be more helpful in their subsequent employment than do humanists. On each of the six options, larger proportions of the former than of the latter say that their graduate education proved to be very useful. Most frequently mentioned among humanists is that the graduate degree was an important factor in their being hired by their current employer (64 percent, compared with 78 percent of the nonhumanists). Humanists are almost equally likely to say that their graduate education provided them with a skill that enabled them to get their first jobs (63 percent of the humanists, compared with 78 percent of the scientists and engineers). In addition, 59 percent of the humanists say that graduate education increased their chances of finding a good job; among nonhumanists, this is the top-ranking reason, mentioned by 80 percent. Over half the humanists (57 percent, compared with 67 percent of the nonhumanists) feel that graduate education gave them knowledge and skills that they use on the current job. Comparatively few in either sample say that graduate education helped them to choose their life goals (44 percent of the humanists, 47 percent of the scientists and engineers) or that a graduate degree is necessary for promotion in their current jobs (38 percent of the humanists, 52 percent of the scientists and engineers).

Looking at particular fields within the humanities, we find that those with doctorates in history are generally more likely than others to find their graduate education helpful in the ways specified, and that those with doctorates in foreign languages are generally least likely to do so. In addition, a relatively large proportion of those with doctorates in other humanities say that their graduate education increased their chances of finding a good job, whereas a relatively small proportion of those with doctorates in philosophy find graduate education to have been helpful in this way. Relatively few of those with doctorates in English believe that the graduate degree was a factor in their being hired by the current employer.

Analysis of the data by employment sector and primary work activity indicates that, among humanists, researchers in libraries, museums, and archives are most likely to have found graduate education valuable in a number of ways; for example, 84 percent (compared with 57 percent of all humanists) say that it gave them the knowledge and skills that they use on the current job. Those humanists performing ''other'' primary work activities in human-services organizations are least likely to feel that their graduate education was useful.

Most-Useful Aspects of Training

To determine the specific aspects of both graduate training and other types of training or education that prove most valuable to humanists and nonhumanists employed in the public sector, the following item was included on both questionnaires. ''To what extent did the following provide knowledge or skills that helped prepare you for your present job?'' Eleven options were listed.

1. Particular course(s) in major area.
2. Courses outside major area.

 3. Graduate study in general.
 4. Extracurricular activities while in graduate school.
 5. Research assistantship.
 6. Teaching assistantship.
 7. Undergraduate study.
 8. Formal training or courses at place of employment.
 9. Formal training or courses other than programs offered by employer.
10. General on-the-job experience.
11. Leisure activities.

The discussion that follows is based on those respondents indicating that a particular option helped them "very much" in preparing for their present jobs.

Once again, scientists and engineers find their graduate education (as well as other training experiences) more useful in their public-sector jobs than do humanists. The rank order of the most frequently mentioned types of training is the same for the two groups, however. Most likely to be considered valuable is general on-the-job experience (67 percent of the humanists, 69 percent of the nonhumanists), followed by graduate study in general (49 percent versus 56 percent); particular courses in the major area (39 percent versus 54 percent); and undergraduate study (36 percent versus 42 percent). The greatest discrepancy between the two samples occurs with respect to research assistantships: 36 percent of the scientists and engineers, but only 9 percent of the humanists, say that this aspect of their graduate training contributed a great deal toward preparing them for their present jobs. The most-obvious explanation of this is simply that few research assistantships exist in the humanities. Courses outside the major are generally more helpful to nonhumanists (28 percent) than to humanists (17 percent); the same is true of teaching assistantships (17 percent of the nonhumanists, compared with only 10 percent of the humanists). On the other hand, 11 percent of the humanists but only 6 percent of the nonhumanists say that their leisure activities constituted useful preparation for the current job. Formal training at the place of employment is found useful by roughly equal proportions of the two samples (14–15 percent), but formal training programs outside the place of employment were useful to larger proportions of scientists (15 percent) than of humanists (10 percent). Least helpful are extracurricular activities in graduate school, mentioned by only 8 percent of the humanists and 7 percent of the scientists and engineers.

Within the humanities, those from different graduate fields find different aspects of training valuable in preparing them for their government jobs. Those with doctorates in English are especially apt to mention general on-the-job experience and teaching assistantships, but less likely to mention particular courses in their major area. Those with doctorates in foreign languages are most likely to mention formal training programs (both at the place of employment and outside it) than are other humanists, but are less likely to feel that graduate study in general or particular courses in their major area were valuable. The pattern for philosophy Ph.D.'s is striking, in that relatively large proportions mention undergraduate study, courses outside their major area, leisure activities, and extracurricular activities in graduate school; relatively small proportions, however, find general on-the-job experience very helpful. Doctorate-level historians tend to cite graduate study in general, particular courses in their major field, and research assistantships as helpful; but very few mention formal training programs offered outside the place of employment. Those with doctorates in other humanities are somewhat more inclined than others to cite undergraduate study and particular courses in their major field as helping to prepare them for their government jobs.

The kinds of education and training experiences found valuable on the current job also vary by employment sector and primary work activity. Thus, graduate study in general is much more likely to be regarded as helpful by researchers in all employment settings and by administrators in state or local agencies, and much less likely to be rated as helpful by humanists employed in human-services organizations. Similarly, researchers—as well as those performing "other" activities in libraries, museums, and archives and in state or local government agencies—tend to say that particular courses in their major area helped prepare them for their current job; relatively few administrators in federal agencies or humanists in human-services organizations make this evaluation. Most likely to regard their undergraduate training as valuable preparation are researchers in libraries and administrators in state and local government, whereas those engaging in other primary work activities for the latter employer type rarely find undergraduate study useful. Administrators in all employment settings are especially likely to mention general on-the-job experience as providing them with the skills and knowledge required for their current jobs. Those humanists engaging in other primary work activities within human-services organization are most apt to say they benefited from formal training programs, whether sponsored by the employer or by some outside agency. Generally, then, the formal aspects of graduate study seem most beneficial to humanists working in libraries, museums, and archives and to those doing research for all employer types. Humanists working in human-services organizations or performing administrative tasks in any settings are less likely to find their graduate education helpful and thus are more likely to mention training programs or on-the-job experience.

The Development and Value of Specific Traits and Abilities

Both humanists and nonhumanists were asked to indicate which of eighteen traits and abilities had, first, improved significantly in graduate school and, second, proved useful in their current jobs. The specific traits and abilities were:

1. General knowledge.
2. Ability to think clearly.
3. Leadership ability.
4. Critical thinking or analytical skills.
5. Self-confidence.
6. Self-discipline and ability to follow rules.
7. Creativity and originality.
8. Writing ability.
9. Insight.
10. Cultural perspective.
11. Understanding of others.
12. Political awareness.
13. Academic ability.
14. Drive to achieve.
15. Mathematical ability.
16. Mechanical ability.
17. Public-speaking ability.
18. Research skills.

The traits and abilities most frequently mentioned as having improved significantly during graduate school are generally the same for the two samples: research skills (cited by 79 percent of the humanists and 85 percent of the scientists and engineers); critical thinking or analytical skills (71 percent and 75 percent); general knowledge (65 percent and 70 percent); ability to think clearly (61 percent and 65 percent); and academic ability (62 percent and 64 percent). Humanists, however, are just as likely to mention improvement in writing ability as improvement in critical ability (71 percent), whereas only half the scientists and engineers think that their writing ability improved during graduate school. Further, larger proportions of humanists than of nonhumanists mention improvements in cultural perspective (50 percent versus 26 percent) and political awareness (33 percent versus 20 percent), whereas larger proportions of scientists and engineers mention improvements in mathematical ability (44 percent, compared with only 5 percent of humanists); mechanical ability (14 percent, compared with 2 percent); and creativity and originality (50 percent versus 38 percent). Those competencies more likely to be gained through graduate work in the humanities are particularly useful for public-sector employment.

Among humanists employed in the public sector, those with doctorates in English are more likely than others to feel that their academic ability and self-discipline had improved in graduate school but are less likely to mention improvements in self-confidence or in creativity and originality. Foreign-language Ph.D.'s mention improvements in insight and cultural perspective; relatively few feel that graduate training improved their general knowledge, ability to think clearly, self-confidence, understanding of others, or political awareness. Those with doctorates in philosophy are distinguished by their tendency to mention improvements in ability to think clearly, leadership ability, critical thinking, creativity and originality, mathematical ability, and public-speaking ability; few, however, cite improvements in cultural perspective and self-discipline. History Ph.D.'s resemble the "average" humanist (understandably, since they far outnumber humanists from other fields and thus influence the average), except that somewhat higher proportions mention improvements in general knowledge and political awareness. Like philosophy Ph.D.'s, those with degrees in other humanities believe that their leadership ability and mathematical ability were improved by graduate study. Lower-than-average proportions, however, mention improvements in ability to think clearly, critical thinking, writing ability, and insight. To summarize, those with doctorates in philosophy seem to have the most-positive view of their development during graduate school, those with doctorates in foreign languages the least-positive attitude.

Turning to those traits and abilities that Ph.D.'s in the public sector consider most useful in their present jobs, we find that neither research skills nor academic ability are mentioned as often as some other skills. Three-fifths of both samples say that research skills are useful (compared with about four in five who say that graduate study developed those skills); and two-fifths of the humanists, but only one-third of the scientists, say that academic ability is very useful (compared with three-fifths who mention improvement during graduate school). Otherwise, the ranking of "useful" traits and abilities not only is essentially the same as the ranking of "improved" traits and abilities but also seems to be consistent for humanists and nonhumanists: general knowledge (cited by about 80 percent of both samples), ability to think clearly (cited by slightly more than 80 percent), critical thinking and analytical skills (cited by about 75 percent), and writing ability (cited by 79 percent of the humanists and by 82 percent of the scientists and engineers). Other traits and skills regarded as useful on the job by at least three-fifths of both groups—but not necessarily viewed as having improved markedly during graduate school—are self-confidence (cited by 68 percent of the humanists and 71 percent of the nonhumanists); self-discipline and the ability to follow rules (cited by 69 percent of the humanists and 62 percent of the scientists and engineers); and understanding of others (64 percent of the humanists, 71 percent of the scientists and engineers).

Generally, scientists and engineers regard a wider range of skills and abilities as useful on the job. Thus, they are markedly more likely than are humanists to mention insight (67 percent of the nonhumanists versus 58 percent of the humanists), public-speaking ability (66 percent versus 53 percent), leadership ability (64 percent versus 57 percent), creativity and originality (64 percent versus 54 percent), drive to achieve (56 percent versus 48 percent), mathematical ability (38 percent versus 16 percent), and mechanical ability (23 percent versus 6 percent). On the other hand, humanists are almost twice as likely as nonhumanists (46 percent versus 24 percent) to say that cultural perspective is useful on the job. The tendency of the nonhumanists to regard more traits and skills as useful may in part reflect the greater heterogeneity of the sample, which includes not only natural scientists and engineers (who are likely to be empirically oriented) but also psychologists and other social scientists (who are likely to be person oriented, to engage in counseling and clinical work as primary activities, and thus to find such traits as understanding of others and insight valuable on the job.)

Government-employed humanists from different graduate fields regard different traits and abilities as useful. Those with doctorates in English are especially likely to mention writing ability, public-speaking ability, and cultural perspective, but not research skills. Like Ph.D.'s in English, those with doctorates in foreign languages find cultural perspective useful; comparatively small proportions, however, say that their jobs demand creativity and originality, writing ability, or research skills. Once again, government-employed humanists with degrees in philosophy present a somewhat distinctive pattern, in that much larger than average proportions say that ability to think clearly, critical thinking and analytical skills, creativity and originality, political awareness, and mathematical ability are useful. Those with doctorates in history are especially likely to find research skills valuable, but not cultural perspective or academic ability. Public-speaking ability and cultural perspective, but not research skills, are cited as useful by those with doctorates in other humanities.

Different jobs in different settings require different traits and abilities. Thus, as might be expected, some distinctive patterns emerge for the different employer types and primary work activities. For example, human-services organizations seem to emphasize such interpersonal traits as self-confidence, insight, and understanding of others (as well as political awareness), but not writing ability. Obviously, many of the humanists working at "other" activities in these organizations come into direct contact with clients in counseling and clinical roles. In striking contrast, jobs in libraries, museums, and archives do not require these skills, nor is drive to achieve important; perhaps this negative pattern reflects the solitary, "ivory-tower" nature of these employment settings. The ability to think clearly and critical thinking or analytic skills are especially important for those with jobs in federal agencies, whereas state- or local-government jobs require political awareness but not general knowledge.

Researchers in all employment settings naturally need to have research skills and writing ability. In addition, research jobs in federal agencies require creativity and originality, political awareness, and insight. Leadership ability and self-confidence are valuable to administrators in all settings. In addition, administrative jobs in federal agencies and human-services organizations (but not in state or local agencies) seem to demand cultural perspective and public-speaking ability; those in human-services organizations and state or local agencies (but not in federal agencies) demand drive to achieve and mathematical ability; and those in state or local agencies demand, in addition, self-discipline and the ability to follow rules, as well as academic ability. Beyond saying that jobs emphasizing "other" primary work activities in state or local agencies require writing ability, no generalizations can be made about the demands of these other jobs, probably because of their heterogeneous nature.

Summary

At the beginning of this chapter, we asked three questions, which now can be answered with some degree of confidence.

First, do government-employed humanists start out with traditional career goals; and, if so, what makes them change their minds? Clearly, the great majority (about 80 percent) enter graduate school expecting to become college teachers—the traditional career for doctorate-level humanists—and change these career goals chiefly because available teaching jobs are limited or are simply not attractive to them. About two in three give this reason. Thus, the tight academic-job market is forcing these highly trained humanists into nontraditional careers. About half of them mention that other job opportunities are more attractive, a reason that is simply the obverse of the first.

Second, how did doctorate-level humanists go about seeking jobs in the public sector; and what methods or contacts proved most effective in getting their current jobs? Civil-service application and direct application to employer are both the most widely used and the most-effective job-search methods, with professional contacts (a somewhat vague category) also being helpful to them. Although humanists say they took a fairly active role, using many different methods and contacts, the only contacts that actually helped them much were friends. Many say they got their current jobs through chance or luck. Except for administrators, few received unsolicited offers. There was considerable variation by employer type and primary work activity in both the methods used and the methods that proved effective.

Third, what do government-employed humanists perceive to be the relation between those jobs and their graduate training? Slightly under half see their current jobs as closely related to their graduate training, and 15 percent see no relation at all between the two. Those in jobs not closely related to their doctoral field most commonly say that they took the jobs because employment opportunities in their field were either scarce or not available at all. Some positive incentives are mentioned as well: better pay (in comparison, presumably, with what they would be making in academe); more opportunity for career advancement; and awakened interest in another field.

Nonetheless, graduate training is not a total waste even for those humanists working in jobs unrelated to that training. About three in five say that the degree itself helped them to get their current jobs, that graduate education provided them with a marketable skill for their current jobs, and that it had increased their chances of finding a good job. True, graduate education is not as helpful as general on-the-job experience in providing the knowledge and skills they need for their current jobs. But it is mentioned as the second-most-helpful type of training, followed by particular courses in the major field and by undergraduate study.

There is some discrepancy between the kinds of skills and abilities developed in graduate school and those found useful in the current job. Four in five of the government-employed humanists say that their research skills developed during graduate school, and two in three mention improvement in academic ability; but neither of these competencies is necessarily very helpful in the current job (except that researchers must, of course, have research skills). But other skills commonly developed during graduate school can be put to good use in the current job: namely, critical thinking ability, writing ability, general knowledge, and the ability to think clearly. Because different kinds of government jobs clearly demand different kinds of competencies, recent Ph.D.'s might do well to consider the specific skills and abilities required by certain kinds of jobs in the public sector and to emphasize their strength in these areas when applying for such jobs.

7 Job Characteristics and Satisfactions

Chapter 6 focused on the reasons that government-employed humanists give for changing their initial career goals of becoming college teachers; the methods and contacts they use in seeking jobs in the public sector and the comparative effectiveness of different job-search methods; and the connections between their graduate education and their current jobs with respect not only to the degree of relation between job and graduate training but also to the usefulness of different aspects of education and training. The chapter ended with a discussion of the particular traits and abilities found to be valuable on the current job. To some degree, these traits and abilities varied by employer type and primary work activity and thus might be said to distinguish among various kinds of public-sector jobs.

This chapter looks more closely at the characteristics of the jobs themselves in an effort to define the nature of public-sector jobs in general—at least, of those jobs that employ doctorate-level humanists—and to distinguish further among particular types of jobs. More specifically, it deals with humanists' views of the most-salient job characteristics, salary, research productivity, perceived underemployment, and assorted job conditions. Finally, it considers the overriding and crucial issue of job satisfaction: its competents and determinants.

As in chapter 6, humanists are compared with scientists and engineers where data for such comparisons are available. in addition, the findings are discussed in terms of the similarities and differences among the five humanities fields (English, foreign languages, philosophy, history, and other humanities) and among employer types and primary work activities.

Job Characteristics Perceived as Salient

Just what do humanities Ph.D.'s regard as the most important characteristics of a job? What specific attractions lead them to choose one job over another? To answer these questions, we looked at responses to an item that appeared on the Higher Education Research Institute (HERI) survey form for humanists (but was not included on the form for scientists and engineers). The item read, "How important were each of the following job characteristics in your decision to choose your current job instead of your next best alternative?" The seventeen job characteristics were:

1. Congeniality of colleagues.
2. Competency of colleagues.
3. Reputation of employer among scholars.
4. Administration and administrators.
5. Research facilities and opportunities.
6. Salary.
7. Fringe benefits.
8. Rank.
9. Opportunities for outside income.
10. Future salary prospects.
11. Nearness to a graduate school.
12. Nearness to friends and relatives.
13. Climate.
14. Cultural opportunities.
15. Courses taught.
16. Teaching load.
17. Quality of students.

Three response alternatives were offered: "very important," "somewhat important," and "not important." The discussion that follows deals with those who said that a given characteristic was very important in their decision to take the current job over the next-best alternative.

In choosing their current jobs, humanists as a group gave top consideration to salary (39 percent), future salary prospects (35 percent), fringe benefits (32 percent), and competency of colleagues (31 percent). This ranking of priorities should do much to discredit the notion that humanists are less interested in money than are scientists and engineers. Clearly, the material benefits of a job are important to them. Lest this point be overemphasized, however, it should be recalled that the specific question was why they chose their present job over the next-best alternative. If one assumes that the job alternatives were roughly equal in a number of characteristics not listed (intrinsic interest in the work, degree of autonomy allowed, and so forth), then it may be that salary, salary prospects, and fringe benefits were decisive but not overriding factors.

Other job characteristics regarded as very important by relatively large proportions are research facilities and opportunities (26 percent), congeniality of colleagues (23 percent), rank (23 percent), cultural opportunities (22 percent), reputation of employer among scholars (19 percent), and administration and administrators (19 percent). Very few government-employed humanists say that nearness to friends and relatives (10 percent), climate (8 percent), opportunities for outside income (4 percent), or nearness to a graduate school (3 percent) were decisive factors in their choosing the current job, furthermore, the three characteristics of academic jobs—courses taught, teaching load, and quality of students—are mentioned by no more than 6 percent of the group overall. Indeed, it is difficult to understand why these three characteristics are cited by even those small proportions, since all the respondents were public-sector employees. Perhaps the next-best alternative for some was an academic job that was unattractive because of the courses involved, the quality of the students, or the teaching load.

Looking at the findings by specific humanities field, we find that those with doctorates in English are somewhat more likely than others to mention competency of colleagues and courses taught as salient factors but that they attach little importance to rank. Especially important to those with doctorates in foreign languages are salary (mentioned by 50 percent, compared with 39 percent of all humanists in the sample) and salary prospects (mentioned by 41 percent, compared with 35 percent of the total humanist sample). Since (as is indicated later on) the mean income of foreign-language Ph.D.'s is the lowest of any group's (humanist or nonhumanist), the implication would seem to be that the salaries and prospective salaries of the "next-best-alternative" jobs were very low indeed. In addition, larger-than-average proportions of those with degrees in foreign languages mention nearness to friends and relatives, climate, teaching load, and quality of students as decisive factors in choosing their current jobs; relatively few mention either administration and administrators or research facilities and opportunities.

Those humanists with doctorates in philosophy tend to give exceptionally high priority to competency of colleagues, administration and administrators, cultural opportunities, and nearness to a graduate school; they are markedly less likely than others to say that fringe benefits and salary were very important factors in their decision to take the current job. Since the jobs they have do not pay especially well (as will be discussed later on), perhaps this group more closely fits the stereotype of the humanist as being relatively unconcerned with monetary rewards.

The only distinctive trait of the history Ph.D.'s is that they tend to regard research facilities and opportunities as very important job characteristics. Those with degrees in other humanities are more likely than the groups already discussed to say that administration and administrators, reputation of employer among scholars, fringe benefits, climate, and opportunities for outside income were very important factors in choosing the current job over the next-best alternative.

The importance attached to particular characteristics varies considerably, depending on the nature of the respondent's current job in the public sector. The following summarizes the three top-ranking factors, by employer type and by primary work activity. (Results are not reported for those job categories where fewer than ten humanists are employed.)

Libraries, museums, and archives:
  Researchers: research facilities and opportunities (79 percent); salary (53 percent); congeniality of colleagues (37 percent); fringe benefits (37 percent).

Administrators: fewer than ten cases.
Others: research facilities and opportunities (43 percent); reputation of
employer among scholars (36 percent); salary (36 percent).

Human-services organizations:
Researchers: fewer than ten cases.
Administrators: competency of colleagues (64 percent); administration
and administrators (50 percent); climate (40 percent).
Others: future salary prospects (48 percent); salary (43 percent); fringe
benefits (43 percent).

Federal agencies:
Researchers: salary (60 percent); competency of colleagues (46 percent);
future salary prospects (43 percent)
Administrators: salary (50 percent); fringe benefits (40 percent); competency of colleagues (39 percent).
Others: future salary prospects (41 percent); salary (37 percent); fringe
benefits (35 percent).

State/local agencies:
Researchers: fewer than ten cases.
Administrators: administration and administrators (38 percent); compe-
tency of colleagues (35 percent); future salary prospects (35 percent).
Others: competency of colleagues (42 percent); congeniality of colleagues
(36 percent); salary (26 percent).

Salary, future salary prospects, or both are among the three top-ranked job
characteristics for all categories except administrators in human-services organizations. Fringe benefits were a major factor in the choice of those humanists
in human-services organizations and federal agencies whose primary work activity was other than research and administration, as well as in the choice of
administrators in federal agencies.

Regardless of primary work activity, those employed in libraries, museums,
and archives mention research facilities and opportunities as very important. In
addition, researchers in these settings give high priority to congeniality of colleagues, whereas "others" regard the reputation of the employer among scholars
as very important. In short, humanists working in the library group seem to
retain a more-academic orientation than humanists employed in other public-
sector jobs.

Curiously, research facilities and opportunities are not among the three top-
ranked job characteristics of researchers in federal agencies; they are, however,
fourth ranked, being mentioned by two in five of this group (compared with 26
percent of all humanists). In interpreting all these results, the reader should bear
in mind that respondents were asked what job characteristics had led them to
choose their current jobs over the next-best alternative.

Salary

As the previous analysis suggests, people with doctorates in the humanities are just as concerned with the financial rewards of a job as are those with doctorates in other fields. Indeed, salary, future salary prospects, or both were often decisive factors in humanists' choice of one job over another. Just what kind of salaries do government-employed Ph.D.'s earn? Table 7–1 shows the mean salaries of humanists and nonhumanists by graduate field; table 7–2 shows the mean salaries of both samples by employer type and primary work activity.

As table 7–1 indicates, doctorate-level humanists employed in the public sector average $25,150 in salary, with those whose doctorates are in "other" humanities having the highest mean salaries and those with foreign-language doctorates making the least. The average salaries of government-employed non-humanists are much higher. The lowest paid (psychologists) nonetheless average over $3,000 more than the highest paid of the humanists; and engineers, who are the most highly paid of all, make over $7,000 more than the average for all humanists. Nonetheless, humanists in the public sector generally earn higher salaries than their counterparts on college faculties—who, according to a recent study (Solmon, Ochsner, and Hurwicz 1979) averaged $18,769 in 1975—and make about the same salaries as their counterparts in academic administration, who average $25,583. Thus employment in the public sector is relatively lucrative for humanists, compared with what they would be making in academe.

As table 7–2 indicates, administrators tend to earn higher salaries than either researchers or those with other primary work activities; this holds true for both the humanities and the science and engineering samples, as well as across em-

Table 7–1
Mean Salary, by Graduate Field

Field	Mean Salary ($)	N
Humanities		
English	22,700	70
Foreign languages	22,246	65
Philosophy	23,222	45
History	25,986	399
Other humanities	26,569	80
Total	25,150	659
Nonhumanities		
Biological sciences	29,942	844
Other natural sciences	31,956	1,658
Engineering	32,306	420
Psychology	29,876	602
Other social sciences	31,855	411
Total	31,233	3,935

Table 7–2
Mean Salary, by Employer Type and Primary Work Activity

	Mean Income ($)	N
Humanities		
Libraries, museums, archives:		
Research	23,289	19
Administration	—	9
Other	23,640	114
Human-services organizations:		
Research	—	4
Administration	30,200	10
Other	24,273	22
Federal agencies:		
Research	26,974	38
Administration	31,819	80
Other	24,738	183
State/local agencies:		
Research	—	6
Administration	25,765	17
Other	18,435	31
Science and engineering		
Libraries, museums, archives:		
Research	33,944	27
Administration	—	—
Other	23,636	11
Human-services organizations:		
Research	29,119	180
Administration	33,633	173
Other	28,703	493
Federal agencies:		
Research	30,228	1,450
Administration	37,327	733
Other	29,366	764
State/local agencies:		
Research	22,885	13
Administration	25,972	18
Other	23,641	32

Note: Percentages not shown for those cells with fewer than ten cases.

ployer types. For humanists, jobs in federal agencies other than libraries or human-services organizations pay the highest salaries.

Multiple-regression techniques were used to identify those personal and job characteristics that best explain salary differences among humanists employed in the public sector. The most-important factor turns out to be years employed since receiving the Ph.D. degree; that is, the longer an individual has been in the labor force, the higher his or her salary tends to be. (Two other variables closely related to the first—age and number of years since receiving the doctorate—are also significantly related to salary, as is number of years in the current job.)

The second-most-important factor is the perception that one is not under-employed. It would seem that those jobs that require the application of the humanist's talents and training also pay high salaries. An alternative interpre-tation of the correlation between not feeling underemployed and salary is pos-sible. Perhaps high salary in and of itself eliminates feelings of being underemployed, regardless of what talents the high-paying jobs require. High salary might make up for certain undesirable job features. Another significant variable is number of publications. Even in the public sector—which presumably does not have the publish-or-perish policy found in academe—those humanists with higher publication rates earn more.

Some of the results confirm what is already obvious from the previous analyses: Administrators, particularly of research-and-development programs, make higher salaries than do researchers or "others." Of the employer types, human-services organizations and federal agencies pay more than do libraries, museums, and archives, or state or local agencies.

Humanists who are married, who work full time, and who are in what they regard as traditional jobs for people with their background generally make higher salaries than the unmarried, the part-time workers, and those in nontraditional jobs. Those who did their graduate work at highly selective institutions also tend to earn high salaries, although the relation is slight. Rank in graduate school, however, had a slight negative relationship to high salary. Apparently the best students do not always get the highest-paying jobs. Perhaps grades do not reflect those competencies likely to result in successful nonacademic careers: Knowledge of course content may be of little help in running a government department. But the reader should bear in mind that the respondents constitute a very homogeneous group in that all have doctorates in the humanities and work in the public sector, a nontraditional area for doctorate-level humanists.

Those who say that their mobility is limited because of their spouse's job make relatively low salaries. Such a constraint on mobility is of course, typical of women rather than of men. Otherwise, after marital status, age, number of years since receipt of the doctorate, and type of job are taken into account, sex differences in salary are not significant; that is, women in government jobs do not earn appreciably less than men of the same age and general qualifications. A National Research Council (NRC) study that covered all employment sectors and did not control for other factors found that in 1977 male humanities Ph.D.'s averaged $22,100, whereas women with humanities doctorates averaged $18,300 (NRC 1978). These salary differences are due in part to other factors: Only recently have large numbers of women been earning the doctorate. Therefore, the typical female Ph.D. is younger than her male counterpart, has been in the labor force for a shorter period, usually has fewer publications to her credit, and so forth. Even allowing for age differences, however, women's salaries remain lower than men's. For instance, of humanities Ph.D.'s in the 45- to 49-year-old group, the men earn $24,300 and the women $19,800 (NRC 1978). The special case of government-employed women with humanities doctorates is discussed in greater detail in chapter 8.

Some of the factors that turn out to be unimportant in explaining salary differences among humanists employed in the public sector are as follows: being currently engaged in research, having a job closely related to graduate training, working full time between the baccalaureate and the doctorate, and changing career goals since graduate school.

On the whole, these findings with respect to salary reinforce the conclusion that doctorate-level humanists who choose to work in the public sector will probably make higher salaries than their counterparts in academe. It does not follow, however, that they must therefore sacrifice other amenities or benefits.

Research Productivity

Graduate training in all fields emphasizes research and scholarly productivity over other possible activities such as teaching or administration. But how much research do humanists (or nonhumanists, for that matter) actually do when they work at nontraditional jobs in the public or the private sector? Do those who are not specifically employed as researchers simply fail to put their graduate training in research to any use? Both the humanities and the science and engineering questionnaires contained an item that read, "Compared with others in your field and at your degree level, how much research/publication per year did you accomplish during (a) first job after completing highest degree; (b) job prior to present position (if different); (c) present position (if different)." The response alternatives were: "great deal," "some," "little," "none." Admittedly, this measure of research productivity is subjective, depending on the respondent's interpretation of how much constitutes (for instance) "a great deal." Nonetheless, it gives some sense of the research activity of Ph.D.'s from different graduate fields and in different jobs.

Of the humanists, one-third say they did no research in their first jobs after receiving the degree, one-third had done no research in their immediately previous jobs, and close to one-third (30 percent) do no research in their current jobs. The figures for scientists and engineers are smaller: 16 percent, 22 percent, and 21 percent, respectively. Thus, for many humanists and some nonhumanists in the public sector, graduate training in research skills seems to be wasted. However, it is likely that research skills are useful even if scholarly research is not being carried out. Writing, critical thinking, and exploration abilities, developed while learning how to do research, are probably valuable in many business activities. Moreover, humanists and nonhumanists are about equally likely to say that their research productivity on their current jobs is high (23 percent and 22 percent, respectively). And the proportions of humanists saying they accomplish a great deal of research was higher for the current job (23 percent) than for the first job (17 percent); this increase in research productivity occurred in all fields except ''other'' humanities.

Current research activity among humanists varies considerably by graduate field. Generally, those with doctorates in history are most likely to engage in research, and those with doctorates in English or foreign languages least likely. For instance, one finds that 28 percent of history Ph.D.'s and 24 percent of philosophy Ph.D.'s—but only 18 percent of those with doctorates in other humanities, 15 percent of English Ph.D.'s, and 11 percent of foreign-language Ph.D.'s—are currently doing what they regard as a great deal of research. Conversely, over two-fifths of those with doctorates in English or philosophy, and half of those with foreign-language doctorates, do no research on the current job; but only 22 percent of the history Ph.D.'s do no research. Findings with respect to those with degrees in other humanities are ambiguous: Only 18 percent see themselves as very active in research, but only 35 percent do no research. Apparently, people from these fields have a greater tendency than others to say that they are doing ''some'' or ''little'' research.

Not surprisingly, those humanists who work as researchers, especially in libraries, museums, and archives, are most likely to report very high research productivity in their current jobs. What is surprising is that 12 percent of the library researchers and 25 percent of the researchers in federal agencies say they do no research in their present jobs; one wonders just what they are doing. About one-third of the administrators do no research. By employer type, human-services organizations seem to be least conducive to research activity.

Underemployment

Although it is often said that the surplus of Ph.D.'s means that many recent graduates will be underemployed if not unemployed, a precise definition of *underemployment* is difficult. Certainly the term implies employment at jobs that are undemanding, routine, below the level of the individual's competencies. To elicit information on just what is involved in the perception of being underemployed, and to assess the extent of the problem among Ph.D.'s employed in the public sector, we looked at responses to an item included on both the humanities and the sciences and engineering questionnaires that listed twelve statements about underemployment and about various job conditions or characteristics that may be related to perceived underemployment. Table 7–3 lists the statements and indicates the proportions of humanists and of scientists and engineers in the public sector who say that a given statement applies to their current situation. The data are presented by employer type and primary work activity, as well as for the total samples.

Table 7–3
Perceptions of Underemployment, by Employer Type and Primary Work Activity
(percent)

	Libraries, Museums, and Archives		
	Research	*Administration*	*Other*
Humanities			
I am *not* underemployed.	58	—	53
I am underemployed and would prefer a more-challenging position.	10	—	22
I am underemployed, but for personal reasons I prefer to remain in this or a similar position.	10	—	8
I am underemployed; my job is not in my field.	5	—	12
I am underemployed; my job is not commensurate with my level of experience.	0	—	14
I am underemployed; my job is not commensurate with my level of training.	16	—	21
I am underemployed; my job is not commensurate with my level of ability.	21	—	27
I have the skills and knowledge necessary for successful performance on my job.	100	—	84
People with less formal schooling are performing well in jobs identical to mine.	26	—	37
If people with less formal schooling were hired, they could do my job as well as I.	10	—	31
I believe my present job is a nontraditional one for people in my doctoral field.	47	—	37
I have held other nontraditional jobs.	32	—	26
N	19	9	115
Sciences and engineering			
I am *not* underemployed.	93	—	46
I am underemployed and would prefer a more-challenging position.	0	—	36
I am underemployed, but for personal reasons I prefer to remain in this or a similar position.	0	—	27
I am underemployed; my job is not in my field.	0	—	9
I am underemployed; my job is not commensurate with my level of experience.	0	—	36
I am underemployed; my job is not commensurate with my level of training.	0	—	27
I am underemployed; my job is not commensurate with my level of ability.	0	—	27
I have the skills and knowledge necessary for successful performance on my job.	79	—	91
People with less formal schooling are performing well in jobs identical to mine.	14	—	18
If people with less formal schooling were hired, they could do my job as well as I.	14	—	9
I believe my present job is a nontraditional one for people in my doctoral field.	14	—	36
I have held other nontraditional jobs.	7	—	18
N	28	7	11

Note: Percentages not shown for those cells with fewer than ten cases.

Human-Services Organizations			Federal Government			State/Local Government			
Research	Administration	Other	Research	Administration	Other	Research	Administration	Other	Total
—	54	18	67	58	50	—	53	38	52
—	36	27	18	29	32	—	29	28	27
—	9	18	10	15	12	—	6	16	11
—	18	23	8	16	23	—	12	16	15
—	27	23	15	25	21	—	18	25	19
—	36	36	13	20	27	—	18	31	23
—	36	32	23	35	31	—	35	31	28
—	91	82	87	85	86	—	88	72	84
—	54	50	38	49	56	—	41	34	44
—	36	46	10	45	38	—	18	28	32
—	91	59	28	61	61	—	65	44	50
—	54	41	28	48	32	—	35	28	34
4	11	22	39	80	185	6	17	32	666
75	65	64	71	70	54	62	78	56	66
13	16	20	13	14	26	15	6	19	17
4	8	11	7	7	8	0	6	9	8
1	4	4	4	3	10	8	0	16	5
10	10	14	10	8	18	23	11	16	12
8	11	14	10	9	24	23	17	22	13
11	19	21	14	13	26	15	11	25	17
75	79	83	79	82	83	100	89	84	81
11	17	17	18	30	40	54	11	44	24
7	14	12	11	18	24	46	11	28	15
16	44	20	16	35	44	54	67	53	28
9	19	12	6	17	17	23	6	25	12
179	171	488	1,436	727	759	13	18	32	3,902

About two-thirds of the scientists and engineers, but just slightly more than half the humanists, indicate that they are not underemployed in their current jobs. Clearly, in the public sector, a large number of humanists—and a somewhat smaller but still substantial number of nonhumanists—consider themselves underemployed. This situation is obviously a source of discontent in that 27 percent of the humanists and 17 percent of the scientists and engineers indicate that they would prefer a more-challenging position; only 11 percent of the humanists and 8 percent of the scientists and engineers said that, for personal reasons, they prefer to remain in their present (or similar) positions, even though they are underemployed.

The pattern of responses to the next four items on the list gives some sense of just what is involved in perceptions of underemployment. The ranking of these "reasons" is the same for humanists as for scientists and engineers. A larger proportion of humanists check each of the statements, as is to be expected, since a larger proportion see themselves as underemployed. Perceptions of underemployment are most commonly related to the feeling that the job is not commensurate with level of ability (28 percent of the humanists, 17 percent of the nonhumanists); with level of training (23 percent of the humanists, 13 percent of the nonhumanists); or with level of experience (19 percent of the humanists, 12 percent of nonhumanists). Relatively few (15 percent of humanists, 5 percent of the nonhumanists) regard themselves as underemployed simply because their current job is not in their doctoral field.

The last five statements on the list, although not directly connected with perceived underemployment, may nonetheless throw some light on the circumstances that generate such feelings. Approximately equal proportions of both samples (84 percent of the humanists, 81 percent of the scientists and engineers) believe that they have the skills and knowledge necessary to perform successfully at their jobs. By implication, very few regard themselves as "in over their heads," overwhelmed by the demands of their jobs. Many more humanists than nonhumanists, however, say that people with less formal schooling are performing well in the same jobs (44 percent versus 24 percent) and that if they were hired, people with less formal schooling could do the job as well as they themselves (32 percent versus 15 percent). Finally, humanists are much more likely than are scientists and engineers to regard their current jobs as nontraditional for people in their fields (50 percent versus 28 percent) and to say that they have held other nontraditional jobs (34 percent versus 12 percent). As was pointed out earlier, humanities Ph.D.'s have almost invariably been limited to academic jobs in the past, whereas science and engineering Ph.D.'s have a long history in certain kinds of nonacademic jobs (for example, as researchers, engineers, counselors, and clinical workers in both government and the private sector).

Among humanists, administrators in human-services organizations are most likely to see their jobs as nontraditional, whereas those engaging in "other" primary work activities in libraries, museums, and archives or in state or local units are least likely to do so. All the researchers in libraries and 91 percent of the administrators in human-services organizations, but only 72 percent of "others" in state or local agencies, believe that they have the skills and knowledge necessary to perform their jobs successfully.

Other findings for humanists, by employer type and primary work activity, may be summarized as follows: Those employed in libraries, museums, and archives are unlikely to perceive themselves as underemployed or to say that they would prefer more-challenging positions, that their jobs are not in their fields, that their jobs are not commensurate with their experience or their training, or that people with less formal education are performing as well in jobs similar to theirs. Only 10 percent of the researchers, but 31 percent of those engaged in other activities, believe that people with less formal education could, if hired, do the job as well.

Humanists working in human-services organizations tend to say that their jobs are nontraditional and that they have held other nontraditional jobs. They are somewhat more likely than others to see themselves as underemployed because their jobs are not in their field or are not commensurate with their experience, training, and ability. About half say that less-well-educated people are performing competently in identical jobs. A larger-than-average proportion of administrators in this employment setting would prefer more-challenging positions; a larger-than-average proportion of "others," even though underemployed, prefer for personal reasons to remain in their present positions.

Most of those humanists working in federal agencies, particularly those employed as researchers or administrators, do not feel underemployed. Higher-than-average proportions of administrators in such agencies, however, believe that their jobs are not commensurate with their experience or ability; close to half have held other nontraditional jobs. Higher-than-average proportions of humanists performing other primary work activities would prefer more-challenging positions and say that their jobs are being done as well by people with less education. They also tend to feel underemployed because their jobs are not in their fields and are not commensurate with their training and ability.

The positions held by humanists in state and local government tend to be regarded as beneath their level of ability. Otherwise, patterns differ by primary work activity. Those engaging in other activities, but not those doing administrative work, are likely to perceive themselves as underemployed, usually because the job is not commensurate with their experience, training, or ability.

By primary work activity, then, researchers are least likely to regard themselves as underemployed or to say that people with less formal training are performing as well in similar jobs. Administrators tend to feel that their jobs are not commensurate with their ability. Except for those in libraries, museums, and archives, humanists engaged in other primary work activities are likely to say that they are underemployed because their jobs are not commensurate with their training or with their level of ability.

Perceptions of the Current Job

The HERI questionnaires for both the humanities and the sciences and engineering samples included one item that was designed to elicit more-specific information about the nature of the current job and, more particularly, about the respondent's perceptions of the appropriateness of the job for a highly trained individual. Respondents were asked to indicate to what extent—"very much," "somewhat," or "not at all"—each of twelve statements applied to their current jobs. The twelve statements were as follows.

1. I am well paid for my work compared with others with the same amount of education.
2. I supervise people trained in my field.
3. Most of my colleagues are trained in my field.
4. I am satisfied with my career progress to date.
5. My job offers good future prospects for further advancement.
6. My job fits my long-range goals.
7. My skills are fully utilized in my job.
8. I am working at a professional level.
9. I would have liked more training outside graduate school before I started working.
10. I received job training inappropriate for the actual requirements of my job.
11. I am glad I had the graduate education I did.
12. My position required on-the-job training.

The discussion that follows is based on those proportions indicating that a statement applied "very much" to their current job.

Overall one gets a positive impression of the public-sector jobs held by both humanists and nonhumanists; that is, the jobs seem generally appropriate for these highly trained individuals. Thus, four in five of both samples say that they are glad to have had a graduate education, and about seven in ten say that they are working at a professional level. With respect to this latter item, older workers are more likely to say that their jobs are of professional status than are younger workers. However, it may not be age that is closely associated with working at a professional level, as much as number of years since receiving the doctorate or number of years on the current job.

Smaller proportions (about two in five of both samples) say that they are satisfied with their career progress and that the job fits their long-range goals. About one-third believe strongly that their skills are fully utilized on the job, and about three in ten say that most of their colleagues are trained in the same field. On the other hand, very small proportions would have liked more training outside graduate school before they started working (5 percent of the humanists, 4 percent of the scientists and engineers) or believe that the job training they received was inappropriate for the actual requirements of the job (10 percent of the humanists, 6 percent of the scientists and engineers). Thus, the two samples seem in virtual agreement on many points.

More humanists (46 percent) than scientists and engineers (38 percent), however, see themselves as well paid compared with others who have the same amount of education. This difference between the groups may seem odd, since (as we have seen) scientists and engineers usually recieve higher salaries than humanists. Two points may clarify this apparent contradiction: First, the item involves perceptions about salary rather than actual salary; humanists probably compare themselves with other humanists (most of whom work in academic jobs, where salaries are lower) rather than with doctorate-level nonhumanists working in government jobs or in the private sector. Second, and perhaps more important, the high proportion is accounted for almost entirely by those with doctorates in history, 53 percent of whom say they are well paid. Only about one-third of the humanists with doctorates in other fields indicate that they are well paid, a proportion well below the proportions of biological scientists (44 percent), psychologists (42 percent), and other social scientists (44 percent) who give this response.

In addition, more humanists (26 percent) than nonhumanists (20 percent) say that their job offers prospects of further advancement. More scientists and engineers (29 percent) than humanists (23 percent) say that they supervise people from their own fields. And many more humanists (34 percent) than nonhumanists (21 percent) say that their position required on-the-job training. This last finding emphasizes that humanists working outside academe are more likely than other doctorate-holders to require additional training in order to function effectively.

Comparing humanists from different fields, we find that those with doctorates in English, although generally glad to have had the graduate education they did, nonetheless are somewhat more inclined than others to say that they would have liked more training outside graduate school before they started working and that their job training was inappropriate to the actual requirements of their jobs. Only 37 percent are satisfied with their career progress. Moreover, Ph.D.'s in English may feel more isolated than do some others: Only 10 percent said that they were working with or supervising people trained in their field.

In many ways, those humanists with doctorates in foreign languages seem most out of place in public-sector jobs. Only 53 percent are working at a professional level. Moreover, much lower than average proportions say that their skills are fully utilized on the job, that most of their colleagues are trained in their field, or that they supervise people in their field; and somewhat lower than average proportions say that they are satisfied with their career progress and that the current job is consistent with their long-range plans. A high of 42 percent say that they required on-the-job training for their current position.

Philosophy Ph.D.'s present a somewhat brighter picture. They are more likely than others to be satisfied with their career progress, to believe that their jobs hold good prospects for advancement, and to work at a professional level. Comparatively few required on-the-job training for their positions, and none would have liked more training outside of graduate school before they started working. On the other hand, like Ph.D.'s in English and in foreign languages, they tend not to be working with or supervising people from their own field.

History Ph.D.'s are perhaps best adapted to government jobs. They are more likely than others to say that their skills are fully utilized and that they are well paid compared with others who have the same amount of education. Finally, a large proportion are working with colleagues from the same field or hold supervisory positions over people in the same field.

The only distinctive points to emerge about those with doctorates in other humanities is that they are more likely than any other group of humanists to say that their job fits with their long-range plans, but they tend not to feel that it offers opportunities for advancement.

Comparisons of humanists in different public-sector jobs indicate that in some ways libraries, museums, and archives are ideal employment settings, especially for researchers, who are generally more likely than any other group to say that most of their colleagues were trained in the same field, that they are satisfied with their career progress, that their job offers good prospects for advancement, that the job is consistent with their long-range goals, that their skills are fully utilized on the job, and that they are working at a professional level. They are much less likely than average to say that the position required on-the-job training or that they would have liked more training outside of graduate school. About one-third of all library-employed humanists are supervising people in the same field.

In contrast, human-services organizations do not seem to be appropriate employment settings for highly trained humanists. Relatively large proportions of both administrators and "other" types of workers say that their job training was inappropriate to the requirements of the job; and relatively small proportions regard themselves as well paid, work with people trained in the same field, are satisfied with their career progress, or believe that their skills are fully utilized on the job. Looking just at administrators in human-services organizations, only 9 percent say they supervise people trained in their field, only 27 percent say their jobs fit their long-range goals, and half needed on-the-job training for the position. Nonetheless, 90 percent (the highest proportion of any group) do not regret having had a graduate education. On the other hand, only 73 percent of the humanists performing other primary work activities in these organizations are glad they had the graduate education they did.

The findings for humanists employed in federal agencies differ by primary work activity. Researchers in this employment setting are more likely than any other group to say that they were well paid, and their actual salaries are, indeed, comparatively high (table 7–2). In addition, unusually large proportions are glad to have had their graduate training; and somewhat larger than average proportions believe they are working at a professional level and that their skills are fully utilized. Somewhat lower than average porportions say that their job training was inappropriate, and relatively few supervise people in their own fields, although they do tend to work with people trained in the same field. Administrators in federal agencies, on the other hand, are more likely than any other group to hold such supervisory positions; in addition, they consider themselves well paid, are satisfied with their career progress to date, say that the job fits their long-range goals, and indicate that their job training was appropriate to the actual requirements of the job. On the other hand, only 17 percent work with colleagues trained in the same field. The only outstanding points about humanists engaged in other primary work activities in federal agencies are that their jobs are very likely to have required on-the-job training, but they rarely supervise people trained in the same field.

State and local agencies seem to be more-compatible settings for humanists doing administrative work than for those performing other activities. Although a large proportion of administrators indicate that their job training was inappropriate to the actual requirements of the job and that they would have liked more training outside graduate school before they started working, unusually large proportions also say that they are working at a professional level, that their job is consistent with their long-range goals, and that their prospects for advancement on the job are good. In addition, they are more likely than average to say that their skills are fully utilized. In contrast, although fairly likely to be working with colleagues from the same field, only 16 percent of humanists engaged in other primary work activities in state or local agencies feel that they are well paid. Lower-than-average proportions are satisfied with their career progress, have jobs that fit their long-range goals, work at a professional level, and are glad to have had their graduate education.

Regardless of employer type, researchers are especially likely to say that they are working at a professional level (usually with colleagues trained in the same field) at a job that fully utilizes their skills and that did not require on-the-job training. Whatever the employment setting, administrators are less likely than average to say that most of their colleagues are trained in the same field; otherwise, however, patterns for administrators are mixed. Unusually large proportions of those working for human-services organizations or in state and local agencies say that they are working at the professional level but that their job training was inappropriate and that they should have had more training outside graduate school; those in federal agencies are less likely than average to work at the professional level but also are less likely to say that their training was inappropriate for the actual requirements of the job. Those in federal, state, or local agencies have jobs that fit their long-range career goals, but relatively few of those in human-services organizations see their jobs in this way. No generalizations can be made about humanists performing work activities other than research or administration.

Job Satisfaction

As the voluminous literature on the subject attests, job satisfaction is perhaps the most important of all career outcomes, whatever the individual's educational level. Because it is a subjective state, however, job satisfaction cannot be identified or evaluated very effectively through objective measures; rather, it must be assessed through retrospective data, gathered from the workers themselves by means of interviews or surveys. Ultimately, only the individual can say to what extent he or she is satisfied with a job.

Once the data are collected, they can be analyzed in two ways. First, because happiness is a major life goal, and because work takes up a substantial proportion of the average person's life, job satisfaction can be seen as an end in itself. Second, because job satisfaction affects other attitudes and behaviors, it can be studied in relation to these outcomes.

With respect to this second approach, Locke (1976) epitomizes one point of view:

> Job satisfaction itself, or in combination with the conditions (both in the individual and the job environment) which bring it about, has a variety of consequences for the individual. It can affect health and possibly how long one lives. It may be related (indirectly) to mental health and adjustment, and plays a causal role in absenteeism and turnover. Under certain conditions, it may affect other types of on-the-job behavior as well. However, some believe that job satisfaction has no direct effect on productivity. [p. 1334]

According to another school of thought, not only will absenteeism, sabotage, turnover, and other productivity-reducing behaviors be lower among more-satisfied workers, but also such workers may be inspired to work more productively. Hence, job satisfaction is a worthy goal from the perspectives of both the employer and the employee.

For the purposes of this book, identification of the kinds of public-sector jobs that prove satisfying to highly educated workers, and analysis of the components, conditions, and determinants of that satisfaction, may be helpful in encouraging recent doctorate recipients and current graduate students to consider seriously employment in the public sector.

Table 7–4 shows the proportions of humanists and nonhumanists who say that they are "very satisfied" overall with their jobs and with nineteen aspects or conditions of their jobs. Data are presented by employer type and primary work activity as well as for the total humanities and science and engineering samples.

More humanists (36 percent) than scientists and engineers (30 percent) are very satisfied overall with their jobs. If we consider those who indicate that they are either satisfied or very satisfied with their jobs, however, this difference disappears; 80 percent of both samples checked one or the other of these alternatives. Only 5 percent of the humanists and 6 percent of the nonhumanists are not at all satisfied; the remainder (about 15 percent) express marginal satisfaction with their jobs. Most likely to express great overall job satisfaction are Ph.D.'s (whether humanists or nonhumanists) employed in libraries, museums, and archives. Thus, these employment settings seem ideal for highly trained people, whatever their graduate field.

These data clearly refute the notion that doctorate-level humanists cannot be happy in nonacademic jobs. Obviously, many of them do find satisfying jobs in the public sector. It should be pointed out in passing that, even though humanists are more likely than scientists and engineers to find jobs in the public sector very satisfying, the data do not permit us to generalize (nor is it within the scope of this book to do so) about the comparative satisfaction of humanists and nonhumanists in private-sector jobs. We do know that many scientists and engineers working in the private sector say that they are very satisfied with their jobs. That humanists are more likely than nonhumanists to be very satisfied with jobs in the public sector should be taken into consideration when government recruiters are seeking highly educated generalists.

Turning to specific aspects or conditions of the job, we find that doctorate-level humanists are most likely to be very satisfied with job security (49 percent, compared with 45 percent of the scientists and engineers), salary and fringe benefits (43 percent versus 35 percent), and prestige of the employer (36 percent versus 26 percent). The markedly greater tendency of humanists to be very satisfied with salary and fringe benefits may seem paradoxical in that their salaries are much lower than those of government-employed scientists and engineers. As was pointed out before, however, the most-likely explanation for this difference is that humanists take as their point of comparison the salaries they could make as faculty, whereas scientists and engineers are thinking of the salaries they could make in the private sector.

Similar proportions of the total samples of humanists and nonhumanists express themselves as being very satisfied with variety in activities (32 and 33 percent, respectively); challenge (32 percent); congenial work relations (30 and 31 percent); opportunity to use training or schooling (28 and 30 percent); status (25 and 28 percent); autonomy and independence (28 and 30 percent); opportunities for creativity (25 and 26 percent); and competency of colleagues (22 and 23 percent). Relatively few in either sample are very satisfied with their opportunities for scholarly productivity (17 and 20 percent), internal politics (6 and 7 percent), or visibility for jobs at other institutions or organizations (13 and 16 percent).

Larger proportions of humanists than of scientists and engineers are very satisfied with resources available to get the job done (26 percent versus 18 percent), with policymaking power (18 percent versus 14 percent), with opportunities for better jobs within the organization (16 percent versus 10 percent), and with pressure to publish (32 percent versus 17 percent). It is difficult to

Table 7–4

Satisfaction with Job and with Aspects of Job, by Employer Type and Primary Work Activity

(percentage responding "very satisfied"

	Libraries, Museums, and Archives		
	Research	Administration	Other
Humanities			
Overall job satisfaction	44	—	40
Salary and fringe benefits	58	—	49
Opportunity for scholarly pursuits	53	—	22
Opportunity for creativity	39	—	31
Opportunity to use training or schooling	61	—	31
Resources to get job done	50	—	31
Pressure to publish	50	—	24
Internal politics	17	—	9
Working conditions (hours, location)	42	—	30
Status	26	—	30
Autonomy and independence	42	—	30
Variety in activities	21	—	33
Policymaking power	36	—	17
Congenial work relationships	42	—	31
Competency of colleagues	37	—	26
Opportunities for different (better) jobs at this institution/organization	20	—	10
Visibility for jobs at other institutions/organizations	24	—	18
Challenge	50	—	35
Job security	53	—	56
Prestige of employer	65	—	47
N	18	9	111
Sciences and engineering			
Overall job satisfaction	75	—	54
Salary and fringe benefits	59	—	18
Opportunity for scholarly pursuits	75	—	36
Opportunity for creativity	75	—	46
Opportunity to use training or schooling	75	—	64
Resources to get job done	43	—	27
Pressure to publish	37	—	—
Internal politics	11	—	50
Working conditions (hours, location)	54	—	46
Status	64	—	36
Autonomy and independence	71	—	36
Variety in activities	73	—	27
Policymaking power	25	—	27
Congenial work relationships	36	—	46
Competency of colleagues	21	—	36
Opportunities for different (better) jobs at this institution/organization	39	—	0
Visibility for jobs at other institutions/organizations	44	—	25
Challenge	64	—	36
Job security	71	—	50
Prestige of employer	68	—	70
N	28	7	11

Human-Services Organizations			Federal Government			State/Local Government			
Research	Administration	Other	Research	Administration	Other	Research	Administration	Other	Total
—	20	24	29	35	33	—	31	28	36
—	30	50	40	50	45	—	38	25	43
—	0	6	29	9	20	—	8	19	20
—	10	10	25	25	24	—	19	20	25
—	11	16	38	28	27	—	27	30	30
—	33	83	33	24	16	—	12	19	26
—	0	0	40	33	30	—	0	80	32
—	11	0	12	11	5	—	7	7	7
—	20	30	34	31	27	—	27	22	30
—	20	16	26	34	23	—	47	16	28
—	30	15	37	33	22	—	25	25	28
—	20	10	22	40	30	—	44	35	33
—	11	12	11	26	13	—	31	10	18
—	20	15	24	28	29	—	38	29	31
—	20	0	24	20	21	—	44	16	23
—	10	18	13	11	15	—	18	14	16
—	10	12	19	13	12	—	53	13	16
—	20	16	26	32	30	—	47	28	32
—	30	42	54	53	55	—	13	29	49
—	20	11	19	42	32	—	31	35	36
4	10	21	38	77	184	6	16	32	653
26	38	26	28	37	28	33	18	34	30
31	44	33	34	43	31	23	11	13	35
19	12	15	20	12	12	23	13	7	17
24	26	20	30	26	22	58	33	30	26
30	27	31	30	25	22	38	40	31	28
20	13	12	22	17	17	8	18	18	18
12	27	25	14	18	18	—	—	—	17
3	7	5	5	5	6	10	6	7	6
23	35	35	38	35	31	27	6	24	35
19	34	24	22	34	20	17	44	24	25
30	37	30	28	29	30	31	22	36	30
26	39	32	28	38	29	17	28	52	32
7	22	10	10	24	13	8	28	28	14
22	37	27	29	34	31	31	22	34	30
17	21	20	22	27	19	17	11	17	22
4	15	9	8	12	10	0	12	16	10
9	24	10	10	18	11	15	31	19	13
25	42	25	30	40	27	41	65	55	32
38	54	56	41	44	46	31	24	36	45
20	31	19	23	32	26	25	24	21	26
178	170	492	1,443	729	758	12	17	29	3,907

know how to interpret this last difference. Does it mean that scientists and engineers are more inclined to believe that they are under too much pressure to publish and that they resent this pressure? Or does it mean that they feel there is not enough pressure to publish and thus that they have too little incentive to be productive? The only aspect of the job with which scientists and engineers are more likely to be very satisfied is working conditions (35 percent, compared with 30 percent of the humanists).

Components of Job Satisfaction

Obviously, the nineteen aspects of the job listed in table 7-4 are not of equal importance in determining overall job satisfaction. To learn which are most significant, we used multiple-regression techniques.

Seven factors seem to make a job in the public sector desirable for doctorate-level humanists; taken together, they explain two-thirds of the individual differences in overall job satisfaction ($R^2 = .642$). The top ranked are satisfaction with challenge, with opportunity for creativity, and with opportunity to use training or schooling. In other words, humanists who hold government jobs that challenge them and that allow them to be creative and to make use of their graduate training are likely to say that they are very satisfied with their jobs overall. Generally, this description is most congruent with jobs in libraries, museums, and archives and is least true of jobs in human-services organizations.

The remaining four factors that proved to be significant are satisfaction with working conditions, with status, with internal politics, and with variety in activities.

On the other hand, satisfaction with salary and fringe benefits, with opportunities for scholarly pursuits, with resources, with pressure to publish, with autonomy and independence, with policymaking power, with congenial working relationships, with competency of colleagues, with opportunities for better jobs within the organization, with visibility for jobs at other organizations, with job security, and with prestige of the employer are not related to overall job satisfaction. It would seem, then, that for highly educated humanists, jobs that are not satisfying with respect to the seven factors first mentioned are less likely to be satisfying overall, whatever other advantages such jobs may offer. The reasons that salary does not emerge as a significant factor in determining job satisfaction will be discussed later.

Determinants of Job Satisfaction

To explore further the personal and job characteristics that make for overall job satisfaction, we again used multiple-regression techniques, finding that nine variables explained 47 percent of individual differences in job satisfaction.

The two most significant turned out to be the perceptions that one's skills are fully utilized on the job and that one's doctoral training was appropriate for the job. These two measures together reaffirm a previous finding (Solmon, Bisconti, and Ochsner 1977) that skill utilization refers to competencies beyond those acquired in higher education. Doctorate-level workers are happiest in jobs that make use of nonacademically acquired skills as well as those skills they learned in graduate school. Nonetheless, the third-best predictor of job satisfaction is the perception that specific courses taken in one's field provided useful job preparation.

In addition, those humanists who believe that self-confidence is both a strong point of theirs and a trait useful in their jobs are more likely to be satisfied, whereas those who feel either that mechanical ability is a strong point of theirs but not useful to them on the job or that the job demands mechanical abilities that they do not have are likely to be dissatisfied.

The more years that have passed since receipt of the doctorate, the higher the job satisfaction, a relationship that is consistent with a mass of evidence (for example, U.S. Department of Labor 1974) that older workers tend to be more satisfied than younger ones. Whites tend to be less satisfied with their jobs than nonwhites, perhaps because they had higher expectations of getting prestigious academic jobs. Those who perceive themselves as well paid compared with others who have the same amount of education are more likely to be satisfied; actual salary, however, is not significant in determining job satisfaction. Finally, those who, at the time of entry to graduate school, expected to be college teachers are less likely to be satisfied with their jobs in the public sector than are those who had had no such expectation.

Equally interesting are some of the variables that proved to be unrelated to job satisfaction. One of these, as already mentioned, is salary per se. Another is the respondent's gender. At the bachelor's-degree level, however, women are typically more satisfied than men in the same position, even though women tend to earn less than men (Ochsner and Solmon 1979a). Field of doctorate, position in the public sector, current involvement in research, overall research productivity, self-ratings of ability, and mother's education are unrelated to job satisfaction. Humanists who supervise people trained in the same fields as themselves or whose colleagues are in the same fields have no particular tendency to be more satisfied with their job.

Utilization of Skills

Because agreement with the statement "My skills are fully utilized on the job" is by far the strongest determinant of job satisfaction, we undertook further analysis, by means of multiple regression, to explicate the meaning of this variable. Ten variables were significant, accounting for about one-third of the variation in perception of full utilization of skills. Nor surprisingly, most of them in some way involved the link between education and work.

The strongest predictor is the perception that one's graduate education provided knowledge and skills useful on the current job. In addition, those government-employed humanists who supervise people trained in their own fields; who find creativity and originality as well as research skills useful in their jobs; who work at a professional level; who say that a graduate degree is necessary for promotion in their current jobs; who believe that general knowledge is both a strong point of theirs and useful to them on the current job; and whose jobs are closely related to their graduate training also tend to feel that the job fully utilizes their skills. Finally, the higher the salary, the more likely the respondent is to feel that the job makes good use of his or her skills. This could be interpreted to mean that the more skills a worker has and uses, the higher that worker's salary. An equally compelling explanation, however, is that the more the respondent is paid, the more likely that respondent is to think that his or her skills are being fully utilized. Earlier, it appeared that salary was not an important determinant of job satisfaction. Now it seems that this apparent lack of relation is the result of a statistical artifact. Both salary and skill utilization are highly related to job satisfaction, but the correlation between utilization and satisfaction is the higher of the two. Since utilization and salary level are correlated in the multiple-regression analysis, utilization is significant but salary is not. In effect, the skill-utilization measure includes the effects of both itself and salary on job satisfaction. In other words, those whose skills are fully utilized earn more and are more satisfied.

Some of the variables that turned out to be unrelated to perception of full utilization of skills are doing research, perceiving oneself as well paid, working with colleagues trained in the same field, saying that one would have liked more outside job training, and feeling that the current position required on-the-job training.

Summary

In choosing their current jobs in the public sector over the next-best alternative, humanists gave greatest weight to such materialistic considerations as salary, future salary prospects, and fringe benefits, although they also say they were concerned about the competency of their colleagues.

Although they receive lower salaries on the average than scientists and engineers in government jobs (the mean salary of the highest-paid nonhumanists, engineers, being over $10,000 higher than the mean salaries of the lowest-paid humanists, foreign-language Ph.D.'s), larger proportions of humanists nonetheless see themselves as well paid compared with others who have the same amount of education. This difference is probably accounted for by differences in reference group; that is, humanists are likely to compare the salaries they make in government with the salaries of humanists in academe, whereas scientists and engineers compare their government salaries with the salaries of their colleagues working in the private sector.

Indeed, actual salary often bears little relation to the perception of being well paid. For instance, close to half of the humanists working as researchers in libraries, museums, and archives say that they are very well paid, even though they rank next to the bottom in actual salary. In contrast, fewer than one in four administrators in human-services organizations feels well paid, although in fact, their average salaries are high, exceeded only by the salaries of humanists working as administrators in federal agencies.

Nor does satisfaction with salary have much direct relation to overall job satisfaction; much more important in determining whether a doctorate-level humanist is happy with the current job are the challenge, opportunities for creativity, and opportunities to use one's training that the job offers. Once again, however, the perception that one is well paid compared with others who have an equal amount of education does contribute to overall job satisfaction. As was the case with skill utilization and salary, the perception of being well paid is correlated with salary; thus, in the multiple regressions, the perception measure takes on the effects of both factors.

Not only can doctorate-level humanists make more money in the public sector than in academe, but also they need not sacrifice other advantages and amenities when they take government jobs. Many humanists in our sample do not use the research skills acquired in graduate school, and many regard themselves as underemployed and would prefer more challenging work; but even so, a substantial majority say they are glad they had the graduate education that they did, feel themselves to be working at a professional level, and are either satisfied or very satisfied with their current public-sector jobs, especially with job security (which, as untenured faculty members, they would not have); salary and fringe benefits; variety and challenge (two important components of overall satisfaction); and congenial work relationships. On the other hand, government jobs do not seem to provide sufficient opportunities for internal advancement or sufficient visibility for jobs in other organizations. The internal politics involved in the government-job situation may also be a source of discontent.

Again and again, the analyses presented in this chapter indicate that libraries, museums, and archives are close to being ideal settings for doctorate-level humanists, perhaps because, of all the employer types, they most closely resemble the academic world. Equally clearly, human-services organizations are generally not congenial work settings for these highly educated humanists. Perhaps the lesson to be emphasized here is that recent humanities Ph.D.'s considering public-sector employment should be warned against taking such jobs unless they really have the interest and the interpersonal skills that would suit them to the environment of these organizations.

8 The Female Ph.D. in the Public Sector

The steady increase in the labor-force participation of women has been called one of the most-significant phenomena of our time, holding heavy implications for the future. By 1977 the proportions of U.S. women who worked outside the home reached a new high of 56 percent (Young 1979). Not only are more women taking paid employment, but also both their patterns of employment and their attitudes towards work are changing. As the proportions of women in the undergraduate population have increased, and as more of these women go on to graduate school, get their doctorates, and take professional positions in the world of work, they are developing a career orientation as opposed to a job orientation.

As table 1–2 indicated, the proportions of women among doctorate recipients in the four leading humanities fields has risen at a fairly steady rate, from 20 percent in 1967 to 39 percent in 1979. The increase in absolute numbers of women receiving the Ph.D. degree over the same period was even more impressive, from 472 in 1967 to 1,004 in 1978, a 113 percent increase. By way of contrast, the number of men receiving the doctorate in these four fields dropped slightly, from 1,849 in 1967 to 1,559 in 1979, a 16 percent decrease.

The representation of women in specific humanities fields has varied. Although history and philosophy have always been strongly male dominated and remain so, the increase in the number of female Ph.D.'s was much larger than the increase for men. Moreover, women constituted close to half of all new doctorate recipients in English/American language and literature in 1979; and they outnumbered men among new doctorate recipients in foreign languages.

With the increased labor-force participation of women, more research attention has been focused on the female worker. Nonetheless, compared with the amount of information we have on the male worker, we know very little about his female counterpart. In particular, we do not know much about the highly trained woman worker.

The sample of government-employed humanists used in this study offers an opportunity to investigate male–female differences with respect to work-related attitudes, goals, and values. It seems especially appropriate to look at government as an employer of women since, of all sectors, it should manifest the least sex discrimination. Given recent affirmative-action legislation emanating chiefly from the federal government, we would expect the public sector to offer greater access opportunities and more equitable salaries to women than are offered either by the private sector or by academe.[1]

127

In this chapter, then, the responses of government-employed doctorate-level humanists to the Higher Education Research Institute (HERI) questionnaire are analyzed by sex and, in some cases, by marital status. No attempt is made to cover all the topics included in chapters 6 and 7. Rather, after describing the sample in terms of employer types, primary work activity, rank or level of position, and certain other characteristics, we will compare men and women on the following points: reasons for career-goal change, perceived relation between current job and graduate training, perceived salient job characteristics, salary, perceived underemployment, other perceptions of the current job, job satisfaction, and mobility. In this way, we may gain some new insights into the characteristics of the highly educated woman worker.

The Sample

Of the HERI sample of doctorate-level humanists employed in the public sector, 13 percent are female.[2] The representation of women within each specific field generally is consistent with the sex differences by field discussed earlier. Women are most heavily concentrated among those with doctorates in foreign languages, constituting 23 percent of that group. One in five of those with doctorates in English is a woman. In the heavily male-dominated fields of philosphy and history, women constitute only 13 percent and 8 percent, respectively, in our sample of government-employed humanists.

Table 8–1 shows the distribution of women and of men by employer type and by primary work activity, and Table 8–2 shows their distribution by rank or level. Larger proportions of women (33 percent) than of men (25 percent) are employed in libraries, museums, and archives; on the other hand, the proportion of men working in federal agencies (58 percent) exceeds that of women (49 percent). In addition, slightly larger proportions of women (9 percent) than of men (6 percent) are employed in human-services organizations.

Women are less likely than are men to be researchers (9 percent, compared with 13 percent of the men) or administrators (19 percent of the women, 22 percent of the men) and are more likely to be engaged in other primary work activities. Among the other activities reported by women are writing and editing, program planning and budgeting, teaching, and library, museum, and archival work.

As table 8–2 indicates, female humanists employed in the public sector are significantly less likely than are men to hold executive, managerial, administrative, and supervisory positions and are more likely to be professionals and research scientists. The lower ranks of the women in our sample may in part be explained by their having been in the labor force for a shorter period: The mean number of years since receiving the doctorate is 10.2 for women and 12.3 for men.

Table 8–1
Employer Types and Primary Work Activities of Male and Female Humanists
(*percent*)

	Women (N = 69)	Men (N = 463)	Total (N = 532)
Libraries, museums, archives:			
Research	13	14	7
Administration	4	7	6
Other	83	80	80
N	23	118	141
Human-services organizations:			
Research	17	10	11
Administration	50	23	28
Other	33	67	61
N	6	30	36
Federal agencies:			
Research	6	14	13
Administration	21	27	27
Other	74	59	60
N	34	267	301
State/local agencies:			
Research	0	12	11
Administration	33	31	32
Other	67	56	57
N	6	48	54

Table 8–2
Rank or Level of Current Position, by Sex
(*percent*)

Rank or Level	Women	Men	Total
Executive	7	12	11
Manager	3	9	8
Administrator	14	16	16
Professional	57	43	45
Research scientist	4	2	3
Technician	0	1	1
Supervisor	1	6	5
Clerical	1	1	1
Other	12	10	10
N	91	556	647

Finally, the marital status of the two sexes is as follows:

	Women (%)	Men (%)
Single (never married)	35	14
Married	50	77
Separated, divorced, widowed	14	9

Reasons for Career Change

As we saw in chapter 6, the great majority of humanities Ph.D.'s (about 80 percent) begin graduate school expecting to become college professors. However, only about three in five of the women in our sample had such expectations; 29 percent say that they did not expect to become college professors, and the remainder say they were undecided at graduate-school entry. It would seem, then, that female humanists are more likely than are their male counterparts to consider careers other than the traditional one of college teaching, perhaps because they believe that sex discrimination still exists in academe. Whatever the reasons for the differences between men and women in their initial career goals, it may be easier to persuade women with humanities Ph.D.'s to consider non-academic careers.

Table 8–3 shows the reasons given by women and by men for having changed career goals at some point after graduate-school entry. The most-important reason, cited by equal proportions, is that available teaching opportunities were limited or unattractive. As to differences between the sexes, female humanists are less likely than men to say that they found more-attractive or challenging job opportunities elsewhere, that they decided they did not enjoy their first-choice career, or that they decided they did not enjoy teaching. With respect to the last of these reasons, it may be that fewer women than men in our sample had ever held teaching jobs. Women are more likely than men to say that they became interested in a different area of study; this suggests that, to some degree, women's changes in career goals are motivated by intrinsic considerations.

Slightly more men than women in the sample changed their career goals for personal or family reasons, a finding that runs slightly contrary to expectation. About equal proportions (slightly over one-tenth) changed goals as a result of job termination.

Table 8–3
Reasons for Changing Career Goals, by Sex
(percent)

Reason	Women	Men	Total
Available teaching opportunities were limited or unattractive.	63	62	63
Decided I did not enjoy teaching.	9	12	12
Available job opportunities in previous field were limited or unattractive.	19	20	20
Decided I did not enjoy first-choice career.	4	9	8
Found more-attractive or challenging job opportunities elsewhere.	41	49	48
Changed career aspirations for personal or family reasons.	22	24	24
Became outdated in my first-choice field.	4	4	4
Became interested in different area of study.	21	16	16
Was terminated in a job.	12	11	11
N	68	416	484

Relationship of Job to Graduate Training

Slightly more women (50 percent) than men (47 percent) in our sample see their current jobs as being closely related to their graduate training, whereas slightly more men (37 percent) than women (34 percent) say they are in somewhat related jobs. Equal proportions (16 percent) say that their current job is not at all related to their graduate training. In general, first jobs are considered to be more closely related to one's education than are later jobs (Ochsner and Solmon 1979a). Since the women in our sample tend to have received the doctorate more recently and thus to have been in the labor force for a shorter period, they are more likely than are the men to hold entry-level jobs; this may explain their slightly greater tendency to see their current jobs as closely related to their graduate training.

Table 8–4 compares the sexes with respect to the reasons they give for working in a job that is less than closely related to their graduate training. Over two in three women and 57 percent of the men say that employment opportunities were scarce for people in their doctoral field; 49 percent of the men and 42 percent of the women cite the very similar reason that jobs related to their

Table 8–4

Reasons for Working at a Job that Is Only Somewhat Related or Is Not Related to Graduate Training, by Sex

(percent)

Reason	Women	Men	Total
Never planned to take a closely related job.	7	3	4
Changed field to one I prefer more.	9	20	19
Exposed to another field and became interested.	17	36	38
Prefer present work.	33	27	28
First job unrelated to doctoral study; became interested in this work.	9	7	7
Tried closely related employment, but did not like it.	2	4	4
Joined family business or firm.	0	0	0
Found job that offers better chance for career advancement.	44	33	35
Pay is better where I am.	51	44	45
No longer in closely related job because of promotion.	4	6	6
Wanted part-time work, flexible hours.	2	0	1
Wanted to work at home.	0	0	0
Jobs related to doctoral study not available where I live, and do not want to move.	33	10	13
Jobs related to my doctoral field not available.	42	49	48
Could not get closely related job but would prefer one.	36	27	28
Limited in job selection by situation of spouse, family responsibilities.	36	7	11
Employment opportunities scarce for people in jobs related to my doctoral study.	69	57	58
Have become technologically obsolete in field of doctoral study.	7	6	6
In the military.	0	2	2
Better-quality work environment where I am.	13	12	12
N	45	292	337

doctoral field were simply not available. In other words, both sexes have been strongly affected by the scarcity or complete unavailability of academic jobs.

Aside from these two most-common reasons, women and men tend to cite different kinds of reasons for working in jobs that are only somewhat related or are unrelated to their graduate training. For instance, substantially larger proportions of men than of women say they changed to a field they prefer more or that they were exposed to and became interested in another field. The explanation here may be that men are more inclined to lose interest in their humanities field once they have the doctorate and move into the world of work. On the other hand, women are more likely to say simply that they prefer their present job, that they never planned to take a closely related job, or that they could not get a closely related job but would prefer one.

Contrary to the popular image of women as more concerned with the intrinsic rewards of a job and less concerned with extrinsic features such as pay and promotion, larger proportions of women (51 percent) than of men (44 percent) say they are working in a job not closely related to their graduate training because it offers better pay; similarly, 44 percent of the women, compared with 33 percent of the men, cite the opportunities for career advancement as their reason for working at their current (unrelated) jobs. Perhaps these differences reflect not so much a difference in values as a difference in employment sectors. As was pointed out in chapter 5, when doctorate-level humanists answer questions like these, they are probably comparing their current jobs with traditional jobs in academe. (Doctorate-level scientists and engineers, on the other hand, are more likely to have in mind jobs in the private sector when they make such comparisons.) It would seem to follow, then, that public-sector jobs offer women better chances for advancement and more-equitable salaries than do academic jobs. Sex discrimination may continue to operate in academe to a greater extent than it does in government.

That women's occupational and geographical mobility is more limited than that of men is evidenced by the greater tendency of women to say that jobs related to their doctoral study are not available where they live but that they do not want to move (33 percent of the women, compared with 10 percent of the men) and that they are limited in their job selection by the situation of their spouse and by family responsibilities (36 percent of the women, compared with only 7 percent of the men).

Salient Job Characteristics

As was indicated in chapter 7, when asked to indicate which of a number of job characteristics were most important in their choosing the current job over the next-best alternative, doctorate-level humanists are most likely to cite such materialistic considerations as salary, future salary prospects, and fringe benefits, although competency of colleagues is also a major concern.

Table 8–5 shows the proportions of respondents, by sex and by marital status, indicating that a given job characteristic was very important. Looking first at overall sex differences, we find that larger proportions of men than of women cite salary, future salary prospects, and fringe benefits as decisive factors in their choosing their current (government) jobs over the next-best alternative. Although this would seem to contradict the findings of the previous analysis, it should be remembered that the question there was why the respondent was working in a job not closely related to his or her graduate training. Moreover, salary is still the top-ranked factor for women, although future salary prospects and fringe benefits seem less important to them than certain other factors.

Men are also somewhat more likely than women to mention rank as a very important factor in job choice and are much more likely to mention administration and administrators, perhaps because they are also more likely to hold executive, managerial, and supervisory positions.

For their part, women are somewhat more concerned than are men with the congeniality and the competency of their colleagues and with research facilities and opportunities; moreover, they are far more likely to cite factors not directly connected with the job itself, namely, cultural opportunities (cited by one in

Table 8–5
Salient Factors in Choice of Current Job over Next-Best Alternative, by Sex and Marital Status
(percentages responding ''very important'')

	Women				Men			
Salient Factor	S	M	D	Total	S	M	D	Total
Congeniality of colleagues	22	27	36	26	23	22	17	22
Competency of colleagues	28	37	36	34	23	32	34	30
Reputation of employer among scholars	13	24	27	21	14	19	22	19
Administration and administrators	7	14	27	13	20	21	12	20
Research facilities and opportunities	30	37	27	33	22	25	24	25
Salary	41	33	36	36	27	42	38	40
Fringe benefits	22	29	27	26	27	34	35	34
Rank	31	13	18	20	22	24	23	23
Opportunities for outside income	3	2	9	3	1	4	6	4
Future salary prospects	31	25	54	31	28	38	37	36
Nearness to a graduate school	7	7	0	6	1	2	6	2
Nearness to friends and relatives	26	16	18	20	19	7	12	9
Climate	3	11	18	9	5	8	10	8
Cultural opportunities	44	30	18	34	22	18	26	20
N	32	45	11	88	74	412	52	538

Note: Key to the column headings: S = single; M = married; D = separated, divorced, widowed.

three women), proximity to friends and relatives, and proximity to a graduate school. When marital status is taken into consideration, some possible interpretations suggest themsleves. For instance, it is the single women who are concerned with their nearness to friends and relatives; and it is the separated, divorced, and widowed women who are concerned with the congeniality of their colleagues. One possible explanation is that the single women (who probably tend to be younger than either the married or the separated, divorced, or widowed) still maintain very close ties with their parents, other relatives, and college friends — ties that members of the other two categories no longer have. In contrast, the woman who has been married but is now separated, divorced, or widowed can no longer turn to her family or old friends as readily; she is more concerned with the congeniality of her colleagues, probably because they constitute her social network. Given the very small numbers involved, however, these interpretations are admittedly tenuous.

Some of the other differences make very good sense. For example, salary tends to be very important to single women and to married men, but not to single men and married women. Similarly, concern with fringe benefits is clearly connected to marital status. Single people of both sexes are not very likely to say that they chose their current job over the next-best alternative because of its fringe benefits, but these are important to the married—as well as to the separated, divorced, and widowed—who are very likely to have families and thus must be more concerned about such matters as health plans and life insurance.

There are several other distinctive patterns among women. Single women are more likely than other women to have chosen their jobs because of salary, rank, and cultural opportunities but otherwise are relatively indifferent to the listed factors. Research facilities and opportunities tend to be important to married women. Separated, divorced, and widowed women are more likely to have been influenced by the reputation of their employer among scholars, administrators and administration, and future salary prospects in choosing their current government jobs over the next best alternative.

Salary

It is common knowledge that the average working woman earns less than the average working man. According to one estimate (Levitin, Quinn, and Staines 1973), she earns only 58 percent of what an equally qualified man would make, or about $3,458 less than her male peer. The higher the occupational level, the greater the salary inequity; 70 percent of the women in professional, technical, or managerial positions; 65 percent in clerical and sales jobs; but only 15 percent in blue-collar jobs (for example, operative work) suffered salary inequities of $3,500 or more.

According to the same study (Levitin, Quinn, and Staines 1973), even though about 95 percent of all working women earn less than they should on the basis of achievement, only 8 percent feel discriminated against because of their gender. But the women who are more discriminated against in terms of the quality of their employment tend to be less satisfied with their jobs than do other women. Similarly, those who are paid less than they should be are more likely to be dissatisfied with their salaries. Such dissatisfaction does not, however, "generalize to other aspects of the job—comfort, challenge, relations with co-workers, or resources" (p. 91).

The Levitin–Quinn–Staines study did not control for differences in educational attainment, except as reflected in the occupations themselves. But even within an educationally homogeneous group of psychology Ph.D.'s, women receive substantially lower salaries than men, an average of $2,607 less (Solmon 1978). Further, comparing humanities Ph.D.'s with science and engineering Ph.D.'s, the National Research Council (NRC) (1978) showed that humanists in the federal government, especially women, earn less than scientists and engineers. In 1977 female humanists earned a median salary of $19,900; male humanists, $29,300; female scientists and engineers, $26,600; and male scientists and engineers, $29,900. The NRC data also show that the older the group of workers, the greater the salary differences between male and female Ph.D.'s in all employment sectors.

The mean salary of the women in our sample of government-employed humanities Ph.D.'s is $20,755; the mean salary of the men is $25,834, a difference of $5,079. As table 8–6 shows, married men receive the highest salaries, whereas separated, divorced, and widowed women earn the least. Interestingly, single women make more than single men. As the last analysis indicated, they are also much more likely than single men (or other women) to say that they

Table 8–6
Mean Salary, by Sex and Marital Status

	Mean Salary ($)	Standard Deviation ($)	N
Women:	20,755	8,822	92
Single	22,197	9,474	33
Married	20,378	8,717	45
Separated, divorced, widowed	18,571	7,468	14
Men:	25,834	10,969	559
Single	18,609	7,693	78
Married	27,635	11,048	429
Separated, divorced, widowed	21,817	8,889	52
Total:	25,117	10,831	651
Single	19,676	8,382	111
Married	26,635	11,048	474
Separated, divorced, widowed	21,129	8,657	66

chose their current job over the next-best alternative because of salary; about two in five of the single women, compared with only 27 percent of the single men and 34 percent of other women, indicate that salary was a very important consideration in their choice.

In the regression equation on salary (see chapter 7), the respondent's sex per se was not a significant predictor once marital status was taken into account. Thus, being married is more important in explaining salary differences for this sample than is being male or female. The most-important predictor was number of years in the labor force since receiving the doctorate. As was pointed out earlier in this chapter, the women, on the average, received their doctorates more recently than the men, although they are not necessarily younger. Rather, they are more likely to have left school to work for a while after completing their baccalaureates but before beginning their doctoral study. Next in importance, those who see themselves as not being underemployed tend to receive higher salaries. As we shall see in the next section, men and women differ significantly on this point, with women being much more likely to feel that they are under-employed. For this sample, then, sex differences in salary are accounted for chiefly by sex differences in number of years employed since receipt of the doctorate, number of years in the current job, number of publications, and number of years since receiving the doctorate.

Underemployment

According to a recent NRC report (1978), not only are women with doctoral degrees less likely than their male counterparts to be employed full time and more likely to be unemployed and seeking work, but also doctoral work in the humanities is less likely than doctoral work in the sciences and engineering to lead to full-time employment. Thus, female humanists suffer a kind of double jeopardy. In 1977, 6.8 percent of the women with doctorates in humanities were unemployed and seeking work, compared with 1.9 percent of the male humanities Ph.D.'s, 3.6 percent of the female science and engineering Ph.D.'s, and only 0.9 percent of the male science and engineering Ph.D.'s (NRC 1978).

Unemployment is underemployment taken to the extreme. Part-time employment can also be considered underemployment (especially if the individual would rather hold a full-time job), but not necessarily. The discussion here focuses on *perceived* underemployment among doctorate-level humanists with full-time jobs in the public sector.

Table 8–7 shows the proportions of respondents, by sex and by marital status, who indicate that a particular statement about perceived underemployment or about other job conditions that may be related to perceived underemployment applies to them. More women than men in our sample of government-employed humanists see themselves as underemployed: 54 percent of the men, compared

Table 8–7

Perceptions of Underemployment, by Sex and Marital Status

(percentages indicating that statement applies)

	Women				Men			
	S	M	D	Total	S	M	D	Total
I am *not* underemployed.	48	52	14	45	47	56	45	54
I am underemployed and would prefer a more-challenging position.	24	33	21	28	35	25	32	27
I am underemployed, but for personal reasons I prefer to remain in this or a similar position.	12	6	21	11	4	12	15	11
I am underemployed; my job is not in my field.	12	15	7	13	30	12	21	15
I am underemployed; my job is not commensurate with my level of experience.	15	26	14	20	23	16	30	18
I am underemployed; my job is not commensurate with my level of training.	15	28	21	23	40	19	24	23
I am underemployed; my job is not commensurate with my level of ability.	21	37	21	29	38	26	38	28
I have the skills and knowledge necessary for successful performance of my job.	73	89	86	83	91	83	89	85
People with less formal schooling are performing well in jobs identical to mine.	36	39	43	39	55	41	57	45
If people with less formal schooling were hired, they could do my job as well as I.	33	20	57	30	41	28	43	32
I believe my present job is a nontraditional one for people in my doctoral field.	48	48	43	47	59	49	58	51
I have held other nontraditional jobs.	18	41	43	33	40	32	45	34
I was employed full-time for a period of time after receiving my bachelor's degree and before starting my doctoral program.	36	46	43	42	31	39	43	38
N	33	46	14	93	78	432	53	563

Note: Key to the column headings: S = single; M = married; D = separated, divorced, widowed.

with only 45 percent of the women subscribe to the statement ''I am *not* underemployed.'' Perceived underemployment is least common among married people of both sexes and most common among the separated, divorced, and widowed, especially the women, only 14 percent of whom feel they are not underemployed.

Overall sex differences on most of the remaining items are slight. Men are somewhat more likely to say that people with less formal schooling are performing well in similar jobs, that their jobs are nontraditional for people in their doctoral field, and that they are underemployed in that their jobs are not in their doctoral field; women are somewhat more likely to perceive themselves as underemployed because their jobs are not commensurate with their experience.

Looking at women grouped according to their marital status, we find the following distinctive patterns. Single women are unlikely to regard their current jobs in the private sector as nontraditional; they seem to be slightly less self-confident than other women in that they are less likely to say that their jobs are not commensurate with their level of training or that they have the skills and knowledge necessary for the successful performance of their jobs. (Nonetheless, 73 percent say that they do have the necessary skills and knowledge, a sizable proportion even though it is lower than the 89 percent for married women and the 86 percent for separated, divorced, and widowed women.)

Married women have less tendency than other women to regard themselves as underemployed. Those who do see themselves as underemployed are likely to say that they would prefer a more-challenging position and are unlikely to say that they prefer to remain in their current positions for personal reasons. Relatively large proportions indicate the following ''reasons'' for their underemployment: job is not in same field; job is not commensurate with experience, with level of training, or with level of ability. Very few feel that people with less formal schooling could do the job as well as they.

Separated, divorced, and widowed women are much more likely than others to say that, although underemployed, they prefer for personal reasons to remain in the same position; they are less likely than other women to say that they would prefer a more-challenging position. Relatively large proportions say that the less educated either could perform or are performing well in jobs similar to theirs.

Other Perceptions of the Current Job

Table 8–8 shows the proportions of respondents, by sex and marital status, who indicate that a particular statement applies very much to their situation. The statements in this list cover a wide range of job conditions, most of them having to do with the appropriateness of the current job to these highly trained humanists.

In some ways, jobs in the public sector seem to offer less to the female humanist than to her male counterpart. Although slightly larger proportions of women than of men say they are working at a professional level, women tend to believe that their jobs do not offer good prospects for further advancement. Only one in three (compared with 43 percent of the men) is satisfied with her career progress to date, and only one in five (compared with one in four men) supervises people trained in the same field. Perhaps the greatest discrepancy between the sexes has to do with salary. Only 30 percent of the women, compared with close to half the men, regard themselves as well paid compared with other people who have the same amount of education. More women than men say that the position required on-the-job training. Nonetheless, women are markedly happier than men with their graduate education, with 92 percent glad to have had the graduate education they did.

On the whole, single women seem to find government jobs most compatible, and separated, divorced, and widowed women to find them least so. Thus, markedly larger proportions of single women than of other women consider themselves well paid (a perception consistent with reality); work with people

Table 8–8

Perceptions of Current Job, by Sex and Marital Status

(percentages indicating that statement "very much" applies)

	Women				Men			
	S	M	D	Total	S	M	D	Total
I am well paid for my work compared with others with the same amount of education.	40	30	8	30	31	50	50	48
I supervise people trained in my field.	25	14	23	19	9	27	18	24
Most of my colleagues are trained in my field.	36	23	17	27	22	31	24	29
I am satisfied with my career progress to date.	37	36	23	34	24	48	28	43
My job offers good future prospects for further advancement.	36	12	17	21	35	24	28	26
My job fits my long-range goals.	45	35	27	38	32	41	35	39
My skills are fully utilized in my job.	33	36	8	31	22	36	17	32
I am working at a professional level.	71	82	50	73	57	73	65	70
I would have liked more training outside graduate school before I started working.	10	5	0	6	7	4	8	5
I received job training inappropriate for actual requirements of my job.	7	7	0	6	11	9	17	10
I am glad I had the graduate education I did.	97	88	93	92	69	81	79	79
My position required on-the-job training.	56	38	38	44	37	31	35	32
N	30	44	13	87	78	422	52	552

Note: Key to the column headings: S = single; M = married; D = separated, divorced, widowed.

trained in the same field; and feel that their jobs fit their long-range goals and offer good prospects for further advancement. At the same time, they are most likely of any group to say that the position required on-the-job training and that they would have liked more training outside graduate school before they started working.

Over four in five married women are working at a professional level; and relatively large proportions feel that their skills are fully utilized on the job, a factor that contributes significantly to overall job satisfaction. But relatively few of these women supervise people trained in the same field. Moreover, they tend to be in dead-end jobs. Only 12 percent say that their jobs offer good prospects for further advancement.

A more-dismal picture emerges for separated, divorced, and widowed women (although the reader should bear in mind that the actual number involved is very small). Very few of these women are working at a professional level, feel that their skills are fully utilized or that they are well paid, find their jobs consistent with their long-range goals, or are pleased with their career progress to date. Their general discontent is given some substance by the finding reported earlier that they are the lowest paid of any group. Otherwise, it is difficult to surmise why their public-sector jobs seem so markedly less desirable than those held by single and by married women.

Job Satisfaction

Consistent with the impression mentioned previously that public-sector jobs may offer more rewards for men than for women, at least within our sample of doctorate-level humanists, 36 percent of the men but only 31 percent of the women declare themselves very satisfied with their jobs overall (table 8–9). Married people of both sexes are likely to feel greater overall job satisfaction than are the unmarried.

About one-third of both sexes are very satisfied with the challenge offered by their jobs, an essential element in overall satisfaction, with single men and with single and separated, divorced, or widowed men and women being slightly less likely to find their jobs challenging. With respect to the two next-most-important job aspects—opportunity to be creative and to use schooling or training—a larger proportion of women than of men express great satisfaction; single women are especially likely to find their jobs satisfying in these ways. A much larger proportion of men than of women are very satisfied with the salary and fringe benefits of their jobs; among women, it is the single women who are most

Table 8–9
Satisfaction with Job and with Aspects of Job, by Sex and Marital Status
(percentages responding "very satisfied")

Job Aspect	Women				Men			
	S	M	D	Total	S	M	D	Total
Overall job satisfaction	28	39	8	31	25	39	29	36
Salary and fringe benefits	42	30	14	32	39	45	47	44
Opportunity for scholarly pursuits	27	22	0	21	14	22	13	20
Opportunity for creativity	38	32	0	30	15	27	19	25
Opportunity to use training or schooling	43	35	8	34	20	32	29	30
Resources to get job done	26	28	20	26	26	27	18	26
Internal politics	3	11	0	7	5	7	12	8
Working conditions (hours, location)	29	35	8	29	26	31	37	31
Status	37	16	9	22	19	30	25	28
Autonomy and independence	36	36	0	31	22	27	33	27
Variety in activities	40	38	17	35	18	35	35	33
Policymaking power	27	21	9	21	12	19	13	17
Congenial work relationships	23	35	15	28	29	31	36	31
Competency of colleagues	19	29	8	22	20	23	23	23
Opportunities for different/better jobs at this institution/organization	16	7	0	8	18	16	22	17
Visibility for jobs at other institutions/organizations	26	11	10	16	19	16	17	16
Challenge	32	33	25	32	29	34	24	33
Job security	45	35	46	40	40	53	48	50
Prestige of employer	37	38	38	38	29	37	35	36
N	32	46	13	91	77	424	51	552

Note: Key to the column headings: S = single; M = married; D = separated, divorced, widowed.

likely to be satisfied, as should be the case since they receive the highest mean salaries of their sex. Men are also more inclined to express great satisfaction with job security; since about two-thirds of the men but only half the women had worked at their current jobs for at least three years, this difference may simply mean that the men have more formal security at their public-sector jobs.

In addition, larger proportions of men than of women are very satisfied with their opportunities for better jobs in government and with their status. In connection with the latter point, it should be remembered that the male humanists in the sample tend to hold higher rank than the female humanists. On the other hand, larger proportions of women are very satisfied with their autonomy and independence and, surprisingly, with their policymaking power.

Further analyses were carried out to see whether satisfaction with various aspects of the job is related to length of time in the current job. For both men and women, the longer they have worked at their current job, the more inclined they are to be satisfied with job security, opportunities for creativity, and opportunities to use training or schooling. In addition, men who have been working at the current job longer are more likely than other men to express great satisfaction with the variety of their work activities, their status, and their policymaking power. This was not the case for women. Those who have worked at their current jobs for more than ten years, as well as those who have less than one year's tenure, tend to be less satisfied than are women with between one and ten years' experience on the job with the variety of their work activities, their status, and their policymaking power. The likely explanation is that women (but not men) who have been in the same position for over ten years have demonstrated a lack of upward mobility; they are in dead-end jobs and foresee no improvement in their status, authority, and responsibility. Relatively recently employed women, on the other hand, may have expressed less satisfaction with these job aspects because they have not yet adjusted their expectations to the realities of the job situation. That is, they may have taken jobs in the public sector expecting to have greater policymaking power and status than they indeed find themselves to have. Finally, the longer the female humanist has worked at her current job, the less likely she is to be satisfied with the competency of her colleagues, her work relationships, and her opportunities for a better job either within or outside the government.

Mobility

It is often asserted that women hold less-attractive jobs than men because they are less geographically and occupationally mobile. The married woman in particular usually defers to her husband's wishes about where the family will live; his job comes first.

The findings in table 8–10 confirm the lesser mobility of women. For

Table 8–10
Job Mobility, by Sex
(percentages responding "agree strongly")

	Women	Men	Total
I would take a job anywhere as long as there were opportunities to travel.	3	38	7
If I were looking for a job now, I would look nationwide.	22	28	36
There are a limited number of cities in which I would live.	55	38	41
Climate would be a major factor in my decision to move.	25	21	21
I would take a job anywhere for a short period, but I have specific preferences for permanent residence.	21	19	19
I would move anywhere if the salary were attractive enough.	8	12	12
I would move anywhere for an extremely satisfying job.	26	35	33
I will be more mobile when my children are out of school.	14	15	15
My mobility is limited because my parents are alive.	6	3	3
My ideal job location is within 500 miles of the community where I grew up.	9	9	9
My occupation severely limits my choice of geographic location.	18	14	14
My mobility is limited because of spouse's job.	24	4	7
My mobility is limited because of spouse's educational plans.	0	2	1
My mobility is limited because of spouse's preferences about locale.	11	6	7
If I could begin my career again, I would like to become a college professor.	20	28	27
I could be equally or more satisfied with a different employer.	32	34	34
N	87	548	635

instance, 38 percent of the men, but only 22 percent of the women, say that if they were looking for a job now, they would look nationwide; 35 percent of the men, but only 26 percent of the women, say that they would move anywhere for an extremely satisfying job; and 12 percent of the men, compared with 8 percent of the women, say that they would move anywhere if the salary were attractive enough.

The kinds of constraints imposed on the mobility of women are reflected in the much larger proportions who say that their mobility is limited because of their spouse's job (24 percent of the women, compared with only 4 percent of the men) and because of their spouse's preferences as to locale (11 percent of the women, 6 percent of the men). Women are also somewhat more likely than men to agree strongly that their occupation severely limits their choice of a geographic location (18 percent of the women, 14 percent of the men) and that there are only a limited number of cities in which they would live (55 percent of the women, 38 percent of the men). Relatively few doctorate-level humanists of either sex indicate that they would take a job anywhere provided they had opportunities to travel; that their mobility is limited by their spouse's educational plans; or that it is limited because their parents are still alive, although women are more likely to be affected by the last of these than are men. Surprisingly large proportions—25 percent of the women and 21 percent of the men—say that climate would be a major factor in their decision to move. Finally, roughly equal proportions (about 20 percent) of women and of men say that they would take a job anywhere for a short period but have decided preferences for a permanent residence. One-third of the humanists in government jobs, regardless of sex, say they could be equally or more satisfied with a different employer. Perhaps many of the individuals in this group are actively seeking (or are on the point of actively seeking) new jobs, either in the public sector or outside it.

Summary

The women in our sample of government-employed humanists are less likely to hold high rank, but their lower positions are probably explained by their not having had the doctorate or been in the current jobs as long as the men. Because relatively few say that they expected, at the time of entry to graduate school, to become college professors, employment in the public sector may represent less of a disjunction for women than for men; thus, they may be easier to attract into government jobs.

Women are only slightly less likely than men to feel that their current jobs are not closely related to their graduate field. Among those who say that the job is only somewhat or not at all related to their training, women are more likely than men to cite better pay and greater opportunity for career advancement as their reasons for taking an unrelated job. In choosing that job over the next-best alternative, women are likely to have given greater weight to the congeniality and competency of their colleagues and to extraneous factors such as cultural opportunities and proximity to friends and relatives.

Although in some ways jobs in the public sector seem to be less fulfilling for women than for men—as is indicated by the smaller proportions who are satisfied with their jobs overall, with their opportunities for other jobs or for advancement in their own jobs, and with their career progress to date—the evidence indicates that the government does not discriminate as much against women in terms of salary as academe (and the private sector?) may. The salaries received by the women in our sample average about 80 percent of the salaries received by men; according to one estimate, women ordinarily make only about 58 percent as much as men with equal qualifications. The smaller salaries made by the women in our sample are probably attributable to the shorter time that has passed since they received their doctorates and to their shorter tenure in the current job. In short, salary inequities between the sexes seem considerably less marked among government workers than among workers in other sectors.

There were a number of intriguing differences by marital status among the women in our sample. On the whole, single women seem to come out best in their government jobs, whereas separated, divorced, and widowed women seem to have the least-desirable jobs. Indeed, generally speaking, the responses of single women—particularly with respect to job satisfaction—more closely resemble the responses of men than those of other women.

This analysis clearly confirms that women have less mobility than men. They are much more likely to defer to the needs and wishes of their spouses than are men, and this seriously hampers their freedom of movement and their ability to take possibly more-desirable jobs that are closely related to their graduate training.

Notes

1. On the other hand, if discrimination reduces profits, it could be argued that profit-seeking entities would be least discriminating (see Becker 1971).

2. The sample used for these female–male comparisons differed somewhat from the sample used in the analyses discussed in chapters 6 and 7; hence, there are differences in totals shown in the tables.

9

How Useful Is Humanities Tracking?

A major policy question addressed in this book is, Does graduate training in the humanities have any practical value in preparing people for employment in the public sector? As chapter 6 indicated, some of the competencies developed in graduate school (by humanists and nonhumanists alike) may not prove to be useful in government jobs; research skills and academic ability are the most notable examples. Conversely, some of the traits and skills called for by such jobs—including self-confidence, self-discipline and the ability to follow rules, creativity and originality, leadership ability, insight, and public-speaking ability—are not always significantly improved by graduate study. Nonetheless, humanities graduate training seems to contribute to effective performance in a public-sector job, as is evidenced by the large proportions of doctorate-level humanists in the Higher Education Research Institute (HERI) sample who report that they are glad they had a graduate education; that many of the talents developed through graduate study (critical thinking and analytical skills, writing ability, general knowledge) are also helpful to them in their current jobs; and that specific academic experiences (graduate study in general, courses in the major, undergraduate study) gave them skills and knowledge that they apply in their work.

Significant Factors in the Preparation of Ph.D.'s

To further our understanding of the ways in which graduate education has instrumental payoffs for publicly employed humanists, we conducted factor analyses of responses to two items on the survey questionnaire. The first item asked humanists to indicate which of eighteen skills and abilities had improved significantly in graduate school. The second item asked them to indicate, on a three-point scale ("very much," "somewhat," "not at all"), the extent to which each of eleven types of training or education had provided skills and knowledge that helped to prepare them for their present jobs. For purposes of comparison, the responses of scientists and engineers to these two items were also subjected to factor analysis.[1] Tables 9–1 and 9–2 show the results of these analyses.

For the 666 doctorate-level humanists on whom this analysis is based, the eighteen skills and abilities developed in graduate school can be combined into three factors: (1) personal and social development, (2) cognitive and academic development, and (3) technical competence.[2]

Table 9–1
Factor Loadings for Skills and Abilities that Improved Significantly in Graduate School

	Humanists (N = 666)			Scientists and Engineers (N = 3,953)			
	Personal and Social Development	Cognitive and Academic Ability	Technical Competencies	Personal Development	Analytical Skills	Awareness	Mathematical Ability
General knowledge		.51					
Ability to think clearly	.56	.65			.58		
Leadership ability				.49			
Critical thinking or analytical skills	.54	.62			.70		
Self-confidence				.50			
Self-discipline and the ability to follow rules	.47						
Creativity and originality	.46			.40			
Writing ability		.63		.46			
Insight	.56						
Cultural perspective	.46					.60	
Understanding of others	.64					.60	
Political awareness	.45					.52	
Academic ability		.55					.37
Drive to achieve	.49			.49			
Mathematical ability			.66				.53
Mechanical ability			.61				
Public-speaking ability	.44			.52			
Research skills		.60			.43		

Note: Only those factor loadings of .4 or higher are shown.

Table 9–2
Factor Loadings for Aspects of Education and Training that Gave Preparation for the Current Job

	Humanists (N = 666)			Scientists and Engineers (N = 3,953)			
	Academic Study	Co- and Extracurricular Activities	External Formal Training	Academic Study	Cocurricular Activities	External Formal Training	Extracurricular Activities
Particular course(s) in major area	.71			.58			
Courses outside major area	.55			.53			
Graduate study in general	.65			.52			
Extracurricular activities while in graduate school		.45					.52
Research assistantships		.39			.65		
Teaching assistantships		.40			.47		
Undergraduate study	.54			.45			
Formal training program at place of employment			.56			.55	
Formal training or courses other than programs offered by employer			.45			.54	
General on-the-job experience							
Leisure activities		.46					.56

Note: Only those factor loadings of .4 or higher are shown.

The first factor, personal and social development, comprises ten of the eighteen listed variables: understanding of others, leadership ability, insight, self-confidence, drive to achieve, self-discipline and the ability to follow rules, creativity and originality, cultural perspective, political awareness, and public-speaking ability.

The second factor, cognitive and academic development, is made up of six variables: ability to think clearly, writing ability, critical thinking or analytical skills, research skills, academic ability, and general knowledge. These are the kinds of competencies that are traditionally regarded as being developed by graduate study.

Mathematical ability and mechanical ability constitute the third factor, technical competency, which one would not expect to be emphasized in the graduate training of humanists.

The factor analysis based on the responses of 3,953 scientists and engineers produced somewhat different results. Fourteen of the eighteen listed skills and abilities clustered into four, rather than three, factors: (1) personal development, (2) analytical skills, (3) awareness, and (4) mathematical skills.

For the nonhumanists, personal development encompasses six variables: public-speaking ability, self-confidence, leadership ability, drive to achieve, writing ability, and self-discipline and the ability to follow rules. Five of these variables also appear in the first factor for humanists, but the sixth—writing ability—does not.

The second factor, labeled analytical skills, consists of critical thinking or analytical skills, ability to think clearly, and research skills. These are the kinds of competencies that one would expect scientists and engineers to have when they enter graduate school; advanced training probably refines these talents.

Three variables—cultural perspective, understanding of others, and political awareness—cluster in the awareness factor. It should be noted that these traits (especially understanding of others and cultural perspective) are important in explaining the personal and social development of humanists. Apparently, they contribute little toward explaining the graduate experience of scientists and engineers.

The fourth factor, labeled mathematical ability, comprises both mathematical ability and academic ability; it seems safe to assume that these two abilities are virtually synonymous for scientists and engineers, whose graduate training emphasizes mathematics.

Four variables—general knowledge, creativity and originality, insight, and mechanical ability—did not cluster into factors in the analysis for the nonhumanists. In a sense, these traits and skills are outside the realm of traditional graduate study in science and engineering.

For humanists, the factor analysis of the types of education or training that provided knowledge and skills that helped prepare them for their current jobs in the public sector yielded three factors, accounting for ten of the eleven variables. The factors were: (1) academic study, (2) cocurricular and extracurricular activities, and (3) external formal training.

The first factor, academic study, seems to constitute the most-important kind of training (at least in terms of job preparation) received by government-employed humanists. It encompasses the following variables: particular course(s) in major area, graduate study in general, courses outside major area, and undergraduate study.

Substantially less of the job preparation for humanists is explained by co-curricular and extracurricular activities (a factor that includes leisure activities, extracurricular activities while in graduate school, teaching assistantships, and research assistantships) or by external formal training (a factor that includes only two variables, formal training at place of employment and formal training or courses other than programs offered by employer). Since on-the-job experience was cited by fully two-thirds of the humanists as a major source of job preparation (chapter 6), this variable did not contribute to explaining variation in the responses of humanists.

As was the case with the factor analysis for skills and abilities improved significantly during graduate study, the factor analysis for scientists and engineers yielded four rather than three factors. They were: (1) academic study, (2) co-curricular activities, (3) external formal training, and (4) extracurricular activities. The first and third of these factors encompass the same variables as were found for humanists. Moreover, on-the-job experience was mentioned by 69 percent of the scientists and engineers as a very important aspect of job preparation and thus does not account for major variations in response.

The second-most-important factor for nonhumanists (after academic study) is labeled cocurricular activities and includes research assistantships and teaching assistantships. The fourth factor, extracurricular activities, comprises leisure activities and extracurricular activities while in graduate school.

These factor analyses indicate that graduate training contributes to affective as well as cognitive development for both humanists and nonhumanists, and that academic study is an important aspect of preparation for jobs in the public sector.

Conclusion

This chapter has clearly demonstrated that humanities Ph.D.'s (as well as science and engineering Ph.D.'s) can find satisfying jobs outside academe, more specifically in the government sector of the economy. It also seems that graduate training helps to develop competencies that are valuable on the job.

This is not to argue that graduate work in the humanities is necessarily the best preparation for government employment. Rather, the point is that taking a job in the public sector does not represent a waste of graduate training. Doctorate-level humanists working in the public sector seem to be better—and more-satisfied—employees because of their educational background:

If, in addition, we accept the common assertion that humanists can bring a fresh perspective and a deeper sense of values to the public (or the corporate) employment sector, then it can also be argued that the employment of more humanities Ph.D.'s in nonacademic jobs might well benefit society as a whole. Such a conclusion warrants the development of mechanisms to encourage the new generation of scholars to consider government jobs and to persuade those who hire government workers to recruit more doctorate-level humanists.

Notes

1. On each item, principal factor analysis with iteration, using varimax orthogonal rotation, was employed separately for the humanists and the non-humanist samples. This method of factor analysis collapses a given set of variables—in this case, eighteen and eleven in number—into a set of factors that are orthogonal to, or uncorrelated with, each other, so that the factors show underlying patterns of relationships among the variables in question.

2. Factor names are, of course, assigned by the authors and are intended to capture the general nature of the variable clusters that make up each factor.

**Part II
Science and Engineering Ph.D.'s
in Nonacademic Jobs**

10 Identifying Nonacademic-Career Options

As chapter 1 indicated, Ph.D. production in science and engineering fields during the coming decades will far exceed the number of faculty openings available. Therefore, more often than in the past, new doctorate holders may have to seek employment outside academe. Although nonacademic employment is an established tradition for Ph.D.'s from some fields (for example, engineering and psychology), for others if represents a departure from the norm.

The purpose of the study reported in chapters 11 through 15 was to identify the nonacademic jobs that doctorate-level scientists and engineers now hold, to describe the characteristics of these jobs, to assess the degree of satisfaction associated with them, and to explore the dynamics of job change.

Twelve fields were selected for study: four in the natural sciences (biology, chemistry, physics, and mathematics); three in engineering (civil, electrical, mechanical); and five in the social sciences (economics, political science, anthropology, psychology, and sociology). Although the study focused on nonacademic jobs (in both the public and the private sectors), academe as an employment sector was included for purposes of comparison.

Sampling and Data Collection

The methods used to compile the rosters fo science and engineering Ph.D.'s to be surveyed, although diverse and somewhat unorthodox, were necessary because no other means were available to obtain truly comprehensive lists of individuals from the groups of interest: academics, government employees, and private-sector employees.[1]

The following steps were taken to draw the sample of academics. First, the 50 largest doctorate-granting institutions were identified (on the basis of the number of doctoral degrees they awarded in 1973). A random sample of 110 additional institutions was drawn from the remaining institutions that award a baccalaureate or higher degree and that report annually to the Higher Education General Information Survey (HEGIS), as nearly all nonprofit postsecondary institutions do. Second, department chairs in the relevant science and engineering disciplines from both groups of institutions were asked to provide the names and addresses of faculty and former faculty who met three conditions: (1) they had changed jobs within the previous three years (that is, had joined or left the department during that period); (2) they had not been hired directly from graduate school; and (3) they had not died or retired from academe. In this way, we hoped to get a sample of still-active faculty members who had recently exhibited job mobility. Of the 2,360 departments contacted, 1,234 (52 percent) complied with our request. As a result, a list was compiled of 3,098 faculty members who met the three conditions.

The roster of federal civil servants was compiled with the aid of the U.S. Civil Service Commission (now the Office of Personnel Management), which maintains a computerized mailing list of all federal civil servants, showing their degree level, discipline, and primary work activity. We surveyed all civil servants with a doctorate in one of the designated science and engineering disciplines, with the exception of biology, physics, and psychology. The large numbers of Ph.D.'s from these fields who hold civil-service positions necessitated our drawing a stratified random sample; every third biologist, physicist, and psychologist whose primary work activity was research was selected, along with all those whose primary work activity was teaching, administration, or "other." The Higher Education Research Institute (HERI) file also contains data on several hundred other government-employed Ph.D.'s (including some who work for state- and local-government agencies) drawn from a variety of sources.

Several methods were used to compile the name-and-address roster of science and engineering Ph.D.'s employed in the private sector. First, advertisements asking for the names of nonacademically (or, in some fields, nontraditionally) employed Ph.D.'s were placed in the journals of the relevant professional societies. Second, the journals of those fields that list job changers were searched. Third, the names of members of the National Research Council's Comprehensive Roster employed "outside science" were included. Finally, three professional societies—the American Psychological Association, the Institute for Electrical and Electronic Engineers, and the American Anthropological Association—provided data on their members that permitted us to draw samples stratified so as to pick up as many private-sector and "nontraditionally" employed people as possible. As this description makes clear, the development of the HERI roster of doctorate-level scientists and engineers employed in the private sector differed considerably for the different fields, with psychologists, electrical engineers, and chemists being overrepresented in our sample.[2] These solicitation methods also resulted in the identification of substantial numbers of science and engineering Ph.D.'s employed in academe and government, whose names were duly included on the relevant rosters.

Collecting the Data

The instrument used to collect the data was the HERI Survey of Mobility and Nontraditional Careers of Ph.D.'s in Science and Engineering, an eight-page questionnaire dealing with education and work experience (including job change). (See appendix A for a copy of the questionnaire.) On the assumption that, if doctorate-level scientists and engineers are to be persuaded to pursue nonacademic careers, they must have information about nonacademic jobs that offer acceptable salaries, opportunities to do research and to publish, and emotional rewards, the survey questionnaire emphasized the career outcomes of salary, research productivity, and satisfaction. Other areas covered were as follows:

1. Educational background (for example, degrees received; self-ratings of comparative ability as a graduate student; field of specialization).
2. Experience with postdoctoral appointments.
3. Experience with unemployment.
4. Characteristics of the current job (for example, type of employer; primary work activity; position or rank; attitudes and opinions about job; perceptions of underemployment).
5. Characteristics of previous job (same types of questions as were asked about current job).
6. Assessments of the value of graduate and other training and of one's own skills and abilities.
7. Changes in career goals.
8. Conditions and outcomes of most-recent job change.
9. Potential mobility.
10. Scholarly productivity.
11. Satisfaction with nonoccupational areas of life.
12. Personal characteristics (sex, age, marital status).

The HERI questionnaire was mailed in March 1977 to all those people whose names were on the three rosters. A second copy was sent out in May 1977 to nonrespondents. As a result of these procedures, a total of 9,450 questionnaires were returned; of these, 8,445 were found to be usable. More specifically, the response rate for faculty job changers identified by department chairs was 65 percent; the response rate for federal workers identified through the U.S. Civil Service Commission was 44 percent.

Representativeness of the Respondent Samples

Just how adequately do the three different respondent groups represent the population of doctorate-level scientists and engineers in each of the three employment sectors?[3] The faculty job changers are not—and were not intended to be—representative of all faculty. They are, however, representative of recently mobile, experienced faculty in the designated disciplines from two important classes of institutions: the largest doctorate-granting institutions and all other baccalaureate- and higher-degree-granting institutions. As a group, they are probably somewhat younger than typical faculty. For the government employees, rates were sufficiently high for all designated disciplines to indicate that this group of HERI respondents is representative of the population. Thus, we can say with some confidence that the samples of faculty and of government workers are representative of important populations. The representativeness of the private-sector employees is considerably less clear, primarily because of the impossibility of compiling a comprehensive roster from which to sample. Nonetheless, the representativeness seems sufficient for most disciplines at least to point the direction for new Ph.D.'s entering the labor force.

Description of the Sample

Table 10–1 summarizes some of the personal characteristics of the sample (sex, age, marital status) and indicates the number of cases, by field and by employment sector. The total number of cases is 8,445.

The fields somewhat overrepresented in the sample (for reasons indicated earlier) are psychology (21 percent of the total sample), biology (15 percent), chemistry (15 percent), and physics (11 percent). Fields that are somewhat underrepresented include civil and mechanical engineering, political science, and sociology (each constituting about 3 percent of the total sample).

About one in three respondents is employed in academe. Of these, 87 percent hold faculty ranks; the rest are labeled *nonfaculty academics* (mostly administrators). Relative to their numbers in the total sample, social scientists (with the exception of psychologists) are especially likely to be working in academe, whereas electrical engineers and natural scientists (with the exception of mathematicians) are relatively unlikely to be so employed. Fields with a larger-than-average proportion of nonfaculty academics (relative to faculty members) are chemistry, electrical engineering, and psychology.

Forty-six percent of the total sample hold government jobs, with biologists and chemists being somewhat overrepresented in this sector, and anthropologists and psychologists being somewhat underrepresented.

The private sector employs 22 percent of all respondents. Relative to their representation in the total sample, psychologists and electrical engineers are more likely to work in this sector, whereas biologists and mathematicians are less likely to do so.

Personal Characteristics

Women constitute about 10 percent of the sample. This figure is identical with their representation among all science and engineering Ph.D.'s in the United States (National Research Council 1978). The proportion of women is highest in the social sciences, especially anthropology (34 percent), sociology (22 per-

Table 10–1
Personal Characteristics of the Sample, by Field and Employment Sector

	Biology				Chemistry				Physics			
	Faculty	Non-faculty Academic	Government	Private	Faculty	Non-faculty Academic	Government	Private	Faculty	Non-faculty Academic	Government	Private
Number of cases	270	35	867	109	148	51	793	248	200	28	559	178
Percentage of women	22	11	6	11	8	16	4	7	5	0	3	2
Average age	37	48	46	44	38	49	46	44	37	49	44	48
Marital status:												
Percentage single	15	9	6	6	9	12	7	5	11	11	5	4
Percentage married	76	86	88	86	86	84	86	91	86	89	91	92
Percentage widowed, separated, divorced	9	6	6	8	5	4	6	4	3	0	4	4

	Mechanical Engineering				Economics				Political Science			
	Faculty	Non-faculty Academic	Government	Private	Faculty	Non-faculty Academic	Government	Private	Faculty	Non-faculty Academic	Government	Private
Number of cases	97	8	131	43	201	24	229	59	151	24	87	20
Percentage of women	1	0	0	0	8	4	7	14	12	25	6	0
Average age	37	48	41	43	38	48	41	43	37	48	43	38
Marital status:												
Percentage single	7	0	4	7	8	0	11	10	14	4	15	20
Percentage married	88	100	92	90	87	96	82	85	76	88	80	70
Percentage widowed, separated, divorced	4	0	4	2	4	4	8	5	9	8	5	10

Table 10–1 continued

	Mathematics				Civil Engineering				Electrical Engineering			
	Faculty	Non-faculty Academic	Government	Private	Faculty	Non-faculty Academic	Government	Private	Faculty	Non-faculty Academic	Government	Private
Number of cases	238	24	211	78	80	8	96	32	54	16	240	313
Percentage of women	9	8	5	6	0	0	3	3	2	0	0	0
Average age	35	43	43	40	37	44	42	42	40	48	43	45
Marital status:												
Percentage single	19	22	11	10	6	12	3	0	6	6	3	2
Percentage married	71	74	78	82	89	62	92	97	87	88	93	92
Percentage widowed, separated, divorced	10	4	11	8	5	25	5	3	8	6	4	6

	Anthropology				Psychology				Sociology			
	Faculty	Non-faculty Academic	Government	Private	Faculty	Non-faculty Academic	Government	Private	Faculty	Non-faculty Academic	Government	Private
Number of cases	318	23	59	61	407	96	570	686	156	11	66	42
Percentage of women	37	35	24	26	24	25	13	19	21	27	21	26
Average age	38	41	41	40	42	46	46	45	38	47	45	41
Marital status:												
Percentage single	17	27	7	13	11	11	6	8	8	18	8	15
Percentage married	66	64	76	74	74	76	84	79	75	82	82	68
Percentage widowed, separated, divorced	17	9	17	13	15	14	11	14	17	0	11	17

cent), and psychology (19 percent). Only 8 percent of the economists and 10 percent of the political scientists in the HERI sample are female. Women are markedly underrepresented in engineering; there are only three women among the 1,118 engineers in the sample. In the natural sciences, the proportions of women are higher among biologists (10 percent) and mathematicians (7 percent) than among chemists (5.6 percent) and physicists (3.2 percent). These differences among disciplines within the HERI sample reflect actual differences in the representation of women in the various science and engineering fields.

By employment sector, the proportion of women is higher in academe (17 percent) than in the nonacademic sectors (8 percent of each). Of those employed in colleges and universities, women with doctorates in biology, physics, and economics are especially likely to be faculty members; those with doctorates in chemistry, political science, and sociology are relatively more likely to be non-faculty academics. Overall, the private sector has a better record than government for employing women with doctorates in science and engineering (11 percent and 6 percent, respectively). However, there are no women among the twenty political scientists identified as working in the private sector; and the proportions of female physicists, mathematicians, and anthropologists are about equal for the two sectors.

The faculty is the youngest group, averaging 37 to 38 years of age, with electrical engineers and psychologists tending to be slightly older (ages 40 to 42) and mathematicians slightly younger (age 35). Nonfaculty academics are the oldest group, averaging 46 to 49 years of age, with the mathematicians and anthropologists among them being slightly younger. That nonfaculty academics with doctorates in the disciplines covered tend to be older than their counterparts who hold faculty ranks is not surprising; most of them are administrators who were probably promoted to their current positions after having served as faculty members. For Ph.D.'s employed in the nonacademic sectors, the average age is 43. Among government workers, biologists, chemists, and physicists tend to be slightly older; mechanical engineers, economists, and anthropologists tend to be slightly younger. Among private-sector employees, physicists, electrical engineers, and psychologists have a higher average age; mathematicians, political scientists, anthropologists, and sociologists are younger.

The overwhelming majority of the sample—over 80 percent—are married; equal proportions (about 8 percent) either are single or are widowed, divorced, or separated. By employment sector, those in academe are twice as likely as those in government and in the private sector to be single; faculty members are the most likely of the four groups to be widowed, separated, or divorced. By field, larger-than-average proportions of mathematicians, political scientists, and anthropologists are single; and larger-than-average proportions of anthropologists, psychologists, and sociologists are widowed, separated, or divorced.

Current Position

One item on the HERI questionnaire asked respondents to indicate their current rank or level, with different alternatives for faculty members, for nonfaculty academics, and for nonacademics. Of those holding faculty ranks, about half are assistant professors, one-quarter are associate professors, and close to one-fifth are full professors. Very few (about 5 percent) are at the lowest rung of the academic ladder (instructor or lecturer), and 2 percent have other titles. By field, two-thirds of the electrical engineers and three-fifths of the economists and the psychologists hold higher academic ranks (associate or full professor); relatively small proportions of biologists, physicists, mathematicians, and anthropologists hold these ranks. In some cases, these differences can be accounted for by differences in average age.

Close to half of the nonfaculty academics check the "other" category of rank or level. In addition, the sample includes twelve presidents/chancellors. Thirty-two others (9 percent) hold vice-presidential positions in college administration. One-fifth are deans or the equivalent; another one-fifth are other types of administrators. Only ten people (3 percent), eight of them psychologists, are counselors.

Among those scientists and engineers employed in government jobs, the largest proportion (34 percent) hold positions as research scientists. Biologists, chemists, and physicists are most likely—and economists, political scientists, anthropologists, and psychologists least likely—to check this alternative. The second-most-frequent response (checked by about one-quarter of the government workers) is simply "professional," with social scientists, civil engineers, and mathematicians most likely, and other natural scientists least likely, to characterize their current position in this way. About 12 percent of the government employees are managers, about 8 percent are administrators, and only 7 percent are executives; the proportion of political scientists checking this last alternative is considerably higher (23 percent). Only 5 percent of the total group, but one-tenth of the mechanical engineers, hold a supervisory position. "Other" positions are indicated by about 9 percent of the government workers, with 20 percent of the anthropologists giving this response. Thirty-three government-employed science and engineering Ph.D.'s are teachers. The number indicating that they are clerical workers, skilled workers, or unskilled workers is negligible.

The picture is somewhat different for those doctorate-level scientists and engineers employed in the private sector. They are more likely than are their counterparts in government to be executives (22 percent) and managers (16 percent) or to hold "other" positions (17 percent), and are less likely to be research scientists (11 percent, compared with 34 percent of government workers). Slightly over one-quarter (the same proportion as among government workers) describe themselves as professionals. By field, engineers of all types, chemists, and physicists are more likely to hold high-status positions (executive or manager); biologists, anthropologists, and sociologists are less likely to occupy such positions. Social scientists (with the exception of political scientists) and mathematicians are markedly more likely, and physicists and electrical engineers markedly less likely, to hold middle-level positions (professionals, research scientists) when they work in the private sector. In short, the private sector seems to offer better opportunities for high-status jobs than does the government, but only for those from certain fields. Nineteen of the private-sector employees are teachers (eight of them in elementary and secondary schools). As was true in the government sector, virtually none hold such low-level positions as clerical worker, skilled worker, or unskilled worker. Finally, biologists and psychologists are much more likely than are those from other fields to characterize their positions as ''other.''

Life Satisfaction

Life satisfaction has been found to correlate highly with job satisfaction (Solmon and Ochsner 1978). As table 10–2 shows, over three in five respondents indicate that they are very satisfied with life in general. Nonfaculty academics are most likely to express this feeling, followed by private-sector employees. In most fields, larger proportions of government workers than of faculty members express great satisfaction with life; the exceptions are chemistry, civil engineering, economics, and political science, where the proportions of faculty expressing great satisfaction are higher by no more than 3 percentage points; and electrical en-

Table 10–2
Satisfaction with Life, by Field and Employment Sector
(percent)

	Academic		Nonacademic	
Field	Faculty	Nonfaculty Academic	Government	Private Sector
Biology	60	74	66	65
Chemistry	60	75	59	58
Physics	55	70	56	65
Mathematics	52	75	55	55
Civil engineering	63	—[a]	62	75
Electrical engineering	66	75	57	65
Mechanical engineering	58	—[a]	61	74
Economics	60	83	57	71
Political science	61	70	58	53
Anthropology	51	70	66	64
Psychology	58	71	60	68
Sociology	59	73	67	62

Note: Percentages indicating they were ''very satisfied.''
[a]Fewer than ten cases.

gineering, where 66 percent of the faculty members but only 57 percent of the government workers report high satisfaction. In short, faculty tend to be less satisfied with life than are other groups; and this is particularly true of those faculty with doctorates in mathematics and anthropology.

Statistical Techniques

The cross-tabulations presented here are based on comparisons by field and by employment sector (academe, government, the private sector). Within academe, a breakdown is made between those holding faculty rank and nonfaculty academics, the latter group composed chiefly of administrators. The other basic type of comparison used in this report involves primary work activity: teaching; administration; research; and "other" (for example, counseling, environmental protection, public relations).[4]

In addition to cross-tabulations, stepwise multiple-regression analysis—a statistical technique that allows the researcher to assess the independent contributions of particular variables to a given outcome—is employed to identify the correlates of certain career outcomes and job characteristics. (See appendix B for a more-detailed discussion of the statistical techniques used.)

Notes

1. This last group includes a small number of people employed in elementary and secondary schools.

2. When fields or employment sectors were combined, weights were employed to ensure that aggregate data were not biased toward high-response groups.

3. A small proportion of the sample, 4.6 percent of the government employees and 8.3 percent of the private-sector employees, did not actually have a doctoral degree. The range by field was from 20 percent of the anthropologists to only 1 percent of the chemists responding to the survey. Because the non-Ph.D.'s made up only 7.2 percent of the total sample, and because preliminary analysis indicated that their responses did not differ significantly from the responses of younger and less-experienced Ph.D.'s, we decided to include them in the study.

4. The full range of "other" activities covered is specified in chapter 2.

11

Where Are the Nonacademic Jobs?

What careers outside of academe are available to doctorate-level scientists and engineers? The easiest way to answer that question is to identify the jobs in government and in the private sector that these people now hold. To be meaningful, such identification must be done on a field-by-field basis. Although we may have overlooked some popular and viable career options, the methods used to compile representative rosters of nonacademically employed science and engineering Ph.D.'s make it unlikely that any large groups were omitted.

The Higher Education Research Institute (HERI) questionnaire asked respondents to identify their primary work activity or occupation (from a list of forty alternatives) and the type of employer they worked for (from a list of nineteen alternatives). (See appendix A, items 21 and 22 of the survey instrument.) Theoretically, a respondent might belong in any one of 760 cells, 640 of them representing nonacademic jobs. A preliminary count shows that, in actuality, members of the sample can be found in 306 of the 640 nonacademic cells (jobs).

To ensure that the nonacademic jobs identified here constitute real career opportunities for science and engineering Ph.D.'s, we decided to limit the discussion to those cells that contain at least five people from a single field. Because the discriminations with respect to work activity and employer are so fine, and because the number of nonacademically employed Ph.D.'s in some fields is so small, it can be assumed that if even five Ph.D.'s from a field appear in a given cell, then that cell represents a viable career option for other Ph.D.'s from the same field; that is, their employment is attributable to something other than chance. A related assumption is that those cells with fewer than five people from a given field represent extremely new and untried jobs or random job placements; thus, they should not be accorded much weight when one is considering alternatives to academic employment.

Table 11-1 gives an overview of the nonacademic-employment situation for science and engineering Ph.D.'s, by employer type and primary work activity. The matrix includes four of the five types of government employers (all except "international agency"); nine of the eleven types of private employers (all except "retail, wholesale" and "agriculture, mining"); and twenty-five of the forty primary work activities, for a total of eighty-five cells, from a maximum of twenty-three under "U.S. government, civilian employee" to only one under "transportation, public utilities."

Table 11-1
Numbers of Science and Engineering Ph.D.'s Employed in Nonacademic Jobs, by Employer Type and Primary Work Activity

Primary Work Activity	Government				Private Sector		
	Military Service	U.S. Government, Civilian Employee	State or Local Government	Federally Funded Laboratory	Commerce, Finance, Insurance, Real Estate	Manufacturing, Construction	Other Business, Service Establishment
Administration or management:	8	818	25	18	5	225	12
Research and development	(8)	(674)	(6)	(18)	—	(142)	(6)
Educational institution	—	(5)	—	—	—	—	—
Other	—	(139)	(19)	—	(5)	(83)	(6)
Clinical work	—	176	28	—	—	—	6
Consulting/professional services	—	29	8	—	—	7	—
Counseling	—	14	—	—	—	—	32
Data processing, computer science	—	33	—	—	—	14	—
Development	—	21	—	—	—	8	—
Engineering	5	121	—	7	—	53	11
Environmental protection	—	126	—	—	—	—	—
Farming, forestry	—	9	—	—	—	—	—
Health services	—	32	—	—	—	—	—
Inspection, testing	—	5	—	—	—	—	—
Mathematical, statistical, actuarial	—	60	—	—	—	—	—
Personnel, employee relations	—	—	—	—	5	—	—
Program planning, budgeting	—	28	—	—	—	—	—
Public safety, law enforcement, community service	—	11	—	—	—	—	—
Research:	7	1,444	9	36	—	67	6
Applied	—	(602)	(9)	(11)	—	(41)	(6)
Evaluation	—	(119)	—	—	—	—	—
Laboratory/experimental	(7)	(609)	—	(25)	—	(26)	—

Primary Work Activity	Transportation, Public Utilities	Elementary, Secondary School	Independent Research Organization	Human-Services Organization	Other Nonprofit Organization	Other	Row Total	Percentage of Total
			Private Sector					
Administration or management:	12	5	43	37	6	5	1,219	27.0
Research and development	(12)	(5)	(43)	—	(6)	(5)	(920)	
Educational institution	—	—	—	—	—	—	(10)	
Other	—	—	—	(37)	—	—	(289)	
Clinical work	—	9	—	142	10	91	462	10.2
Consulting/professional services	—	—	12	23	6	57	174	3.8
Counseling	—	5	—	17	—	12	48	1.1
Data processing, computer science	—	—	—	—	—	—	47	1.0
Development	—	—	—	—	—	—	29	0.6
Engineering	—	—	6	—	—	9	212	4.7
Environmental protection	—	—	—	—	—	—	126	2.8
Farming, forestry	—	—	—	—	—	—	9	0.2
Health services	—	—	—	21	—	—	53	1.2
Inspection, testing	—	—	—	—	—	—	5	0.1
Mathematical, statistical, actuarial	—	—	—	—	—	—	60	1.3
Personnel, employee relations	—	—	—	—	—	—	5	0.1
Program planning, budgeting	—	—	—	—	—	—	28	0.6
Sales, marketing, purchasing, merchandising	—	—	—	—	5	9	(114)	
Theoretical/other	—	—	—	—	—	—	—	
Training	—	—	—	—	—	—	11	
Other activities	—	—	—	—	—	8	75	
Multiple activities	—	7	—	—	5	12	219	
Total number employed	20	77	61	15	72	403	3,232	
Total, work activities[a]	3	6	4	7	3	11	23	

Table 11-1 (continued)

Primary Work Activity	Transportation, Public Utilities	Elementary, Secondary School	Independent Research Organization	Human-Services Organization	Other Nonprofit Organization	Other	Row Total	Percentage of Total
			Private Sector					
Public safety, law enforcement, community service	—	—	—	—	—	—	11	0.2
Research:	—	—	66	11	5	—	1,651	36.5
Applied	—	—	(45)	(5)	(5)	—	(715)	
Evaluation	—	—	(9)	(6)	—	—	(143)	
Laboratory/experimental	—	—	(12)	—	—	—	(679)	
Theoretical/other	—	—	—	—	—	—	(114)	
Sales, marketing, purchasing, merchandising	—	—	—	—	—	—	14	0.3
Training	—	—	—	—	—	—	11	0.2
Other activities	—	—	—	—	—	5	88	1.9
Multiple activities	—	—	—	19	—	5	267	5.9
Total number employed	12	19	127	270	27	184	4,519	
Total, work activities[a]	1	3	6	8	4	7	86	

Note: Figures are shown only for those cells (jobs) that employ at least five Ph.D.'s from a single field.

[a]The three types of administration and the four types of research are each counted as a separate primary work activity in this analysis.

One might be led to conclude from this table that the federal civil service is the most-promising place for science and engineering Ph.D.'s to look for nonacademic jobs, in that it offers a wide variety of work activities and employs relatively large numbers of doctorate-level personnel. But such a conclusion is unwarranted. The apparent predominance of the U.S. government as an employer of Ph.D.'s can be explained by the methods used in drawing the sample. As noted earlier, the U.S. Civil Service cooperated in providing the names of all the doctorate holders it employs from the fields under study; and we surveyed all of them in every field except biology, physics, and psychology, where samples were drawn. In contrast, the names of other government employees (for example, in state and local government or in federally funded laboratories) were provided by other sources, which may have been less thorough. Similarly, the methods used to identify those employed in the private sector were necessarily more haphazard; and the resulting sample from this employment sector is much less comprehensive. Nonetheless, the relative showing made by various types of private-sector employers may be significant. Manufacturing and construction would seem to offer the most opportunities, followed by human-services organizations such as social-welfare agencies and hospitals, then "other" employers, independent research organizations, and "other" business and service establishments.

Nonacademic Employment, by Field

The number of cells containing at least five people with doctorates from a given field varies by field, as follows: psychology, 43; electrical engineering, 32; chemistry, 28; biology, 22; physics, 21; economics, 12; mechanical engineering, 9; mathematics, 9; civil engineering, 6; anthropology, 5; political science, 4; and sociology, 4.

Again, it is tempting to view these numbers as a rough index of the effectiveness of various fields in preparing their graduates for a wide variety of jobs. But this temptation again should be avoided, since these numbers really indicate nothing more than our relative success in collecting the names of nonacademically employed Ph.D.'s from the various fields. The American Psychological Association and the Institute of Electrical and Electronics Engineers provided us with complete name-and-address files; therefore, the distribution of nonacademically employed respondents from these two fields is probably representative of the overall distribution of psychologists and electrical engineers in nonacademic jobs. Because the rosters from other fields were much less complete, however, it is difficult to say whether the numbers of nonacademically employed Ph.D.'s from these fields is in fact very small or whether our procedures failed to identify many of these people.

The remainder of this section gives a more-detailed description of the kinds of nonacademic jobs available for Ph.D.'s in each field.

Biology	*N*

Government

Military service, active duty
Research, laboratory/experimental — 7

U.S. government, civilian employee

Administration or management, R&D	142
Administration or management, other than R&D or education	40
Clinical work	14
Consulting/professional services	5
Environmental protection	81
Farming, forestry	9
Health services	22
Mathematical, statistical, actuarial	5
Research, applied	114
Research, evaluation	21
Research, laboratory/experimental	223
Research, theoretical/other	19
Training	5
Other activities	14
Multiple activities	62

Federally funded laboratory
Research, laboratory/experimental — 11

Private sector

Commerce, finance, insurance, real estate
Sales, marketing, purchasing, merchandising — 5

Independent research organization
Research, laboratory/experimental — 6

Human-services organization
Health services — 8

Other

Other activities	5
Multiple activities	5

Of the 823 biological scientists in our sample who were working at nonacademic jobs that employed at least five people from the field, the vast majority (96 percent) work for the U.S. government as civilian employees performing a wide range of work activities. Seven others are on active duty in the military service, and eleven work in federally funded laboratories. The private-sector employers of biological scientists are few: independent research organizations, human-services organizations, and "other" employers.

Close to half of all the nonacademically employed biological scientists in our sample are primarily researchers, whatever the employment setting. Of these researchers, 62 percent do laboratory/experimental research; 28 percent, applied research; 5.2 percent, evaluation research; and 4.7 percent, theoretical/other research.

The next-most-common work activity is administration or management (22 percent), usually of research and development (R&D), although slightly over one-fifth of these administrators head programs other than R&D or education. Environmental protection constitutes the primary work activity of 10 percent; health services, 3.6 percent; "other" activities, 2.3 percent; and multiple activities, 8.1 percent. Small numbers of biological scientists are also employed by the federal government to do clinical work; consulting; farming or forestry; training; and mathematical, statistical, or actuarial work.

Chemistry   *N*

Government

   U.S. government, civilian employee

Administration or management, R&D	159
Administration or management, education	5
Administration or management, other than R&D or education	32
Clinical work	6
Consulting/professional services	6
Development	10
Engineering	5
Environmental protection	33
Program planning, budgeting	7
Public safety, law enforcement, community services	11
Research, applied	101
Research, evaluation	24
Research, laboratory/experimental	262
Research, theoretical/other	15
Other activities	21
Multiple activities	37

Federally funded laboratory   *N*
   Administration or management, R&D   6
   Research, applied   5
   Research, laboratory/experimental   5

Private sector

  Manufacturing, construction
   Administration or management, R&D   44
   Administration or management, other than R&D or education 23
   Research, applied   14
   Research, laboratory/experimental   26
   Sales, marketing, purchasing, merchandising   9
   Other activities   8
   Multiple activities   6

  Independent research organization
   Administration or management, R&D   6
   Research, laboratory/experimental   6

Under the criterion set for considering viable nonacademic job opportunities, a total of 897 chemists in our sample were identified as working for four types of employers at eighteen primary work activities. Over four in five of the nonacademically employed Ph.D.'s in chemistry are civilian employees of the U.S. government, although manufacturing and construction provide jobs to about one in seven; the rest are employed in federally funded laboratories and independent research organizations.

Research is the primary work activity for 51 percent of these chemists. About two in three of the researchers conduct laboratory/experimental research; one in four, applied research; 5.2 percent, evaluation research; and only 3.3 percent, theoretical/other research.

Three in ten of the total group are administrators or managers, most often of research and development (78 percent) or of programs other than R&D or education (20 percent), although five chemists employed by the federal government administer some kind of educational program. Slightly under 5 percent of the total group perform multiple activities; 3.7 percent are concerned with environmental protection; and 3.3 percent checked ''other'' activities. The federal government also provides opportunities for small numbers of chemists to do clinical work; consulting/professional services; development; engineering; inspection and testing; program planning and budgeting; and public safety, law enforcement, and community services. A few chemists in the private sector work in sales and marketing.

Physics	*N*

Government

U.S. government, civilian employee
Administration or management, R&D	152
Administration or management, other than R&D or education	12
Data processing, computer science	7
Development	11
Engineering	18
Environmental protection	7
Research, applied	108
Research, evaluation	16
Research, laboratory/experimental	81
Research, theoretical/other	41
Other activities	12
Multiple activities	24

Federally funded laboratory
Administration or management, R&D	7
Research, applied	6
Research, laboratory/experimental	9

Private sector

Manufacturing, construction
Administration or management, R&D	40
Administration or management, other than R&D or education	19
Engineering	5
Research, applied	12

Transportation, public utilities
Administration or management, R&D	7

Independent research organization
Administration or management, R&D	13

Of the 607 nonacademically employed physicists in our sample who work in jobs that meet the criterion of employing at least five people from the field, 16 percent work in the private sector, mostly in manufacturing and construction. Most of the rest work for the U.S. government as civil-service employees.

As with biologists and chemists, research is the predominant primary work activity, performed by 45 percent of the physicists. But unlike these other natural scientists, physicists focus on applied research (46 percent) rather than on laboratory/experimental research (33 percent); 15 percent conduct theoretical or other research, and about 6 percent do evaluation research.

Two-fifths of the physicists are administrators, the majority in research and development, although about one in eight administer programs other than R&D or education. About 2 percent of the group performed "other" activities; 4 percent performed multiple activities; and 3.8 percent are in engineering.

Mathematics	*N*

Government

U.S. government, civilian employee
Administration or management, R&D	29
Administration or management, other than R&D or education	5
Data processing, computer science	17
Mathematical, statistical, actuarial	50
Research, applied	40
Research, evaluation	10
Research, theoretical/other	11
Multiple activities	10

Private sector

Manufacturing, construction
Data processing, computer science	7

The application of our criterion for discussing nonacademic career opportunities resulted in the identification of 179 mathematicians, only 7 of them employed in the private sector, by manufacturing and construction firms. The rest work for the federal government.

Again, research is the primary work activity, performed by 34 percent; about two in three conduct applied research, and the others are evenly divided between evaluation research and theoretical or other research. Almost three in ten work at mathematical, statistical, or actuarial tasks. Close to one-fifth are administrators, chiefly in research and development; 13 percent are in data processing and computer science, and 6 percent perform multiple activities.

Civil engineering	*N*

Government

U.S. government, civilian employee
Administration or management, R&D	14
Engineering	21
Research, applied	28

	N
Multiple activities	6

Private sector

Manufacturing, construction
Engineering   6

Other business or service establishment
Engineering   5

Eighty civil engineers in our sample were identified as working at nonacademic jobs that employ at least 5 people from the field. The federal government provides work for 69 of them, and the private sector for 11. Engineering is the primary work activity of two in five civil engineers; one-third are involved in applied research; 18 percent administer research and development programs; and the remainder perform multiple activities.

Electrical engineering	N

Government

Military service, active duty
Administration or management, R&D   44
Engineering   5

U.S. government, civilian employee
Administration or management, R&D
Administration or management, other than R&D or education   8
Data processing, computer science   9
Engineering   52
Research, applied   34
Research, laboratory/experimental   10
Research, theoretical/other   11
Multiple activities   12

Federally funded laboratory
Administration or management, R&D   5
Engineering   7

Private sector

Manufacturing, construction
Administration or management, R&D   53
Administration or management, other than R&D or education   35
Data processing, computer science   7

	N
Development	8
Engineering	36
Research, applied	9
Multiple activities	6

Other business or service establishment
Administration or management, R&D	6
Administration or management, other than R&D or education	6
Consulting/professional services	5
Engineering	6
Research, applied	6

Transportation, public utilities
| Administration or management, R&D | 5 |

Independent research organization
Administration or management, R&D	18
Consulting/professional services	5
Engineering	6
Research, applied	11

Other
Administration or management, R&D	5
Consulting/professional services	7
Engineering	9

Four hundred fifty-four electrical engineers in our sample work in nonacademic jobs employing at least five people from the field. The private sector accounts for 55 percent, and government for 45 percent; this difference probably reflects our greater success in identifying electrical engineers in business and industry. Of private-sector employers, manufacturing and construction firms provide jobs for the largest number, followed by independent research organizations. Government employers include the U.S. Civil Service, the military, and federally funded laboratories.

Over two in five electrical engineers are administrators; of this group, three in four direct R&D programs. The second-most-common work activity is engineering, practiced by 27 percent. About one-fifth are researchers, most of them (74 percent) in applied research, although a few conduct laboratory/experimental or theoretical/other research. Other fairly common work activities are consulting (3.7 percent), data processing (3.5 percent), development (1.8 percent), and multiple activities (4 percent).

Mechanical engineering   N

Government

U.S. government, civilian employee
| Administration or management, R&D | 23 |

	N
Engineering	25
Research, applied	23
Research, laboratory/experimental	11
Research, theoretical/other	7
Multiple activities	14

Private sector

Manufacturing, construction

Administration or management, R&D	5
Administration or management, other than R&D or education	6
Engineering	6

Of the mechanical engineers in our sample, 120 hold nonacademic jobs that employ at least five people from the field; most of these (86 percent) working for the federal government. The only private-sector employers identified are manufacturing and construction firms.

Over one-third are researchers, focusing chiefly on applied research, although some do laboratory/experimental or theoretical/other research. Slightly more than one-tenth perform multiple activities. The rest are about evenly divided between engineering and administration (usually of research and development) as primary work activities.

Economics   N

Government

U.S. government, civilian employee

Administration or management, R&D	24
Administration or management, other than R&D or education	6
Environmental protection	5
Mathematical, statistical, actuarial	5
Program planning, budgeting	16
Research, applied	84
Research, evaluation	20
Research, theoretical/other	10
Other activities	13
Multiple activities	14

Private sector

Commerce, finance, insurance, real estate

Administration or management, other than R&D or education	5

Independent research organization

Research, applied	11

Over nine in ten of the economists in our sample holding nonacademic jobs that employ at least five Ph.D.'s from the field work for the federal government as civil-service employees. Only 16 percent of the total group of 213 work in the private sector.

Political science	*N*
U.S. government, civilian employee	
Administration or management, R&D	12
Administration or management, other than R&D or education	13
Program planning, budgeting	5
Other activities	15

The U.S. government is the sole employer of the forty-five political scientists in our sample working at nonacademic jobs that employ more than five Ph.D.'s from the field. Over half are administrators, being about evenly split between R&D and other types of programs. One-third perform ''other'' work activities, and the remainder are in program planning and budgeting.

Anthropology	*N*
Government	
U.S. government, civilian employee	
Administration or management, R&D	10
Multiple activities	5
Private sector	
Independent research organization	
Research, applied	5
Other nonprofit organization	
Administration or management, R&D	6
Research, applied	5

By our criterion for inclusion, only thirty-one nonacademically employed Ph.D.'s in anthropology were identified, about half of them working for the federal government and half in the private sector. The administration of research-and-development programs is a primary work activity for sixteen of the thirty-one, ten others conduct applied research, and the remainder perform multiple activities.

Psychology	*N*

Government

U.S. government, civilian employee

Administration or management, R&D	51
Administration or management, other than R&D or education	23
Clinical work	156
Consulting/professional services	18
Counseling	14
Health services	10
Research, applied	58
Research, evaluation	22
Research, laboratory/experimental	22
Training	6
Multiple activities	35

State, local, other government

Administration or management, R&D	6
Administration or management, other than R&D or education	19
Clinical work	28
Consulting/professional services	8
Research, evaluation	9
Multiple activities	7

Private sector

Commerce, finance, insurance, real estate

Personnel, employee relations	5

Manufacturing, construction

Consulting, professional services	7
Research, applied	6

Other business and service establishments

Clinical work	6
Consulting/professional services	27
Multiple activities	5

Elementary, secondary school

Administration or management, education	5
Clinical work	9
Counseling	5

Independent research organization

Administration or management, R&D	6

	N
Consulting/professional services	7
Research, applied	12
Research, evaluation	9
Human-services organization	
Administration or management, other than R&D or education	37
Clinical work	142
Consulting/professional services	23
Counseling	17
Health services	13
Research, applied	5
Research, evaluation	6
Multiple activities	19
Other nonprofit organization	
Clinical work	10
Consulting/professional services	6
Other	
Clinical work	91
Consulting/professional services	50
Counseling	12

Having access to the American Psychological Association's complete name-and-address file allowed us to identify 1,032 nonacademically employed psychologists working at jobs that employ more than 5 from the field. Of this group, 48 percent are in government and 52 percent in the private sector. Although the great majority of the former work for the federal government, about 16 percent are employed by state or local governments, making psychologists the only group in our sample represented in those employment settings. It seems probable that many of these people—especially the clinicians and the administrators of programs other than R&D or education—work in state hospitals or state departments of mental health.

The range of private-sector employers is wide. Human-services organizations provide jobs for 262 psychologists; "other" employers, 153; other business and service organizations, 38; independent research organizations, 34; other nonprofit organizations, 16; manufacturing and construction, 13; and commerce and finance, 5. Finally, 19 psychologists work in elementary or secondary schools.

The range of primary work activities is similarly wide. Over two in five of the psychologists in our sample do clinical work. About one-seventh are researchers, with the majority (54 percent) in applied research, although 31 percent do evaluation research and 15 percent do laboratory/experimental research. About 14 percent of the total group are administrators or managers, usually of programs other than research and development or education; 43 percent, however, administer R&D programs; and five people are administrators in elementary or secondary schools. Consulting/professional services constitute a primary work activity for 13 percent. About 5 percent are counselors; 3 percent perform multiple work activities; and the remainder are in health services, training, or personnel/ employee relations. In short, the preparation of Ph.D.'s in psychology seems to qualify them for a wide variety of tasks, some of them (counseling, personnel/ employee relations) not performed by doctorate holders from the other fields under study.

Sociology	*N*
Government	
U.S. government, civilian employee	
Administration or management, R&D	14
Research, applied	12
Research, evaluation	6
Private sector	
Independent research organization	
Research, applied	6

The nonacademic jobs held by the thirty-eight sociologists in our sample in cells with more than five people from the field are limited to two employer types and to administration and research as primary work activities. Of the twenty-four who are researchers, 75 percent are involved in applied research and the rest in evaluation research.

Summary

In the government sector, the U.S. Civil Service offers job opportunities to Ph.D.'s from every field under study. Overall, about 95 percent of the government-employed Ph.D.'s in our sample were identified as civilian employees of the federal government. Federally funded laboratories employ electrical engineers, biologists, chemists, and physicists, but no social scientists. Relatively few people in the sample—seven biologists and thirteen electrical engineers—are on active duty in military service. State and local governments employ psychologists at a variety of jobs, but no Ph.D.'s from other fields. Again, the reader is reminded that these differences probably reflect our greater success in identifying civil-service employees, as well as the overrepresentation of certain fields. Thus, these figures may not parallel the actual distribution of doctorate-level scientists and engineers in government jobs.

In the private sector, manufacturing and construction firms provide jobs to all three types of engineers, to natural scientists from all fields except biology, and to psychologists. Independent research organizations are especially likely to employ electrical engineers, natural scientists (with the exception of mathematicians), and social scientists (with the exception of political scientists). The range of science and engineering Ph.D.'s working for other private-sector employees is more limited and may be summarized as follows:

Commerce, finance, insurance, real estate: Biologists, economists, psychologists.

Other business or service establishments: Electrical engineers, psychologists.

Transportation, public utilities: Physicists, electrical engineers.

Elementary and secondary schools: Psychologists.

Other nonprofit organizations: Anthropologists, psychologists.

Other employers: Biologists, electrical engineers, psychologists.

The majority of nonacademically employed science and engineering Ph.D.'s in our sample are either researchers (37 percent) or administrators/managers (27 percent), although there is some variation by broad disciplinary area. Thus, close to half of all those with doctorates in the natural sciences are researchers, making this the predominant primary work activity for that group; of these, 53 percent conduct laboratory/experimental research, and 34 percent conduct applied research. One-fourth of the engineers are in research, making it the second-most-common work activity for this group, after administration or management (a primary work activity for one in three engineers). Although the largest proportion conduct applied research, engineers are more likely than others to do theoretical/other research. Research is also second ranked among social scientists, being the primary work activity for 23 percent. Again, most of the social scientists do applied research; but they are more likely than others to do evaluation research as well. In short, it is clear that for scientists and engineers, accepting a job outside academe does not necessarily mean abandoning one's hopes of conducting research. (For a more-detailed discussion of research as a primary work activity, and of the types of research conducted, see chapter 3.) Clinical work is the top-ranked primary work activity among social scientists, but that is accounted for entirely by the psychologists in the sample.

Of those in the sample who are administrators or managers, about three in four conduct research-and-development programs, ranging from 82 percent of the natural scientists in administration to only 54 percent of the social scientists. Social scientists are much more likely than are engineers or natural scientists to administer programs other than R&D or education, probably counseling or clinical programs of some sort. Psychologists are the only group to work as administrators in elementary or secondary schools, although five chemists were identified as administrators of education programs within the federal government.

About 6 percent in each broad disciplinary area perform multiple activities. Three in ten of the engineers—but only 1.1 percent of the natural scientists and none of the social scientists—report engineering as their primary work activity. One-tenth of the social scientists—but only 2.8 percent of the engineers and 0.4 percent of the natural scientists—work primarily as consultants. Other relatively common work activities are as follows:

Natural scientists: Environmental protection; mathematical, statistical, and actuarial work; health services; data processing; "other" activities.

Engineers: Data processing.

Social scientists: Counseling; health services; development; program planning and budgeting; "other" activities.

In summary, natural scientists (except mathematicians) and psychologists seem to have the broadest range of primary activities available to them in nonacademic jobs, whereas engineers and other social scientists have a relatively narrow range.

12 What Are the Nonacademic Jobs Like?

In chapter 11, we identified nonacademic jobs that are held by science and engineering Ph.D.'s and that employ enough people from a given field to make them viable career options for others from the same field. This chapter describes some of the basic characteristics of these jobs: salary, research and publication, nontraditionality, relation of job to graduate training, and underemployment. Whereas chapter 11 dealt exclusively with nonacademic jobs, this chapter also discusses jobs in academe so that comparisons can be made.

Salary

Salary is an important attribute of any job as well as a major career outcome. Academic employment has never been regarded as especially lucrative, and a comparison of mean salaries (table 12–1, second row) confirms this impression. In every field, faculty rank at the bottom in salary, with the lowest salaries going to anthropologists ($16,400) and mathematicians ($17,400) and the highest to electrical engineers ($24,300). It should also be noted, however, that the faculty members in our sample tend to be younger and to have received the doctorate more recently than the academic administrators and the nonacademically employed scientists and engineers; these differences account partially but not entirely for their lower salaries.[1]

Although faculty rank at the bottom in every field, the group earning the highest salaries varies by field. Those who received their doctorates in biology or political science receive the highest salaries when they are employed as nonfaculty academics; mathematicians, anthropologists, psychologists, and sociologists are best paid when they work for the government; and chemists, physicists, all types of engineers, and economists make the most money when they work in the private sector. By broad disciplinary group, engineers in the private sector are the most highly paid. Generally speaking, employment in the private sector and employment in academic administration are about equally lucrative, with government employment only slightly less so.

Predicting Current Salary

It seems logical that the salary one makes would be determined in part by age and experience, as well as by employer type and primary work activity. But exactly what importance do these factors have, and what other factors influence salary level? To answer these questions, we conducted a series of multiple-

Table 12–1
Basic Job Characteristics, by Field and Employment Sector

	Biology				Chemistry			
	Faculty	Nonfaculty Academic	Government	Private	Faculty	Nonfaculty Academic	Government	Private
Number of cases	270	35	867	109	148	51	793	248
Mean salary (in thousands of dollars)	18.6	33.8	30.1	26.5	20.3	30.6	31.3	35.6
Mean year of doctorate	70	59	63	63	67	57	61	61
Percentage whose primary work activity is research	13	9	47	19	12	6	54	29
Percentage currently engaged in research	92	62	76	52	84	59	76	41
Percentage highly productive	26	6	28	20	31	9	31	12
Percentage in nontraditional job	13	27	27	51	8	29	27	42
Percentage same field doctorate/job	99	100	95	89	93	90	88	88
Percentage in job closely related to graduate training	83	20	68	35	83	28	49	32
Reasons not in closely related job:								
Percentage all voluntary	52	73	54	49	56	78	44	67
Percentage all involuntary	18	0	16	25	16	0	19	5
Percentage mixed	30	27	30	26	28	22	37	28
Percentage *not* underemployed	77	74	71	57	80	72	66	71

	Physics				Mathematics			
	Faculty	Nonfaculty Academic	Government	Private	Faculty	Nonfaculty Academic	Government	Private
Number of cases	200	28	559	178	238	24	211	78
Mean salary (in thousands of dollars)	19.1	35.8	33.1	40.2	17.4	29.2	31.0	28.3
Mean year of doctorate	69	58	64	58	70	64	65	66
Percentage whose primary work activity is research	27	7	50	20	11	0	36	10
Percentage currently engaged in research	87	52	68	44	84	42	70	58
Percentage highly productive	30	14	22	12	26	4	22	10
Percentage in nontraditional job	6	44	29	47	5	26	42	61
Percentage same field doctorate/job	91	67	79	57	98	92	88	71
Percentage in job closely related to graduate training	80	21	44	26	85	33	44	27
Reasons not in closely related job:								
Percentage all voluntary	41	82	45	61	34	75	41	48
Percentage all involuntary	18	4	17	7	29	0	20	14
Percentage mixed	41	14	39	32	37	25	39	38
Percentage not underemployed	82	85	69	73	73	78	55	56

Table 12–1 continued

	Civil Engineering				Electrical Engineering			
	Faculty	*Nonfaculty Academic*	*Government*	*Private*	*Faculty*	*Nonfaculty Academic*	*Government*	*Private*
Number of cases	80	8	96	32	54	16	240	313
Mean salary (in thousands of dollars)	22.5	28.5	30.1	33.7	24.3	39.3	33.2	39.4
Mean year of doctorate	70	65	68	66	68	59	66	63
Percentage whose primary work activity is research	5	0	43	9	9	0	28	14
Percentage currently engaged in research	90	75	72	50	82	31	59	38
Percentage highly productive	23	25	25	7	22	0	18	12
Percentage in nontraditional job	9	13	27	34	7	33	27	32
Percentage same field doctorate/job	99	100	91	86	94	82	90	94
Percentage in job closely related to graduate training	91	71	77	71	80	40	49	49
Reasons not in closely related job:								
Percentage all voluntary	67	100	65	89	73	78	65	72
Percentage all involuntary	0	0	22	0	9	11	11	7
Percentage mixed	33	0	13	11	18	11	24	21
Percentage *not* underemployed	75	75	70	66	76	67	55	68

	Mechanical Engineering				Economics			
	Faculty	Nonfaculty Academic	Government	Private	Faculty	Nonfaculty Academic	Government	Private
Number of cases	97	8	131	43	201	24	229	59
Mean salary (in thousands of dollars)	22.1	37.9	31.7	38.8	22.9	35.1	33.8	36.1
Mean year of doctorate	70	61	68	65	69	62	67	65
Percentage whose primary work activity is research	5	0	40	16	12	4	53	41
Percentage currently engaged in research	91	71	71	43	94	54	69	66
Percentage highly productive	34	0	11	18	28	24	8	22
Percentage in nontraditional job	8	0	22	43	4	21	20	40
Percentage same field doctorate/job	88	100	87	88	99	96	96	96
Percentage in job closely related to graduate training	80	38	59	55	96	62	78	66
Reasons not in closely related job:								
Percentage all voluntary	71	100	50	74	75	89	64	70
Percentage all involuntary	12	0	16	5	12	11	16	5
Percentage mixed	18	0	34	21	13	0	20	25
Percentage *not* underemployed	76	75	60	69	84	88	67	78

Table 12–1 continued

	Political Science				Anthropology			
	Faculty	Nonfaculty Academic	Government	Private	Faculty	Nonfaculty Academic	Government	Private
Number of cases	151	24	87	20	318	23	59	61
Mean salary (in thousands of dollars)	18.9	33.7	32.2	27.9	16.4	21.9	24.6	20.7
Mean year of doctorate	70	61	65	69	72	66	69	68
Percentage whose primary work activity is research	4	4	14	35	7	22	14	36
Percentage currently engaged in research	95	79	50	84	98	81	72	87
Percentage highly productive	30	21	13	44	29	26	14	33
Percentage in nontraditional job	8	25	55	40	12	26	62	72
Percentage same field doctorate/job	99	100	90	100	97	100	91	90
Percentage in job closely related to graduate training	88	42	41	30	88	52	56	48
Reasons not in closely related job:								
Percentage all voluntary	50	85	54	57	27	30	38	39
Percentage all involuntary	17	0	17	7	36	30	4	19
Percentage mixed	33	15	29	36	36	40	58	42
Percentage not underemployed	81	83	64	75	67	65	64	54

	Psychology				Sociology			
	Faculty	*Nonfaculty Academic*	*Government*	*Private*	*Faculty*	*Nonfaculty Academic*	*Government*	*Private*
Number of cases	407	96	570	686	156	11	66	42
Mean salary (in thousands of dollars)	22.4	25.6	29.4	28.9	19.4	28.3	29.8	22.1
Mean year of doctorate	65	62	64	64	70	63	66	68
Percentage whose primary work activity is research	9	16	23	9	12	9	41	33
Percentage currently engaged in research	87	69	59	52	94	89	87	76
Percentage highly productive	27	10	12	8	32	10	16	26
Percentage in nontraditional job	19	34	25	25	8	27	46	69
Percentage same field doctorate/job	97	96	98	99	98	100	93	92
Percentage in job closely related to graduate training	76	56	69	68	91	27	59	34
Reasons not in closely related job:								
Percentage all voluntary	55	73	62	70	58	88	58	58
Percentage all involuntary	9	12	9	10	33	0	15	4
Percentage mixed	35	15	29	20	8	12	27	38
Percentage *not* underemployed	73	74	66	70	76	64	58	67

regression analyses, with current salary as the dependent variable. The independent variables were of several kinds: demographic items (age, sex, marital status); educational background, including field of the doctorate; characteristics of the current job; employment history; and mobility items. The analyses were performed not only for the entire group of respondents but also separately for each field. The latter analyses proved to produce more-clear-cut and more-succinct explanations of salary differences. In all but three fields (electrical engineering, psychology, and anthropology), more of the variance was explained by the analyses for the individual fields than by the analysis for the total sample. In other words, different variables predict salary in different fields. Here we will discuss the findings for the total sample, referring where appropriate to findings for specific fields.

In the analysis for the total sample, one set of dichotomous variables was included to determine whether field of the doctorate is related to current salary. As it turned out, the relation is slight after other factors are taken into account. Economists tend to make the highest salaries, followed by electrical engineers and mechanical engineers. The lowest paid are biologists, anthropologists, and chemists. These differences probably reflect the market situation. For instance, the field of biology has been a big producer of Ph.D.'s in recent years, leading to an apparent oversupply; conversely, economists can be utilized in a variety of employment settings, which drives up the demand.

More important in explaining salary differences are employment sector and primary work activity. Administrators in the private sector earn by far the highest salaries, followed by government administrators. Also relatively well paid are teachers in government (of whom there are only thirty-three in our sample); private-sector employees engaged in "other" activities (that is, *not* in teaching, research, or administration); academic administrators; and researchers in the private sector. At much the greatest disadvantage with respect to salary are academics whose primary work activity is teaching. Being a researcher in academe or in government or an academic performing "other" activities is also associated with making a low salary. These findings confirm what table 12–1 suggests: A nonacademic job carries considerable pecuniary benefit, as does being an administrator.

Other Predictors of Salary

Certain other characteristics of the current job—besides employment sector and primary work activity—are associated with salary, the strongest predictor being full-time (as opposed to part-time) employment. In addition, those people whose current job is closely related to their graduate training are likely to earn higher salaries.[2] It seems, then, that the knowledge and skills acquired in graduate school may quite literally pay off later. Moreover, the implication is that science and engineering Ph.D.'s concerned with finding "related" jobs need not confine themselves to (low-paying) academic teaching and research jobs. Jobs that are both high paying and related to graduate training are available in both government and the private sector. Finally, the more productive the worker (as measured by career publication index), the higher his or her salary tends to be.[3] The relationship between the publication index and salary is strongest for economists and sociologists, but it holds for all fields except electrical engineering. Perhaps the criteria for electrical engineers are different than those for other fields, with publications simply not counting as much.

As common sense suggests, several variables indicative of age and experience are related to salary. Years in the labor force (working full time since receiving the doctorate) is an important factor in all fields except civil engineering (where age per se is more important); this factor is especially important for chemists, political scientists, biologists, and sociologists. A somewhat less important but still significant predictor for all fields except anthropology and sociology is years in the current job. In short, both general experience in the labor force and firm-specific on-the-job training contribute to earning a high salary, but general experience is the more important. Age itself is not closely connected with salary (after the two experience factors are taken into account), except among civil and mechanical engineers. Finally, mathematicians and electrical engineers who worked full time at some period between the baccalaureate and the doctorate make higher salaries in their current jobs; perhaps such employment gives them practical experience that proves useful later.

Two variables related to educational background predict current salary in some fields: institutional selectivity and respondents' self-ratings. Those electrical engineers who did their graduate work at highly selective institutions are likely to make better salaries than those who attended less-selective institutions; the same is true, to a lesser extent, of physicists, chemists, and mathematicians. Similarly, anthropologists, sociologists, political scientists, electrical engineers, and physicists who rate themselves high compared with other students in their graduate program tend to be well paid in their current jobs. These findings are consistent with previous studies showing that individual ability and institutional quality are significant determinants of income (Solmon 1975).

The regressions for individual fields reveal that the subfield in which a person is trained may affect current salary. Specialties leading to large paychecks (within a given discipline) included biochemistry (biology), statistics (mathematics), administration and finance (economics), and applied psychology. Underpaid relative to others in their discipline are those Ph.D.'s who specialized in zoology (biology), organic and analytic chemistry, computer and power engineering (electrical engineering), power (mechanical engineering), individual psychology, and social change (sociology).

In the analysis for the total sample, sex was found to be related to current salary; women receive lower salaries than men. One common explanation for sex differentials in salary is that, because women leave their jobs to raise families, they spend less time overall in the labor force than men do. Another explanation is that, in order to defer to her husband's preferences and her children's needs, a woman must often accept a lower-paying job rather than a higher-paying one that would entail a residential move. As it happens, only one "mobility" variable—"My mobility is limited because of spouse's job"—is significant in the analysis: An affirmative answer is associated with a lower salary. However, sex remains a significant predictor of salary even after controlling for this variable and for years of full-time employment. In other words, even when the woman's shorter work history and more-limited mobility are taken into account, she is still paid less than the man. Thus, both "explanations" would seem to be inadequate; other factors, perhaps including sex discrimination, operate to keep women's salaries low.

Looking at the analysis for the individual fields, one gets a slightly different picture. The only fields in which women receive significantly lower salaries than men are physics, mathematics, economics, and psychology. In all four of these fields, salaries are generally high. Why do women in these fields (but not in the others under study) earn substantially less than their male counterparts? Probably no single explanation can be given because of the different conditions in each field.

About one in four doctorate-level psychologists is a woman, and typically she makes $2,607 less than the male psychologist. Since the net sex differential in salary for all Ph.D.'s is $1,555 in the man's favor, the female psychologist is obviously at a strong disadvantage, perhaps partly because women are concentrated in lower-paying subspecialties such as counseling and school psychology (a concentration that in itself may reflect not so much the preferences of women as the sex bias of the advisors who encourage them to go into these subfields). Or it may be that—in contrast to employers in other fields who are concerned about complying with affirmative-action requirements—the employers of psychologists feel no great need to offer high salaries in order to attract women. Becker (1971) suggests a third possible reason: "It has been argued that an increase in the numerical importance of a minority group increases the prejudice against them, since the majority begin to fear their growing power" (p. 16). Thus, the very prevalence of women in psychology may arouse the anxiety of the majority, with the result that women's salaries are kept low.

This line of reasoning does not seem to hold, however, for other fields where the proportion of women is high but the salary differential is not significant (for example, sociology). Nor does it account for the markedly lower salaries paid to the relatively few women in physics, mathematics, and economics. Perhaps the academic women in these fields take jobs at colleges where salaries are low. Or perhaps their numbers are so small that pressures for affirmative action have yet to be felt. But why, then, is the salary difference by sex not evident in engineering, where women are drastically underrepresented? Obviously, additional research is needed to clarify these sex differences in salary by field.

Research and Publication

Graduate education in virtually all fields emphasizes training in research, intended to culminate in publications that presumably add to the body of knowledge in the field. To what extent do science and engineering Ph.D.'s continue to exercise their research skills and to produce scholarly work once they embark on their careers? Does research output remain an objective even when it is not required by the job and does not improve salary? More specifically, do jobs in the nonacademic sector offer opportunities to do research and to publish, and how does the productivity of those employed in government and in private organizations compare with that of their counterparts in academe?

To get some sense of the answers to these questions, we looked at several kinds of data: the proportions of the sample whose primary work activity is research; the proportions who give an affirmative response to the item "Are you currently engaged in any scholarly or research work that you expect to lead to publication?"; and the proportions who say that they accomplish a "great deal" of research or publication in their current jobs (a subjective measure of productivity). The fourth, fifth, and sixth rows of table 12–1 show the results. In addition, a regression analysis was performed to identify the correlates of productivity, as reflected in high publication rates over the course of the career.

Comparing the figures in the fourth and the fifth rows of table 12–1, we find that far more of the sample report that they are currently engaged in research than are employed specifically as researchers. Thus, these highly trained people continue to keep their hand in, so to speak, even when their current jobs offer no direct opportunity for research. It is not clear whether their current research is an offshoot of their primary work activity (teaching, administration, clinical work, consulting, or whatever), or whether it is something they do in their spare time away from the job; this probably varies with the individual.

Research as a Primary Work Activity

Ph.D.'s employed in nonacademic jobs are much more likely to be working primarily as researchers than are those employed in academe. This is logical since teaching is the primary work activity for most faculty members, and administration for most nonfaculty academics. Only among physics faculty and anthropology nonfaculty academics are the proportions of researchers substantial (27 percent and 22 percent, respectively).

Generally, the government employs more science and engineering Ph.D.'s as researchers than does private industry. For instance, about half of all government jobs held by biologists, chemists, physicists, and economists are in research. For political scientists and anthropologists, however, research jobs are more common in the private sector than in government.

There are some variations by field, across sectors, in the proportions of Ph.D.'s whose primary work activity is research. Chemists, physicists, biologists, and economists are more likely than others to work as researchers; psychologists, electrical engineers, and mathematicians are less likely to do so.

Types of Research Conducted

Although somewhat peripheral to our main concern—that of identifying and describing nonacademic-job opportunities for science and engineering Ph.D.'s— the question of what types of research are conducted is a vital policy issue. Unless a proper balance is maintained, the nation may find itself suffering from serious inadequacies in some research areas, however great the overall support for research.

Those in the sample whose primary work activity is research are distributed as follows:

	N	Percentage
Applied	874	40.2
Evaluation	21	9.9
Laboratory/experimental	835	38.4
Theoretical/other	252	11.6

Obviously, the majority do either applied or laboratory/experimental research; relatively few are engaged in the theoretical/other or the evaluation areas. Different fields are associated with different types of research. Thus, biologists and chemists are most likely to work in the laboratory/experimental area; physicists are about evenly divided between applied and laboratory/experimental research; and mathematicians are most likely to do applied research, although they are also more likely than any other group to do theoretical/other research. Engineers of all types are concentrated in applied research, although about one in four mechanical engineers does laboratory/experimental work. Social scientists, too, are likely to be in the applied field, although relatively large proportions of sociologists, political scientists, and anthropologists engage in theoretical/ other research; and a relatively large proportion of psychologists do laboratory/ experimental research. Evaluation research is almost entirely the territory of the social scientists.

As table 12–2 indicates, most theoretical/other research is done in colleges and universities. The private sector favors applied research, and the government sector emphasizes both applied and laboratory/experimental research. As more young Ph.D.'s take jobs outside of academe, then, the amount of applied research is likely to increase, and the amount of basic research (that is, research that, at least in the short run, is commercially nonviable) to decline. Exact estimation is difficult, since some laboratory/experimental research belongs to the "basic" rather than the "applied" category. Nonetheless, the danger is clear. The amount of "pure" research done in this country could easily drop below acceptable levels if larger proportions of Ph.D.'s take nonacademic jobs, and such a situation would be against the national interest. Moreover, if it is true that researchers in some fields do their best work when they are young, then the channeling of new Ph.D.'s out of academe and into government and the private sector carries certain dangers of which policymakers should be aware.

Current Research Effort

As was mentioned, the proportions of Ph.D.'s reporting that they are currently engaged in research far exceed the proportions reporting that research is their primary work activity. Overall, about seven in ten science and engineering Ph.D.'s have kept active in research, from a low of 31 percent of electrical engineers in nonfaculty academic positions to a high of 98 percent of anthropology faculty. Indeed, in all fields it is the faculty group that is most likely to be doing research for eventual publication—understandably, in view of the publish-or-perish policies of most colleges and universities. Nonetheless, research activity is also high among the nonacademically employed, especially those who work for the government. Generally, private-sector employees are the least likely of the four groups to be engaged in research. The exceptions are political scientists and anthropologists working in the private sector, large proportions of whom (84 percent and 87 percent, respectively) report current research efforts. Finally, the research activity of nonfaculty academics varies widely by field. Social scientists (except for economists), biologists, and civil and mechanical engineers are very likely to engage in research even when they hold nonfaculty academic positions.

Current involvement in research varies considerably by field as well as by employment sector. Sociologists, anthropologists, and political scientists are especially likely to be engaged in research, whereas electrical engineers are markedly less likely than others to be so engaged. These differences no doubt reflect differences in the demands of the fields themselves.

Perceived Productivity

The HERI questionnaire contained one item asking respondents to indicate how much research/publication per year they accomplish in their current position; the

Table 12–2
Types of Research Conducted, by Employment Sector and Field
(percent)

	Biology	Chemistry	Physics	Mathematics	Civil Engineering
Academe:					
Applied	17	5	5	0	75
Evaluation	3	5	0	4	0
Laboratory/experimental	77	65	63	4	0
Theoretical/other	3	25	32	92	25
Government:					
Applied	29	26	43	60	78
Evaluation	6	6	7	14	8
Laboratory/experimental	60	64	33	6	5
Theoretical/other	5	4	17	21	10
Private:					
Applied	33	27	61	67	50
Evaluation	14	8	3	0	0
Laboratory/experimental	48	65	32	11	50
Theoretical/other	5	0	3	22	0

Note: Percentages of those indicating that their primary work activity is research.

response categories were "a great deal," "some," "little," and "none.' The sixth row of table 12–1 indicates the proportions who say that they accomplish a great deal of research or publication (or both) in their current jobs. Although this measure of productivity is admittedly somewhat vague and subject to individual interpretation (exactly how does one distinguish, for example, between "a great deal" and "some"?), it nonetheless gives a sense of the differences among employment sectors and fields.

Roughly one-fifth of all science and engineering Ph.D.'s say that they do a great deal of research/publication on the current job, ranging from only 4 percent of mathematicians in nonfaculty academic positions to 44 percent of political scientists working in the private sector. As one would expect, faculty members are most likely, and nonfaculty academics least likely, to see themselves as highly productive. Among the nonacademically employed, there is considerable variation by field. Of those working in government, natural scientists and civil engineers tend to say that they produce a great deal, whereas social scientists and electrical and mechanical engineers tend to rate themselves low on productivity. Of those working in the private sector, social scientists (with the exception of psychologists) and biologists are most likely to see themselves as highly productive. In short, some jobs in government and the private sector do offer opportunities for research and publication, but apparently not to all fields equally.

Although it is not shown in the table, a surprising number of Ph.D.'s say they do no research or publication, and this response is most frequent among

Electrical Engineering	Mechanical Engineering	Economics	Political Science	Anthropology	Psychology	Sociology	Total
40	20	50	43	41	25	13	20
0	0	4	0	7	20	13	7
40	40	0	0	26	41	0	39
20	40	46	57	26	14	75	34
60	54	74	27	43	50	50	40
6	8	17	46	29	25	31	10
16	23	0	0	0	22	0	41
18	15	9	27	29	2	19	9
86	50	79	71	68	62	64	57
9	17	13	14	14	33	7	14
3	17	0	0	0	5	7	24
3	17	8	14	18	0	21	5

those employed in the private sector, followed by those in government jobs. For instance, about half the chemists, civil engineers, and mechanical engineers working in the private sector check "none." Apparently jobs in the private sector either provide ample opportunity for the science and engineering Ph.D. to be productive, or provide no opportunity at all. Except for natural scientists, relatively few of the nonfaculty academics say they accomplish no research/publication.

Predicting Career Publication Rates

Productivity over the course of an individual's career was also assessed by means of a publication index developed by assigning different weights to different kinds of publications, as follows.

Scholarly book, single authorship	10
Scholarly book, joint authorship	6
Scholarly book, editor	5
Other book	6
Chapter or article in scholarly journal	3
Article in nonscholarly journal	2
Book review, editorial, abstract, other short work	1

Published report	3
Unpublished report or article of	
monograph length	1
Patentable invention	4

A publication index—based on total (weighted) publications over the course of the career—was developed for each respondent, and this publication index then became the dependent variable in a multiple-regression analysis.

Current involvement in research expected to lead to publication is the best single predictor of a high career-publication index, followed by year of full-time employment since receipt of the doctorate and years since receiving the doctorate; age per se is relatively unimportant once the "experience" variables are taken into account. Although it is not surprising that those who have been out of graduate school and in the labor force longer should have published more, it is worth noting that research and scholarly effort are apparently lifetime involvements; that is, doctorate holders who have been highly productive in the past continue to be active in research at the present time.

Administrators in all three employment sectors (academe, government, private) tend to have published more than others, even when their greater age and experience are taken into account. This finding, which contradicts the popular notion that administrators are a breed apart from scholars, suggests that a substantial list of publications is an important qualification for becoming an administrator in the first place. Clearly, those who have demonstrated this type of productivity are viewed as having skills that are applicable in other work settings.

Psychologists, mathematicians, and economists tend to have lower publication indexes than do others, although their apparent lack of productivity may reflect differences in the types of publications connected with various fields. Producing a journal article in mathematics (for instance) may require as much time and effort as producing an entire book in some other field.

Men are likely to have higher publication indexes than women; and the more-mobile Ph.D.'s (as indicated by willingness to look nationwide for a job and by distance of the current job from home town) are likely to have higher publication rates than the less mobile. In addition, those who rate themselves high compared with other students in the same graduate program, who have held a number of jobs since the doctorate, who did their graduate work at selective institutions, and who have full-time jobs are likely to have published substantially over the course of their careers.

Nontraditionality

The concept of nontraditionality is difficult to pin down. According to the National Science Foundation (1975, p. 4), the federal agency charged with monitoring the nation's supply of science and engineering manpower, a "nontraditional" job is one that is outside academe and that does not involve research and development. By implication, a traditional job is any job in a college or university or a research job in any employment setting. This definition seems inadequate, however. Jobs that are neither academic nor research oriented are traditional for some fields, notably engineering and psychology.

Traditionality seems to have two dimensions: frequency and history. A job that employs relatively large numbers of doctorate-level personnel will probably not be seen as nontraditional, even if it represents a relatively new occupation (for example, data processing or environmental protection). Similarly, a job that has consistently employed doctorate-level personnel over time will probably not be seen as nontraditional, even though the actual numbers who hold such jobs are small (for example, museum curatorships).

Very roughly, about one in four respondents considers his or her job non-traditional, from a low of 5 percent of mathematicians who are faculty members to 72 percent of anthropologists employed in the private sector. As one would expect, faculty members are least likely to view their jobs as nontraditional. Generally, those employed in the private sector, followed by those employed in government, are most likely to perceive their jobs as nontraditional, although there is some variation by field. Thus, biologists, chemists, and economists are more likely to see their jobs as nontraditional if they work in the private sector than if they are nonfaculty academics and government workers; to electrical engineers and psychologists, however, jobs in either government or the private sector are less likely to be seen as nontraditional than are nonfaculty academic positions. In virtually every field, however, a larger proportion of those working in the private sector than of those working in government see their jobs as nontraditional. The only exceptions are psychology, where the proportions are equal, and political science, where 55 percent of the government workers, but only 40 percent of the private-sector employees, consider their jobs nontraditional.

Relevance of Primary Work Activity

The perception that one holds a nontraditional job probably depends less on whom one works for than on what one does—the primary work activity involved in the job. Table 12–3 indicates the proportions saying that their jobs are non-traditional, by primary work activity: teaching, research, administration, and "other."

Teaching, an activity confined almost entirely to faculty members, is most likely to be perceived as traditional by science and engineering Ph.D.'s. Even so, as many as 15 percent of the psychologists and 13 percent of the biologists see their teaching jobs as nontraditional for people in their fields.

Research is perceived as a traditional activity by most respondents, especially if it is done in an academic setting. Researchers in government are more likely than those in the private sector to view their jobs as traditional, except in the fields of chemistry (where 14 percent of those in government, as opposed to 13

Table 12–3
Proportion Perceiving Job as Nontraditional, by Field, Primary Work Activity, and Employment Sector
(percent)

	Teaching					Research				
	Faculty	*Nonfaculty Academic*	*Government*	*Private*	*Total*	*Faculty*	*Nonfaculty Academic*	*Government*	*Private*	*Total*
Biology	13	—	50[a]	100[a]	14	11	—	11	22	12
Chemistry	8	100[a]	—	—	9	0	—	14	13	6
Physics	3	0[a]	—	—	3	4	—	21	30	19
Mathematics	4	—	—	—	4	12	—	36	50[a]	31
Civil engineering	2	—	—	—	2	25[a]	—	11	0[a]	12
Electrical engineering	0	—	—	0[a]	0	40[a]	—	21	22	23
Mechanical engineering	7	—	—	—	7	20[a]	—	17	20[a]	18
Economics	5	—	—	—	5	0	—	12	33	14
Political science	7	—	100[a]	—	8	17[a]	—	40	43[a]	35
Anthropology	7	—	50[a]	—	8	35	50[a]	50[a]	85	53
Psychology	15	—	—	—	15	25	100[a]	24	36	27
Sociology	5	—	—	100[a]	6	15	—	44	40	35

[a]Based on fewer than 10 cases.

	Administration					Other					Total
	Faculty	Nonfaculty Academic	Government	Private	Total	Faculty	Nonfaculty Academic	Government	Private	Total	Total
Biology	46	19	37	61	38	25[a]	50[a]	52	71	55	30
Chemistry	17[a]	33	34	45	37	100[a]	100[a]	59	72	64	25
Physics	33[a]	50	33	41	37	80[a]	100[a]	56	75	63	29
Mathematics	0[a]	38	59	58	48	4	0[a]	42	73	43	31
Civil engineering	50[a]	0[a]	40	50[a]	36	14[a]	—	48	41	41	21
Electrical engineering	14[a]	44[a]	32	25	28	0[a]	—	23	41	33	26
Mechanical engineering	25[a]	0[a]	30	54	33	0[a]	—	32	38	28	21
Economics	20[a]	8	23	57	27	0[a]	—	43	38[a]	40	16
Political science	0[a]	14	65	67[a]	43	0[a]	—	60	0[a]	53	27
Anthropology	20[a]	43[a]	71	80	62	20[a]	0[a]	75	82	66	26
Psychology	42	36	43	45	43	19	23	17	23	21	25
Sociology	50[a]	50[a]	44	100[a]	57	—	—	83[a]	73	76	27

[a]Based on fewer than 10 cases.

percent of those in the private sector, say their jobs are nontraditional); civil engineering (11 percent compared with 0 percent); and sociology (44 percent compared with 40 percent). The natural scientists (except mathematicians), engineers of all types, economists, and psychologists are especially likely to view research as a traditional activity for their field; but rather large proportions of mathematicians (31 percent), political scientists (35 percent), anthropologists (53 percent), and sociologists (35 percent) see their research jobs as nontraditional.

Overall, about two in five of the science and engineering Ph.D.'s working in administration and close to half of those working in "other" activities see their jobs as nontraditional. Among mathematicians, mechanical engineers, and psychologists, administration tends more often to be regarded as nontraditional than do "other" activities.

Academic administration is more likely to be accepted as traditional than are administrative jobs in the nonacademic sectors, although as many as 50 percent of the physicists and sociologists and 44 percent of the electrical engineers who are academic administrators consider their jobs nontraditional. In most fields, an administrative job in the private sector is more likely than an administrative job in government to be viewed as nontraditional. Exceptions are mathematics and electrical engineering. Administration seems most firmly established as a traditional activity among economists, engineers of all three types, chemists, and physicists. Most likely to see their administrative jobs as nontraditional are anthropologists (62 percent), sociologists (57 percent), biologists (50 percent), and mathematicians (48 percent).

In some fields, involvement in "other" activities represents a traditional use of training: for example, engineering activities among engineers, clinical work and counseling among psychologists. Of those with nonacademic jobs, private-sector employees are more likely than are government workers to find such jobs nontraditional. The exceptions are civil engineers, economists, political scientists, and sociologists. Perceptions of the nontraditionality of jobs involving "other" activities are greatest among anthropologists, sociologists, and natural scientists (including mathematicians).

Field Response to Market Pressures

Mathematicians, anthropologists, sociologists, and political scientists in other than teaching jobs are most likely to indicate that their jobs are nontraditonal for their fields. The finding with respect to the three social sciences is not surprising, considering that doctorate holders in these fields have traditionally been absorbed in academe and are only now being forced to look outside as college enrollments level off. For mathematicians, however, the job market may have tightened as early as 1967 or 1968, along with the job market for physicists (Cartter 1976,

p. 21). That mathematicians do not seem to have expanded their options since that time may indicate that their training has only limited application, or may mean that the market has already improved for them.

Engineers, on the other hand, are relatively unlikely to feel that the jobs they hold are nontraditional. Certainly their record of involvement in all sectors of the economy during the space race and, more recently, the energy crisis—to name only two examples—substantiates this finding. The continuing strong job market for engineers has permitted them to avoid taking nontraditional jobs.

Biologists, chemists, and physicists have had a long history of employment in government jobs (and, in the case of chemists, in the private sector) as well as in academic jobs. Thus, they tend to find both teaching and research jobs traditional. In the case of chemists and physicists, but not of biologists, administrative jobs are also likely to be regarded as traditional.

Of the social scientists, economists and psychologists are the most likely to have been involved in jobs other than teaching long enough, and in large enough numbers, to consider them traditional. As Cartter (1976, p. 21) observed, economists first became aware of the changing job market in 1969. In addition, *The American Psychologist* devoted its entire May 1972 issue to manpower concerns, suggesting that psychologists recognized very early that the job market in their field was on the decline.

By 1970, doctorate holders in every field were feeling the constriction, from members of the Modern Language Association to engineers and scientists experiencing the effects of aerospace cutbacks and the slowdown in federal expenditures for research (Cartter 1976, p. 21). It is not easy to explain why some fields have only recently attempted to expand their employment alternatives. For example, anthropologists as a group did not seem to be aware that a problem existed until Walter Goldschmidt's tenure as president of the American Anthropological Association in 1975. For this field, at least, the label *nontraditional* is applied to most jobs outside of academe, and even to those within it that do not involve teaching or research in an anthropology department.

To this sample of doctorate-level scientists and engineers, the "history" dimension of the concept of traditionality seems to be more pertinent than the "frequency" dimension. If Ph.D.'s in a given field were not seeking (or being encouraged to seek) jobs in a given sector or activity before the market constricted, then they were likely to consider such jobs nontraditional in a tight labor market. In that sense, such jobs represent new directions for this group.

Predicting Perceived Nontraditionality

According to the regression analysis conducted to determine the correlates of perceived nontraditionality, the strongest predictor is agreement with the statement "I have held other nontraditional jobs." Two explanations are possible here. Those who now hold nontraditional jobs may have been pursuing nontraditional careers for some time; that is, they were not forced to look for other than traditional jobs by the recent job crisis. Alternatively, those in nontraditional jobs may change jobs more often than others, perhaps in an attempt to find a job more closely related to their graduate training.

The second strongest predictor (in a negative direction) is the perceived relationship of the current job to graduate training. Those respondents who feel that their jobs are not related to their graduate training are more likely to see those jobs as nontraditional for people with degrees in their field. Several other significant variables support this finding. Those who see their jobs as nontraditional are also likely to say that neither courses in their major nor graduate study in general helped to prepare them for their jobs. Further, they indicate that the doctorate itself played little part in their getting the nontraditional job in the first place. In other words, nontraditional jobs are those for which graduate school does not provide the requisite credentials or training.

Nonetheless, those in such jobs believe that they have the skills and knowledge needed for successful performance. However, they also tend to say that people with less formal training are performing well in the same jobs.

When the foregoing factors are taken into account, people in nontraditional jobs are not likely to feel underemployed. When they do say they are underemployed, it is because the job is not in the field of the doctorate or because it is not commensurate with their level of training. They are less likely than are those in traditional jobs to say that they are underemployed in that their jobs are unchallenging. Further, they are more likely than not to express overall satisfaction with their jobs. Since they also tend to say that they have changed career goals since entering graduate school, their job satisfaction may reflect a change in their expectations, that is, because they do not expect to find jobs that match their training, they may not be disappointed. In short, although the concept of "nontraditionality" implies a lack of fit between graduate training and current employment, nontraditional jobs are by no means "bad" jobs; they may be both challenging and satisfying.

The variable "years since receiving the doctorate" is negatively related to nontraditional jobs; that is, recent graduates are more likely to hold nontraditional jobs than are older cohorts, probably because of the tight academic-job market in recent years. Anthropologists, sociologists, and biologists are more likely than those from other fields to hold nontraditional jobs, when other factors are taken into account. In these fields, perhaps, concern about identifying alternative jobs is greater precisely because doctorate holders were previously channeled into a relatively narrow range of jobs.

As was suggested by the cross-tabulations, those who consider their jobs to be nontraditional are not likely to be teaching or doing research. Further, they are unlikely to hold faculty ranks or to have the title of research scientist, college or university vice-president/provost, or supervisor. To some degree, then, the results of the regression analysis support the National Science Foundation's implicit definition of a nontraditional job as one that is outside academe and that does not involve research and development.

Relationship of Job to Graduate Training

Presumably, people who spend time, money, and effort to get the doctorate do so with the hope and expectation of pursuing careers in the doctoral field; to do otherwise would seem to be a waste of their extensive training. How many of those in our sample of science and engineering Ph.D.'s have succeeded in realizing that aim? How many now hold jobs that are closely related to their graduate education? More specifically, do the government and private sectors offer opportunities to pursue "related" careers, or must those who seek nonacademic employment settle for jobs that are only peripherally related—or even completely unrelated—to their doctoral field?

Two different questionnaire items were used to answer these questions. The first asked the respondent to indicate both the doctoral field and the field of the current job; a comparison of the two responses provided an objective measure of relatedness. The second item, which was broader and more subjective, asked the respondent to indicate whether the current job was "closely related," "somewhat related," or "not related" to his or her graduate training.

As the eighth row of table 12–1 indicates, the current jobs of about nine in ten respondents are in the same field as their doctorates. Most likely to be working in an entirely different field are physicists in academic administration and in the private sector. Overall, academics are slightly more likely than are nonacademics, and government workers slightly more likely than private-sector employees, to be working in the field of their doctorates. Generally, then, relatively few people in the sample are working in unrelated jobs, at least in one sense of that term.

But a different impression emerges when one looks at the figures in the next row of the table. Just slightly more than half of all respondents say that they are working in jobs closely related to their graduate training. In all fields, faculty members are most likely to give this response. Nonfaculty academics are least likely to perceive a close relation between their graduate training and their current jobs, and this holds true for all fields except mathematics, political science, and anthropology, where private-sector workers are most likely to feel that their jobs are only slightly related or are not related to their graduate education. Comparing fields, we find that civil engineers, economists, and psychologists have the greatest tendency to say they work in closely related jobs. On the other hand, biologists, physicists, mathematicians, and chemists are relatively unlikely to view their jobs as being closely related to their doctoral study.

There are also differences by primary work activity, which are not shown in the table. Predictably, teaching faculty and researchers in all sectors most frequently consider their jobs to be related to their graduate training. Administrators are most apt to say their jobs are not closely related, although many of this group (probably those administering research and development programs in their own fields) indicate that their jobs are "somewhat" related. The responses of those in the "other"-activity category vary somewhat by field. Since this category includes counseling, clinical work, and engineering, it is not surprising that psychologists and engineers performing ''other'' activities are most likely to say that their jobs are closely related to their graduate training, whereas chemists and physicists doing ''other'' things are much less likely to find a close relationship between their jobs and their graduate training.

Reasons for Working in a Less than Closely Related Job

Those respondents working in jobs only somewhat related or not related to their graduate training were asked to indicate, from a list of twenty-one possible reasons, why they took those jobs. Overall, slightly more than three in four cite only voluntary reasons; about one in ten cite only involuntary reasons; and the remainder mention both types of reasons. By far the most likely to say that they chose their unrelated jobs voluntarily are nonfaculty academics; this is true for all fields except anthropology, where only 30 percent say that the choice was voluntary. Indeed, in all employment sectors, those anthropologists whose jobs are only slightly related or not at all related to their graduate training are less likely than those from other fields to cite voluntary reasons and more likely to cite involuntary reasons. Generally, people working in the private sector are more likely than are their counterparts working as government employees or faculty members to give voluntary reasons for taking unrelated jobs. Economists and engineers, especially, tend to take unrelated jobs by choice.

Of the specific reasons given for taking an unrelated job outside of academe, the most common is being exposed to and becoming interested in another field; this is cited particularly often by those in the private sector working at ''other'' activities. Other common reasons are better pay, a better chance for career advancement, and promotion to a nonrelated field; all three reasons are cited most often by those holding administrative positions in government and in the private sector. Obviously, many of the Ph.D.'s were promoted into administrative slots, with resulting salary increases.

Other frequently mentioned reasons of a voluntary nature are ''changed field of science or engineering to one I prefer more,'' ''never planned to take a closely related job'' (both reasons frequently given by researchers in nonacademic jobs), and ''first job unrelated to doctoral study; became interested in this work.'' A fairly large proportion, especially of those carrying out ''other'' work activities in the private sector, say that the work environment of their current job is of ''better quality.''

Of the reasons that can be classified as involuntary, the three most important are ''employment opportunities scarce for people in jobs related to my graduate study,'' ''jobs related to my graduate field not available,'' and ''could not get a closely related job but would prefer one.'' Obviously, the employment crunch is being felt by many Ph.D.'s in our sample. In addition, administrators in government are more likely than others to say that they became technologically obsolete in their doctoral field. One explanation for this finding is that the government has the least stake in keeping up with the "state of the art" in any field, since its goal is neither to make a profit (as in the private sector) nor to train future professionals (as in academe). Alternatively, it may be that once a doctorate holder becomes involved in the federal bureaucracy, he or she finds it increasingly difficult to find the time to keep up with developments in the field.

Reasons infrequently cited as explanations for taking a less than closely related job include preferring one's current work in a nonscience or nonengineering position; joining the family firm or business; and trying but not liking related work. Further, relatively few of the Ph.D.'s in our sample mention wanting part-time, flexible jobs; wanting to work at home; not wanting to move in order to get a related job; or being limited by spouse and family responsibilities.

Generally, then, being in a job less than closely related to one's graduate training is most often the result of a change in interest or a desire for better working conditions (pay, opportunities for advancement). Nonetheless, enough respondents mention limited employment opportunities to make it clear that the job market for Ph.D.'s is indeed tight; it will almost certainly continue to be so, and many doctorate holders will be *forced* to take jobs that are only somewhat related, or not at all related, to their graduate training.

Predicting Job Relatedness

To learn the correlates of perceiving that one's job is closely related to one's graduate training, we undertook a multiple-regression analysis with relatedness as the dependent variable. The strongest predictors turned out to be saying that one's graduate education was very useful in giving "knowledge and skills that I use in current job" and that "particular courses in major area" are very useful on the current job. People who believe that their jobs are nontraditional or who say that they have changed career goals since entering graduate school are less likely to say that they hold closely related jobs. Perhaps these two negative predictors measure similar concepts. That is, a job seen as related may be one that lives up to the expectations that the individual had in graduate school, whereas a job perceived as unrelated is one that does not. It would seem that relatedness is more than just a matter of matching the substantive content of course work with employment-related activities.

When other factors are taken into account, economists, psychologists, civil and electrical engineers, and sociologists are most likely, and chemists are least likely, to perceive their jobs as closely related. By sector, faculty members have the smallest tendency to see their jobs as unrelated to their graduate study; by work activity, those engaged in administration are most likely to have this perception.

Older workers are more inclined than are younger workers to feel that they hold related jobs; this finding confirms that newer Ph.D.'s have more difficulty getting traditional, closely related work. But when age is taken into account, those who perceive that their jobs are closely related to their graduate training have spent fewer years in the labor force but more years on the current job; they are also likely to be male. One can only speculate about the meaning of these relationships. Since people tend to get promoted out of related jobs (usually into administration), it is logical that those who have worked for fewer years have had less opportunity for advancement out of their field. The findings also imply that moves into unrelated jobs are likely to involve a change of employers. That men are more likely to hold related jobs is consistent with the view that women are at a disadvantage, especially in the academic-job market.

Being currently engaged in research and agreeing with the statement "I am not underemployed" also predict relatedness. Other variables significantly related to the outcome measure involve the link between education and work. Thus, those who say that the doctorate was necessary for promotion in their current jobs and that graduate school in general helped prepare them for these jobs are also likely to say that their work is related to their graduate training, whereas those who say that formal training at the place of work helped prepare them for the current job are likely to see these jobs as unrelated.

Finally, those in relatively unrelated jobs tend to disagree with the statement "If I could begin my career again, I would be a college professor"; this finding suggests that once the doctorate holder has made the break from related work, he or she is no longer eager to work at the prototypical doctorate-level job, namely, as a faculty member. The converse is also true: Many in related jobs (including, of course, a large number of college professors) would become professors again if they could begin their careers anew.

Underemployment

The perception of being underemployed seems even more subject to the vagaries of individual interpretation than does the perception of holding a nontraditional job. What precisely does the concept of *underemployment* imply? Evidence suggests that perceived underemployment has an economic component, that is, people working less than full time or earning relatively low salaries tend to feel underemployed (Solmon, Bisconti, and Ochsner 1977). Moreover, as some of the regression analyses reported in this chapter have indicated, those in nontraditional jobs are likely to say that they are underemployed because their jobs are not in their fields or are not commensurate with their level of training but not that they are underemployed because they would prefer a more challenging position. Those in jobs closely related to their graduate training tend to say that they are not underemployed. Finally, as will be indicated in the next chapter, the perception that one is not underemployed is positively correlated with overall job satisfaction.

The last row of table 12–1 shows the proportions of respondents, by field and employment sector, who agree with the statement "I am *not* underemployed." The majority of the sample—roughly seven in ten—do not suffer from feelings of underemployment. The range is from 54 percent (of anthropologists working in the private sector) to 88 percent (of economists holding nonfaculty academic positions).

Generally, those in academe—whether in faculty or nonfaculty positions—are more likely to say they are not underemployed than are those in nonacademic jobs. Nonetheless, the proportion of faculty members who feel underemployed ranges from 16 percent (of economists) to 33 percent (of anthropologists). The implication is that all faculty positions are not ideal; an individual may be giving up superior opportunities by holding out for "any" faculty position. Those in the private sector less frequently feel underemployed than do those in government jobs, except in the fields of biology, civil engineering, and anthropology, where the reverse is true. Of science and engineering Ph.D.'s employed in government, perceived underemployment is highest among mathematicians, electrical engineers, and sociologists. Of private-sector employees, mathematicians, biologists, and anthropologists most frequently suffer from a sense of underemployment.

In addition to the statement "I am *not* underemployed," item 37 of the HERI questionnaire listed six statements beginning "I am underemployed . . ." and concluding with what may be regarded as an amplification of that assertion or a "reason" for the perception of underemployment. Inasmuch as academics are more likely than nonacademics to say that they are *not* underemployed, it is not surprising that a larger proportion of those in nonacademic jobs than of those in academe agree with each of the statements.

The two most-common reasons—cited by about 13 percent of the overall sample—are: "I am underemployed and would prefer a more-challenging position" and "I am underemployed; my job is not commensurate with my level of ability." The desire for a more-challenging position is expressed by about one in six of those in government and private-sector jobs but by only one in ten of those in academic jobs. Among government employees, the most likely to indicate that they are underemployed because of lack of challenge are mathematicians, political scientists, and anthropologists. On the other hand, civil engineers and biologists in government are less likely than average to give this response. Among those employed in the private sector, relatively large proportions of biologists, political scientists, and sociologists—but a relatively small proportion of economists—want more-challenging positions. Close to one-fifth of the government employees and one-sixth of the private-sector employees, but only one-tenth of the academics, feel that their jobs are not commensurate with their ability. Mathematicians in both nonacademic sectors are particularly prone to feel that their abilities are not being put to good use. Relatively few biologists or civil engineers in government, and relatively few economists in the private sector, cite this reason.

The next-most-common reason for feeling underemployed is the perception that one's job is not commensurate with one's level of training, cited by about 11 percent of the total group—15 percent of government employees, 13 percent of private-sector employees, and 7 percent of academic employees. Political scientists in both nonacademic sectors; electrical engineers and anthropologists in government; and mathematicians, biologists, civil engineers, and sociologists in the private sector are most apt to feel that their training is being wasted. Relatively small proportions of biologists and sociologists in government and of economists in the private sector agree with this statement.

About 9 percent of the total sample link perceived underemployment to their job's not being commensurate with their level of experience. Those in government (especially anthropologists), followed by those in the private sector (most notably biologists), are most likely to feel this way. Very few economists employed in either government or the private sector check this response; apparently, nonacademic jobs for economists offer them full scope to draw on their past experience.

About 8 percent of the total sample check "I am underemployed but for personal reasons I prefer to remain in this or a similar position." The proportions in government and in the private sector are roughly similar; very few academics agree with this statement. Among government workers, mathematicians and sociologists are most likely to say that they have personal reasons for remaining in their jobs; among private-sector employees, mathematicians and biologists most frequently give this reason.

Conclusion

The following is a summary, by field, of the most-notable characteristics of nonacademic jobs for doctorate-level scientists and engineers.

Biologists typically earn higher salaries when they work *in government* than when they work in the private sector, although in both cases their salaries are only moderately high.[4] Three-quarters of government-employed biologists are currently engaged in research expected to lead to publication; and a fairly large proportion (28 percent) perceive themselves as having accomplished a great deal of research and publication on the current job, which they are inclined to regard as traditional for their field and as closely related to their graduate training. More than half of those working at a job that is other than closely related cite only voluntary reasons for doing so. Government biologists are not especially likely to experience feelings of underemployment.

In contrast, just over half the *biologists in the private sector* are currently engaged in research; and only a moderate proportion perceive themselves as highly productive on the current job. Moreover, fully half say that their jobs are nontraditional for people in their field; about two-thirds say that they are in jobs not closely related to their graduate training (often for involuntary reasons); and over two-fifths perceive themselves to be underemployed, often because their jobs are not commensurate with their training.

Chemists in government earn relatively high salaries compared with other government workers. They also have a strong tendency to say that they have been very productive on their current jobs. Only about three in ten see their jobs as nontraditional, and about one-third feel underemployed. Only half are in jobs closely related to their graduate training.

Chemists in the private sector make higher salaries than their counterparts in government (perhaps because they are more likely to be administrators, especially of research-and-development programs). They are somewhat unlikely to be engaged in research, to see themselves as highly productive on the current job, or to regard their jobs as nontraditional; but they are somewhat more inclined than other private-sector workers to say that their jobs are not closely related to their graduate training. Seven in ten (about the average for the private sector) say that they are not underemployed.

Physicists in government are very well paid, averaging $33,100 per year. They are less likely than are government-employed biologists and chemists to see themselves as highly productive, and only two-thirds are currently engaged in research expected to lead to publication. Relatively few regard themselves as underemployed, and an average proportion (29 percent) see their jobs as nontraditional. Only 44 percent, however, say that their current jobs are closely related to their graduate study.

Physicists are the most highly paid group *in the private sector,* averaging $40,200 annually (over twice the mean salary of physicists who are faculty members). Only 44 percent report current research activity, and only 12 percent perceive themselves as highly productive on their current jobs. Close to half regard those jobs as nontraditional, and only one-fourth (the lowest figure for any group in the private sector) are in jobs closely related to their graduate study. Their reasons for taking nonrelated jobs are likely to be voluntary. Finally, about three in four (slightly above the average) say they are not underemployed.

Mathematicians typically earn higher salaries *in government* than in the private sector, although their salaries are only moderate. Over half are in jobs not closely related to their graduate field, often for involuntary reasons. Two in five regard their government jobs as nontraditional for people in their field. The proportion currently engaged in research is about average for government workers (70 percent), although they are less likely than others to see themselves as doing a great deal of research and publication on the current job. Finally, an unusually large proportion (about 45 percent) see themselves as underemployed.

Jobs held by *mathematicians in the private sector* are likely to be nontraditional and not closely related to graduate training. These jobs seem to have several other negative features as well: They pay rather low salaries, and they frequently generate feelings of underemployment. In addition, even though an average proportion of mathematicians (relative to other private-sector workers) are currently engaged in research, only 10 percent (about half the average) regard themselves as highly productive in their current jobs.

About three in four of the *civil engineers in government* hold jobs they regard as traditional and as closely related to their graduate training. Many of those in unrelated jobs, however, cite involuntary reasons. About three-quarters are currently engaged in research, and they are more likely than are other government-employed engineers to see themselves as highly productive. Seven in ten say that they are not underemployed. Their salaries are only moderate, with a mean of $30,100 per year.

The average annual salary of *civil engineers* employed *in the private sector,* on the other hand, is $33,700. They too are likely to regard themselves as being in closely related jobs; the 30 percent who are not usually cite only voluntary reasons for being in a less than closely related job. One-third regard their jobs as nontraditional. But only half are currently engaged in research, and only 7 percent see themselves as highly productive at the current job.

Electrical engineers in government earn mean salaries of $33,200, higher than any other group in government except economists but lower than their counterparts in the private sector. The proportion saying that their jobs are nontraditional is slightly lower than average for government workers, and the proportion saying they are highly productive is about average. But only 59 percent are currently engaged in research, and about half are in jobs not closely related to their graduate training, although usually for voluntary reasons. Moreover, this group has a marked tendency to feel underemployed, usually because the job is not commensurate with their training or ability.

The mean salary of *electrical engineers in the private sector* is very high, second only to that of physicists. Comparatively few report current research involvement, see themselves as highly productive, or regard their jobs as nontraditional, even though half are in jobs not closely related to their graduate training (usually by choice). They have no particular tendency to see themselves as underemployed.

Only 22 percent of the *mechanical engineers in government* consider their jobs to be nontraditional; in this respect, they resemble the other two types of engineers. (As has been pointed out previously, engineers have a more-established tradition of nonacademic employment than do Ph.D.'s from most other fields.) In most respects, this group is typical of government-employed scientists and engineers, except that their perceived productivity is very low, with only 11 percent saying they have accomplished a great deal of research and publication at their current jobs. Their salaries are in the average range.

By contrast, *mechanical engineers in the private sector* are very well paid, averaging about $7,000 more per year than their counterparts in government.

They are much less likely than either their counterparts in government or most other private-sector groups to be currently engaged in research. Over two-fifths view their jobs as nontraditional (an unusually high proportion among nonacademically employed engineers), and 45 percent say that their jobs are not closely related to their graduate training (although they usually take such jobs for voluntary reasons).

Economists earn higher salaries than any other group of doctoral-level scientists and engineers employed *in government*. Moreover, a higher proportion (78 percent) see their jobs as closely related to their graduate training, and the few in unrelated jobs tend to cite voluntary reasons. Conversely, only one-fifth see their jobs as nontraditional. Their perceived productivity is rather low, however, with only 8 percent saying they have done a great deal of research or publication at the current job.

Economists in the private sector earn even higher salaries than their counterparts in government, although lower than some other private-sector groups. Their current research activity and perceived productivity are slightly higher than average. Twice as many economists in the private sector as in government regard their jobs as nontraditional. About two-thirds (a relatively high proportion) see their jobs as closely related to their graduate training, and those in unrelated jobs took them by choice. Finally, a higher proportion of economists than of any other group of private-sector employees say that they are not underemployed. Thus, in terms both of salary and of challenge, the private sector seems to offer good opportunities for economists.

Political scientists in government earn slightly higher than average salaries. They are markedly less likely than others to be currently engaged in research and are unlikely to see themselves as highly productive. In addition, fully 55 percent see their jobs as nontraditional; and only 41 percent (a low among government workers) see their jobs as closely related to graduate training. Slightly over one-third (an average for the sector) feel underemployed, frequently on the grounds that the job is not commensurate with their experience. It is strange that political scientists seem to fit so poorly in government jobs; perhaps their graduate training results in unrealistically high ideals and expectations that are frustrated by their actual experience in the day-to-day pace of their jobs.

A different picture is presented by the small number (twenty) of *political scientists* identified as working *in the private sector*. Although they tend to make lower salaries than their counterparts in government, and although they are even less likely to be working in closely related jobs, their involvement in research is high; and they are more likely than any other group of private-sector scientists and engineers to see themselves as very productive. Moreover, relatively few suffer from feelings of underemployment.

Anthropologists are the lowest-paid group of science and engineering Ph.D.'s employed *in government*, perhaps partly because they also tend to have received their doctorates most recently. Moreover, a larger proportion than average view their jobs as nontraditional. Of the 44 percent working in jobs not closely related to their field, only about two in five do so for voluntary reasons only. Although 72 percent are currently engaged in research expected to lead to publication, only 14 percent view themselves as highly productive. The proportion saying they are not underemployed (64 percent) is about average for government workers.

Anthropologists employed *in the private sector* earn even lower salaries than those in government, with a mean of $20,700. (This is also the lowest mean-salary figure in the private sector.) They are also more inclined than others to see their jobs as nontraditional, to say that they took less than closely related jobs for involuntary reasons, and to perceive themselves as underemployed. On the bright side, 87 percent (a high for the private sector) are currently involved in research; and 33 percent regard themselves as highly productive.

Psychologists earn slightly higher salaries *in government* than in the private sector. A relatively small proportion (25 percent) feel that their jobs are nontraditional, and a relatively large proportion (69 percent) say that they work in jobs closely related to their graduate training. Few of those working in nonrelated jobs cite involuntary reasons only. The proportion of psychologists reporting current research activity is slightly below the average for government workers, and only 12 perceive themselves as highly productive. Nonetheless, they have no marked tendency to feel that they are underemployed; those who do are more likely than other groups to say that, despite this feeling, they prefer to stay in their current jobs for personal reasons; one possible explanation here is that psychology is a field with a relatively high proportion of women, who are usually less mobile than men because of family responsibilities.

Psychologists in the private sector average only moderately high salaries. They differ very little from their counterparts in government, except that slightly smaller proportions say that they are currently involved in research expected to lead to publication and that they have accomplished a great deal of research/publication in their current jobs. The one-third working in jobs not closely related to their graduate training are likely to cite voluntary reasons.

The salaries of *sociologists in government* are moderately high. Although 87 percent (a high for the government sector) are currently engaged in research, only 16 percent (a rather low proportion) see themselves as highly productive. Close to half say that their jobs are nontraditional, about two in five say that their jobs are not closely related to their fields, and two in five see themselves as underemployed.

After anthropologists, *sociologists* typically make the lowest salaries of any group *in the private sector,* with a mean of $22,100, substantially less than they make in government. An unusually high proportion (69 percent) regard their jobs as nontraditional, and a rather low proportion (34 percent) say their jobs are closely related to their graduate training. Nonetheless, they are not particularly inclined to see themselves as underemployed. The group is distinguished by its relatively strong research involvement (76 percent are currently engaged in research) and its relatively high perceived productivity (26 percent said they have done a great deal of research/publication at the current job).

Notes

1. In the regressions on current salary (discussed in the following section), the beta coefficients from the final step indicate that being a faculty member is more than three times as important in explaining salary differences as the combined effects of age, years since receiving the doctorate, and years of full-time employment.

2. The simple correlation between job relatedness and salary is negative, probably because of the low salaries made by faculty members. When employment sector is controlled, however, the sign becomes positive.

3. The publication index used as a proxy for productivity is discussed in more detail later in the chapter.

4. When considering salary data, readers should refer back to Table 12–1, which shows differences in years since receiving the Ph.D. Although this variable is correlated with salaries, high salaries do to some extent represent generally good job opportunities.

13 How Satisfying Are the Nonacademic Jobs?

Most authorities would agree that Ph.D.'s who find satisfying jobs have achieved a major goal of their graduate education. Some would probably assume, however, that such jobs can be found only, or chiefly, in academe. How valid is this assumption? How satisfied are those doctorate-level scientists and engineers who take jobs, either by choice or by necessity, in government or the private sector? How does their job satisfaction compare with that of their counterparts who hold faculty or nonfaculty positions in colleges and universities? What are the components of job satisfaction? What are its correlates? This chapter attempts to answer these questions.

Overall Job Satisfaction

The Higher Education Research Institute (HERI) questionnaire included a number of items geared toward understanding the elusive concept of job satisfaction. One of these items asked respondents to indicate their overall job satisfaction, as well as their satisfaction with twenty-one aspects of their jobs. This section focuses on overall job satisfaction.

Table 13–1 shows the proportions of respondents—by field, employment sector, and primary work activity—who say that they are very satisfied overall with their current jobs. (For purposes of comparison, academics are included in the table.)

Roughly two in five science and engineering Ph.D.'s say that they are very satisfied with their current jobs, although the range is considerable. For instance, only 20 percent of the sociologists employed in government as researchers, but 100 percent of the economists in academic administration, report high overall job satisfaction.

Those working in the private sector are most likely to express great overall job satisfaction, and those in government are least likely. In academe, administrators are most likely to be very satisfied, contradicting any allegation that Ph.D.'s are primarily interested in teaching and research. Of those two primary activities, research seems to be more satisfying than teaching, except among chemists, physicists, and mechanical engineers. Among government workers, administrators again are usually the most likely to express great satisfaction with their jobs, followed by those working at "other" activities; those doing research

217

Table 13–1

Overall Job Satisfaction, by Field, Employment Sector, and Primary Work Activity

(percent)

	Academe			
Field	*Teaching*	*Research*	*Administration*	*Other*
Biology	35	55	53	—
Chemistry	38	27	46	—
Physics	35	26	64	—
Mathematics	32	33	43	39
Civil engineering	40	—	—	—
Electrical engineering	24	—	60	—
Mechanical engineering	32	—	75	—
Economics	33	39	100	—
Political science	42	—	41	—
Anthropology	24	30	—	—
Psychology	31	33	40	39
Sociology	29	50	—	—

Note: Percentages indicating that they are "very satisfied." Cells with fewer than 10 respondents to the item were omitted.

are least likely. In the private sector, administration and "other" activities hold about equally high potential for giving satisfaction, depending on the field.

Perhaps the most-important conclusion to be drawn here is that teaching, the only primary work activity almost exclusively confined to academe, does not seem to be as satisfying to most doctorate-level scientists and engineers as administration, research, and other activities, all of which are available in the nonacademic sectors. Jobs in the private sector can be very satisfying to many Ph.D.'s. Even in government, relatively large proportions indicate that they are very satisfied with their jobs. In short, the contention that science and engineering Ph.D.'s can find happiness only in academe is not confirmed by these findings.

The question of the relative satisfactions provided by academic and by non-academic jobs was approached by means of another item asking respondents whether they would like to become college professors if they could begin their careers again. Table 13–2 shows the proportions who strongly agree that they would. Generally, those currently employed in the academic sector are much more likely than those currently employed in the nonacademic sectors to indicate strong agreement with this statement. Indeed, only about one-tenth of the science and engineering Ph.D.'s who currently work in government or the private sector have any great yearning for a life in academe, although the range is considerable: from only 3 percent of the mechanical engineers in the private sector to 23 percent of the anthropologists in the private sector. Thus, one may conclude that most of these nonacademically employed Ph.D.'s do not feel that they have suffered any great deprivation by taking jobs outside colleges and universities. Or does their attitude reflect "sour grapes?"

Government				Private Sector				
Teaching	Research	Administration	Other	Teaching	Research	Administration	Other	N
—	33	41	31	—	33	50	28	1,142
—	24	37	21	—	31	60	40	1,047
—	20	34	24	—	37	41	65	858
—	26	26	35	—	—	50	39	487
—	35	33	36	—	—	—	—	205
—	24	39	39	—	39	49	55	593
—	25	28	28	—	—	50	60	256
—	33	45	35	—	58	—	70	436
—	38	39	41	—	—	—	—	238
—	—	44	26	—	33	—	33	319
—	26	32	27	54	33	54	52	1,617
—	20	33	27	—	38	—	47	231

The responses of the academics would indicate that it does not. Some of them too have reservations about becoming college professors if they were starting out all over again. Except in the fields of mechanical engineering and economics, faculty members are more likely than nonfaculty academics to agree strongly that they would like to become college professors. Roughly three in five faculty members, but only two in five nonfaculty academics, strongly agree with the statement, although the proportion is as low as 7 percent among electrical

Table 13–2
Proportion Agreeing Strongly with the Statement "If I Could Begin My Career Again, I Would Like to Become a College Professor," by Field and Employment Sector

Field	Faculty	Nonfaculty Academic	Government	Private Sector
Biology	65	52	12	14
Chemistry	61	47	10	11
Physics	52	32	13	6
Mathematics	62	46	14	13
Civil engineering	55	29	10	4
Electrical engineering	58	7	9	7
Mechanical engineering	59	63	10	3
Economics	60	70	9	11
Political science	61	32	16	21
Anthropology	55	52	14	23
Psychology	51	35	6	10
Sociology	62	44	14	13

engineers in nonfaculty positions. It appears that the role of college professor is not so highly coveted after all, once doctorate holders are actually embarked on their careers.

Analysis, by Employer Type and Primary Work Activity

So far, the data have indicated that many science and engineering Ph.D.'s who take jobs outside of academe find them satisfying, especially if they are in the private sector or if they involve administration. But precisely what kinds of nonacademic jobs are most likely to prove satisfying to these highly trained people? Tables 13–3 through 13–8 show more specifically—by employer type within the two sectors and by primary work activity—the most potentially rewarding jobs. Data for these tables came from the responses of those nonacademically employed Ph.D.'s who were identified in chapter 11. It will be recalled that the criterion for regarding a particular job as a viable option was that it employ at least five Ph.D.'s from a given field; therefore, the group discussed here is a subsample of the total group of science and engineering Ph.D.'s employed outside of academe.

Two further warnings should be noted. First, some of the cells contain a very small number of people (for the Ns, see chapter 11); thus, any conclusions about the potential satisfaction of a given job are very tentative in some cases. (On the other hand, if four out of the five biologists who work for the federal government in training activities, for example, say that their jobs are satisfying, that at least suggests that other biologists will react similarly to such jobs.) Second, these tables show the proportions saying that they are either ''satisfied'' or ''very satisfied'' with their jobs, whereas table 13–1 showed only those who are ''very satisfied,'' which seems an overly stringent standard for the purpose of identifying viable options.

The majority of the natural scientists working in the government sector express overall satisfaction with their jobs. At least three in five give such a response (table 13–3). The only exceptions are biologists working for the federal government at ''other'' activities (only 43 percent of whom say they are satisfied or very satisfied); chemists working for the federal government in engineering activities (only 20 percent, or one of the five people so employed); and physicists working for the federal government in environmental protection (57 percent, or four in seven).

Natural scientists are even more likely to express satisfaction with jobs in the private sector (table 13–4). In no case does the proportion giving such a response fall below 75 percent; and in several cases, all the respondents working at a particular job say they are satisfied or very satisfied. This is true of biologists and chemists doing laboratory/experimental research for independent research organizations; chemists engaged in sales and marketing for manufacturing and

Table 13–3
Job Satisfaction of Natural Scientists in Government, by Employer Type, Primary Work Activity, and Field
(percent)

	Biology	*Chemistry*	*Physics*	*Mathematics*
Military service				
Research laboratory/experimental	100	—	—	—
U.S. government, civilian employee				
Administration, R&D	83	85	82	59
Administration, education	—	60	—	—
Administration, other	85	81	75	60
Clinical work	85	—	—	—
Consulting/professional services	100	83	—	—
Data processing/computer science	—	—	86	62
Development	—	60	64	—
Engineering	—	20	61	—
Environmental protection	73	61	57	—
Farming, forestry	89	—	—	—
Health services	82	—	—	—
Mathematical, statistical, actuarial	60	—	—	69
Program planning, budgeting	—	67	—	—
Public safety, law enforcement, community services	—	91	—	—
Research, applied	87	85	79	77
Research, evaluation	86	78	67	80
Research, laboratory/experimental	67	84	82	—
Research, theoretical/other	95	87	82	91
Training	80	—	—	—
Other activities	43	81	82	—
Multiple activities	79	80	88	—
Federally funded laboratory				
Administration, R&D	—	83	71	—
Research, applied	—	80	83	—
Research, laboratory/experimental	73	80	89	—

Note: Proportions indicating that they are "satisfied" or "very satisfied" overall with their jobs.

construction concerns; mathematicians doing data processing for such concerns; physicists administering R&D programs in independent research organizations; and biologists working at "other" activities for "other" types of employers.

The level of satisfaction is also high among engineers employed by the government, with at least three in four reporting themselves satisfied or very satisfied in most cases (table 13–5). The exceptions—all of them working as civilian employees of the federal government—are civil engineers performing multiple activities (67 percent); electrical engineers administering programs other than R&D or education (62 percent), engaged in data processing (44 percent), or doing theoretical/other research (64 percent); and mechanical engineers whose primary work activity is engineering (72 percent).

The relatively few civil and mechanical engineers identified by our study

Table 13–4

Job Satisfaction of Natural Scientists in the Private Sector, by Employer Type, Primary Work Activity, and Field

(percent)

	Biology	Chemistry	Physics	Mathematics
Manufacturing, construction				
Administration, R&D	—	86	92	—
Administration, other	—	87	95	—
Data processing, computer science	—	—	—	100
Engineering	—	—	80	—
Research, applied	—	77	83	—
Research, laboratory/experimental	—	88	—	—
Sales, marketing, purchasing, merchandising	—	100	—	—
Other activities	—	75	—	—
Multiple activities	—	83	—	—
Transportation, public utilities				
Administration, R&D	—	—	86	—
Independent research organization				
Administration, R&D	—	83	100	—
Research, laboratory/experimental	100	100	—	—
Human-services organization				
Health services	75	—	—	—
Other				
Other activities	100	—	—	—
Multiple activities	80	—	—	—

Note: Proportions indicating that they are "satisfied" or "very satisfied" overall with their jobs.

Table 13–5

Job Satisfaction of Engineers in Government, by Employer Type, Primary Work Activity, and Field

(percent)

	Civil	Electrical	Mechanical
Military service			
Administration, R&D	—	88	—
Engineering	—	100	—
U.S. government, civilian employee			
Administration, R&D	93	—	78
Administration, other	—	62	—
Data processing, computer science	—	44	—
Engineering	90	77	72
Research, applied	89	79	74
Research, laboratory/experimental	—	80	82
Research, theoretical/other	—	64	100
Multiple activities	67	83	79
Federally funded laboratory			
Administration, R&D	—	100	—
Engineering	—	71	—

Note: Proportions indicating that they are "satisfied" or "very satisfied" overall with their jobs.

as working in the private sector are almost all satisfied with their jobs (table 13–6). The jobs most likely to be satisfying to electrical engineers (at least four in five) include administration (of R&D or "other" programs), applied research, and consulting, whatever the specific private-sector employer.

At least four in five economists working for the government are happy with their jobs (table 13–7). The single exception occurs among economists conducting evaluation research, only 70 percent of whom indicate they are satisfied or very satisfied overall. Political scientists working for the government are somewhat less likely to be content. For instance, only about two-thirds of those engaged in "other" activities, and 77 percent of those administering programs other than R&D or education, report themselves satisfied or very satisfied. All fifteen of the anthropologists identified as working for the federal government (at jobs that employ at least five anthropologists) are satisfied; but the sociologists are less likely to feel favorably about their jobs. For instance, only 71 percent of those administering R&D programs for the federal government are satisfied or very satisfied. The best government jobs for psychologists (rated as satisfying

Table 13–6
Job Satisfaction of Engineers in the Private Sector, by Employer Type, Primary Work Activity, and Field
(percent)

	Civil	*Electrical*	*Mechanical*
Manufacturing, construction			
Administration, R&D	—	89	80
Administration, other	—	94	100
Data processing, computer science	—	83	—
Development	—	75	—
Engineering	100	72	100
Research, applied	—	88	—
Multiple activities	—	100	—
Other business/service establishment			
Administration, R&D	—	100	—
Administration, other	—	83	—
Consulting/professional services	—	80	—
Engineering	80	83	—
Research, applied	—	80	—
Transportation, public utilities			
Administration, R&D	—	88	—
Independent research organization			
Administration, R&D	—	88	—
Consulting/professional services	—	100	—
Engineering	—	83	—
Research, applied	—	82	—
Other			
Administration, R&D	—	100	—
Consulting/professional services	—	100	—
Engineering	—	67	—

Note: Proportions indicating that they are "satisfied" or "very satisfied" overall with their jobs.

Table 13–7
Job Satisfaction of Social Scientists in Government, by Employer Type, Primary Work Activity, and Field
(percent)

	Economics	Political Science	Anthropology	Psychology	Sociology
U.S. government, civilian employee					
Administration, R&D	83	91	100	82	71
Administration, other	100	77	—	87	—
Clinical work	—	—	—	81	—
Consulting/professional services	—	—	—	78	—
Counseling	—	—	—	71	—
Environmental protection	80	—	—	—	—
Health services	—	—	—	90	—
Mathematical, statistical, actuarial	100	—	—	—	—
Program planning, budgeting	88	80	—	—	—
Research, applied	87	—	—	66	75
Research, evaluation	70	—	—	71	83
Research, laboratory/experimental	90	—	—	96	—
Research, theoretical/other	—	—	—	—	—
Training	92	67	—	67	—
Other activities	93	—	—	—	—
Multiple activities	—	—	100	76	—
State/local government					
Administration, R&D	—	—	—	33	—
Administration, other	—	—	—	79	—
Clinical work	—	—	—	89	—
Consulting/professional services	—	—	—	50	—
Research, evaluation	—	—	—	78	—
Multiple activities	—	—	—	86	—

Note: Proportions indicating that they are "satisfied" or "very satisfied" overall with their jobs.

by at least four in five) are doing administrative or clinical work; conducting laboratory/experimental research; and being involved in health services for the federal government, as well as doing clinical work or performing multiple activities for state or local governments. The least-promising jobs for psychologists involve counseling, applied research, and training in the federal government (only about two-thirds with such jobs find them satisfying), and administering R&D programs (33 percent) or consulting (50 percent) for state and local government.

Although few in number, all the economists, anthropologists, and sociologists identified as working in the private sector express satisfaction with their jobs (table 13–8). The great majority of psychologists working in the private sector also are happy with their jobs, although those who do evaluation research for independent research organizations are somewhat less likely to be so (only 56 percent express satisfaction), along with those conducting applied research or evaluation research for a human-services organization (60 and 50 percent, respectively).

In summary, most of the science and engineering Ph.D.'s working in the nonacademic world seem to enjoy their jobs. In support of the findings from the analysis of the larger group, those working in the private sector are somewhat more likely than those working in government to have positive feelings about their jobs. Even among government workers, however, roughly four in five say that their jobs are satisfying. Administration—especially of research and development—tends to be a source of satisfaction, with research only slightly less so. The very few involved in the administration of educational programs outside of academe are less likely than other types of administrators to express satisfaction; and those administering some kind of program other than R&D or education tend to be less satisfied than the R&D administrators. For some reason, evaluation research seems to produce less satisfaction than other types of research. Interestingly, those who perform multiple activities for nonacademic employers tend to be satisfied with their jobs, perhaps because of the scope and variety of their work tasks.

Components and Correlates of Job Satisfaction

The conclusion that academic employment is not the only potentially satisfying career option open to science and engineering Ph.D.'s leads inevitably to a set of related questions: What is it that makes a specific job satisfying? How important is the "fit" between the person and the job, and how can that fit be assessed? What characteristics of the tasks involved, the work environment, and the individual are most important in determining job satisfaction? What kinds of tradeoffs exist among various types of jobs?

According to the regression analysis performed to learn the relationship

Table 13–8
Job Satisfaction of Social Scientists in the Private Sector, by Employer Type,
Primary Work Activity, and Field
(percent)

	Economics	Anthropology	Psychology	Sociology
Commerce, finance, insurance, real estate				
Administration, other	100	—	—	—
Personnel, employee relations	—	—	100	—
Manufacturing, construction				
Consulting/professional services	—	—	86	—
Research, applied	—	—	83	—
Other business/service establishment				
Clinical work	—	—	83	—
Consulting/professional services	—	—	93	—
Multiple activities	—	—	100	—
Elementary/secondary school				
Administration, education	—	—	80	—
Clinical work	—	—	89	—
Counseling	—	—	100	—
Independent research organization				
Administration, R&D	—	—	100	—
Consulting/professional services	—	—	100	—
Research, applied	100	100	83	100
Research, evaluation	—	—	56	—
Human-services organization				
Administration, other	—	—	83	—
Clinical work	—	—	83	—
Consulting/professional services	—	—	96	—
Counseling	—	—	82	—
Health services	—	—	77	—
Research, applied	—	—	60	—
Research, evaluation	—	—	50	—
Multiple activities	—	—	79	—
Other nonprofit organization				
Administration, R&D	—	100	—	—
Clinical work	—	—	80	—
Consulting/professional services	—	—	80	—
Other				
Clinical work	—	—	94	—
Consulting/professional services	—	—	98	—
Counseling	—	—	100	—

Note: Proportions indicating that they are "satisfied" or "very satisfied" overall with their jobs. No private-sector jobs employing 5 or more political scientists were identified.

between overall job satisfaction and satisfaction with twenty-one different aspects of the job, the four most-important components of overall satisfaction are satisfaction with challenge, with opportunity for creativity, with congenial work relationships, and with status. To a lesser extent, those respondents who are satisfied with the opportunity to use their training and schooling, with the variety of their work activities, with internal politics, and with their own policymaking power tend to find overall satisfaction with their jobs. Much less important, once these other job aspects are taken into account, are salary and fringe benefits, job security, and working conditions. The competency of one's colleagues—along with such "academic" job characteristics as teaching load, quality of students, and pressure to publish—are not related to overall satisfaction. The most-satisfying jobs, then, seem to be those that offer a mix of intrinsic, "expressive" rewards (challenge, opportunity for creativity, task variety) and extrinsic, "instrumental" rewards (status, policymaking power, salary).

To get a more-comprehensive picture of the correlates of job satisfaction, we conducted a series of multiple-regression analyses, first for the total sample and then by broad disciplinary groups within the three employment sectors. As independent variables in these analyses we used personal background characteristics as well as factors related to educational background, employment history, and characteristics of the current job. Items involving respondents' opinions and perceptions of, for example, the nontraditionality of their current jobs and the usefulness of certain aspects of their graduate training were also considered.

Predicting Job Satisfaction for the Total Sample

As it turned out, three of the four most important predictors of overall job satisfaction involve "perception" or "opinion" items. Those respondents who agree with the statements "My skills are fully utilized on the job" and "I am not underemployed" but who do not agree that "I could be equally or more satisfied with a different employer" are most likely to be satisfied with their current jobs. The last item seems self-explanatory: If one is very happy with one's present job, one will probably not expect that another job could be as good or better. The first two statements may represent different versions of the same perception; that is, underutilization of the individual's skills seems almost to define underemployment. Moreover, dissatisfaction and the perception of underemployment may be two sides of the same coin; seeing oneself as underemployed means seeing one's job as lacking in challenge, status, and opportunity for creativity—the very components that make a job rewarding. If underemployment were synonymous with less-than-full utilization of skills, however, only one of these variables would be significantly correlated with job satisfaction. Since both were significant in the regressions, the conclusion is that they measure somewhat different perceptions.

The fourth-most-important predictor of current job satisfaction is satisfaction with life in general. The interesting question here is whether job satisfaction substitutes for, or complements, other aspects of life. Recent evidence (Solmon and Ochsner 1978) indicates that job satisfaction is an important component of life satisfaction and that job dissatisfaction cannot be canceled out by satisfaction with other aspects of life. That is, the person who is unhappy with his or her job will be generally unhappy.

Neither any of the demographic variables (age, sex, marital status) nor any of the employment-history variables is related to job satisfaction, except that those people who were seeking a job change while on their previous jobs are more likely to be satisfied with their current jobs. The implication is that they were discontented with the previous jobs and deliberately chose the current job with the intention of correcting this situation.

Several educational-background variables are related to overall job satisfaction. First, the selectivity of the institution where the individual took his or her graduate training is important. The more selective the institution, the greater the satisfaction with the current job, independent of salary and other characteristics. At least two (by no means exclusive) interpretations may be offered here. Perhaps a "high-quality" degree enables its holder to get a better and potentially more-satisfying job in the first place. People with doctorates from less-prestigious institutions may have fewer offers of good jobs. As degrees proliferate at all levels, the prestige of a degree is perhaps becoming more important than the degree per se as the credential for entry into many jobs and for progress thereafter (Solmon 1979). The other interpretation is that the person with a prestigious degree is treated with more respect by her or his coworkers and thus finds the work environment more pleasant.

The second educational-background variable of significance is a self-rating. Those people who rate themselves high compared with other students in their graduate program are more likely to be satisfied with their current jobs. Perhaps those people who think well of their own abilities also have enough self-confidence to go after, and get, the best jobs. Or perhaps such self-ratings have substantial validity, and these people are indeed the cream of the crop and thus able to get such jobs on their own merits.

Third, even though age per se is not related to job satisfaction, years since receiving the doctorate is significantly and positively related. The implication is that the longer one has been out of graduate school, the more likely one is to get the kind of job that will be satisfying (for example, an administrative or managerial position). This finding is consistent with human-capital theory, which argues that the full payoff of formal schooling is not realized until several years after entry into the labor force (Mincer 1970). It also implies that one should not try to evaluate the efficacy of advanced training by looking at its labor-market outcomes (like income or job satisfaction) for graduates immediately after they receive the degree or begin the first job. This point is often ignored by writers (for example, Freeman 1976) who focus on the experiences of new entrants to the labor force in analyzing alleged "overeducation" in the United States.

Finally, those people who believe that their graduate training gave them skills that enabled them to get their first jobs are more likely to be satisfied with their current jobs. It appears that people whose careers began in jobs where they could benefit from the human capital they acquired in graduate school end up more satisfied than others do.

Doctoral field of study is related to overall job satisfaction in only two cases. Those with doctorates in economics are more inclined, and those with doctorates in psychology less inclined, to be satisfied with their current jobs. It is hard to know whether the reason for this difference has to do with temperament or with the nature of the current job market. Thus, it may be that those people who go into economics are predisposed to take a positive attitude toward life, whereas those who go into psychology are generally more jaundiced in their views. If the explanation lies with personality differences among people in various fields, however, one would expect that other graduate fields of study would be related to satisfaction or dissatisfaction. The alternative explanation—that the outcome is related to differing market conditions for different fields—works better for economists than for psychologists. Economists seem to have the kind of expertise that is currently in great demand in many employment settings. On the other hand, psychologists also exhibit considerable versatility in the types of jobs they take. But perhaps the kinds of primary activities in which they frequently engage (counseling, clinical work) are not as satisfying as, for example, administration.

The regression analyses for the total sample confirm differences in satisfaction by employment sector and primary work activity already revealed by the cross-tabulations. Thus, being an administrator in academe or in the private sector is associated with high overall job satisfaction, as is being a private-sector employee engaged in some "other" (single) activity or in multiple activities and being a faculty member engaged in some "other" activity (that is, besides teaching, research, or administration). Working for the government—particularly in research or at some "other" activity—is related to dissatisfaction.

The rank or level of one's current position also has some pertinence. Being an executive in the nonacademic sector or a full professor or vice-president/provost in academe is associated with job satisfaction. It would seem that the higher up the ladder one is (short of a college presidency or chancellorship), the happier one is likely to be; it makes little difference whether the "ladder" is academic or nonacademic.

Not surprisingly, salary is positively associated with satisfaction. Moreover, independent of the effects of actual salary, agreement with the statement "I am well paid compared with others with the same amount of education" is positively related to satisfaction. Apparently, then, either actually making good money or perceiving that one is making good money (or both) contributes to favorable feelings about the job.

The relationships between job satisfaction and research activity or productivity are more complex. The publication index—an objective measure of publication over the course of one's career (see chapter 12)—bears no relation to satisfaction with the current job. But a subjective measure of productivity—the respondent's perception that he or she has accomplished a "great deal," "some," "little," or no research/publication in the current job—does have such a relationship. Those respondents who believe themselves to be highly productive are likely to be satisfied with their jobs. Somewhat surprisingly, however, current engagement in research or scholarly work is associated with dissatisfaction. Of course, saying that one has been highly productive while in the current job does not necessarily mean that one is now actively engaged in research, although the two items are in fact highly correlated. Perhaps productive scholars who at the time of the survey had taken a respite from their somewhat trying research efforts are simply less pressured and hence more satisfied with their jobs.

A close relationship between the current job and graduate training is strongly and positively associated with satisfaction. That is, those people working in closely related jobs are more inclined to express job satisfaction than are those who are not. Nonetheless, job satisfaction is also related to the belief that one's current job is a nontraditional one for people in the same doctoral field. There is not necessarily any contradiction involved here. People working as administrators may regard themselves as being in a nontraditional job and yet (depending on the kind of program they administer) may feel that the job is related to their graduate training.

Certain other characteristics of the current job are associated with satisfaction. For instance, people working in jobs where they have no formal security arrangements tend to be more satisfied; perhaps this correlation reflects the kinds of jobs that typically offer security (tenured faculty positions, civil-service appointments) compared with those that do not (corporate-executive positions, high-level academic administrative positions). In addition, even though the variable "years since receiving the doctorate" is positively associated with satisfaction, the variable "years on the current job" has a negative correlation. This finding—that the longer one works at a given job, the more likely one is to feel dissatisfied with it—seems intuitively logical. Almost inevitably, over time, even the most-exciting job loses its initial challenge and becomes routine; moreover, the longer one stays in the same job, the more likely one is to feel that one's career is not advancing properly and that a dead end has been reached.

Supervising people trained in the same field, which may be regarded as a sign of status, is positively related to satisfaction. Moreover, people who say that their leisure activities provide them with knowledge and skills useful for their current jobs are more inclined to be satisfied. Perhaps this statement indicates simply that the individual's overall interests are consistent with the job and that no conflict exists between extracurricular and job activities. Those who say that their job training was inappropriate to the actual requirements of the job are less likely to be satisfied. Those agreeing with the statement "My position required on-the-job training" are more likely to be satisfied. Since the importance of having a job related to one's graduate training has already been established, this finding confirms the notion that people benefit both from their general training as graduate students and from more-job-specific training.

One item on the HERI questionnaire listed eighteen personal traits (for example, self-confidence, understanding of others) and abilities or skills (for example, academic ability, mechanical ability) and asked respondents to indicate which are their strong points and which are useful on the current job. Looking at those attributes that are both strong points and useful competencies, we find that self-confidence, leadership ability, self-discipline and ability to follow rules, creativity and originality, public-speaking ability, and mathematical ability are all positively related to satisfaction. In other words, people who regard themselves as superior in these qualities and who at the same time believe that their jobs require such qualities are more likely to be satisfied. On the other hand, writing ability, general knowledge, and the ability to think clearly are negatively related to satisfaction. Interpretation here is more difficult. Either people feel that they are strong in these qualities but that their jobs do not demand that they use them, resulting in a waste of talents; or people feel that the job demands such qualities but they are lacking in them, resulting in feelings of inadequacy and anxiety. In either case, the result is job dissatisfaction.

Finally, one mobility variable is significant. Agreement with the statement "If I were looking for a job now, I would look nationwide" is positively correlated with satisfaction. Taken in conjunction with the previously mentioned finding that satisfaction is associated with seeking a job change while on the previous job, this relationship suggests that the more mobile (psychologically and geographically) one is, the better able one may be to find a job that is satisfying.

Predicting Job Satisfaction, by Employment Sector

Because analyses of more-homogeneous groups usually yield results that are both more economical and more precise than those emerging from analysis of the larger and more-heterogeneous group, multiple-regression techniques were further applied to identify the variables associated with job satisfaction in each of the three employment sectors: academe, government, and the private sector. The sample was subdivided into natural scientists and engineers, on the one hand, and social scientists, on the other. The most-important finding to emerge from these analyses is that, in all cases, the perception that one's skills are fully utilized in the job was strongly and positively related to job satisfaction. No other single variable proved to be significant across employment sectors and broad disciplinary groups; therefore, the remainder of the discussion will be presented by sector.

Academe

Those variables that predict job satisfaction among natural scientists and engineers in academe differ from those predicting job satisfaction among social scientists, with three exceptions. Years since receiving the doctorate and the perception that self-discipline is both a strong point and a trait useful on the job are positively related to job satisfaction for both groups. The third common variable is the self-rating of rank in the graduate program, but the direction of the correlation differs for the two groups. Social scientists who rate themselves high relative to others in their academic program tend to be satisfied with their current jobs, whereas natural scientists and engineers who rate themselves high tend to be dissatisfied. One interpretation of this difference in the sign of the correlation is that social scientists who see themselves as superior look on college and university jobs as more suited to their abilities than the kinds of jobs available to them outside of academe, whereas scientists and engineers with highly favorable self-images believe that the options available to them outside of academe offer more scope for their talents than do academic jobs.

The next-most-important predictor of job satisfaction among natural scientists and engineers in academe (after the perception that their skills are fully utilized on the job) is the perception that they are well paid compared with others who have the same amount of education. However, salary per se is not related to job satisfaction. Those who supervise people trained in the same field and who perceive themselves as having accomplished a good deal of research and publication while in their current positions are more likely to express satisfaction. Satisfied natural scientists and engineers also tend to say that having a research assistantship while in graduate school did not help to prepare them for their present jobs. Besides self-discipline, the following traits that are regarded both as strong points and as useful on the job are related to job satisfaction: mathematical ability, self-confidence, and political awareness (all positive); and general knowledge (negative). Those natural scientists and engineers who are married are more likely to be satisfied with their jobs than those who are not. Finally, biologists and civil engineers are more likely than those with doctorates in other natural-science and engineering fields to have positive feelings about their jobs.

Among social scientists employed in colleges and universities, the selectivity of the institution where they took their graduate training and (actual) salary are strongly related to satisfaction. The more selective the institution and the higher the current salary, the more likely is the social scientist to be happy with his or her academic job. Satisfied social scientists also tend to feel that they have leadership ability that is useful in their jobs and that their graduate training provided them with the skills necessary to get their first jobs. Cultural perspective as a "useful strong point" is negatively related to satisfaction for this group; either they feel that such perspective would be useful to them on the job but that they lack it, or they believe that they have cultural perspective but that they cannot apply it in their current job. Whichever the case, such a combination produces dissatisfaction.

Government

Among those employed in government jobs, natural scientists and engineers have little in common with social scientists in terms of variables predicting job satisfaction. For both groups, those who believe that their graduate training gave them the skills necessary to get their first jobs and that their job training was appropriate for the actual requirements of their job are likely to express satisfaction.

Natural scientists and engineers who are happy in their government jobs are also likely to supervise others trained in their fields, to see themselves as well paid, and to believe that particular courses in their major field helped to prepare them for their current jobs. Those who believe that their self-confidence, creativity and originality, and political awareness are useful to them tend to be satisfied, whereas those who believe that they have strong research skills that are not being tapped, or that their jobs demand research skills that they lack, are likely to be dissatisfied.

Psychologists with government jobs are strongly inclined to be dissatisfied with them. In addition, government-employed social scientists who did their graduate work at highly selective institutions tend to be dissatisfied, perhaps because they feel that their superior abilities are wasted or are unappreciated by their colleagues. (By contrast, those social scientists in academe who got their doctorates at highly selective institutions are happy with their jobs, perhaps because in such an environment they are accorded high respect for their credentials.) "Useful strong points" positively associated with satisfaction for this group are leadership and public-speaking ability; writing ability is negatively related to satisfaction.

Private Sector

Besides the "utilization of skills" variable, the only predictors of satisfaction among natural scientists and engineers employed in the private sector are the perceptions that their high drive to achieve is useful in their current jobs and that their leisure activities provide them with the knowledge and skills necessary for their present jobs.

Those social scientists satisfied with their jobs in the private sector are also likely to regard their high drive to achieve as a useful trait. Moreover, like their counterparts in academe and government, the satisfied social scientists in the private sector believe that their graduate training gave them the skills necessary to get their first jobs. Researchers and female social scientists are unlikely to be happy working in the private sector. Those whose jobs are related to their graduate field and who have jobs with no formal security arrangements are likely to express satisfaction.

Utilization of Skills

Because the perception that one's skills are fully utilized in the job proved to be such a strong correlate of overall job satisfaction, both for the total sample and across employment sectors and broad disciplinary groups, another series of regression analyses was performed to learn more about what is implied by this variable. It was hypothesized that "skills" here mean more than just the competencies acquired in graduate school. The feeling that all of one's skills and abilities are being used is probably more essential to job satisfaction than is the feeling that course requirements and work requirements are closely linked (Solmon, Bisconti, and Ochsner 1977).

"My skills are fully utilized in my job" served, then, as the dependent variable. The independent variables were of five categories:

1. Three general characteristics of the job (relationship to field of graduate study, salary, current research activity).
2. A series of factual and opinion statements about the current job.
3. A series of statements about the ways in which the respondent's graduate education proved to be useful in the world of work.
4. The "useful strong points" included in the previous analyses (that is, the traits and abilities that are regarded both as personal strong points and as useful on the current job).
5. The same list of traits and abilities regarded simply as useful on the current job.

The fourth category was included on the assumption that jobs calling for the use of traits and abilities regarded by the individual as personal strong points will be perceived as fully utilizing one's skills; the fifth category was included on the assumption that the greater the number of competencies seen as useful on the job, the more likely the individual will be to feel that his or her skills are fully utilized. The regression analyses were performed both for the total sample and by employment sector (academe, government, private), with respondents again subdivided into natural scientists and engineers, on the one hand, and social scientists, on the other.

The most consistent and generally strongest predictor of "full utilization of skills" is the perception that graduate education "gave me skills and knowledge that I use in current job." Thus, even though competencies developed in other ways (for example, prior to graduate school, on the job) are theoretically relevant, respondents are nonetheless inclined to view their graduate education as providing the most-important training. A close relationship between the job and graduate training is also a factor in the perception that one's skills are fully utilized, both for the total sample and for all subgroups except natural scientists and engineers in the private sector; this relationship suggests, again, that respondents view their graduate training as the most-important source of skills. Jobs that call for creativity and originality are seen as fully utilizing skills by all groups—not surprising, in that satisfaction with opportunities for creativity constitutes a major component of overall job satisfaction. Supervising others trained in the same field (a measure both of job relatedness and of status) is a significant predictor among all but social scientists in the private sector.

The perception that one is well paid compared with others who have the same amount of education is important to all but natural scientists and engineers in academe; for this group, however, actual salary is related to full utilization of skills, although no such relation was found for social scientists either in academe or in the private sector. One comment is in order here: The causal connections between salary, relatedness, and full utilization of skills are not at all clear, although it seems likely that full (meaning efficient and effective) utilization of skills in the workplace leads both to higher salaries and to the perception that one's job is related to one's graduate training. All these factors go together to promote job satisfaction, and no doubt have feedback relationships that would have to be taken into account in any causal argument.

For all those employed in academe, and for social scientists working in government, the perception that one is working at a professional level is important to the feeling that one's skills are being fully utilized. Beyond that, the specific traits and skills judged to be useful in such jobs vary by subgroup. All those employed in government, as well as social scientists in the private sector, are likely to mention insight as a useful trait. All those employed in academe, as well as social scientists in government, cite research skills. Somewhat curiously, political awareness is a negative predictor for those in academe and for natural scientists and engineers in government. It would seem that those jobs that call for political awareness are not the same jobs that make full use of the individual's skills, or, perhaps, that a lack of political awareness is an absolute asset in certain situations.

Most of the findings for this outcome seem obvious. Perhaps the most-important point to emerge is that jobs perceived as fully utilizing the skills of these science and engineering Ph.D.'s are also jobs that call for creativity and originality. Moreover, full skill utilization involves the use of skills beyond those acquired in graduate school, although academically acquired competencies are very important in the evaluation of total skill utilization.

Conclusion

Despite the highly publicized scarcity of academic jobs, new science and engineering Ph.D.'s usually seek employment in colleges and universities and often fail to give serious consideration to alternative employers. The evidence presented in this chapter indicates, however, that academic jobs may not in reality be the most emotionally rewarding. Indeed, those academics whose primary work activity is teaching tend to be dissatisfied. Academic administrators, to be sure, are generally happy with their work, but people with doctorates in science and engineering usually do not have the option of stepping into such positions directly on completion of graduate study.

The conclusion that faculty positions may appear less desirable to the experienced worker than to the new entrant to the labor market is confirmed by the responses of our sample of doctorate-level scientists and engineers to the question of whether they would like to become college professors if they could begin their careers again. Very few of those currently employed in government or the private sector say that they would choose to be college professors; further, fairly large proportions of those who are faculty members indicate that they would not be college professors if they could begin their careers again. Clearly, new science and engineering Ph.D.'s would be well advised to consider jobs in government and in the private sector.

Of those two nonacademic employment sectors, the private sector seems to offer the greatest potential for satisfying jobs. Nonetheless, even though government-employed scientists and engineers are less likely to be satisfied with their jobs than are their counterparts in business and industry, sizable proportions do express satisfaction.

The results of the regression analyses throw further light on the components and correlates of satisfaction and thus may be helpful to those considering alternative careers. Jobs that are challenging, that offer opportunities for creativity, that provide congenial work relationships, and that carry high status are most likely to be satisfying. In addition, doctorate-level scientists and engineers are most likely to be satisfied by jobs that are related to their graduate training but at the same time are nontraditional for people from their field, and by jobs that pay well or are perceived as paying well. Those satisfied with their jobs also tend to be satisfied with life in general. Economists are somewhat more likely, and psychologists less likely, than those from other fields to find their jobs satisfying. Administrative jobs are usually more satisfying than jobs involving other primary work activities, although faculty members and private-sector employees carrying out "other" activities also tend to regard their jobs as satisfying.

Not all the variables considered in the regression analyses are amenable to any kind of manipulation or control by the individual, of course; but even so, a few obvious morals can be drawn from the findings for the different fields. First, psychologists should perhaps think twice before taking government jobs. Second, natural scientists and engineers are likely to find satisfaction in government jobs that pay high salaries and offer opportunities to supervise others from their field. Third, social scientists interested in government jobs should have leadership and public-speaking abilities; but their writing abilities are likely to be wasted. Natural scientists and engineers who are self-confident, creative, and politically aware are likely to be happy in government jobs; but their research talents are likely to be wasted. Fourth, high drive to achieve is helpful to anyone employed in the private sector. Finally, social scientists stand a chance of being unhappy with research jobs in the private sector; but they should not necessarily avoid jobs that offer no formal security arrangements.

14 The Dynamics of Job Change

The last chapter indicated that overall job satisfaction is associated to some extent with mobility, as reflected by agreement with the statement "If I were looking for a job now, I would look nationwide." Common sense suggests that people who, finding themselves in unhappy job situations, are able and willing to seek out and move into new jobs stand a good chance of eventually finding satisfying jobs (although excessive job mobility may become counterproductive). Moreover, in light of the main focus of this book—viable nonacademic-job options for science and engineering Ph.D.'s—consideration must be given to such questions as why people in this highly trained group change jobs (especially when they take jobs in government or the private sector); how they go about seeking new jobs (and with what degree of success); what they look for when they make job changes; and what other kinds of changes result.

This chapter, then, looks at various aspects of mobility and job change: the potential mobility of different subgroups; changes in career goals as they relate to actual job change; the "push" and "pull" components of job change and the mechanics of seeking a job; and the outcomes of job change with respect to salary and satisfaction.

To perform the analyses required for this chapter, the sample was subdivided into *paths*, defined by the employment sector(s) to which the previous job and the current job belonged. Thus, respondents whose current job is the only one they had held since receiving the doctorate (or who did not give information on their previous jobs) were excluded. Further, for purposes of simplification, non-faculty academics were omitted from all the analyses by path; thus "academe" encompasses only those who hold faculty rank. Table 14–1 lists the nine paths so defined and indicates for each path the number of cases, the mean year of the doctorate, and the average number of years spent on the current jobs.

As the table indicates, people changing jobs are more likely to stay in the same employment sector than to move to a different sector. *Within-sector* changes account for about two-thirds of the job changes reported here. The two most common types of *between-sector* changes are moves from academe to government and from the private sector to government, each accounting for about 10 percent of the job changes. (The reader is reminded that, because of the way in which the samples were selected, science and engineering Ph.D.'s in government are better represented than those in academe or the private sector.) Moves from academe to the private sector account for about 7 percent of the job changes. Relatively uncommon—at least for this sample—are moves from government

Table 14–1
Basic Characteristics of Different Paths

Path	Number of Cases	Year of Ph.D.		Years on Current Job	
		Mean	Standard Deviation	Mean	Standard Deviation
Academe to academe	1,771	69	6	3	4
Government to academe	115	66	8	4	5
Private sector to academe	274	66	9	4	5
Academe to government	731	64	8	7	7
Government to government	2,227	64	8	7	7
Private sector to government	749	62	9	7	6
Academe to private sector	509	66	7	5	6
Government to private sector	141	60	9	6	6
Private sector to private sector	1,160	61	9	6	6

to academe (1 percent), from government to the private sector (2 percent), and from the private sector to academe (4 percent).

Although the range within each path is considerable, those now employed in academe and those who moved from academe to the private sector tend to have received their doctorates most recently, whereas those whose previous and current jobs are in the private sector or who moved to the private sector from government tend to be the most experienced (in terms of years since receiving the doctorate).

Academics tend to have held their current jobs for the shortest period, an average of three or four years; government workers have been at their current jobs longest, an average of seven years; and those now working in the private sector average five or six years on the current job. To the extent that the variable "mean years on the current job" represents group differences in mobility, faculty members were clearly the most mobile, and government workers the least so. (It should be recalled that one of the criteria used in the initial selection of faculty was a mobility factor: having changed jobs within the last three years.) Although not shown in the table, there were some field differences. Biologists, chemists, and physicists in government service are especially likely to have been at their current jobs for a long period; their relative lack of mobility may reflect the rapidity with which knowledge in these fields becomes obsolescent. Psychologists are the least mobile of the social scientists, perhaps because of the constraints imposed by having a clinical practice.

Potential Mobility

Because of the methods used to identify the various paths, virtually all the people in our sample—except for those who have held the same job since receiving the doctorate—can be regarded as job changers and thus as being to some extent mobile. To make valid comparisons of the actual mobility of individuals or groups would require tracing lifetime, or at least long-term, career patterns, a task well beyond the scope of this book. One can, however, get some sense of the potential mobility of the subgroups within the sample by looking at their responses to a series of statements indicative of mobility. Table 14–2 lists the statements and shows the proportions, by employment sector, who say that they strongly agree with each. Note that in some cases agreement with a statement indicates relatively high mobility, whereas in other cases agreement reflects constraints on mobility.

Fewer than 10 percent of the total sample (with nonfaculty academics excluded from the analysis) agree strongly with some statements. For instance, the proportion saying that their mobility is limited because of their spouse's educational plans or because their parents are still alive is very small. Although sex differences are not shown in the table, women are more than twice as likely as men to be affected by these factors. Similarly, about one-third of the women, but only about 3 percent of the men, say that their spouse's job limits their mobility; agreement with this statement is most frequent among those with doctorates in the social sciences (with the exception of economics), fields in which women are fairly well represented. Women are also more likely than men to be constrained by their spouse's preference as to locale. Nonetheless, for the sample as a whole, these family considerations rarely constitute serious impediments to mobility.

The considerable geographical mobility that typifies U.S. society today is reflected in the relatively small proportions who agree that their ideal job location is within 500 miles of the community where they grew up; obviously, most people in the sample do not feel strong loyalties toward their home region. Nor is the opportunity to travel considered a worthwhile compensation for taking a job in an undesirable location; the only subgroups to indicate that they particularly value travel opportunities are anthropologists in the nonacademic sectors and sociologists in the private sector. Those employed in academe and in the private sector are not inclined to feel that their occupation severely limits their choice of a geographical location. This feeling is much more prevalent among those with government jobs; indeed, one in five of the political scientists in government agrees strongly with this statement. The obvious explanation is that these people can practice their profession only in Washington, D.C.

Only about 9 percent of the sample agree strongly that they would move anywhere if the salary were attractive enough; the proportions are largest among economists in academe and government (13 percent) and among anthropologists in the private sector (21 percent). What constitutes an "attractive" salary is, of course, a matter of individual opinion. Economists in academe and in government are very well paid (mean salaries of $22,900 and $33,800, respectively), whereas anthropologists in the private sector are poorly paid (mean salary of $20,000), relative to their coworkers from other fields. Perhaps economists are generally more motivated than others by salary considerations. On the other hand, an-

Table 14–2
Proportions Indicating Strong Agreement with Mobility Statements, by Field and Employment Sector

	Biology			Chemistry			Physics			Mathematics			Civil Engineering			Electrical Engineering		
	Academe	Government	Private	Academe	Government	Private	Academe	Government	Private	Academe	Government	Private	Academe	Government	Private	Academe	Government	Private
I would take a job anywhere as long as there were opportunities to travel.	3	3	3	2	3	4	7	3	2	4	2	3	3	1	0	2	2	2
If I were looking for a job now, I would look nationwide.	40	33	32	50	31	40	51	32	27	45	24	16	34	30	25	35	21	24
There are a limited number of cities in which I would live.	42	43	42	37	37	30	30	40	45	31	41	43	45	50	48	59	46	50
Climate would be a major factor in my decision to move.	21	25	23	16	21	16	12	20	20	16	26	16	25	21	27	24	24	25
I would take a job anywhere for a short period, but I have specific preferences for permanent residence.	16	21	16	15	19	12	19	21	16	18	15	15	18	18	17	22	17	21
I would move anywhere if the salary were attractive enough.	6	9	10	8	10	12	9	9	7	8	10	8	9	5	10	8	7	10
I would move anywhere for an extremely satisfying job.	26	26	26	34	24	31	32	26	26	33	23	24	22	20	10	19	20	17
I will be more mobile when my children are out of school.	14	21	23	12	16	19	11	17	15	9	17	15	15	18	21	21	22	19
My mobility is limited because my parents are alive.	2	2	4	2	3	1	1	2	0	1	3	4	1	1	3	2	3	2
My ideal job location is within 500 miles of the community where I grew up.	11	7	8	4	8	7	5	5	5	11	8	9	6	6	14	8	8	6
My occupation severely limits my choice of locale.	12	14	9	9	11	7	17	16	9	8	14	9	2	11	10	6	13	9
My mobility is limited because of spouse's job.	11	4	5	4	6	4	6	3	5	8	5	4	1	4	3	8	3	3
My mobility is limited because of spouse's educational plans.	2	1	3	1	1	1	2	1	0	2	2	4	0	1	0	4	2	1
My mobility is limited because of spouse's preferences about locale.	6	6	7	4	7	4	7	7	10	6	6	7	4	10	7	15	8	9
I could be equally or more satisfied with a different employer.	38	23	27	39	27	22	37	29	19	38	34	25	17	27	27	29	22	18

Note: Nonfaculty academics are excluded from this table. *Academe* refers only to current faculty.

	Mechanical Engineering			Economics			Political Science			Anthropology			Psychology			Sociology		
	Academe	*Government*	*Private*	*Academe*	*Government*	*Private*	*Academe*	*Government*	*Private*	*Academe*	*Government*	*Private*	*Academe*	*Government*	*Private*	*Academe*	*Government*	*Private*
I would take a job anywhere as long as there were opportunities to travel.	3	2	0	2	4	2	6	5	5	8	12	14	5	3	3	5	0	13
If I were looking for a job now, I would look nationwide.	34	23	24	39	19	28	40	25	35	42	26	47	33	20	17	45	18	33
There are a limited number of cities in which I would live.	46	47	48	45	43	43	34	42	40	42	54	46	44	51	56	32	55	44
Climate would be a major factor in my decision to move.	25	24	27	20	13	24	21	21	10	18	22	30	22	33	35	23	24	22
I would take a job anywhere for a short period, but I have specific preferences for permanent residence.	17	14	25	24	12	14	22	14	10	26	20	22	13	15	18	20	22	17
I would move anywhere if the salary were attractive enough.	9	8	5	13	13	6	8	6	0	8	7	21	4	7	6	7	2	12
I would move anywhere for an extremely satisfying job.	20	18	17	18	18	22	28	33	35	30	29	37	20	16	15	26	16	28
I will be more mobile when my children are out of school.	16	14	18	18	18	11	16	11	7	12	24	18	18	19	21	22	13	21
My mobility is limited because my parents are alive.	2	3	3	3	2	8	4	0	0	4	9	5	2	6	3	3	0	8
My ideal job location is within 500 miles of the community where I grew up.	12	13	8	9	7	6	11	7	5	8	12	10	9	8	8	8	6	8
My occupation severely limits my choice of locale.	12	13	2	4	11	4	9	21	5	8	5	9	6	5	7	7	13	12
My mobility is limited because of spouse's job.	3	5	3	8	8	6	10	4	18	12	15	15	13	8	8	11	10	14
My mobility is limited because of spouse's educational plans.	1	1	0	1	2	0	2	0	0	4	4	0	1	1	1	3	2	0
My mobility is limited because of spouse's preferences about locale.	6	8	12	11	10	17	7	8	12	8	13	8	8	8	8	9	3	11
I could be equally or more satisfied with a different employer.	31	26	20	37	24	18	38	30	28	47	30	36	41	31	22	33	28	34

Note: Nonfaculty academics are excluded from this table. *Academe* refers only to current faculty.

thropologists may perceive themselves as so badly underpaid that they are willing to take any job that pays more; even a salary that is only slightly higher may be attractive to them.

Although not usually willing to take any job that offers an attractive salary, respondents are somewhat inclined to say that they would move anywhere for an extremely satisfying job, with slightly over one in five agreeing strongly with this statement. Natural scientists in all three sectors, and social scientists in the private sector, are particularly likely to give this response. In addition, close to one-fifth of the total group say they would take a job anywhere for a short period, even though they have specific preferences for a permanent residence. Social scientists in academe (except psychologists) are especially likely to express such a willingness.

Nonetheless, geographical preferences do block mobility to some extent. About two in five of the total group agree that there are a limited number of cities in which they would live, psychologists and engineers of all three types being most apt to have such preferences; faculty members seem somewhat more flexible on this point than do those employed in the nonacademic sectors. Similarly, about one-fifth overall say that climate would be a major factor in the decision to move, with psychologists again being most likely to give high priority to this factor. Interestingly, smaller proportions of women than of men are concerned about climate, indicating that on this point they are potentially more mobile.

Responses to the item "I will be more mobile when my children are out of school" are difficult to interpret, especially when one considers that fewer women than men agree strongly. Apparently, disagreement with the statement can indicate either that the respondent does not feel particularly constrained now by the needs of school-aged children or that the children's completing school will not necessarily bring increased freedom in the future, because other factors that limit mobility (for example, spouse's job) will continue to operate.

Perhaps the most-direct gauge of mobility is the statement "If I were looking for a job now I would look nationwide." Differences among the employment sectors on this item are rather marked. About two-fifths of the faculty, but only one-quarter of the government workers, agree strongly with this statement; those employed in the private sector are in the middle. Again, the bias toward Washington, D.C.–based jobs may explain the more-limited mobility of government workers. Field differences are of less importance; chemists, physicists, and anthropologists are most likely to say they would look nationwide for a job, and psychologists are least likely.

Overall, about three in ten agree strongly with the last statement on the list, "I could be equally or more satisfied with a different employer," suggesting a willingness at least to consider changing jobs. The proportion is highest among faculty, followed by government workers. Social scientists (except for economists) and mathematicians are most likely to agree, whereas engineers and economists are least likely.

Generalizing broadly, one may conclude that faculty members are the most potentially mobile group, and government workers the least so. By broad discipline, natural scientists—especially chemists and physicists—seem more mobile than either engineers or social scientists; and social scientists (except for psychologists) are more mobile than engineers.

Predicting Willingness to Change Jobs

Approaching the question of mobility from a slightly different angle, we conducted regression analyses designed to elucidate the actual effects of various factors on willingness to change employers. The dependent variable was agreement with the statement "I could be equally or more satisfied with a different employer." The independent variables—chosen on the basis of the results of earlier analyses and of the work of Brown (1967)—included personal factors (sex, age, marital status); educational-background factors (self-ratings as a graduate student, selectivity of the institution where graduate work was done); characteristics of the current job (salary, formal security arrangements, amount of research and publication accomplished, relationship of job to graduate training, traditionality of job, and perceived underemployment); and variables involving satisfaction not only with different aspects of the current job but also with other aspects of life such as the quality of community cultural life. Finally, dichotomous variables indicating the respondent's field, employment sector, and primary work activity were included in the analysis.

Surprisingly few variables entered the equation. Salary, formal job security, and amount of research or publication accomplished seem to have no bearing on a person's willingness to consider changing jobs, nor does satisfaction with various aspects of life. Rather than being prime motivators, these factors may be what makes a job more or less attractive once the decision to change jobs has been made.

Almost all the variables that did enter the equation carried a negative weight. The most-potent predictor is overall job satisfaction. The greater the satisfaction with the current job, the smaller the tendency to agree that one could be equally or more satisfied with a different employer. Women are less likely than men, and older people less likely than younger, to consider a job change. Those who have worked at the current job for a relatively long time are less likely to indicate an interest in changing jobs. This finding would seem to contradict the earlier finding (reported in chapter 4) that the longer the worker has been on the current job, the less likely he or she is to be satisfied with it. The explanation may be that long-time stability results in inertia—an unwillingness to move regardless of degree of satisfaction. Since level of job satisfaction had already been accounted for when years on the job entered the regression equation, it is likely that longer-term workers are less satisfied and so will consider moving; for a given satisfaction level, however, the longer the worker has been on the job, the less likely he or she is to believe that another job could be equally or more satisfying.

Anthropologists are somewhat more inclined, and biologists less inclined, than those from other fields to agree that they could be as satisfied with a different employer. Those working in the private sector are less apt than those working in academe or government to exhibit high potential mobility; and those whose primary work activity is teaching, research, or administration seem somewhat more mobile than those who engage in some ''other'' single activity or in multiple activities. Finally, those who see themselves as being underemployed or who are dissatisfied with their future prospects are likely to say that they could be as happy or happier with a different employer.

Certain components of job satisfaction are also negatively related to the dependent variable, the most important being satisfaction with the prestige of one's employer and with one's opportunities for different (better) jobs at the institution or organization. Apparently, those Ph.D.'s who believe that their employer is not well known or not highly regarded and that their upward mobility on the current job is limited are more willing to consider taking other jobs. Satisfaction with internal politics and with work relationships (two closely related job aspects that have a zero-order correlation of .48) are also important. People who are not happy with patterns of personal interaction at their place of employment are more potentially mobile. Dissatisfaction with salary and fringe benefits, challenge, opportunity for scholarly pursuits, visibility for jobs at other institutions and organizations, and resources to get the job done is also associated with the belief that one could be equally or more satisfied with a different employer.

Changes in Career Goals

The next major topic addressed in our consideration of job change and mobility among science and engineering Ph.D.'s was that of changes in career goals. How common are such changes? When do they occur? How closely related are they to actual job changes? Why do people change their career goals? Are such changes internally motivated, or do they tend to be forced on the individual by circumstances?

Although it is tempting to assume that virtually all science and engineering Ph.D.'s initially plan on and expect careers in academe and that any change in career goals therefore represents a decision to aim for success in other than the professorial role, such an assumption is unwarranted. Many science and engineering Ph.D.'s probably intend from the beginning to take jobs in government or in the private sector; some of them may end up as faculty members even though this was not their original goal. Moreover, a change in career goals does not necessarily imply either a change of jobs or a move from one employment sector to another.

The Higher Education Research Institute (HERI) questionnaire contained several items related to goal change. The first simply asked respondents to indicate whether their career goals had changed since they entered graduate school; the second inquired about the timing of such a change (those who had changed their career goals more than once were told to refer to their most-recent decision); and the third asked respondents to indicate the reason(s) for the change. Table 14–3 summarizes the responses of the different ''paths'' to these questions.

Table 14–3
Summary of Information on Changes in Career Goals, by Path
(percent)

	Academe			Government			Private Sector		
	1	*2*	*3*	*4*	*5*	*6*	*7*	*8*	*9*
Changed career goals since entering graduate school	26	40	39	56	44	51	67	55	56
Timing of career-goal change:									
While in graduate school	31	20	22	12	16	13	9	15	8
At completion of graduate study	6	9	7	6	9	10	3	12	8
Within three years after completing graduate study	27	28	27	27	28	23	22	18	25
From three to nine years after completing graduate study	29	29	34	44	33	28	46	24	36
Ten or more years after completing graduate study	7	15	10	11	14	25	19	31	22
Factors influencing career-goal change:									
Available job opportunities in previous field were limited or unattractive	32	19	17	46	39	38	43	22	26
Decided I did not enjoy first-choice career	26	19	30	24	16	15	24	12	18
Found more-attractive or challenging job opportunities elsewhere	40	45	53	58	52	49	65	64	66
Changed career aspirations for personal or family reasons	24	20	25	17	19	13	25	25	22
Became outdated in my first-choice field	3	5	2	2	5	7	4	4	6
Became interested in a different area of study	43	31	36	24	29	28	30	34	25
Was terminated in a job	11	6	6	16	6	12	21	4	5

Note: The paths were as follows:

1 = academe to academe
2 = government to academe
3 = private sector to academe
4 = academe to government
5 = government to government
6 = private sector to government
7 = academe to private sector
8 = government to private sector
9 = private sector to private sector

About half the sample report that they had changed career goals since entering graduate school. Such changes are most common among those currently employed in the private sector (especially if their previous jobs were in academe), followed by those now in government jobs (again, those government workers who were previously faculty members are most likely to report having changed career goals). Overall, only about one in three faculty members reports changing career goals; for those moving from one academic job to another, the figure is one in four. Thus, these findings tend to confirm the notion that most (but not necessarily all) science and engineering Ph.D.'s initially intend to take academic jobs; current employment in a nonacademic job is usually associated with career-goal change. Although not shown in the table, those with degrees in engineering or psychology are generally less likely than are other social scientists or natural scientists to have changed career goals.

With respect to timing, about one-third changed career goals from three to nine years after completing graduate study (with the proportions highest among former academics), about one-fourth changed career goals within three years of graduate-school completion; approximately equal proportions (about one in six) changed goals either during graduate school or at least ten years after receiving the doctorate; and under one in ten changed career goals while in graduate school. Most likely to have changed goals while in graduate school are those now employed in academe. The implication is that many people enter graduate school more or less tentatively, uncertain of what they want to do, and then during graduate study make the commitment to be faculty members. Most likely to have changed goals during graduate school are private-sector employees who previously held government jobs. Late decisions (that is, those made ten years or more after graduate-school completion) are most typical of those moving from the private sector to government, those moving from government to the private sector, and those changing jobs within the private sector.

The Sequence of Change

Do people first change their career goals and then seek out new jobs in accordance with the new goals? Do they take the jobs and then redefine their career goals to accommodate to their changed circumstances? Or do the two types of change occur more or less simultaneously? To answer these questions, we compared the time of the most-recent goal change with the time of the most-recent job change. Overall, the first and the third sequence are about equally common (48 percent and 46 percent, respectively, of the total sample).

Most likely to report changing goals before changing employers—a sequence that suggests deliberate decision and careful planning—are current faculty members (approximately 58 percent, whatever their previous employer), those making job changes within the private sector (54 percent) or within government (52 percent), and those moving from the private sector to government (52 percent).

Most likely to have changed their goals at about the same time they changed employers are those moving from academe into the private sector (66 percent) or into government (58 percent) and those moving from government to the private sector (57 percent). This sequence has three possible interpretations. First, these people may have changed their career goals and then been lucky in finding the kinds of jobs they wanted almost immediately. Second, these people may have had a job change forced on them and thus changed their career goals out of necessity; in such cases, the altered goals may represent a kind of ex post facto rationalization. Third, they may have taken the new jobs and then almost at once discovered that those jobs offered unexpected opportunities and benefits; their new perceptions of the jobs may have caused them to alter career goals.

Rarely did a change of employers substantially precede a goal change: The proportions reporting this sequence are highest among those moving from faculty to government jobs (11 percent) or making intragovernment (9 percent) or intra-private-sector (8 percent) changes. The most-likely interpretation of this sequence is that these people changed jobs (perhaps because they were forced out of their previous ones) while maintaining their earlier goals; then, after learning about their new positions, they decided that they preferred them. Or this group may represent people who are ready to change jobs again because of their altered career goals.

Reasons for Goal Change

Respondents were asked directly which of seven possible reasons influenced their latest change of career goals; they were instructed to mark all reasons that applied. The top-ranked reason for all paths except the intra-academic changers was finding more-attractive or more-challenging job opportunities elsewhere; those who currently work in the private sector are most likely, and those whose current jobs are in academe are least likely, to cite this reason.

Becoming interested in a different area of study is also mentioned frequently, especially by those making intra-academic job changes, those moving from the private sector to academe, and those moving from government jobs to the private sector. On the other hand, current government workers (whatever their previous jobs) and those making job changes within the private sector are less likely than others to cite this reason.

The next-most-important reason—particularly for those moving from academic to nonacademic jobs and for those currently holding government jobs— is that available job opportunities in the previous field were limited or unattractive. Thus, the tight academic-job market seems to have been a factor in goal change. A relatively small proportion of those moving from nonacademic jobs to faculty positions, moving from government jobs, or making changes within the private sector give this reason. In short, limited or unattractive job opportunities are more typical of academe than of the nonacademic sectors.

About one-fifth of the total group cite personal or family reasons as underlying their change in career aspirations. Those currently employed in the private sector are most likely, and those currently employed in government least likely, to check this alternative. It is impossible to say for certain whether this factor should be regarded as predominantly positive or negative. That is, in some cases, "personal and family reasons" may represent intrinsic changes within the individual (for example, a change in values) that pull him or her into a different kind of career; in other cases, they may represent altered circumstances that force the individual into a different career (for example, pressure to take over the family business).

Another one-fifth say simply that they did not enjoy their first-choice career. This reason is most common among those changing academic jobs, those moving from academe into government or the private sector, and those moving from the private sector to academe. It is relatively rare among those changing government jobs, those moving from government to the private sector, and those moving from the private sector to government. It seems, then, that faculty members are somewhat more likely than are the nonacademically employed to become disenchanted with their first-choice careers, suggesting that academic jobs may not turn out to be as attractive as expected.

Perhaps because being fired from a job is not an easy situation to acknowledge, only about one in ten of the total group mentions termination in a previous job as a factor in career-goal change. The proportions giving this reason are highest among those moving from faculty to nonacademic jobs and lowest among those changing jobs within government or within the private sector, those moving from government to the private sector, and those moving from nonacademic jobs to faculty positions. In short, government employees are least likely, and academics most likely, to be fired from their jobs. In the case of faculty members, "termination" can probably be taken to mean that they were not granted tenure in their previous position.

The least-common reason for goal change is becoming outdated in one's first-choice field. The highest proportions citing this reason are 7 percent of those moving from the private sector to government and 6 percent of those changing jobs within the private sector. Obsolescence, then, does not seem to be a potent factor in career-goal change for the scientists and engineers in our sample.

Setting aside the item "personal and family reasons" because of its ambiguity and the item "become outdated" because of its infrequency, we can classify these reasons as either "push" factors (limited or unattractive job opportunities; lack of enjoyment of first-choice career; job termination) or "pull" factors (the discovery of more-challenging and more-attractive opportunities elsewhere; the development of interest in a different field). Viewed in this way, it is clear that "push" factors are most important for former faculty members who move into nonacademic jobs and that "pull" factors operate more frequently among those moving into the private sector from government or changing jobs within the private sector. Those making changes within academe or moving from government to academe are more likely than others to cite the "push" factor of not enjoying their first-choice career and the "pull" factor of becoming interested in a different field; these two factors would seem to be two sides of the same coin. The group who moved from the private sector to government are most likely to be "pushed" by termination of employment and by limited or unattractive job opportunities.

Analysis of Goal Change, by Cohort

The findings so far suggest, first, that changes in career goals are indeed connected with actual job changes and, second, that both types of change are connected with changes in the job market. To learn more about the extent to which goal changes reflect market conditions—or, to put it another way, to assess the market responsiveness of science and engineering Ph.D.'s—we undertook a somewhat different type of analysis based on *cohorts,* defined by the period in which the doctorate was received. Of the total sample, 46 percent had received the doctorate prior to 1965; 32 percent, between 1965 and 1970, the period of a strong academic-labor market; and 22 percent in 1971 or later, at a time when the market was taking a turn for the worse (Cartter 1976). These three groups are referred to as the older, middle, and younger cohorts, respectively. Information about changes in career goals for each of the three cohorts is summarized in table 14-4.

Those in the older and middle cohorts are more likely to have changed their career goals since entering graduate school than are those in the younger cohort. This difference is partly a function of age and of years spent in the labor force; more-recent graduates simply have not had as much time in which to change their minds. In addition, many in the younger cohort probably were aware of and prepared for a tight labor market even before they entered graduate school; that is, they entered graduate school knowing that academic jobs would be scarce, and they set their career goals accordingly. Nonetheless, close to half of those in the younger cohort have changed their career goals since entering graduate school.

If the likelihood of changing career goals were no more than a function of career length, then a higher proportion of the older than of the middle cohort would report such change. But the proportions are almost identical, indicating that other factors—including market forces—influence goal change. Indeed, when we consider that 46 percent of the younger cohort (none of whom could

Table 14–4
Summary of Information on Changes in Career Goals, by Cohort
(percent)

	Older Cohort	Middle Cohort	Younger Cohort
Changed career goals since entering graduate school	57	58	46
Timing of career-goal change:			
While in graduate school	6	11	30
At completion of graduate study	5	9	15
Within three years after completing graduate study	19	28	41
From three to nine years after completing graduate study	35	51	14
Ten or more years after completing graduate study	36	1	0
Factors influencing career-goal change:			
Available job opportunities in previous field were limited or unattractive	26	44	51
Decided I did not enjoy first-choice career	15	22	24
Found more attractive or challenging job opportunities elsewhere	65	59	52
Changed career aspirations for personal or family reasons	23	20	23
Became outdated in my first-choice field	6	4	3
Became interested in different area of study	31	26	25
Was terminated in a job	7	13	6

Note: "Older" cohort received doctorate prior to 1965; "middle" cohort received doctorate between 1965 and 1970; "younger" cohort received doctorate after 1970.

have received the doctorate more than eight years earlier) report career-goal changes since entering graduate school, it becomes clear that the incidence of goal change is relatively high for this group.

With respect to the timing of the most-recent goal change, one would expect that, if change depended exclusively on age and career length, then the distribution of responses across the various alternatives shown in the table would be the same for each cohort (except, of course, that none of the respondents in the younger group, and fewer in the middle than in the older cohort, would report changing career goals ten or more years after completing graduate study). If, on the other hand, people change career goals in response to changing market conditions, then one would expect a higher proportion of changes to be made during periods of drastic change in the market. The latter is indeed the case. Most frequently, those in the older cohort report changing goals either ten or more years after graduate-school completion (36 percent) or three to nine years after (35 percent). Those in the middle cohort are most likely to have changed goals from three to nine years after receiving the doctorate (51 percent) or within three years of graduate school completion (28 percent). The younger cohort tends to have changed goals either within three years after the doctorate (41 percent) or while still in graduate school (30 percent). In short, whatever the cohort, the majority of career-goal changes took place in the early and middle 1970s, when academic jobs were becoming scarce and the market for highly trained manpower generally was tightening up.

For all three cohorts, the top-ranked factor in goal change was finding more-challenging and more-attractive job opportunities elsewhere; proportionately more of the older cohort, and proportionately fewer of the younger, cited this reason. Among those in the older cohort, the second-ranked reason was the other "pull" factor: becoming interested in a different area of study. About three in ten of the goal-changers in the older cohort, compared with about one in four of those in the two other cohorts, mention this reason. In contrast, close to half the goal changers in the younger cohort (who had received their doctorates during the period of a tight labor market) say that available job opportunities in their previous field were limited or unattractive; goal changers in the middle cohort were also affected by this factor, to a much greater extent than those in the older cohort, only one-quarter of whom mention this reason. Goal changers in the middle and younger cohorts are about equally likely to say that they decided they did not enjoy their first-choice career, but this factor was relatively unimportant among those in the older cohort. In short, the more-recent doctorate recipients seem to have been more subject to "pushing" influences, and the older cohort to "pulling" influences, probably because the latter felt secure in the first-choice field and changed goals only when they were attracted into other areas. Younger Ph.D.'s may not have had time to become settled in their careers or to develop the professional contacts that might lead them into new and challenging areas.

Approximately equal proportions of each cohort say that they changed their career aspirations for personal or family reasons. Very few cite becoming outmoded in their first-choice field, although this reason is more common among people in the older cohort (6 percent) than among those in the middle or younger cohorts (4 percent and 3 percent, respectively).

Finally, being terminated in a job—the most obvious "push" factor—is mentioned almost twice as frequently by goal changers in the middle cohort as by those in the other two cohorts. The people who had received their doctorates during the academic-boom period may have had the highest expectations. Of those in the total group who were faculty members, members of the older cohort would have achieved tenure already and members of the younger cohort probably had not reached the point of being considered for tenure. Those in the middle cohort, however, would probably have come up for tenure; and "termination" may represent the denial of tenure, with a subsequent change in career goals.

In summary, this analysis by cohort suggests strongly that science and engineering Ph.D.'s change their goals not only because of the passage of time and the development of new interests, but also in response to market pressures and the actual employment situation.

Push and Pull: Seeking a Job

As the preceding section indicated, both "push" and "pull" factors operate to influence goal change. The next steps in our consideration of mobility among science and engineering Ph.D.'s were to examine more closely the relative importance of these factors in influencing actual job change, to determine the frequency with which various kinds of jobs are sought (and with what degree of success), and to identify effective job-search methods.

To what extent do these highly trained people change jobs because they are forced to, and to what extent because they are attracted to new jobs? How much initiative do they take in finding a new job? The HERI questionnaire included two items designed to provide answers to these and similar questions. One of them asked respondents to indicate whether they could have stayed on at their previous jobs if they had so desired; the second asked whether they had been actively seeking a job change while on their previous jobs or whether they had received an unsolicited offer. Table 14–5 indicates their responses, by path. (The reader is reminded that nonfaculty academics are excluded from these analyses.)

More job changes were voluntary. Overall, only about one-quarter of the respondents say that they could not have stayed on in their previous jobs. The government sector seems to offer the most security; fewer than one in five of those whose previous jobs were in government (columns 2, 5, and 8) could not have stayed on in those jobs. Academe offers the least security, with almost one-third from that sector (columns 1, 4, and 7) indicating that they were forced to leave their jobs. The proportion was highest (36 percent) among those making intra-academic changes; apparently many faculty members who are not granted tenure by their institutions move on to other colleges and universities. It should be noted that 30 percent of those moving from the private sector to government, but only 17 percent of those moving from the private sector to academe, say that they had to leave their previous jobs; the implication is that academe receives the more-desirable private-sector employees, whereas government receives the less desirable.

Although not shown in the table, there were some differences by field on this item. Economists and engineers are most likely—and political scientists, anthropologists, sociologists, and mathematicians least likely—to indicate that they could have stayed on in their previous jobs. These differences are consistent with the latest data on field differences in job openings for Ph.D.'s.

In addition, the three cohorts differed. Close to three-quarters of the older

Table 14–5
Push and Pull Factors in Job Change, by Path
(percent)

	Academe			Government			Private Sector		
	1	*2*	*3*	*4*	*5*	*6*	*7*	*8*	*9*
Could not have stayed at previous job	36	17	17	28	19	30	31	18	24
Was actively seeking a job while on previous job	48	45	46	39	33	39	41	25	31
Was actively seeking a job but could have stayed at previous job	47	64	73	47	73	64	51	86	71
Received an unsolicited offer	16	20	24	25	24	21	20	19	22

Note: The paths were as follows:

1 = academe to academe
2 = government to academe
3 = private sector to academe
4 = academe to government
5 = government to government
6 = private sector to government
7 = academe to private sector
8 = government to private sector
9 = private sector to private sector

cohort (pre-1965 doctorates) and the younger (post-1970 doctorates), say that they could have stayed on in their previous jobs. As was pointed out earlier in connection with goal change, members of the older cohort are most likely to have achieved tenure (or seniority) in their positions; these cohort differences probably reflect this fact.

As the second row of table 14–5 indicates, faculty members—especially those making intra-academic changes—are most apt to say that they had been actively seeking a new job while still in their previous (academic) jobs (columns 1, 4, and 7). The probable explanation here is that these faculty members anticipated that they would not be granted tenure at their institutions and so were on the lookout for jobs either at other colleges and universities or in the nonacademic sectors. This interpretation is supported by the figures in the next row of the table; relatively few of the "active seekers" in academe say that they could have stayed on at the previous job. By contrast, of the relatively large proportions of active job seekers who moved into academe from government or from the private sector (columns 2 and 3), very few indicate that they could not have stayed on at their previous jobs. Actively seeking a job while at the previous job was less common among those changing jobs within the government or within the private sector (columns 5 and 9) and among those moving from government to the private sector (column 8); moreover, a high proportion of these people could have stayed on at their previous jobs, suggesting that their search for another job was internally motivated. By field, the most likely to initiate a job search while still holding their previous jobs were mathematicians and political scientists (except for those whose previous jobs were in government); least likely were sociologists, electrical and mechanical engineers, and economists. Such a job search was voluntary in the case of large proportions of economists and engineers; on the other hand, the awareness that they could not stay on at their previous jobs was the motivating factor among many of those physicists, mathematicians, and biologists who actively sought jobs while still in their previous positions. Finally, about one-third of the middle and younger cohorts, but only one-quarter of the older cohort, say that they were actively seeking a job while at their previous jobs.

On the other hand, members of the older cohort are much more likely to have received unsolicited job offers (25 percent) than are members of either the middle (16 percent) or the younger cohort (11 percent). These differences make sense in that those who have been working longer are more likely to have established reputations and a wide network of professional contacts. As the last row of table 14–5 shows, there were only slight differences by path on this point, except that those making job changes within the academic sector are markedly less likely than others to report having received an unsolicited job offer.

By field, relatively large proportions of engineers, physicists, and economists—but relatively few mathematicians and anthropologists—were directly wooed by other employers. It would seem that the government sector seeks to recruit biologists and electrical engineers but has little interest in chemists, mathematicians, and political scientists; private-sector employers are most likely to make unsolicited offers to mechanical engineers and political scientists, but not to mathematicians, anthropologists, and biologists.

What Kinds of Jobs Are Sought?

So far, we have considered some of the conditions of job change: the extent to which such change is voluntary, the degree of personal initiative involved, and the amount of direct "pull" that is manifested through unsolicited job offers. But exactly what kinds of jobs do science and engineering Ph.D.'s seek, and how successful are they? The HERI questionnaire included one item that read, "When you were offered your current position, were you actively seeking employment in the following areas?" Ten employment settings were listed. The response alternatives included, "Sought position and received offer" and "sought position but no offer." Table 14–6 presents the results by path.

Overall, the most-sought-after jobs were in the following employment settings: universities (mentioned by roughly two in five of the total group), the

Table 14–6
Type of Job Sought, and Success Rates, by Path
(percent)

	Academe			Government			Private Sector		
Employer Type	*1*	*2*	*3*	*4*	*5*	*6*	*7*	*8*	*9*
University:									
Successful	61	56	60	14	6	6	15	3	6
Not successful	17	9	11	28	14	20	31	10	10
Four-year college:									
Successful	23	14	19	4	2	2	5	0	1
Not successful	14	10	7	17	8	9	21	6	4
Two-year college:									
Successful	3	3	3	0	0	1	2	0	1
Not successful	5	3	6	5	3	4	8	4	2
Elementary or secondary school:									
Successful	0	0	0	0	0	1	2	1	1
Not successful	1	2	0	1	1	1	2	2	0
Federally funded R&D center:									
Successful	1	1	0	7	2	3	2	4	0
Not successful	6	9	5	9	8	8	15	6	3
Federal government:									
Successful	2	1	1	52	62	68	5	4	6
Not successful	8	9	9	6	4	4	17	15	7
State or local government:									
Successful	1	1	1	5	5	4	3	6	1
Not successful	3	3	2	5	4	6	6	3	3
Other nonprofit organization:									
Successful	1	1	2	4	2	5	14	18	7
Not successful	6	5	6	7	7	13	9	4	4
Private business or industry:									
Successful	2	3	7	6	7	11	44	45	46
Not successful	7	4	10	13	11	22	11	5	6
Employment abroad:									
Successful	1	1	0	1	1	1	1	1	1
Not successful	3	3	4	4	3	5	4	1	3

Note: The paths were as follows:
1 = academe to academe
2 = government to academe
3 = private sector to academe
4 = academe to government
5 = government to government
6 = private sector to government
7 = academe to private sector
8 = government to private sector
9 = private sector to private sector

federal government (about three in ten), private business and industry (slightly less than three in ten), four-year colleges (slightly less than one in five), other nonprofit organizations (about one in eight), and federal research-and-development centers (about one in ten). Very small proportions say that they sought jobs in state or local government, in two-year colleges, in elementary or secondary schools, or abroad. Of course, this result is due in part to the appropriateness of various employment settings for doctorate holders and in part to some of the biases involved in drawing up the rosters, which resulted in differential coverage of different fields and employer types (see chapter 10).

Those whose previous jobs were in academe are more likely than those from government and the private sector to seek academic jobs (universities, four-year colleges, two-year colleges) as well as jobs in federally funded research and development centers. Those whose previous jobs were in the private sector are more likely than others to look for jobs in business and industry. Approximately equal proportions from academe, government, and the private sector sought jobs with the federal government, other nonprofit organizations, state and local governments, and elementary and secondary schools; or looked for employment abroad.

Obviously, success rates are closely connected with the employment sector of the current job; that is, those currently working in academe are more likely than those currently working in the nonacademic sectors to report that their search for a job in a university, four-year college, or two-year college was successful in that they received an offer. The same holds true for those currently holding government jobs who say that they had sought employment with the federal government, in federally funded research laboratories, or in state and local governments; and for those now in the private sector who had looked for jobs in business and industry, other nonprofit organizations, and elementary or secondary schools (which, it will be recalled, are included in the private sector). The correspondence was not perfect; the person who received an offer from a particular employer did not necessarily accept that offer. Nonetheless, because of this close relationship, the discussion of success rates will emphasize the employment sector of the *previous* job.

Generally, those seeking jobs in private business and industry stand the best chance of receiving an offer. Of those currently employed in the private sector who say that they looked for such jobs, about nine in ten of those whose previous jobs were in government or the private sector, and about four in five former faculty members, report success.

Success rates are also fairly high among those seeking jobs with the federal government (especially if they were previously employed in the private sector) and in universities (especially if they moved to academe from government or the private sector.) Of those making intra-academic job changes, 78 percent say they sought jobs in universities; and 61 percent say they received a job offer. Apparently, the 17 percent who were not offered the sought-after university job are currently teaching in other types of institutions. Only about one-third of the people seeking jobs in four-year colleges are offered such jobs. The chances of receiving an offer are highest for former private-sector employees, followed by former faculty; but they are relatively low for former government workers.

State or local governments and nonprofit organizations offered jobs to about two in five of those who sought them. In the case of state and local governments, those who already held government jobs are much more likely to report success than are those whose previous jobs were in the private sector or academe. Curiously, about two-thirds of those moving from government to the private sector who sought state- or local-government jobs received job offers; since they ended up in the private sector, we can conclude that they decided to reject those offers. In the case of state and local governments, the sector of previous employment seems to have made little difference to the success rate.

Very few in the sample report seeking jobs in two-year colleges or in elementary and secondary schools; in both cases, however, those from the private sector have the highest success rates. Of the small number in our sample who wanted employment abroad, former government employees had a slight edge over those from academe and the private sector. Finally, relatively few of those looking for jobs in federally funded research-and-development centers report success. Least likely to be offered such jobs are those from the private sector, whereas former faculty members and government workers have about the same degree of success.

In summary, those whose previous jobs were in the private sector generally have a competitive advantage, especially when it comes to getting job offers from two-year and four-year colleges, elementary and secondary schools, and the federal government. Those coming from government are, overall, somewhat more successful than academics, being especially likely to receive job offers from universities, state and local governments, other nonprofit organizations, and business and industry. They were also the most successful in seeking employment abroad.

Although not shown in the table, members of the older cohort (those who had received the doctorate before 1965) were more likely than were those in the other two cohorts to receive job offers from the sought-after employer, especially when that employer was a university or four-year college, the federal government, private business and industry, or a federally funded research-and-development center. None of the small number in the older cohort who sought jobs in two-year colleges were successful, however, reflecting the resistance of these institutions to "traditional" academics. Those in the middle cohort had relatively high success rates when they applied for jobs in nonprofit organizations, state and local governments, and four-year colleges, but relatively low success rates with respect to jobs in universities and federally funded R&D centers. Members of the younger cohort were as successful as those in the older cohort with respect to university jobs (about two in five of those who sought such jobs received offers) and about as successful as those in the middle cohort with respect to two-year-college jobs (about one-fifth of those seeking such jobs got offers). However, they were at a disadvantage in seeking jobs in four-year colleges, the federal government, and state and local governments. In addition, they seldom succeeded in getting employment abroad.

The HERI questionnaire also inquired about the frequency and the degree of success with which jobs involving various work activities were sought. Slightly under half of the total group say they looked for R&D jobs; of these, about four in five received offers. Teaching jobs are the next most sought after—by about one in four of the total group—but fewer than half of those looking for such jobs report success. Administration is the third-most-popular choice, actively sought by about one in seven of the total group; about three in five of these active seekers report success. Although relatively few say they had wanted jobs involving such nontraditional work activities as sales, marketing, advertising, and public relations, success rates are fairly high for this group of activities; about two in three who had looked for such jobs got job offers. Similarly, slightly over three in five of the very few people who sought jobs involving accounting and data processing were successful. Finally, slightly over one-tenth of the total group say that they had looked for jobs involving activities other than those mentioned here; about four in five of them received offers, making this the most-promising choice. These findings indicate that science and engineering Ph.D.'s would be well advised to go after R&D jobs or jobs involving nontraditional activities when they look for employment in government and the private sector.

Successful Job-Search Methods

Although the discussion of the types of jobs sought and of the success rates can serve as a guide for recent science and engineering Ph.D.'s, giving them a general idea of what kinds of jobs to look for in what employment settings, it does not tell them what methods to use in their job search. Communications between buyer and seller in the market for highly qualified manpower are poor, to say the least. Just how did the doctorate holders in the sample go about getting their current jobs? What particular resources proved most valuable to them? One item on the HERI questionnaire asked respondents to indicate which of eighteen possible job-search methods or contacts they had used in securing their current jobs, and which had proved successful. (Respondents were instructed to mark all that applied.) Table 14–7 shows the proportions in each path reporting that a particular method or contact helped them.

Overall, the most-successful methods/contacts seem to be direct personal application to the employer and professional contacts (each mentioned by about three-tenths of the total group). Colleagues at one's own institution or organization and colleagues at other institutions are also important resources (each mentioned by about one-fifth of the total group). Another one-fifth say that they

Table 14–7
Successful Job-Search Methods, by Path
(percent)

Job-Search Method	Academe			Government			Private Sector		
	1	*2*	*3*	*4*	*5*	*6*	*7*	*8*	*9*
Former professors	32	30	20	18	9	6	11	5	5
Colleagues at my organization/institution	24	23	15	15	23	15	16	16	16
Colleagues in other institutions	31	25	25	18	15	16	17	18	11
College/university placement offices	4	3	2	2	1	1	4	2	1
Public/state employment services	0	0	0	0	1	1	0	0	0
Private employment agency	0	0	0	1	1	1	2	3	7
Civil-service application	1	1	0	36	34	41	1	2	3
Recruiting teams from government, industry	0	0	0	4	4	5	5	1	3
Professional contacts	26	28	24	32	28	27	36	27	25
Direct personal application to employer	36	26	35	25	27	27	36	27	25
Professional organizations, meetings	12	8	7	9	3	6	8	3	4
Newspaper advertisements	2	1	4	1	1	2	7	4	5
Professional journals, periodicals	24	22	24	5	2	5	6	4	5
Met new employer through previous job	5	11	4	14	16	12	11	9	13
Unsolicited offer	19	22	17	24	24	17	23	18	24
Parents/other relatives	1	0	1	0	1	1	3	2	2
Friends	6	4	11	10	9	13	12	13	13
Luck/chance	14	11	11	12	10	11	14	10	10

Note: The paths were as follows:

1 = academe to academe
2 = government to academe
3 = private sector to academe
4 = academe to government
5 = government to government
6 = private sector to government
7 = academe to private sector
8 = government to private sector
9 = private sector to private sector

received an unsolicited offer, but this "method" is not one that can be deliberately used or applied; similarly, about one-tenth attribute their success in getting their current jobs to luck or chance, elements beyond the control of job-seekers.

Very few people in the sample report successful use of such formal job-finding services as college placement offices (used mostly by new entrants to the labor market), public or state employment agencies, and private employment agencies. The highest proportion is the 7 percent of those making job changes within the private sector who say that private employment agencies proved useful to them. Few people, likewise, mention recruiting teams from government and industry (again, used mostly by new entrants); newspaper advertisements; or parents or relatives. Professional organizations and meetings are of most value to faculty members changing jobs within academe; very few respondents from the other paths cite them.

To some extent, successful job-search methods/contacts vary according to the employment sector of the current job. Thus, those now in academe—and especially those moving from other academic jobs or from government jobs— and those now in government who were previously faculty members are most likely to indicate that former professors had helped them to get their current jobs. Faculty members are also much more likely than those now working in government or the private sector to mention colleagues at other institutions. Moreover, close to one-quarter, in contrast to about 5 percent of government and private-sector workers, cite professional journals and periodicals as being of value to them in their search for academic jobs.

People currently employed in government, are, logically enough, the only group to indicate that civil-service application was an important job-search method. In addition, relatively large proportions say that they met their new employers through their previous jobs.

This method was also mentioned by about 11 percent of current private-sector employees. Otherwise, this group is best distinguished from those now in academe and government by the tendency to cite friends as a valuable contact in their job search. Those moving *from* the private sector to academe or government are also inclined to mention friends. Very rarely are former professors cited as a useful contact by those now employed in the private sector.

Summary

What conclusions can be drawn from this discussion of the actual job search? The most obvious is that job seekers should not limit their range of alternatives. There are many markets for highly trained manpower and many nonacademic jobs that can be sought successfully. Moreover, conventional job-search methods (for example, civil-service applications, newspaper advertisements, employment agencies) can work in securing entry-level positions in government and the private sector, although the best opportunities still come through informal networks. Job seekers should keep their eyes and ears open and, most important, should be willing to entertain a variety of possibilities.

Outcomes of Job Change

Presumably, when people change jobs—especially when they do so voluntarily— they hope to benefit in some way from the change. In a constricted job market, however, they may have to give up one benefit in order to gain another. Exactly what kinds of tradeoffs characterize different types of job change? In this section, we will look at two general categories of outcomes: monetary and affective. More specifically, the outcomes under examination are changes in income (both salary and nonsalary) and changes in satisfaction that result from job change.

Changes in Income

The HERI questionnaire included one item that asked respondents to indicate the extent to which the starting salary of their current jobs differed from the salaries they would have received had they stayed in their previous jobs. A second item asked about the effects of job change on other (nonsalary) income. Table 14–8 shows the proportions in each path indicating various changes in income as a result of job change.

Approximately two in five of the sample considered here (again, nonfaculty academics are excluded from the analysis) say that their salaries had increased by more than 10 percent (a figure selected because it represents a real increase in purchasing power, or did before the recent years of double-digit inflation) when they switched from their previous jobs. The proportions reporting such increases are highest among those moving out of academe into government (68 percent) or into the private sector (66 percent) and lowest among those moving

Table 14–8
Changes in Salary and Other Income as a Result of Job Change, by Path

	Academe			Government			Private Sector		
	1	2	3	4	5	6	7	8	9
Percentage whose salary increased (by more than 10 percent)	39	28	23	68	33	30	66	44	46
Percentage whose salary decreased	20	34	46	10	10	24	16	27	18
Percentage whose other (nonsalary) income increased	41	55	43	39	30	29	32	50	40
Percentage whose other (nonsalary) income decreased	15	16	22	14	10	15	24	12	10

Note: The paths were as follows:
1 = academe to academe
2 = government to academe
3 = private sector to academe
4 = academe to government
5 = government to government
6 = private sector to government
7 = academe to private sector
8 = government to private sector
9 = private sector to private sector

into academe from government (28 percent) or from the private sector (23 percent). These findings merely confirm what has been obvious from other analyses. Whatever the benefits of being a college professor, a high salary is not usually one of them. Nonetheless, those faculty members changing jobs within academe had some advantage, in terms of salary increases, over those making intragovernment changes or moving from the private sector into government. Finally, those changing jobs within the private sector, or moving from government to the private sector, are somewhat more likely than average to report that their salaries rose by at least 11 percent.

About one-fifth of the sample indicate that they suffered a drop in salary when they changed jobs. Logically, the pattern is almost the reverse of the pattern for salary increases. Thus, relatively large proportions of those moving into academe from the private sector (46 percent) or from government (34 percent) report a decrease in salary. The proportions reporting salary drops are also fairly high among those moving from government to the private sector (27 percent) and from the private sector to government (24 percent). Least likely to experience salary declines are those changing jobs within the government sector (10 percent), moving from academe to government (10 percent), and moving from academe to the private sector (16 percent). One conclusion to be drawn from this analysis of salary increases and decreases is that the promise of higher salaries is often used to attract doctorate-level scientists and engineers into nonacademic jobs.

The overall proportion reporting increases in other (nonsalary) income is about the same as the proportion reporting salary increases: roughly 40 percent. About 15 percent say that their other income declined when they changed jobs. In this case, government workers are clearly at a disadvantage compared with private-sector employees, and even more so compared with faculty. Thus, 55 percent of those moving from government to academe, and 50 percent of those moving from government to the private sector, say that their outside income increased, compared with only about 30 percent of those making intragovernment changes or leaving the private sector to take government jobs. The most-obvious explanation for these differences is that faculty members are in the best position to get outside consulting jobs (which probably account for most of the nonsalary income); private-sector employees are slightly less so; and government workers are in most cases prohibited from earning outside income through consulting.

Although not shown in the table, there were some differences by field with respect to income changes resulting from job change. The highlights are as follows.

Biologists are somewhat less likely than average to report decreases in salary or increases in nonsalary income. Biologists moving from the private sector into college and university jobs are somewhat more likely than those from most other fields to experience salary increases and markedly less likely to experience salary decreases. Those moving from academe into the private sector are less likely than average to report increases in either salary or nonsalary income and are more likely to report decreases in nonsalary income.

Chemists usually benefit monetarily when they change jobs. For instance, four in five of those moving from academe to the private sector, and over three in five of those moving from government to the private sector, report salary increases of at least 11 percent. On the other hand, moves from the private sector to academe frequently result in income decreases.

Physicists are generally less likely than others to report decreases in nonsalary income as a result of job change. Those moving into academe from the private sector or making intra-academic changes are most likely to benefit in terms of salary. In addition, over three in four of the physicists who left faculty positions to take jobs in the private sector report salary increases of more than 10 percent.

Only about one-third of the *mathematicians* in the sample report increases in either salary or nonsalary income as a result of job change. Job changes within the private sector tend to be most lucrative in terms of increased salaries, but mathematicians making intra-academic changes or moving from academe to the private sector are less likely than average to benefit in terms of income.

Civil engineers are somewhat more likely than average to report that their nonsalary incomes dropped as a result of job change. Exceptions are those making intra-academic or intragovernment job changes, about half of whom report increases in nonsalary income. In addition, three-quarters of those leaving academe for the private sector experience salary increases. On the other hand, those moving from the private sector to academe are more likely than average to report declines in nonsalary income and are less likely to report salary increases.

The overall pattern for *electrical engineers* resembles the norm for the total sample. About half of those changing jobs within academe report salary increases. Of those moving from the private sector to academe, a relatively high proportion report increases in other income; but decreases in salary are also fairly common.

Mechanical engineers are somewhat less likely than average to report declines in salary as a result of job change. Four in five of those moving from academe to government, three in five of those making changes within the private sector, and 55 percent of those making intra-academic changes report salary increases of at least 11 percent.

The favorable job market for *economists* is reflected in their general tendency to command salary increases when they change jobs. For instance, over nine in ten of those making job changes within the private sector or moving from academe to government, and four in five of those moving from academe to the private sector, report salary increases of at least 11 percent. Those making intra-academic changes or moving from the private sector to government are more likely than average to report increases in nonsalary income.

The overall pattern for *political scientists* is not especially distinctive. Those changing jobs within the government are more likely than average to increase their salaries. Unusually large proportions of those leaving faculty jobs to work in government or the private sector report increases in nonsalary income.

Anthropologists are somewhat more likely than average to report increases in both salary and nonsalary income and somewhat less likely to report declines in salary as a result of job change. Over two-fifths of those leaving the private sector to become faculty members experience increases in salary. Conversely, about two-fifths of those leaving academe to take jobs in the private sector take cuts in salary, although this path often leads to an increase in income from other sources.

Psychologists tend to benefit financially when they take jobs in the private sector (whatever their previous job) in that their nonsalary income increases. Moves from government to academe are unfavorable in that a relatively large proportion report decreases in salary.

Over three in four of the *sociologists* leaving academe to take government jobs report salary increases of at least 11 percent. On the other hand, moves within the government or from academe to the private sector tend to have unfavorable effects on both salary and nonsalary income.

So far, the discussion has centered on actual increases and decreases in salary and nonsalary income. But what of respondents' perceptions of changes in their incomes? Because the HERI questionnaire item on degree of satisfaction with various job aspects covered the previous job as well as the current job, it was possible to assess changes in satisfaction. Table 14–9 shows the proportions, by broad disciplinary area and by path, who indicate that their satisfaction with salary had increased as a result of job change.

Overall, slightly more than half of the sample considered here (with non-faculty academics again excluded) say that their satisfaction with salary increased. Most likely to be more satisfied are those moving out of academe into

Table 14–9

Increases in Satisfaction with Salary as a Result of Job Change, by Broad Disciplinary Group and Path

(percent)

Broad Disciplinary Group	Academe			Government			Private Sector		
	1	2	3	4	5	6	7	8	9
Natural sciences	46	37	30	77	61	61	66	47	55
Engineering	50	36	32	59	61	55	76	59	59
Social sciences	49	39	40	80	61	58	67	59	60
Total	48	38	36	77	61	60	68	57	58

Note: The paths were as follows:

1 = academe to academe
2 = government to academe
3 = private sector to academe
4 = academe to government
5 = government to government
6 = private sector to government
7 = academe to private sector
8 = government to private sector
9 = private sector to private sector

government (77 percent) or the private sector (68 percent), those making intra-government changes (61 percent), and those moving into government from the private sector (60 percent). Least likely to indicate increased satisfaction are those moving into academe from the private sector (36 percent) and from government (38 percent) and those making intra-academic changes (48 percent).

There are slight differences by broad disciplinary area. Thus, social scientists currently employed in academe (particularly those coming from the private sector) are more likely than are engineers or natural scientists to say that their satisfaction with salary increased; and engineers currently employed in government are less likely than others to indicate increased satisfaction, whereas engineers employed in the private sector, especially those coming from academe, are more likely than others to report increased satisfaction with salary.

What is somewhat surprising in this table is that those doctorate-level scientists and engineers currently working in government more often register increased satisfaction with salary than do those currently working in the private sector, even though the proportions whose salaries actually increased by at least 11 percent are higher among current private-sector employees than among current government employees (table 14–9). Whatever the explanation for this discrepancy, one point emerges clearly: The rewards of being a faculty member are not monetary, whether one considers actual salary or satisfaction with salary.

Changes in Satisfaction

Does being a faculty member confer nonmonetary benefits unavailable to those highly trained people working in nonacademic jobs? What kinds of rewards do the three sectors provide? What kinds of sacrifices or disadvantages do they entail? To answer these questions, we noted increases in overall job satisfaction between the previous and the current job, as well as increases in satisfaction with challenge, with opportunities for creativity, with congenial work relationships, and with status—the four components found to be most closely related to overall job satisfaction (see chapter 13). Table 14–10 reports the findings by path.

Generally speaking, the majority of the sample register increased satisfaction with various aspects of their new jobs; perhaps this tendency reflects a human desire to see one's present situation as better than one's past situation. For each of the five aspects considered, over half the respondents indicate greater satisfaction on the current job than on the previous job. Indeed, almost two-thirds indicate that they are, overall, more satisfied with their current than with their previous jobs. Those now working in the private sector—whatever their previous employer—and the relatively small group moving from government to academe are most likely to experience increases in overall job satisfaction, whereas those now working in government are least likely to do so.

Increased satisfaction with challenge, with congenial work relationships,

Table 14–10
Increases in Job Satisfaction as a Result of Job Change, by Path
(percent)

	Academe			Government			Private Sector		
	1	*2*	*3*	*4*	*5*	*6*	*7*	*8*	*9*
Overall	64	70	64	59	62	59	70	71	71
Challenge	57	66	57	53	59	52	66	73	72
Opportunities for creativity	57	67	66	44	52	49	58	62	60
Congenial work relationships	61	59	53	54	55	54	62	66	62
Status	55	57	53	52	55	51	60	65	61

Note: The paths were as follows:

1 = academe to academe
2 = government to academe
3 = private sector to academe
4 = academe to government
5 = government to government
6 = private sector to government
7 = academe to private sector
8 = government to private sector
9 = private sector to private sector

and with status follow the same general pattern, except that intragovernmental job changes more frequently result in greater satisfaction than do moves into government from academe or the private sector. The pattern with respect to satisfaction with opportunities for creativity is somewhat different, in that those who become faculty members after working in government or the private sector are more likely than any other group of job changers to feel more satisfied. About two-thirds report such increases in satisfaction, compared with 57 percent of those changing jobs within academe.

In summary, although more likely to offer opportunities for creativity than the other two sectors, academe does not seem to be as desirable an employment setting as new Ph.D.'s may suppose. Private-sector jobs are more likely to be satisfying to doctorate-level scientists and engineers, especially in terms of their challenge and status. Government jobs seem to offer fewer rewards, primarily because they are less challenging and allow less scope for creativity than jobs in the other two sectors; when it comes to status and congenial work relationships, they are about as satisfying as faculty jobs.

Doctorate holders in different fields vary in their tendency to report increased satisfaction as a result of job change. The distinctive patterns for each field can be summarized as follows.

Among *biologists,* job changes are more likely to result in increased satisfaction with status than is the case for Ph.D.'s from most other fields. Moves from the private sector to academe are especially likely to result in greater overall satisfaction and greater satisfaction with all four of the relevant components. Intra-academic changes also lead to increased overall satisfaction and satisfaction with congenial work relationships. Job changes within the private sector, however, are less likely than average to produce greater satisfaction.

Generally, the patterns for *chemists* with respect to changes in satisfaction resulting from job change resemble the norm. Chemists are especially likely to report increased satisfaction overall, as well as with opportunities for creativity and congenial work relationships, when they move from the private sector to academe. Comparatively small proportions report improvements when they move from academe or government to the private sector.

Physicists are least likely of any group to say that their satisfaction with challenge increased as a result of job changes; they are also less likely than average to report greater satisfaction with opportunities for creativity. Moves from the private sector to academe tend to result in increased satisfaction with challenge, congenial work relationships, and status, but not with opportunities for creativity. Over four in five physicists moving from academe to the private sector say that their overall job satisfaction increased. Moves from government to academe or to the private sector are relatively unlikely to have positive effects on satisfaction.

Among *mathematicians,* job change is less likely than average to result in greater satisfaction with status, opportunities for creativity, and congenial work relationships. The most-favorable kind of job change involves moves from the private sector to government, and the least favorable are moves from academe to the private sector. In addition, relatively few mathematicians making intra-academic changes report increased overall satisfaction or increased satisfaction with challenge; and only 11 percent of those moving from the private sector to academe say that their satisfaction with status increased.

Generally, *civil engineers* are less likely than average to find new jobs more satisfying than their old jobs. Overall job satisfaction is most likely to increase among those making intra-academic changes, moving from the private sector, or moving from academe to the private sector. Only one-fifth of those moving from the private sector to government report increased overall satisfaction, although a relatively large proportion took greater satisfaction from work relationships.

Electrical engineers tend more than most others to say that their satisfaction with challenge and with status increased as a result of job change, but they are relatively unlikely to report improvements in work relationships. The most-favorable kind of change is a move from academe to the private sector; the most unfavorable, a move from academe to government.

Mechanical engineers are less likely than average to report greater satisfaction with status in their current jobs. The most-favorable kinds of job change are moves from academe into the nonacademic sectors. Those making changes within the private sector are also very likely to indicate that their satisfaction with challenge and creativity improved but are unlikely to register greater satisfaction with status. Intra-academic changes and moves from the private sector to academe also tend to be unfavorable in terms of increased satisfaction.

Economists are distinguished by their marked tendency to report increased overall satisfaction and satisfaction with the four relevant job components as a result of job change. The most-positive effects are associated with job changes within the private sector, from the private sector or government into academe, from the private sector to government, and from government to the private sector. Indeed, the single exception to the general pattern is that only two in five of those moving from academe to government express greater satisfaction with status.

Political scientists are more likely than most other groups to report increased overall job satisfaction but are less likely to find work relationships more congenial at their current jobs. Relatively few of those moving from the private sector to academe, from academe to government, or from one government job to another report increased satisfaction with challenge. The most satisfying kinds of job change are those within each of the three sectors (with the single exception just noted) and moves from the private sector to academe or government.

Among *anthropologists*, job change is associated with increased satisfaction with work relationships and status. A relatively large proportion of those moving from the private sector to academe, but a small proportion of those moving from academe to the private sector, report increased overall satisfaction. Satisfaction with opportunities for creativity tends to increase among those making intra-governmental changes or moving from academe to the nonacademic sectors.

Psychologists are perhaps the most-typical group in their patterns of increased satisfaction. Those who take faculty jobs after working in the private sector are relatively unlikely to report increases in overall satisfaction or in satisfaction with challenge, whereas those moving from government to the private sector are very likely to feel that work relationships are more congenial in their current jobs.

Sociologists are generally less likely than others to indicate that their satisfaction with opportunities for creativity increased as a result of job change. Those moving from academe to government are more likely than average to report increased overall satisfaction and satisfaction with work relationships and status. Moves from academe to the private sector tend to increase satisfaction and challenge, and intragovernmental changes result in greater overall satisfaction and greater satisfaction with challenge.

15 Summary

The study reported in chapters 10 through 14 was intended to explore nonacademic career options for science and engineering Ph.D.'s, who are faced with a shortage of faculty jobs both now and in the foreseeable future. The data come from the responses of over 8,000 doctorate holders from twelve fields (biology, chemistry, physics, mathematics, civil engineering, electrical engineering, mechanical engineering, economics, political science, anthropology, psychology, and sociology) to an eight-page questionnaire, the Higher Education Research Institute (HERI) Survey of Mobility and Nontraditional Careers of Ph.D.'s in Science and Engineering. This survey instrument focused on three career outcomes—salary, research productivity, and job satisfaction—and covered the respondent's educational background and work history.

The sample comprised three groups: those currently employed in higher-education institutions who had changed jobs within the three years prior to the survey (a group that included both faculty members and nonfaculty academics, the latter chiefly administrators); those currently employed in government (for example, the U.S. Civil Service, state- and local-government agencies, and federally funded laboratories); and those currently employed in the private sector (for example, business and industry, human-services organizations, other nonprofit organizations; this group also included a small number of people employed in elementary and secondary schools). In addition to being classified by current employment sector, respondents were classified by primary work activity: teaching; research; administration; and "other" (the last category including, for instance, clinical work, data processing, engineering, environmental protection, program planning and budgeting, and multiple activities).

Because of the methods used to draw up the separate rosters for the three employment sectors, several caveats should be observed. First, the fields of psychology, biology, chemistry, and physics are somewhat overrepresented; and the fields of civil engineering, mechanical engineering, political science, and sociology are underrepresented. Second, the faculty respondents are generally a younger and more-mobile group than are faculty nationwide. Third, science and engineering Ph.D.'s employed by the U.S. Civil Service are more thoroughly covered than are those working for other types of public-sector employers (for example, state and local governments). Finally, the representativeness of the private-sector respondents is uncertain because there was no way to compile a comprehensive roster from which to sample; the distribution of electrical engineers and of psychologists among the various public-sector employer types probably comes closest to reflecting the actual employment situation for doctorate holders from these fields. Despite these limitations, the data collected are useful in adding to our knowledge of the characteristics and rewards of nonacademic jobs for science and engineering Ph.D.'s.

Of the total sample of respondents, the largest proportion (46 percent) are in government; and the smallest proportion (22 percent) are in the private sector. The remainder work in colleges and universities, 87 percent of these as faculty and 13 percent as nonfaculty academics. The representation of women in the sample (10 percent) is identical with their representation in the U.S. population of science and engineering Ph.D.'s. The respondents average 43 years of age, with faculty tending to be younger (mean age of 37 to 38) and nonfaculty academics older (mean age of 47). Most of the respondents are married; however, 8 percent are single, and another 8 percent are separated, divorced, or widowed.

Approximately 43 percent of the faculty members hold tenured ranks (associate or full professor). Of the nonfaculty academics, 14 percent are in top-level administrative positions (president/chancellor, vice-president/provost); about 38 percent are middle-level administrators; and close to half hold "other" (unclassified) positions. About one-quarter of those in government, but over two-fifths of those in the private sector, are executives, managers, or administrators. Thus, the private sector seems to offer the best opportunities for high-status jobs, especially for engineers, chemists, and physicists.

Nonacademic Employment: The Current Situation

To identify the most-promising nonacademic careers for science and engineering Ph.D.'s, we looked at those jobs—classified by specific employer type (nineteen alternatives) and by primary work activity (forty alternatives)—that currently employ at least five doctorate holders from a given field. Eighty-six such jobs, employing 4,519 respondents in our sample, were identified.

In the public sector, the U.S. Civil Service employs Ph.D.'s from every field and offers a wide variety of work activities. Smaller numbers of the sample are found in state- and local-government agencies, federally funded laboratories, and the military services.

In the private sector, manufacturing and construction firms employ the largest number of Ph.D.'s identified by our criterion, followed by human-services organizations, "other" (unclassified) employers, and independent research organizations.

Overall, research is the most-common primary work activity, accounting for about 37 percent of those employed in nonacademic jobs. Administration or management is the next-most-common activity, reported by 27 percent overall. About 6 percent perform multiple activities.

Salary

Faculty members in the sample receive the lowest mean salaries, in part because they are the youngest group and received the doctorate more recently. Ph.D.'s employed in the private sector tend to earn slightly higher salaries than their counterparts in academe. Administration—especially in the private sector—is the most-lucrative primary work activity, and teaching the least so. Researchers in the private sector are relatively well paid, whereas researchers in government and academe earn relatively low salaries. Those performing "other" activities (that is, *not* teaching, research, or administration) in the private sector tend to earn high salaries, whereas their counterparts in academe have low salaries on average. Thus, it is clear that, whatever the advantages of a faculty position, a high salary is not one of them.

Research and Productivity

Taking a nonacademic job does not mean sacrificing one's chances to do research and to publish. Indeed, doctorate-level scientists and engineers in government (42 percent) and in the private sector (17 percent) are more likely than those in colleges and universities to report that research is their primary work activity. Of course, the primary work activity of faculty is teaching, and that of nonfaculty academics is administration.

The types of research conducted vary by employment sector as well. The private sector emphasizes applied research; the government, both applied and laboratory/experimental research; and academe, laboratory/experimental and theoretical/other research. These data confirm the now common observation that, as more Ph.D.'s take nonacademic jobs, the amount of basic or "pure" research done in the United States could drop to dangerously low levels, unless positive incentives to stimulate this type of research in nonacademic settings are strengthened.

About seven in ten science and engineering Ph.D.'s say that they are currently engaged in research that they expect will lead to publication. Although faculty members are most likely to indicate such involvement, research activity is also high among the nonacademically employed, especially government workers. On a subjective measure of productivity—perceived amount of research/publication done on the current job—faculty members are most likely, and nonfaculty academics least likely, to see themselves as accomplishing "a great deal." In the nonacademic sectors, perceived productivity varies considerably by field. On a publication index designed to measure the individual's output over his or her entire career, those currently engaged in research that is expected to lead to publication, those who have been in the labor force for a relatively long time, and those whose primary work activity is administration tend to score high. Psychologists, mathematicians, and economists have relatively low career publication rates, as do less-mobile Ph.D.'s and women.

Nontraditionality, Relatedness, and Underemployment

Colleges and universities are, of course, the traditional employers of doctorate holders; research-and-development activities outside of academe are also generally considered "traditional" for this group. In addition, doctoral graduates in some fields have an established history in jobs that are neither academic nor research oriented. For instance, psychologists do clinical work and counseling; engineers engage in engineering activities. Our findings with respect to the perceived nontraditionality of the current job reflect these common-sense notions. About one-quarter of the total sample view their jobs as nontraditional for people in their fields, with private-sector workers, followed by government workers, most apt to give this response. By primary work activity, teaching (which is virtually confined to academe) and research (especially in an academic setting) are usually seen as traditional. Conversely, about two in five of the administrators, and close to half of those engaging in "other" activities, feel that their jobs are nontraditional, although academic administration is more likely to be accepted as traditional than is administration in a government or a private-sector setting.

Only about one-tenth of the total sample are working in fields totally different from their doctoral field. Nonetheless, close to half see their jobs as being just somewhat related, or not at all related, to their graduate training, with nonfaculty academics most likely, and faculty least likely, to indicate a less-than-close relationship between education and the current job. Not surprisingly, teaching and research jobs tend to be considered closely related to graduate training, whereas administration does not. Of those performing "other" primary work activities, psychologists and engineers are most likely to see the current job as closely related to graduate training.

Three-fourths of the respondents in less than closely related jobs check only voluntary reasons for taking the job; one-tenth check only involuntary reasons; and the remainder indicate that their reasons were mixed. Nonfaculty academic jobs are usually chosen voluntarily. Private-sector workers are more likely than government workers or faculty to have taken unrelated jobs purely by choice. Among the nonacademically employed, the most-common reason for taking a job not closely related to graduate study was being exposed to and becoming interested in another field. In addition, those holding administrative positions in government or the private sector are especially likely to cite such factors as better pay, better opportunities for career advancement, and promotion to an unrelated job. Of the involuntary reasons, the most frequently mentioned are the scarcity or unavailability of jobs that are closely related to graduate training; many respondents say that, although they are not in a closely related job, they would prefer one. Clearly, the shortage of faculty positions is being felt by the nation's science and engineering Ph.D.'s.

The regression analyses performed to explore the correlates of holding a nontraditional job and the correlates of holding a job closely related to graduate training indicate that, as one would expect, the two outcomes have somewhat antithetical patterns. Those who see their current jobs as nontraditional for people in their field tend to say that they have held other nontraditional jobs, that the current job is not closely related to their graduate training, that neither graduate study nor specific courses in their major helped to prepare them for their current jobs, and that the doctorate itself played no part in their getting the job in the first place. Nonetheless, when these factors are controlled, they have no particular tendency to feel dissatisfied with their jobs or to see themselves as underemployed. Conversely, those in jobs closely related to their graduate training usually feel that both their graduate training in general and specific courses in their major gave them the knowledge and skills that they use in their current jobs. They are unlikely to say that those jobs are nontraditional, that they have changed their career goals since entering graduate school, or that they are underemployed.

Another concept examined in the study was that of underemployment. Seven in ten of the sample say they are *not* underemployed, with those in academe most likely to endorse this statement, and those in government least likely. The two reasons most frequently cited for feeling underemployed are wanting a more-challenging position and perceiving that the current job is not commensurate with one's level of ability. Very few indicate that their perception of underemployment is attributable simply to holding a job not in their graduate field.

Job Satisfaction

Job satisfaction is, obviously, desirable from the perspectives of the individual, the employer, and society at large. One's overall satisfaction with life depends to a considerable extent on one's satisfaction with work. Moreover, unhappy workers are often unproductive and rebellious. Thus, a major focus of the study was overall job satisfaction, its components and correlates.

Generally, the respondents are happy with their work. Two in five say that they are very satisfied overall, the proportions being highest among private-sector workers and lowest among government workers; nonetheless, about four in five of the latter say that they are satisfied (if not very satisfied) with their jobs. Of the primary work activities, administration is most likely, and teaching least likely, to prove very satisfying. The obvious conclusion is that faculty jobs may turn out to be less fulfilling than new Ph.D.'s expect. This finding, if made known to recent doctoral graduates, could provide them with a strong incentive to look for employment in the nonacademic sectors.

Jobs that are challenging, that offer opportunities for creativity, that provide congenial work relationships, and that carry high status are also likely to be satisfying. To a lesser extent, satisfaction with opportunities to use one's training, with variety of work activities, with internal politics, and with policymaking power all contribute to overall job satisfaction. Relatively unimportant, once these other aspects of the job are taken into account, are salary and fringe benefits, formal job security, good working conditions, and the competency of one's colleagues.

The best single predictor of overall job satisfaction for this sample of doctorate-level scientists and engineers is the perception that one's skills are fully utilized on the job. In addition, those people who are satisfied with life in general, who supervise people trained in the same field, and who work at a professional level are likely to be satisfied with their jobs, whereas those who feel underemployed are likely to be dissatisfied. Earning a high salary and seeing oneself as well paid compared with others of the same educational level are both related to overall job satisfaction. Being in a job closely related to one's graduate training produces satisfaction, but so does working in a nontraditional job. Although other significant predictors of overall job satisfaction vary somewhat by employment sector and by broad disciplinary area, the general implication is clear: Highly educated people tend to be happy with jobs that challenge them to use their talents (including creativity and originality) and their training, that pay well, and that carry some status; they are bored and unhappy with routine and undemanding jobs. This can hardly be regarded as big news. The point is that challenging and rewarding jobs are available outside of academe—especially in the private sector, although many public-sector jobs offer satisfactions as well. Moreover, the evidence suggests that teaching faculty are often relatively unhappy with their lot and thus that the few academic jobs projected to be available to new science and engineering Ph.D.'s in the coming years may be less desirable (compared with nonacademic jobs) than they are often presumed to be.

Mobility and Job Change

Another area of concern in the study was the career mobility of science and engineering Ph.D.'s: how and why they change jobs, what kinds of job changes they make, and what the outcomes of these changes are. In these analyses, nonfaculty academics were excluded, and nine types of changes (or ''paths'') were defined on the basis of the employment sectors of both the previous and the current job. *Within-sector* changes (for example, from one government job to another) occur about twice as frequently as *between-sector* changes. The most-common types of the latter, at least for this sample, are moves from academe to government, from the private sector to government, and from academe to the private sector.

Responses to a series of questions designed to assess potential mobility indicate that, as might be expected, women are much more constrained than are men by such considerations as spouse's job and spouse's preference for a locale. By employment sector, faculty seem to exhibit the most potential mobility and government workers the least, as reflected in the relative proportions responding affirmatively to such statements as "If I were looking for a job now, I would look nationwide" and negatively to such statements as "My occupation severely limits my choice of a geographical location."

About half the sample report that they have changed career goals since entering graduate school, with the nonacademically employed—especially those whose previous jobs were in academe—most apt to have done so; this finding confirms the assumption that most science and engineering Ph.D.'s initially intend to become faculty members and that current employment in a nonacademic job tends to represent a change in goals. With respect to timing, most of the sample indicate that they most recently changed their career goals in the early or middle 1970s, a period when higher education was first becoming aware of the "oversupply" of Ph.D.'s; thus, goal change is prompted not only by the passage of time and the development of new interests but also by the actual market situation. As to the sequence of change, the great majority either change goals before changing jobs, or experience the two types of change almost simultaneously. Very few in our sample report changing goals after changing jobs. The implication is that most job changes are deliberate and planned rather than forced on the individual.

The most-common reasons given for job change are finding more-attractive or more-challenging job opportunities elsewhere (mentioned most often by those whose current jobs are in the private sector and least often by current faculty) and becoming interested in a different area of study. Larger-than-average proportions of those moving from academic to nonacademic jobs cite the negative reason that available job opportunities in their area were limited or unattractive. Thus, some job changes are obviously forced by the tight academic-job market. Nonetheless, in most cases job change seems to be voluntary, since about three-quarters of the total sample indicate that they could have stayed on in their previous jobs had they so desired, a response most common among those employed in government and least common among faculty.

The most-popular employer types (as measured by the proportions of the total sample saying that they had sought a job there) are, in descending order, universities, the federal government, private business and industry, and four-year colleges. Respondents are most likely to have received an offer from the sought-after employer if their previous employer belonged to the same employment sector; otherwise, private-sector workers seem to have a slight advantage over government workers and faculty in getting the desired offer. Generally, respondents were most successful when they sought jobs in private business and industry, universities, the federal government, state or local government, and nonprofit organizations.

Overall, the most-effective job-search methods or contacts are direct personal application to the employer, professional contacts, and colleagues at one's own or other institutions and organizations. Current faculty are more likely than others to have found contacts with colleagues an effective means of getting jobs; they are also more likely than others to cite former professors and professional organizations or meetings as valuable resources in the job search. On the other hand, the nonacademically employed more often say that friends were helpful, that they met the new employer through their previous jobs, or that they were recruited by teams from government and industry. Not surprisingly, civil-service application was a successful job-search method for government workers. A modest proportion of private-sector employees cite newspaper advertisements and private employment agencies as useful. However, the sample as a whole made little use of such formal, impersonal channels as public or private employment agencies and university placement offices.

With respect to the outcomes of job change, moves from academe into government or the private sector carry clear monetary advantages; not only does actual salary tend to increase as a result of such job changes, but satisfaction with salary also is likely to increase. As for nonsalary income, government workers are clearly at a disadvantage; that is, moves from government to academe or the private sector usually entail increases in such income, whereas moves into government from the other two sectors tend to result in decreases.

Almost two-thirds of the total sample indicate that their overall job satisfaction increased as a result of almost any type of job change; the increase is most evident among current private-sector workers and is least characteristic of current government workers. Moreover, changes in satisfaction with challenge, with congenial work relationships, and with status follow the same pattern. Increased satisfaction with opportunities for creativity, however, is most closely associated with a move into academe from the nonacademic sectors. Thus, it seems that faculty members have more chances to exercise their creativity than do those employed in government or the private sector. Nonetheless, private-sector jobs seem to offer the most in terms of both challenge and status; and, on the whole, government jobs seem at least as desirable as faculty jobs in the satisfactions they provide.

A Final Word

When the study reported in this book was initiated, the climate was one of anxiety about the oversupply of Ph.D.'s in relation to academic-job openings. But in the early 1980s, new fears are surfacing. As the energy crisis worsens, as problems with the economy grow more severe, and as international relations deteriorate, policymakers are now starting to worry about a potential shortage of highly trained manpower in the United States. The concern is that declining college enrollments, due to the shrinkage of the traditional college-age population and to increased publicity about the poor job market for college graduates, mean that higher-education institutions will be producing fewer doctoral graduates than are needed to carry out the nation's work. These concerns are dealt with in the final part of this book.

Whatever the future holds—whether a shortage or an oversupply of science and engineering Ph.D.'s—the research reported here has important implications for policy. Better information, a wider perspective about potential jobs, and greater interaction between the academic and nonacademic spheres cannot fail to benefit both the nation as a whole and the most talented among its citizens.

16

A New Crisis? Dealing with Prospective Shortages of Scientists and Engineers

As was pointed out in chapters 1 and 15, some experts—far from being concerned about a current and continuing oversupply of doctorate-level manpower—maintain that the "crisis" is quite the opposite. The United States, they say, faces a prospective shortage of scientists and engineers that may seriously hamper the nation's defense capability and its capacity to solve pressing domestic problems.

Just how realistic are these anxieties? Should the leaders of the United States be concerned about a possible shortage of personnel in certain scientific and technical areas during the next twenty years? As mentioned earlier, the available data provide no definite answers to these questions. Too many imponderables enter the equation. Changes in the international situation, with a return to a Cold War mentality; continued preoccupation with balancing the federal budget by, among other things, cutting expenditures for science education by 20 percent (as has just been proposed by the Reagan administration); and major reorderings of national priorities—any or all of these factors, among others, could reverse the situation overnight.

In this final chapter, then, we will consider the potential problem of shortages, first weighing the pros and cons of "letting the market work" and then exploring ways of intervening in the natural market-adjustment process. The following discussion parallels the one in chapters 3 and 4. That analysis suggested how to deal with an oversupply of Ph.D.'s. Here, a future shortage is the focus.

Reliance on Natural Market Adjustments

Despite, or perhaps because of, the empirical evidence available, some argue that reliance on natural market forces will be the most-effective (and certainly the least-expensive) way to ensure a sufficient supply of scientists and engineers. When shortages arise in certain areas, the salaries of professionals in these fields will be bid up, more people will enroll, and more new scientists and engineers will become available. Moreover, higher salaries will encourage those trained to work in areas of shortages but now working elsewhere to switch employment fields to help fill the immediate void. However, despite the appeal of this "market solution," particularly to classical economists, letting the market work without intervention raises some problems.

First, we are uncertain about the market responsiveness of prospective students, current students, and professionals with various types of science and engineering training. Although work by Richard Freeman (1971) and others has shown quite convincingly that economists, engineers (especially those with degrees lower than the doctorate), and physicists in particular do respond to market forces, we know less about adjustments in other fields, and very little about market responsiveness to shortages (or surpluses) in subfields that might be vital to the pursuit of future national interests. It is clear that most fields are less supply elastic than engineering.

Second, even if we could determine that scientists and engineers are reasonably responsive to salary adjustments, it is not obvious that employers today are able to react to shortages by adjusting salaries offered. Universities are facing increasingly tight budgets and also find it difficult to differentiate faculty pay schedules according to field. Government employees are more inclined to attempt to balance budgets now than in the past. Even the private sector must make salary decisions in a context of fighting inflation, keeping product prices under control, and achieving some "reasonable" equity between their highly trained research staff and unionized production workers. Moreover, in a highly inflationary era, huge dollar increases would be required to achieve "real" increases in purchasing power. If job changes required geographic moves, high costs of housing might be limiting. Thus, the costs of letting the market work may be larger than they initially appear.

Third, the market responsiveness evidenced by most of the research to date involves serious lags. Assuming that shortages do give rise to adequate salary adjustments (and we have questioned this), it has been shown that the time between salary increases and the influx of new scientists and engineers into the labor force is both lengthy and variable. It takes considerable time for a high-school or college graduate who "responds to the market" by pursuing additional science and engineering training to enter the labor force. By the time he or she does so, the shortage may have disappeared. Hence, Freeman has argued that "cobweb" cycles are the result. Moreover, institutions may be unable to provide additional seats in high-demand classes on short notice without seriously sacrificing educational quality.

Fourth, we must question the assumption that those who have been highly trained in science and engineering but are working elsewhere can be lured back by high salaries within the feasible range. Many scientists and engineers leave their fields for administrative posts in academe, government, and industry. These jobs can be exceptionally high paying; research positions may never be able to offer sufficient salaries, prestige, autonomy, and status to induce reentry into research activities. And those who have moved out of science and engineering research may have obsolete skills that would require extensive investment in retraining before they could be utilized for research during times of need.

Finally, there is a serious question about whether the types of long-run societal "needs" we are addressing in this chapter will be reflected in the present labor market. We probably are now in a situation where few shortages exist for scientists, with the possible exception of certain types of engineers. The National Science Foundation (NSF) projects that this excess-supply situation may continue over the next decade. The "need" we are anticipating has not yet been reflected by new research funds or by new financial commitments to the areas of national concern noted in the first paragraphs of this chapter. Hence, if we allow the market to "work," it is possible that present salary rates will *not* encourage growth of the science and engineering labor force. As William Zumeta has pointed out: "the societal need based case for a new doctoral program or for retention or expansion of an existing one will invariably claim that a strong market for program graduates will materialize, but there may be little or no solid evidence of this at the time the case is being made" (Zumeta 1978, p. 509). This divergence between true social need in the long run and current market demands and projections could lead to market responses that reflect present willingness and ability to pay by the labor market, but *not* long-run needs. That is, if we let the market work now, labor supplies might fall; and the market's ability to respond later might be hurt.

For all these reasons, blind reliance on market forces could be a serious abdication of national responsibility. There is no guarantee whatsoever that highly trained scientists and engineers would become available as national needs are articulated and funds to support them are made available. Unfortunately, alternative courses of action are equally troublesome.

General Problems with Intervention Strategies

The presumption underlying the federal concern with future availability of scientists and engineers is that some action needs to be taken. Yet any new policies have inherent problems that must be considered. Most important, in one way or another, policy is made in a context or in reaction to a current set of circumstances. And it is rarely clear what that context is. Several illustrations are appropriate here. First, there are several projections of future availability of scientists and engineers (from NSF 1979; Bureau of Labor Statistics 1975; National Center for Education Statistics 1978; and Cartter 1976). These, however, are based on a variety of assumptions about enrollments, field choice, progression rates of students, and so on. Thus, estimates of labor supply diverge widely.

Second, projections of demand are generally based on rather arbitrary assumptions about the rate of growth, usually some type of extrapolation from the past. Current advocates of new support for science apparently do not accept prevailing demand-side projections. However, little evidence, other than rhetoric, is available to tell us what new demands will develop, when these will arise, and how much money will support them. Thus, those seeking intervention wish to alter assumptions about future demand; but how these assumptions should be modified is unclear. And national priorities involving highly trained manpower are subject to rapid and unpredictable changes (Zumeta 1978, p. 604). These factors lead some to argue that we know the *direction* of changes we desire, that is, that *more* support is needed. However, the form of that support is unclear, as will be discussed later. And it is still unclear how one should argue that public funds should go to science, rather than to welfare recipients, highway construction, or foreign aid.

An alternative to the general argument for increased funding for science and engineering is the advocacy by some of a "fine-tuning" approach. Some still would have us await concrete evidence of a problem (if not a crisis) and then act in response. The obvious problem here is that delays will probably limit the effectiveness of any fine-tuning efforts or even make them counter-productive (Freeman 1971). Four types of delays will occur: the lag in recognizing the problem; the delay in deciding on an appropriate policy; the time it takes to implement the policy (set-up time); and the time the policy takes to have an effect (in particular, the gestation period required to produce a new scientist, particularly one of high quality). These lags are especially probable when so much depends on action by government and universities, which have never been the most flexible of institutions.

These problems were graphically illustrated during the post-Sputnik period. By the time the massive federal science-support programs had an effect, our major objectives had been achieved by other means; the newly minted scientists and engineers were forced into other endeavors. But the current circumstances differ from those that existed in the late 1950s and early 1960s. A major problem at that time was to *develop* capacity for training and research. Currently, the declining cohort of traditional-aged college attenders has left us with *excess* capacity, particularly in the many universities that have seen enrollments fall.

The difficulties with fine tuning lead to the advocacy of intervention *now,* based on the sense that social need for science and engineering research will develop later. Although the basic assumption here might be incorrect, it is true that current public support of science and scientists will insure us against a possible future shortage. The costs of the efforts to support unknown future needs must be weighed against alternative uses of scarce federal funds and against the costs of relying on the market.

In one sense, then, a current policy consideration should be how to maintain existing capacity cheaply in a system facing short-term demand declines. Given a prospective need to "tool up" quickly in the future, and the obvious problems (including high start-up costs) inherent in developing "crash programs," it might be reasonable to maintain at least some high-quality, low-demand graduate programs in order to ensure that we can respond quickly to future needs. The costs of maintenance are like those of insurance, in that we will be prepared for future unknowns. Moreover, benefits of diversity and competition will be derived from the existence of more than a few institutions. Particular care should be taken before allowing cuts in relatively high-quality science and engineering doctoral programs that are experiencing enrollment declines or anticipate these in the next few years.

As Zumeta has argued, surpluses may be less costly than shortfalls (Zumeta 1978, p. 545). If future social needs are to be met, it may be less expensive to subsidize research and training facilities in the short run than to incur the costs of starting over when demand expands. These start-up costs could include the possibly disastrous ones of failing to respond fast enough to urgent crises. Moreover, there is some evidence that in science, supply creates its own demand (Zumeta 1978). If more highly trained scientists and engineers are produced than can be hired at usual salary levels for traditional science and engineering jobs, then we will see more Ph.D.'s moving into jobs where previously only a few had worked; or, perhaps at lower salaries, they will accept jobs in new areas for science and engineering Ph.D.'s. In a sense, these highly trained individuals will be "stockpiled" for reentry into science when the demand arises. Of course, problems of obsolescence will have to be addressed; and social benefits of research capacity will have to be balanced against individual despair at being "underemployed" in the short run. However, some believe that obsolescence was not a problem when stockpiled scientists returned to science to participate in the space race. And, as pointed out in chapter 13, surprisingly few scientists and engineers indicate high levels of dissatisfaction with "alternative careers." This might be explained by several factors. First, our credential-oriented society tends to value highly the capacities of those trained in science, and so is willing to structure jobs for these people that utilize their talents in some way. Second, the high salaries and other job amenities available to highly trained persons working outside their fields continue to lead to job satisfaction.

The Young-Investigator Problem for Academe

Before we discuss specific proposals to ensure adequate availability of science and engineering talent, we should address the concerns of those worried about a "lost generation" of scholars. This concern is otherwise known as the "young-investigator problem." To state the problem simply, some argue that since most basic research is done by young scholars, and most basic research is done in the university, if university positions are unavailable for young Ph.D.'s, then the United States will be seriously hurt by the lack of high-quality research, particularly basic research. The key words underlying this argument are *young Ph.D.'s, doing research,* and *in academe.*

Hence, a set of proposals has been put forth, involving direct input of new financial resources into academic departments of science and engineering. The suggestions of postdoctoral fellowships and related programs for new Ph.D.'s have both a short-term and a long-term rationale. Postdoctorate fellowships, it is argued, are necessary in the short run to find places for new Ph.D.'s who entered graduate school before the publicity about current or near-future over-supply was provided and who now, on graduation, face a poor job market. Many feel that we "owe" jobs to those who entered graduate schools at a time when the job situation was different than at present. The long-term argument is that unless we find a mechanism that enables young scholars to enter academe, the science and engineering disciplines will wither and die because they will be deprived of the vitality and new ideas of the younger generation.

The argument about a social responsibility to new graduates who entered graduate school during a period of high demand for Ph.D.'s does have some appeal. However, the volatility of the labor market in various science and engineering fields makes this rationale less compelling than it is for humanities Ph.D.'s, for whom the job-market crisis is more general; and the question remains whether or not better alternatives can be developed. Does establishing short-term academic positions merely delay the inevitable, postponing by two, three, or five years the time when certain Ph.D.'s will be thrown into the poor job market? And why should the nation compensate Ph.D.'s for their bad luck in training for a profession that has become oversubscribed? After all, we do not advocate the same remedy for the person who invests in a new restaurant that goes bankrupt.

The long-term argument rests on the conviction that young scholars are necessary to maintain the vitality of science. The graduate institutions provide evidence that only 25 percent of college-faculty members are young, compared with 45 percent ten years ago. The proportion of young faculty members, defined as those who received the doctorate less than eight years previously, fell by 24.4 percent between 1968 and 1974. From an aggregate of 39.2 percent young people in 1968, the range was from 42.4 percent in sociology to 18.2 percent in physics in 1974.

Our problem with these solutions is that very little is known about the effect of postdoctoral programs during a period of retrenchment. Most people can accept the argument that, during the boom times of the 1960s, those holding postdoctoral appointments carried out productive research. However, if new postdoctoral programs are developed during a time of job scarcity, no one knows whether or not those holding appointments will spend their time on their own research, serve as research associates on the projects of their senior colleagues, or search for permanent jobs in order to have something to do at the end of their appointments. Moreover, since the size of graduate programs is declining, postdoctoral appointees may spend more time teaching undergraduates than doing research, that is, doing what graduate students used to do. Similarly, arguments for new faculty positions are weakened by the fact that fewer students are enrolling and that, hence, teaching demands are lower now. Since one of the prime functions of the university is to teach, if there are fewer students, then why should there be more professors?

In considering funding for postdoctoral programs, the first question is, Why do we need *young* researchers? One answer is that old researchers become outdated. They have not been trained in nor do they keep up with the newest developments in their fields. If the problem is the outdated knowledge of some senior faculty, it might be more efficient to provide incentives for the established top researchers to "retool" than to hire large numbers of Ph.D.'s, only some of whom will ultimately be productive—unless, of course, the obsolescence phenomenon is due to some uncontrollable factor. The relative costs of hiring a large number of young faculty members must be compared with the relative cost of "retooling" a smaller number of older faculty members. Given that only a small proportion of young faculty members are ultimately productive, a case might be made that the payoff from retooling some of the older "stars" would be greater.

Another possible answer to the question is that the mind deteriorates with age, as do energy and enthusiasm; hence, new ideas are not developed after a certain age. Older researchers may not be physically or mentally capable of doing research of as high a quality as do younger researchers. Although it is generally accepted that brain cells do die throughout the human lifetime, most scientists think that only a small fraction of the total is lost and that in any case the relationship between productivity and number of cells is uncertain. Most evidence supporting decreased productivity is based on behavioral, rather than physiological, evidence; the methodology of most of these studies has been seriously questioned (Reskin 1979); and there are many examples of intellectually productive older people.

Some people also argue that since older faculty members already have tenure and may be at the top of the salary scale, they do not have the incentive to work harder in order to increase their incomes. That is, older faculty may not have the desire to do high-quality research to achieve the rewards of academe. If the problem is lack of incentives for senior researchers, then the most-efficient solution might be to change the incentive system. Salary ceilings, particularly in public universities, could be reconsidered. Recently, there has been some talk of amending tenure regulations so that tenured faculty members are reviewed periodically.

Finally, evidence in most fields indicates that people do their best research when they are young. Peaks of productivity occur at different ages—earliest in mathematics, latest in the humanities. However, who is to say that if young people were not entering research in continuously larger numbers, older re-searchers would not continue to produce at their earlier rates? A person receiving the Ph.D. degree in 1961 has had to compete with more new candidates for research funds in each successive year during the past twenty years. University funds are usually provided as seed money for young faculty members; if estab-lished faculty members received this money, they might be at least as productive. Success in obtaining other grants depends, in large part, on the number as well as the quality of competitors. Mature researchers have seen the probability of obtaining any grant decline precipitously over the last two decades. Hence, they compete for fewer grants and do less research. If there were less competition, competent older researchers would have a higher probability of getting grants, would apply more often, and would do more research. As a result, their age-publication profiles might not decline.

Senior faculty members also seem to move into administrative positions that preclude conducting research at the rate possible for full-time faculty. Part of the reason for moving into administration is the ever increasing difficulty of competing for grants and contracts. It is clear that the day a senior faculty member becomes an administrator, his or her research productivity declines; however, research *capability* has not necessarily declined with it. If the payoff to competing for and conducting research were greater, then perhaps some of the best researchers would forego administrative positions to continue their research.

It might be argued that we need enough young scientists now to ensure that there will be enough older ones later. Senior scientists make great synthetic contributions, and they will always be needed. But demand to replace those who die, retire, or leave academe will always exist. Hence, as long as the most-able Ph.D.'s can be retained in academe, a source of senior faculty members will exist.

The second major question in considering postdoctoral funding is this: If we want faculty positions for young Ph.D.'s, must these be new or additional positions, or can young Ph.D.'s replace older faculty members? The answer to the last part of that question today is "no." A large proportion of older faculty is tenured and, with new policies that delay retirement, these faculty members may remain in the university longer than they have in the past. However, it is possible that if senior faculty members move to government or industry, they can be at least as satisfied with their jobs there as are those who remain in academe. Moreover, a great number are able to continue their research in non-academic sectors. If facilities and incentives to do "needed" research were available outside academe, then some faculty members might move to industry, freeing academic positions for their younger colleagues.

Another question is whether new Ph.D.'s would be as productive outside academe as they might be within. Since much of a young faculty member's time is devoted to teaching and administrative work, a case could be made that with the proper facilities and incentives, the brightest new Ph.D.'s could advance their research more rapidly outside academe. It has been shown that research productivity is unimpaired as long as faculty devote no more than 25 percent of their time to other activities. The question is whether or not young academic faculty can restrict their nonresearch time commitments. Moreover, some fear that as the graduate-student population declines, Ph.D.'s and young faculty will be more likely to work in subservient positions on their senior colleagues' research projects, rather than developing their own independent research activities.

Finally if faculty jobs are artificially "created" for new doctorate recipients, increased pressure might be felt to augment enrollments to fill their classes. Although this might in turn provide a "reserve army" to meet future national needs, a short-term effect could be increased underutilization of science and engineering Ph.D.'s. Since all graduate training is subsidized, these short-term dislocations could be viewed as wasteful of public funds; this might make legislators hesitant to support graduate education later on.

Even if we could accept the argument that if there are fewer young researchers, there will be less research conducted, the question remains, Do we need as much research as was conducted during peak funding periods? The answer to this might be "no." Perhaps if science and engineering Ph.D.'s took nonacademic jobs that forced them out of traditional research activities, neither the doctorate holders nor society would be worse off. Much basic research is an esoteric extension of useful earlier research. However, another response to this question, which everyone from researchers to politicians is asking, is that we do not know which projects will be fruitful until they have all been conducted. Some research will yield great payoffs to the relevant professors. But if only 5 percent of the basic research is valuable, then one cannot be sure that something of value will not be lost unless all of it is funded. In addition, good unknown talent would be lost if only "sure things" were funded. Some apparently irrelevant projects might turn up results of value later.

Of course, some screening of research projects exists. Certainly not all proposed research is funded. If the base of research funding were cut back or if fewer researchers were available, most important basic research might still be done. Those in a position to do research might even have more resources to help them. In countries such as Great Britain and the USSR, the number of researchers per capita is much lower than in the United States. Nevertheless, there is no evidence that the United States is proportionately more productive. Perhaps review procedures for funding could be improved to ensure a higher yield of value per dollar or per researcher. Also, no one knows how much research is duplicative.

Also, why must needed research be done only *in the universities* rather than in other research settings? Proponents of university research argue that universities have always done basic research, whereas government and industry have focused on applied research. The corporate world, they say, will only do research that has a relatively short-term profit potential. Why should a particular corporation invest in basic research if the results then become available without cost to competitors? Further, some people claim that red tape in government hinders creativity there.

According to the American Council of Education's 1972–1973 faculty survey, 43.2 percent of faculty members in universities spent nine or more hours per week in "research and scholarly writing." The range is from less than 26 percent in the humanities, to 38.8 percent in engineering, to 53.2 percent in physics. About one-third of the faculty members said they did no research at all. Some 41.5 percent of those in universities who did research said it was "pure or basic." The range was from 29.8 percent in engineering, to 41.9 percent in the humanities, to 76.8 percent in physics. Hence, the percentage of university faculty doing basic research ranged from 11.6 percent in engineering, to 11.9 percent in the humanities, to 40.9 percent in physics. Apparently, even humanists in academe do relatively little basic research.

Although basic research is conducted in universities, the average faculty member has at most a 40-percent chance of doing it. Thus, the creation of faculty positions does not seem to be a clear and efficient way to encourage basic research. However, young faculty members might be more likely to do basic research than the faculty as a whole; and incentives to induce faculty members to conduct basic research could increase the chances of their doing so. The fact remains, however, that if ten new junior-faculty positions are created, probably not more than four of the Ph.D.'s who get them will conduct useful basic research. Consideration should be given to whether or not alternative approaches to ensure adequate basic research for our society would be more efficient.

The share of time devoted to research by faculty members, government employees, or those in the corporate world may vary. Those outside of faculties may spend more time per year actually conducting research, since faculty members are diverted to teaching and administrative tasks. Those in government whose primary work activity is research may be deflected into bureaucratic activity more often than those in corporations.

There are several advantages of stimulating research activity outside academe. First, full time could be devoted to this effort. Second, Ph.D.'s could be employed in a setting that does not require more students to survive. Third, resources for research might be more accessible in specialized research institutions than in universities in which scientists must compete with members of other disciplines for funds.

Planned Programs for Stimulating Research Output

In response to the projected social need for more research in science and engineering than would automatically be forthcoming without intervention, the scientific community and the academic institutions have come forth with a variety of proposals. These proposals, which usually involve massive expenditures of public money, will be considered under four headings.

1. The most-basic approach is to *fund more science and engineering research.*
2. In order to ensure that the best young minds are available to carry out the research, it is argued that *more students should be encouraged to enroll.*
3. Because of concern that new and existing scientists and engineers be employed where they can be effective, suggestions have been put forth to *create more jobs in academe.*

4. For the same reasons, suggestions have been put forth to *create more jobs in nonacademic settings*.

These will now be discussed in order.

Fund More Research

At first, it appears that the simplest way to ensure that adequate research is available is to increase research funding. From an economic perspective, if research—particularly basic research—is a public good, then without subsidy, a suboptimal amount will be available from a social-welfare-maximization viewpoint. As Klitgaard (1979) indicates, "if research is a public good and if the research effort will also decline [in terms of quantity or quality] in a declining academic labor market, there is a case for governmental concern" (p. 70). However, Klitgaard also argues that it is uncertain whether fewer jobs in academe necessarily will lead to less research or to lower-quality research.

The apparently straightforward advocacy of increased research funding involves a number of complexities. Most obviously, it assumes that enough researchers will be available to carry it out. This takes us back to the issues of enrollments and job availability, which will be discussed later. More subtle, perhaps, is the question of how research gets funded. More and more, research funding means the awarding of contracts for specific projects, to be performed under monitoring constraints, sometimes severe, imposed by federal bureaucrats and by the Office of Management and Budget. It is naive to assume that under current federal funding procedures, an increase in research funding will automatically result in the production of high-quality basic-research findings that will prepare the United States for the crises of the future.

Certainly, more research funds are preferable to fewer. But it is hard to imagine that enough foresight and creativity exists in the federal funding agencies to ensure that the Request for Proposal (RFP) process will procure the needed research. Further, the competitive bidding process, which gives excessive weight to proposal preparation in the award process, may not ensure that the best researchers (as opposed to the best writers of proposals) will win the contract. The federal government is often obligated to award contracts or grants to the lowest bidders, and in many cases it gets only what it pays for. Finally, pressures for geographical representation, rather than quality of ideas, prevail in many grant-making activities.

Hence, serious reviews are needed of federal contracting, monitoring, and topic-selection procedures should precede any blind advocacy of increased research funding. If funds with few strings attached could be made available to proven or promising researchers, who were then allowed to pursue whatever paths their research suggested, then increased funding programs would offer more promise.

Encourage More Students to Enroll

To some, the most-reasonable reaction to the fear that fewer of the best and the brightest will be available to science and engineering over the coming decades is to encourage more able students to enroll in science and engineering. Questions immediately arise about whether standards of student quality will have to be lowered in order to increase numbers. As we shall see, it is very difficult to identify at the admissions stage those who will be most productive later on. Nevertheless, we might want to advocate merit-scholarship programs, which have had the desired effect in the past.

However, many merit-fellowship programs were terminated in the 1960s because of the protests of antielitists who claimed that screening procedures favored white males to the exclusion of minorities and women. It was argued that equally capable women, minority-group members, and low-income students had not been trained to do well on (culturally biased?) achievement tests, which were the basis for many merit awards. Hence, any massive merit-fellowship programs will have to combat programs fostering movement toward equal-access that are now in vogue (such as the Basic Educational Opportunity Grants and similar federal and state programs). Of course, these non-merit-based programs could also be expanded to attract students for whom costs have been a constraint. But if students less likely to contribute to future national needs were thereby attracted, resources would be wasted or at least would not be achieving the ends with which we are concerned in this chapter.

Another question concerns the ability of U.S. universities to absorb new enrollees. Many of the best departments have not yet experienced excess capacity. Would we accept increased student/faculty ratios that might reduce the effectiveness of the educational experience? Or would we prefer that newly attracted students be allocated among second-line departments that could more readily absorb them? Surely efforts to develop new programs or expand nonelite ones would meet with resistance from state legislators who have been reacting to the poor job market and to declining enrollments by trying to terminate or reduce many programs.

The prospect of expanded enrollments also raises the question of where these new clients will be employed before projected national needs are translated into new jobs. Again, the notion of stockpiling scientists and engineers must be evaluated.

It has been suggested that if more students were exposed to the scientific disciplines throughout their educational careers, then more of the best would choose to study science or engineering at higher levels. Hence, arguments are made for improving the teaching of science in the elementary and secondary schools. Of course, the gestation period involved for an elementary student to become a productive scientist may make this policy irrelevant for needs anticipated for the near future.

It has also been suggested that one way of stockpiling surplus scientists and engineers in the short run is to enrich elementary- and secondary-school faculty by employing science Ph.D.'s there. This would be exceedingly expensive, particularly if salary schedules at institutions at these educational levels require higher pay for those with more-advanced degrees. It should be remembered that there is no shortage of elementary- or secondary-school teachers; there is no basis for the assumption that Ph.D.'s can be more-effective teachers at these levels or that they are more capable of teaching basic skills than are those trained for elementary or secondary teaching.

Related to these ideas about precollegiate enrichment are proposals for revising undergraduate curricula in order to enable more students to sample science or engineering courses and for development of interdisciplinary programs to attract the most able from other disciplines into science. Although these proposals have often been put forth by humanities departments in an attempt to fill their empty classrooms by offering service courses to science or engineering majors, the reverse flow might have some utility in attracting additional bright students to science. Science and engineering programs are justifiably viewed by many liberal-arts students as exceedingly demanding of both effort and prerequisites. But for certain bright students who might recognize their capability to study in these areas, a taste of science might make the extra effort required to succeed seem worthwhile.

A final set of recommendations for increasing science and engineering enrollments involves seeking out new audiences: returning adults who have been out of school for years, minority-group members, women, part timers, and foreign students. Several problems are evident immediately. Members of some of these groups will not have had sufficient preparation for graduate, or even undergraduate, work in science and engineering. Remediation costs might outweigh the benefits of discovering a certain number of late-blooming stars. This, coupled with the long time it takes working adults enrolled part time to complete their studies, may make the "new-clientele response" both long term and problematic.

Most working adults who return to college choose to study business or management; if they choose science, they do so usually to update their skills rather than to develop a new capability in scientific research. As for foreign students, any investment in their education carries the risk that they will return home upon graduation, and thereby be unavailable for the U.S. science and engineering labor force.

In conclusion, efforts to expand science and engineering enrollments, if they do not threaten educational quality, may be worthwhile. But the conflict between merit-based and access-expanding motives for fellowship awards must be addressed. And efforts to attract new audiences into science are problematic.

Create More Jobs in Academe

Although new research money and more students could in themselves expand job availability, it is argued that enrollments will not pick up *until* the job market improves, and that research activity depends not only on funding but also on an existing pool of competent scholars to carry out the funded projects. As noted earlier, the near-term demand for scientists and engineers probably will lead to excess applicants compared with available traditional jobs, particularly in academe, which is limited in its employment potential because of declining undergraduate enrollments. Hence, the problem is one of utilizing our science and engineering talent until projected social needs are translated into jobs. Although this book continually questions the arguments that those jobs must be in the academic sector, many of the proposed job-creating interventions involve the creation of jobs in academe.

The creation of academic jobs can be accomplished either directly, by funding additional positions, or indirectly, by changing procedures or incentives within the current academic system in ways that will make more money available either for replacement or for new hires. At least five types of academic jobs have been suggested for subsidized funding: postdoctoral fellowships, junior-faculty positions, senior-faculty positions, senior-faculty research posts, and nonfaculty research positions. The goals of these programs are to ensure a continued flow of young scholars into academic positions during the transition to a steady state, and to find other ways to stimulate the flow of new ideas and new research thrusts into academic departments (National Research Council 1979).

Funding postdoctoral fellowships has been a traditional part of the advanced-training process for scientists and engineers for decades, as the National Science Foundation and other agencies have provided high-quality doctorate recipients with opportunities to hone or redirect their research interests, to work with new senior colleagues, and generally to begin their scientific careers without the burden of the teaching and administrative responsibilities that accompany traditional junior-faculty assignments. However, since these programs already are widespread in many fields, further expansion may reduce their quality and stature.

Recently, concerns have been expressed that the poor academic-job market will divert postdoctoral fellows from their research by forcing them to spend excessive amounts of energy trying to secure tenure-track positions for the time when the fellowship ends. It is also feared that since fewer graduate students are enrolling, postdoctoral fellows will replace them as teachers of undergraduates, laboratory assistants, and research assistants on the research projects of senior faculty. Moreover, as postdoctoral appointments have proliferated at less-than-first-rate institutions, the utility of the postdoctoral fellow as a training vehicle is becoming suspect. Thus, the question arises whether in today's academic environment postdoctoral fellows can pursue their own independent research, both to advance their careers and to revitalize the research capacity of the United

States. It is argued that regular assistant professors are more independent and thus potentially more productive. Moreover, faculty members are likely to see their research have more-lasting effects if it is integrated both with teaching and with the research of their colleagues.

In contrast to the foregoing concerns, proposals have been put forth to build a teaching component into postdoctoral work, in part to prepare postdoctoral fellows better for future faculty responsibilities and in part to compensate for declining numbers of junior faculty and graduate students. Also, some argue that more research will get done if the term of the postdoctoral appointment is lengthened, perhaps even to five years. Of course, these delays will push the Ph.D.'s into the job market at even more-treacherous times. Finally, some argue that postdoctoral appointments provide an effective and relatively inexpensive screening device, a way of determining which of the recent graduates will grow into leading researchers. And postdoctoral fellowships provide a good, quick response mechanism whereby young scholars can move into new research positions when national needs materialize.

Funding new junior-faculty positions seems to have a number of desirable traits that are lacking in postdoctoral appointments. They give a sense of permanence to the job holder and permit him or her to combine research, teaching, and collegial interactions productively. Yet if a public agency were to select "winners" of regular tenure-track positions, the normal university process for selecting assistant professors would be violated. And there might be no assurance that the new positions would be net additions to the faculty rather than subsidized replacements of faculty who would have been hired anyway.

Although all proposals to establish new faculty positions are predicated on the need for a continued research capability, it is undeniable that teaching represents a major aspect of most faculty jobs. Hence, it may be difficult to convince federal or state legislators that subsidizing faculty is justified during a period when the number of students who must be taught is declining. Moreover, it is difficult to be certain that the young people given subsidized faculty positions will be sufficiently productive in their research over the years to warrant the subsidy.

These arguments have led then to the advocacy of *support for more senior-faculty positions*. New positions are not available for qualified untenured assistant professors who in other times would justifiably be awarded tenure; nowadays, when universitywide budgets are being made, resources are being reallocated from some fields of science to others; declining undergraduate enrollments in general and declining proportions of undergraduates choosing certain fields of science are jeopardizing the jobs of already entrenched senior faculty.

These situations appear to be portents of declining opportunities for certain senior science and engineering faculty members to conduct important research (which cannot be that important if we accept the arguments for the need for *new* Ph.D.'s), as well as increasing insecurity among senior faculty, which may mean the loss of senior scholars who serve as synthesizers for their disciplines. Hence, new support programs are being advocated that would create new research professorships and senior postdoctoral fellowships to permit research, career development, renewal, or career change for senior faculty. A related type of program would increase research funding for senior scholars; this, it is argued, would free up faculty by buying their time and hence would permit the hiring of replacements as well as providing jobs on research projects for recent doctorate recipients.

These proposals are questionable on several counts. First, what is the point of subsidizing senior-faculty positions if these faculty will have too few students—particularly undergraduates but also graduate students—to teach? Creation of faculty positions generates a need for more students, who, on graduation, will be left with poor job prospects. The response that these faculty will conduct important research is sufficient only if this research could not be accomplished in nonacademic settings that do not require students to be trained as a byproduct. And surely senior faculty are more expensive than are their junior colleagues, if that choice had to be made.

Senior postdoctoral fellowships thus seem more appropriate, since in theory those holding them would be able to retrain either for nonacademic jobs or for faculty positions in more-marketable areas. At least they would be able to update their skills in their field. The question here is whether or not qualified and deeply entrenched senior faculty would indeed be motivated to change fields or to acquire new skills. Will tenured faculty feel the need to do so? On the contrary, it seems likely that senior postdoctoral fellows will simply use their fellowships to delay their inevitable displacement while they search for other academic jobs.

Even if a few senior faculty took the opportunity to retrain for nonacademic careers, their success might be questioned. In only a year or two, would they acquire adequate preparation to enable them to compete in the nonacademic-job market with younger graduates from programs in science, business, or public policy? Would nonacademic employers be willing to hire older former faculty members, who would require higher salaries and would already be set in their ways? The latter question becomes particularly pertinent when there are also surpluses of younger graduates and of graduates from fields more relevant for nonacademic employment.

Finally, the provision of research grants to senior faculty probably would result in some good research. However, the social worth of that research compared with research in the medical fields would have to be evaluated before funds should be reallocated. And the byproduct of being able to buy off the time of senior faculty and replace them with new Ph.D.'s seems doubtful. In this era of tight budgets, it is more likely that advanced seminars of the newly funded faculty member would be shelved for the period of the grant, or that other existing faculty members would teach them; it is less likely that new faculty would be hired who would have to be terminated at the end of the grant. Similarly, unless very long-term research-grant commitments were made, any doctoral-level research associates hired for the grants would find themselves quickly back among the job seekers at the end of the research project.

Despite these reservations, we should explicitly acknowledge the National Research Council's (NCR's) proposal for a "Research Excellence Award Program" (REAP). This would provide periodic five-year stipends in support of the salaries of full-time faculty members on regular appointments (either tenured or nontenured in a tenure-track position). The released university funds would then have to be used to support the employment of new faculty members (NRC 1979). This program retains for individual departments their historical autonomy in deciding whom to hire for faculty positions. It rewards productive senior scholars whose research potential is already known. And, although the NRC estimates that the minimum bill over the program's nineteen-year life will be $381 million, this amounts to a relatively small amount of the National Science Foundation's budget for basic research and development in colleges and universities in any one year.

Our major reservation about the REAP proposal is the assumption that freed-up funds from salaries of senior faculty would be used to hire *additional* junior tenure-track faculty members. If university administrators are seeking to save money during a period of retrenchment, particularly one in which enrollments are declining, then surely they will be clever enough to use the funds saved to hire the few faculty they would have hired in the absence of the REAP. Departments, in anticipation of National Science Foundation (NSF) funds, could simply project lower hiring rates than they would expect in the absence of the grant. On receipt of the grant, the department could hire up to the level it would have sought without the funds. From the university's point of view, this is more reasonable than is the spirit of REAP, if enrollments are declining. Finally, it is not clear how the NSF would be assured that the "additional" young faculty members would be given an "adequate" chance for tenure. These decisions are extremely subjective and variable; five or seven years in the future, if enrollments are down, tenure standards might be so elevated that virtually no one could meet them.

To some, funding the expansion of nonfaculty doctoral research staff in universities seems a preferable policy option to the expansion of faculty positions. Universities could make new research talent available on their campuses without having to justify new-faculty hiring during a period of enrollment declines. These researchers could devote full time to research without competition from teaching or committee work. And there might be an opportunity to get around rigid faculty salary schedules, which may have to be kept in line with faculty salaries in nonscience areas, particularly the humanities.

One advantage of nonfaculty employment is actually seen as a negative factor by some observers. It should be an advantage to the universities to be able to hire top scholars when research funds are available and then to terminate them at the end of a project. On the other hand, it is argued that the irregularity of employment of research staff will detract from their research efforts in that they constantly will be trying to secure more-permanent positions. Perhaps programs need to be developed that would cover periods between grants for nonfaculty academic research staff. This would facilitate continuity, perhaps at not too great a cost. It could be argued, however, that, just as in most nontenurable jobs, research staff will have great incentives to maximize their efforts in order to be kept on after the end of the present project.

Many universities have regulations stipulating that only regular faculty can serve as principal investigators on research grants or contracts. Hence, it is argued that nonfaculty research staff will be unable to pursue independent, innovative lines of their own research, but instead will be forced to serve in support positions to faculty members. This is a weak objection; surely the opportunity to utilize high-quality research associates will enhance the research efforts on a project. On balance, nonfaculty doctoral research appointments seem to be a viable way for the universities to retain a research capability during depressed times.

It is obviously possible, although usually expensive, to finance new jobs in academe. In many situations these subsidies are necessary because of rigidities in the system that in some sense do not let the market work naturally. In academe most of the rigidities, such as tenure, are either long-established traditions that have come to be seen as employee rights or policies of long standing that would be very difficult to change.

Finally, *geographic immobility* often restricts academic-job opportunities for productive scholars. Frequently, productive scholars forego academic careers and move to other sectors, into jobs that may or may not permit productive research, so that they may remain in a particular city or region. At the same time, academic jobs may go unfilled in more-remote, less-desirable, or more-expensive parts of the United States. Departments with good resources may be forced to hire second-rate faculty, whereas well-located departments may house faculty who are working below their potential. For some faculty, mobility is also limited because of jobs held by spouses. Hence, it seems reasonable that a "national mobility center" be set up that would enable individual scholars or departments to apply for funds to allow or encourage productive scholars to move. Funding could be used to cover differentials in housing or other costs, to permit a spouse to search for a job or take one at reduced pay, to pay moving costs, and so on. The applicant would have to show that the move had the potential to enhance national research productivity, perhaps by locating a scholar in an environment more conducive to him or her. The costs of such subsidies surely would be lower than the costs of creating new faculty positions, and the need for such a center should be studied.

Creating More Jobs Outside Academe

Our work has shown that science and engineering doctorate holders and other science and engineering researchers who work in industry and government are often as satisfied and productive as are faculty (Solmon, Hurwicz, and Kent 1980). Social benefits clearly can derive from jobs outside academe. But although new jobs might be subsidized in nonprofit research institutes or in government agencies, it would be difficult to advocate direct subsidy of jobs for scientists and engineers in industry. Nevertheless, funding agencies might be encouraged to give more-serious consideration to contract applications of private industry (particularly in the basic-research area). Other incentives for industry are discussed later. Moreover, advising and information services might be provided to science and engineering researchers in order to break down the stereotype that academe is the only respectable or desirable place to work.

Although there are a variety of nonacademic science- and engineering-research settings, the pros and cons are quite similar for most of them. Let us first consider briefly the positive aspects of nonacademic research jobs. Outside academe, there is the need constantly to produce useful work, lest one be terminated. Since tenure restricts this possibility in universities, more resources are wasted on "dead wood." Whereas campuses face space problems and have outdated equipment, in industry these limitations may be overcome more easily. Nonacademic researchers, because they are not burdened by "diversionary" teaching and committee work, can focus more on their research. It may be easier to tailor jobs around individual interests and abilities in industry than it is in academe. Finally, even if science and engineering Ph.D.'s are not directly involved in (basic) research, they can be stockpiled, to be updated and moved back into research when needs arise.

Those arguing against nonacademic research careers for scientists and engineers make a number of points. First, it is highly unlikely that public subsidy can be directed to private industry. Indeed, regulations for awarding research contracts to for-profit organizations are quite different from the rules applicable to nonprofit corporations. It is argued that the environment for research is less desirable outside academe. Obsolescence is more likely to occur. Research positions in government and, particularly, in industry are thought by some to be too unstable and temporary; however, policies could be developed to ensure continuity. Some argue that in universities teaching and research are joint products, lowering the costs of both types of activities. (On the other hand, it is likely that university overhead derived from science and engineering research projects is in part used to shore up humanities programs, thereby adding unnecessary costs to scientific research.) The nonacademic research enterprise does not have the cheap labor of graduate students, which lowers costs. A critical mass of doctoral students may be needed to permit senior faculty to most effectively pursue their research interest. (However, may academic departments may have reached the point of diseconomies of scale.) In general, nonacademic science-research enterprises are alleged to provide less training as a byproduct of their research; hence, it is argued that, if research is moved off campus, we will be deprived of the opportunity to encourage a new generation to enter science and engineering and to train those who do enter.

On balance, it seems that the potential for "creating" nonacademic jobs is less than the opportunities available for subsidizing academe. However, given the inevitable decline in the need for a teaching professoriate, and the fact that for the most part university budgets are enrollment driven, planners should do whatever is possible to make nonacademic researchers full partners in any national efforts to use science to solve our society's problems.

Two Proposals to Enhance the Working of the Market

The proposals discussed so far involve different types of public intervention to ensure that the science- and engineering-research capacity of the United States will be adequate to meet projected national needs. Our initial assessment of the market mechanism (nonintervention) and intervention approaches was mixed: laissez faire alone is probably insufficient, but the effects of intervention are both costly and uncertain. However, our discussions so far have taken as given the present "state of the market" in the United States. It must be acknowledged that one reason that the "market system" does not operate efficiently in this country is that many of the conditions that the classical market model assumes exist are not evident in the U.S. economy today. In particular, the classical model assumes *perfect information, profit maximization,* and *absence of government regulations.* Perhaps efforts to enable the United States to move toward the classical model would, more than anything else, ensure our capability to produce research to meet national needs. This final section elaborates on this point.

Improving Information for Better Decision Making

Better information is needed in at least five areas. First, our ability to estimate *future science- and engineering-labor supply and demand* is poor. This is a common complaint, which needs little elaboration here. It should be noted simply that disaggregated field estimates need to be improved and that we require fewer innovative mathematical models and more discussions of projected social needs and of the implications of political actions. Likewise, there should be more discussion of how to react if the forecasts prove to be wrong.

Second, *students, potential students, and graduates must be provided with better data* with which to make decisions. Most of their advice comes from faculty who may know little about the nonacademic world and who at times feel ambivalent about giving correct information that might cause students to transfer out of their area. News media may also be an information source to some, but these tend to stress the dramatic (Ph.D.'s driving taxis) over the useful. And counseling offices are often ill prepared to deal with graduate students, particularly those interested in nontraditional career paths. Perhaps subsidized training programs to provide information sources with adequate information would be worth their cost.

Third, we must improve our *ability to select* students for admission to graduate programs. If admissions committees were able to select students who would turn out to be the most productive, then declining application rates would not hurt the quality of scientific research. But many students must be admitted in order ultimately to discover a few "stars." If the best students could be more easily identified, a declining pool might not be a problem. Additionally, we need to develop better mechanisms for *screening during graduate school,* to ensure that those who drop out are not potentially high producers.

Finally, we must improve the *academic hiring process and review procedures* to ensure that only the best applicants are chosen to fill the increasingly scarce number of openings. In the natural- and social-science fields, important discoveries are very disproportionately made by the top researchers. For example, in many subfields, the top 2 percent of researchers produce 25 percent of the research; and their output is also of higher quality (Klitgaard 1979, quoting Price 1962 and Cole and Cole 1973). Also, if research funds that go to weaker scientists who leave when academic jobs get scarce were instead granted to the stronger ones who remain, it is theoretically possible that total research output would increase. This is unlikely, however, because the leavers probably would have done no research (that is, would only have taught).

The effects of a cutback in faculty will depend on who is cut, not on how many leave. In general, the proportionate decline in research will be less than the decline in the number of faculty jobs.

To summarize, decisions by funders, students, job seekers, admissions committees, hiring committees, and promotion committees are often made unsystematically, without adequate data and without formulas that will optimize the results. Research on how these decisions can be improved will surely make the free-market process more effective.

Taking the Constraints Off Private Industry

It is clear to almost everyone that research-and-development activity in the United States has lagged behind that of many other nations. The slowing of productivity improvement during the past few years parallels the discouraging decline in the rate of investment in plant and equipment (*Chemical Marketing Reports,* 24

March 1980, p. 2). If incentives can be developed to stimulate research and development in the private sector, then new activities are likely to open up new jobs for scientists and engineers. The availability of increased employment opportunities is then likely to encourage more highly qualified students to enroll in these fields.

The Committee for Economic Development (CED) (1980) has recently made a series of policy recommendations that are intended to help industry help the nation reassert its dominance in research and development. If these were considered in the present context, then perhaps some of the labor-supply constraints could be better understood.

First, the level of investment in plant and equipment should be raised in order to increase the diffusion of new technology into the industrial processes. This would provide the structural change necessary for permanent impact on productivity growth and thereby on the control of inflation. The CED recommends that this be accomplished immediately by the removal of certain tax disincentives. In particular, the CED report identifies the urgent need for a more-rapid capital-recovery allowance as the highest-priority measure to stimulate investment in new plant and equipment (this contradicts the traditional concept that depreciation be spread over the entire useful life of an asset).

The CED suggests that capital-recovery allowances be based on the inflation rate to approximate the rising costs of replacing plant and equipment. They advocate flexible depreciation of all research-and-development (R&D) assets to take into account the inherent uncertainty of the usefulness of R&D assets.

Second, the CED recommends that all nonessential regulatory constraints on, and uncertainties inherent in, productive investments should be reduced. This, in conjunction with the improved economic performance that will result from more-rapid productivity growth, would create the essential climate for investment in all phases of technological innovation to be increased as the natural response of the entrepreneurial process.

The CED points out that compliance costs reduce resources available for technological innovation. Regulatory delays and court challenges to the legality of regulatory policy have reduced the rate of innovation. Uncertainty about acceptability of advanced technological applications should be reduced.

An example of ways in which other nations are less constrained in R&D might stress this point. In Japan, the five leading semiconductor-computer manufacturers (Nippon Electric, Hitachi, Toshiba, Mitsubishi Electric, and Funjitsu) formed a cooperative research laboratory to pool their resources in order to conduct R&D more efficiently. The research group, which holds 600 patents, recently disbanded (in part because of protest from the United States); the research has now shifted to the Computer Basic Technology Research Association. In the United States, this approach would not be possible because of antitrust regulation. (*Inside R&D,* 26 March 1980).

There are several reasons that relatively little basic research is conducted in private corporations. The costs are high. The payoffs are uncertain and are likely to accrue only in the long run. Further, results from basic research are difficult to monopolize through patent procedures. Hence, the incentives to collaborate with competitors (as in the foregoing Japanese example) might increase incentives for U.S. corporations to expand their basic-research efforts. Also, since basic research generally has been conducted in the universities and has been available to the corporate sector at little or no cost, there has been little incentive to pursue basic research outside academe. If basic-research activity declines at the universities, however, then the corporate sector might feel compelled to pick up the slack. This would open doors for the employment of scientists and engineers in basic-research activities in government.

The last major recommendation of the CED is that appropriate tax, patent, and regulatory changes be made to provide support that would foster private R&D. In addition, adequate support of basic research should be a high-priority item in the federal budget. The CED favors moves toward increased government support for basic research, but recommends that federal involvement in selection and management of technological development aimed at commercial applications be undertaken only under extremely limited circumstances.

Conclusion

The concerns that underlie this book seem, on balance, justified. Jobs in academe will grow scarcer; and academe has become the home of science in this nation, as it has long been the home of the humanities. Market adjustment will not solve all the problems, particularly because markets are unable to adjust because of inadequate information and burdensome regulations that pervade the United States. Interventionist strategies must be considered, particularly in the short run. But these are costly and will meet heavy resistance from budget-conscious legislators and bureaucrats. Perhaps our best long-run hope is to try to reestablish a national economic system that allows the market (and its several sectors, particularly private industry) to function again as it did when U.S. scientific research was a model for the world. A prosperous nation based on high technology and productivity should support the arts and humanities both in the academy and in the broader society. Just as partnerships—between academe on one hand and government and industry on the other—are a theme of this book, so it should be stressed that the interdependence among all the scholarly disciplines is an important reality.

Appendix A:
Questionnaire Forms

SURVEY OF MOBILITY AND NONTRADITIONAL CAREERS OF PhDs IN SCIENCE AND ENGINEERING

HIGHER EDUCATION RESEARCH INSTITUTE ● 4555 WEST 77TH STREET ● MINNEAPOLIS, MINNESOTA 55435

DIRECTIONS: Your responses will be read by an optical mark reader. Your careful observance of these few simple rules will be most appreciated.

● Use only a black lead pencil (no. 2½ or less).
● Make heavy black marks that fill the circle.
● Erase cleanly any answer you wish to change.
● Make no stray markings of any kind.
● Where write-in responses are necessary, please confine your writing to the limits of the lines provided.

EXAMPLE: Will marks made with ball-point or fountain pen be properly read?   ○ Yes   ● No

PLEASE DO NOT WRITE IN THIS AREA

16868

NOTE: A postdoctoral appointment should not be classified as a job. A separate section considers postdoctoral appointments.

Any reference to "previous job or position" means your most recent former job with a different company or institution.

1. On the following list, please mark (A) all degrees you have earned and (B) the degree(s) for which you are currently working, if any.

	(A) Now hold	(B) Working on
Bachelor's	○	○
Master's	○	○
Doctor of Arts or equivalent	○	○
EdD	○	○
PhD	○	○
Other professional degree (MD, DDS, LLB)	○	○
Other	○	○
None		○

2. What were the areas of concentration for (A) your bachelor's and (B) your master's degree? (Mark all that apply)

	Bachelor's	Master's
Arts & humanities	○	○
Social science	○	○
Biological science	○	○
Physical science	○	○
Business	○	○
Education	○	○
Engineering	○	○
Other professional	○	○
Other	○	○
Same major field as highest degree	○	○

3. Bachelor's degree-granting institution: (Please write within the lines)

Name of Institution		City	
		State	

4. Doctoral degree-granting institution:

Name of Institution		City	
		State	

5. Mark each of the following (if applicable).
(Please write the year in the boxes, and mark the corresponding circle below each box)   **EXAMPLE**

19 | 7 0

Year of Bachelor's   Year of Master's   Year of Doctorate

6. Were you employed full-time for a period after you received your bachelor's and before you started to study for your PhD or equivalent degree? (Mark one)
   ○ No
   ○ Yes, at a job unrelated to both undergraduate and graduate studies
   ○ Yes, at a job related to my undergraduate studies
   ○ Yes, at a job related to my subsequent doctoral studies

7. As a graduate student, did you receive or attain: (Mark all that apply)
   ○ Woodrow Wilson fellowship
   ○ Other national fellowship based on merit
   ○ University fellowship based on merit
   ○ Academic prize
   ○ Publication of scholarly article
   ○ Completion of dissertation subsequently published as book or monograph

8. When you were in graduate school, how did you rate yourself compared with other students in your academic program?
   ○ Top 20%
   ○ Next 20%
   ○ Average
   ○ Next 20%
   ○ Lowest 20%

(Please check that your pencil markings are completely darkening the circles. Do not use pen or make ✓'s or X's. THANK YOU)

9. Listed below are 13 broad fields followed by their specializations. (A) Mark the specialization that most closely represents the major for your highest earned degree. If your training was interdisciplinary, mark all that apply and then mark "interdisciplinary major" at the end of the column. If your specialization does not appear on the list, mark "other" in your broad field. (B) Mark the specialization you use most in your current position. (C) Mark the specialization you used most in your previous position. If not currently employed, mark only A and C. If you have no previous employer, mark only A and B.

(A) Specialization closest to highest-degree major

(B) Specialization — Current position

(C) Specialization — Previous position

BIOLOGICAL SCIENCE

Biochemistry	(A)(B)(C)
Microbiology & Bacteriology	(A)(B)(C)
Physiology	(A)(B)(C)
Molecular Biology	(A)(B)(C)
Genetics	(A)(B)(C)
Ecology	(A)(B)(C)
Entomology	(A)(B)(C)
Zoology	(A)(B)(C)
Botany	(A)(B)(C)
Other	(A)(B)(C)

ENGINEERING

CIVIL ENGINEERING

Transportation	(A)(B)(C)
Construction	(A)(B)(C)
Environmental engineering	(A)(B)(C)
Geo-technical (solid mechanics)	(A)(B)(C)
Structural	(A)(B)(C)
Highway	(A)(B)(C)
Hydraulics	(A)(B)(C)
Urban planning and development	(A)(B)(C)
Other	(A)(B)(C)

ELECTRICAL ENGINEERING

Power engineering	(A)(B)(C)
Computer engineering	(A)(B)(C)
Circuits and systems	(A)(B)(C)
Control systems	(A)(B)(C)
Communication technology	(A)(B)(C)
Aircraft and missiles	(A)(B)(C)
Other	(A)(B)(C)

MECHANICAL ENGINEERING

Applied mechanics	(A)(B)(C)
Design	(A)(B)(C)
Heat transfer	(A)(B)(C)
Management	(A)(B)(C)
Plant engineering and maintenance	(A)(B)(C)
Power	(A)(B)(C)
Production	(A)(B)(C)
Other	(A)(B)(C)

PHYSICAL SCIENCE AND MATHEMATICS

CHEMISTRY

Agricultural	(A)(B)(C)
Analytical	(A)(B)(C)
Biochemistry	(A)(B)(C)
Chemical engineering	(A)(B)(C)
Environmental	(A)(B)(C)
Inorganic	(A)(B)(C)
Macromolecular (Polymer)	(A)(B)(C)
Organic	(A)(B)(C)
Pharmaceutical/ Medicinal	(A)(B)(C)
Physical	(A)(B)(C)
Other	(A)(B)(C)

MATHEMATICS

A. Pure Mathematics

Analysis and functional analyses	(A)(B)(C)
Algebra and number theory	(A)(B)(C)
Geometry and topology	
Other	(A)(B)(C)

B. Other Mathematics

Statistics	(A)(B)(C)
Computer science	(A)(B)(C)
Applied mathematics	(A)(B)(C)
Other	(A)(B)(C)

PHYSICS

Astronomy and astrophysics	(A)(B)(C)
Atomic and molecular	(A)(B)(C)
Elementary particles and fields	(A)(B)(C)
Nuclear physics	(A)(B)(C)
Solid state physics	(A)(B)(C)
Other	(A)(B)(C)

SOCIAL SCIENCE

ANTHROPOLOGY

Ethnology (Social/ cultural)	(A)(B)(C)
Archeology	(A)(B)(C)
Physical (Biological)	(A)(B)(C)
Linguistics	(A)(B)(C)
Applied (Anthropology of modern life)	(A)(B)(C)
Other	(A)(B)(C)

ECONOMICS

Theory, History, Systems	(A)(B)(C)
Economic growth	(A)(B)(C)
Economic statistics	(A)(B)(C)
Monetary, Fiscal, International	(A)(B)(C)
Administration, Finance, Marketing, Accounting	(A)(B)(C)
Industrial Organization, Agriculture, Natural Resources	(A)(B)(C)
Manpower, Labor, Population, Welfare, Consumer, Urban & Regional	(A)(B)(C)
Other	(A)(B)(C)

HISTORY

A. Area

U.S.	(A)(B)(C)
Latin America	(A)(B)(C)
Western Europe	(A)(B)(C)
Eastern Europe and Russia	(A)(B)(C)
Africa	(A)(B)(C)
Asia	(A)(B)(C)
Near and Middle East	(A)(B)(C)
International Relations	(A)(B)(C)
Other	(A)(B)(C)

B. Period

Contemporary (20th Century)	(A)(B)(C)
Pre-20th Century	(A)(B)(C)

POLITICAL SCIENCE

American government	(A)(B)(C)
Public administration	(A)(B)(C)
Public policy	(A)(B)(C)
Political theory	(A)(B)(C)
Comparative/cross national politics	(A)(B)(C)
International relations/ world politics	(A)(B)(C)
Other	(A)(B)(C)

PSYCHOLOGY

Individual: Personality, social, educational, developmental	(A)(B)(C)
Physiological and Experimental: Parapsychology, psychopharmacology	(A)(B)(C)
Quantitative: Mathematical, psychometrics, statistical	(A)(B)(C)
Work-applied: Industrial, organizational, personnel	(A)(B)(C)
Person-applied: Clinical, counseling, school, psychotherapy, theoretical, historical	(A)(B)(C)
Other	(A)(B)(C)

SOCIOLOGY

Theory/methods	(A)(B)(C)
Social psychology	(A)(B)(C)
Social organizations	(A)(B)(C)
Deviance/crime	(A)(B)(C)
Social change	(A)(B)(C)
Population/demography	(A)(B)(C)
Applied sociology	(A)(B)(C)
Other	(A)(B)(C)

OTHER

SCIENCE, GENERAL	(A)(B)(C)
BUSINESS	(A)(B)(C)
OTHER FIELD (Specify)	
_____	(A)(B)(C)

INTERDISCIPLINARY MAJOR   (A)(B)(C)

10. Have you ever held or do you now hold a postdoctoral appointment?

○ Yes, I have completed one period of postdoctoral work ⌉
○ Yes, I have had more than one period of postdoctoral work |
○ Yes, I am now engaged in postdoctoral work ⌋
                              Continue with Question 11 ◄
○ No ──► Proceed to Question 14

11. Why did you accept your latest postdoctoral appointment?
(Mark all that apply)

○ To continue working at the institution where I received my PhD
○ Employment not available elsewhere
○ To complement knowledge and skills in doctoral field
○ To update knowledge and skills in doctoral field
○ To obtain knowledge or training in a different specialization than doctorate but in same field
○ To obtain knowledge or training in a field other than doctorate
○ To become more "employable"
○ To carry out a specific research project
○ To stay in an academic environment
○ To work with a specific faculty member
○ To get a permanent job at the university where I held the postdoctoral appointment

12. After your most recent postdoctoral work, did you: (Mark one)

○ Accept your first job after PhD
○ Return to your previous job at the same level and salary
○ Return to your previous job at a lower level and/or salary
○ Return to your previous job at a higher level and/or salary
○ Return to your previous employer, but to a different job
○ Accept a new position at the same level and salary as position held prior to postdoctoral work
○ Accept a new position at a lower level and/or salary
○ Accept a new position at a higher level and/or salary
○ Become unemployed

13. What was the year of (A) your first or only postdoctoral appointment and (B) your latest postdoctoral appointment if different from first?

First Postdoctoral Appointment

19 ☐☐

(Write the year in the boxes and mark the corresponding circles)

⓪⓪ ①① ②② ③③ ④④ ⑤⑤ ⑥⑥ ⑦⑦ ⑧⑧ ⑨⑨

Mark here ○ if latest appointment is the same as the first.

Latest Postdoctoral Appointment

19 ☐☐

⓪⓪ ①① ②② ③③ ④④ ⑤⑤ ⑥⑥ ⑦⑦ ⑧⑧ ⑨⑨

14. How many full-time jobs with different employers have you held since receiving your highest degree?

○ None   ○ Two–three   ○ Six–eight
○ One   ○ Four–five   ○ Nine or more

15. Have you been unemployed and seeking employment for more than one month at any time since receiving your highest degree?

○ No ──► Proceed to Question 17
○ Yes, once ⌉
○ Yes, more than once ⌋──► Continue with Question 16

16. What is the most recent year during which you were unemployed and seeking work for more than one month since receiving your doctorate?

(Write the year in the boxes and mark the corresponding circles)

19 ☐☐ ──► ⓪①②③④⑤⑥⑦⑧⑨
              ⓪①②③④⑤⑥⑦⑧⑨

17. Are you presently employed for pay? (Mark one)

○ Yes, employed full-time ⌉
○ Yes, employed part-time ⌋──► Proceed to Question 21
○ No, seeking full-time work
○ No, seeking part-time work
○ No, not seeking employment but plan to look within a year
○ No, not seeking employment but plan to look within five years
○ No, not seeking or planning to seek employment
                              Continue with Question 18 ◄

18. If you are not currently employed, when did you last hold a job? Do not include part-time jobs held while in graduate school.
(Mark one)

○ Within last three months   ○ Over a year ago
○ Within last four–twelve months   ○ Never

19. How long have you been unemployed and looking for a job?
(Mark one)

○ Not looking   ○ Six months–one year
○ Less than one month   ○ One–two years
○ One–two months   ○ More than two years
○ Three–six months

20. Why are you presently unemployed? (Mark all that apply)

○ Pursuing postdoctoral study
○ Do not like jobs available
○ Not seeking work because I would be unable to find a job
○ Do not know what I want to do
○ Lack certain skills now considered vital in desired job area
○ Do not have the proper education
○ Job market too tight, not enough jobs available
○ Do not have required work experience
○ Would like a part-time job or a job with flexible hours, but I am unable to find one
○ Spouse discourages employment
○ Moved to new location, have not found job
○ Institution/company cut-back (due to enrollment decline, sales decline, loss of research grants, etc.)
○ Illness, accident, health problems
○ Do not want to be employed
○ Travel, extended vacation
○ Prefer volunteer or community activity
○ Involved with home, child care
○ Prefer leisure
○ Have not looked hard enough
○ Employers are reluctant to hire people like me because of age
○ Employers are reluctant to hire people like me because of sex
○ Employers are reluctant to hire people like me because of race
○ Employers are reluctant to hire people who have as much education as I have

For the next two questions, (A) refers to your current job, (B) refers to your previous job, and (C) refers to your first job after completing the PhD or highest degree. If your current position is your only job since completing your highest degree, mark only A. If you are currently unemployed, mark B and C if applicable.

21. Indicate your primary work activity or occupation in:

(C) First job
(B) Previous job
(A) Current job

	A	B	C
Accident prevention	Ⓐ	Ⓑ	Ⓒ
Accounting	Ⓐ	Ⓑ	Ⓒ
Administration or management of:			
research & development	Ⓐ	Ⓑ	Ⓒ
educational institution	Ⓐ	Ⓑ	Ⓒ
both	Ⓐ	Ⓑ	Ⓒ
other than research & development and education	Ⓐ	Ⓑ	Ⓒ
Advertising	Ⓐ	Ⓑ	Ⓒ
Clerical	Ⓐ	Ⓑ	Ⓒ
Clinical work	Ⓐ	Ⓑ	Ⓒ
Consulting/professional services	Ⓐ	Ⓑ	Ⓒ
Counseling	Ⓐ	Ⓑ	Ⓒ
Data processing, computer science	Ⓐ	Ⓑ	Ⓒ
Development	Ⓐ	Ⓑ	Ⓒ
Engineering	Ⓐ	Ⓑ	Ⓒ
Environmental protection	Ⓐ	Ⓑ	Ⓒ
Farming, forestry	Ⓐ	Ⓑ	Ⓒ
Health services	Ⓐ	Ⓑ	Ⓒ
Inspection, testing	Ⓐ	Ⓑ	Ⓒ
Mathematical, statistical, actuarial	Ⓐ	Ⓑ	Ⓒ
Performing, creative arts	Ⓐ	Ⓑ	Ⓒ
Personnel, employee relations	Ⓐ	Ⓑ	Ⓒ
Production, quality control	Ⓐ	Ⓑ	Ⓒ
Program planning, budgeting	Ⓐ	Ⓑ	Ⓒ
Public relations	Ⓐ	Ⓑ	Ⓒ
Publications	Ⓐ	Ⓑ	Ⓒ
Public safety, law enforcement, community service	Ⓐ	Ⓑ	Ⓒ
Research (applied)	Ⓐ	Ⓑ	Ⓒ
Research (evaluation)	Ⓐ	Ⓑ	Ⓒ
Research (laboratory/experimental)	Ⓐ	Ⓑ	Ⓒ
Research (theoretical/other)	Ⓐ	Ⓑ	Ⓒ
Sales, marketing, purchasing, merchandising	Ⓐ	Ⓑ	Ⓒ
Skilled worker	Ⓐ	Ⓑ	Ⓒ
Speaking to groups, leading discussions	Ⓐ	Ⓑ	Ⓒ
Teaching	Ⓐ	Ⓑ	Ⓒ
Technological design, construction	Ⓐ	Ⓑ	Ⓒ
Technology (other)	Ⓐ	Ⓑ	Ⓒ
Training	Ⓐ	Ⓑ	Ⓒ
Unskilled worker	Ⓐ	Ⓑ	Ⓒ
Writing, editing	Ⓐ	Ⓑ	Ⓒ
Other	Ⓐ	Ⓑ	Ⓒ

22. Indicate the type of employer that best describes:

(C) First job
(B) Previous job
(A) Current job

	A	B	C
Commerce, finance, insurance, real estate	Ⓐ	Ⓑ	Ⓒ
Manufacturing, construction	Ⓐ	Ⓑ	Ⓒ
Retail, wholesale	Ⓐ	Ⓑ	Ⓒ
Other business, service establishments	Ⓐ	Ⓑ	Ⓒ
Transportation, public utilities	Ⓐ	Ⓑ	Ⓒ
Agriculture, mining	Ⓐ	Ⓑ	Ⓒ
Four-year college, university, professional school	Ⓐ	Ⓑ	Ⓒ
Technical institute	Ⓐ	Ⓑ	Ⓒ
Two-year college	Ⓐ	Ⓑ	Ⓒ
Elementary, secondary school	Ⓐ	Ⓑ	Ⓒ
Federally funded lab (e.g., Brookhaven)	Ⓐ	Ⓑ	Ⓒ
Independent research organization	Ⓐ	Ⓑ	Ⓒ
Human services organization (social welfare, hospital)	Ⓐ	Ⓑ	Ⓒ
International agency	Ⓐ	Ⓑ	Ⓒ
Military service, active duty	Ⓐ	Ⓑ	Ⓒ
U.S. government, civilian employee	Ⓐ	Ⓑ	Ⓒ
State, local, other government	Ⓐ	Ⓑ	Ⓒ
Other nonprofit organization	Ⓐ	Ⓑ	Ⓒ
Other	Ⓐ	Ⓑ	Ⓒ

23. Indicate the kind of appointment or job security you have/had in:

(B) Previous position
(A) Current position

(Mark one in each column)

College/University Faculty

	A	B
Tenured	Ⓐ	Ⓑ
No tenure, but on tenure ladder	Ⓐ	Ⓑ
Acting	Ⓐ	Ⓑ
Visiting	Ⓐ	Ⓑ
Fixed-term contract (more than 2 years)	Ⓐ	Ⓑ
Short-term contract (2 years or less)	Ⓐ	Ⓑ
Other	Ⓐ	Ⓑ

Non College/University Faculty
(i.e. college administration or nonacademic job)

	A	B
Tenured	Ⓐ	Ⓑ
Seniority rights	Ⓐ	Ⓑ
Civil service tenure	Ⓐ	Ⓑ
Formal security arrangement	Ⓐ	Ⓑ
No formal security or seniority arrangements	Ⓐ	Ⓑ
Other	Ⓐ	Ⓑ

24. What was the year you were awarded tenure at current institution (if applicable)?
(Write year in boxes and mark the circles)

19 ☐ ☐ → ⓪①②③④⑤⑥⑦⑧⑨
→ ⓪①②③④⑤⑥⑦⑧⑨

25. Indicate the rank or level most closely representing your:

(B) Previous position
(A) Current position

(Mark one in each column)

College/University Faculty

	A	B
Professor	Ⓐ	Ⓑ
Associate professor	Ⓐ	Ⓑ
Assistant professor	Ⓐ	Ⓑ
Instructor/lecturer	Ⓐ	Ⓑ
Other	Ⓐ	Ⓑ

Other College/University Position
(i.e., non faculty)

	A	B
President/Chancellor	Ⓐ	Ⓑ
Vice-president/Provost or equivalent	Ⓐ	Ⓑ
Dean or equivalent	Ⓐ	Ⓑ
Other administrator	Ⓐ	Ⓑ
Counselor	Ⓐ	Ⓑ
Other	Ⓐ	Ⓑ

Non-College/University Position

	A	B
Executive	Ⓐ	Ⓑ
Manager	Ⓐ	Ⓑ
Administrator	Ⓐ	Ⓑ
Professional	Ⓐ	Ⓑ
Research scientist	Ⓐ	Ⓑ
Technician	Ⓐ	Ⓑ
Supervisor	Ⓐ	Ⓑ
Clerical	Ⓐ	Ⓑ
Teacher (elementary, secondary)	Ⓐ	Ⓑ
Skilled/semi/unskilled worker	Ⓐ	Ⓑ
Other	Ⓐ	Ⓑ

26. What was the year you obtained your current rank or level?
(Write year in boxes and mark the circles)

19 ☐ ☐ → ⓪①②③④⑤⑥⑦⑧⑨
→ ⓪①②③④⑤⑥⑦⑧⑨

27. What was the year you most recently changed employers?
(Write year in boxes and mark the circles)

19 ☐ ☐ → ⓪①②③④⑤⑥⑦⑧⑨
→ ⓪①②③④⑤⑥⑦⑧⑨

28. What is your job title and the name of your employer for (A) your current <u>primary</u> position, (B) your current <u>secondary</u> position (if applicable), and (C) your <u>previous</u> position. If self-employed, write "self" for employer.

(A) <u>Current primary position</u>

    Job Title: _____

    Employer: _____

    City/State: _____

(B) <u>Current secondary position</u>

    Job Title: _____

    Employer: _____

    City/State: _____

(C) <u>Previous primary position</u>

    Job Title: _____

    Employer: _____

    City/State: _____

29. What proportion of your working time is devoted to your current <u>primary</u> position?

  ○ Unemployed   ○ 26 – 50%   ○ 76 – 99%
  ○ 1 – 25%   ○ 51 – 75%   ○ 100%

30. How satisfied are you with the following aspects of (A) your current job and (B) your previous job?

	(A) Current job	(B) Previous job
	Very satisfied / Satisfied / Marginally / Not satisfied / Not applicable	Very satisfied / Satisfied / Marginally / Not satisfied / Not applicable
Overall job satisfaction	○○○○○	○○○○○
Salary and fringe benefits	○○○○○	○○○○○
Opportunity for scholarly pursuits	○○○○○	○○○○○
Opportunity for creativity	○○○○○	○○○○○
Opportunity to use training or schooling	○○○○○	○○○○○
Resources to get job done	○○○○○	○○○○○
Teaching load	○○○○○	○○○○○
Quality of students	○○○○○	○○○○○
Pressure to publish	○○○○○	○○○○○
Internal politics	○○○○○	○○○○○
Working conditions (hours, location)	○○○○○	○○○○○
Status	○○○○○	○○○○○
Autonomy and independence	○○○○○	○○○○○
Variety in activities	○○○○○	○○○○○
Policy-making power	○○○○○	○○○○○
Congenial work relationships	○○○○○	○○○○○
Competency of colleagues	○○○○○	○○○○○
Opportunities for different (better) jobs at this institution/organization	○○○○○	○○○○○
Visibility for jobs at other institutions/organizations	○○○○○	○○○○○
Challenge	○○○○○	○○○○○
Job security	○○○○○	○○○○○
Prestige of employer	○○○○○	○○○○○

31. How many years have you been (were you) employed full- and/or part-time?

(Mark <u>one</u> on <u>each</u> line)

	None	Less than one year	1 – 3 years	3 – 6 years	6 – 10 years	10 – 15 years	15 – 20 years	20 – 30 years	30 – 40 years	More than 40 years
At your current job	○	○	○	○	○	○	○	○	○	○
At your previous job	○	○	○	○	○	○	○	○	○	○
At your first job after you received your highest degree	○	○	○	○	○	○	○	○	○	○
In colleges and universities since you received your highest degree	○	○	○	○	○	○	○	○	○	○
Total years employed since you completed your highest degree	○	○	○	○	○	○	○	○	○	○

32. What will your basic salary from primary employment be, before tax and deductions, for 1977? If self-employed, indicate your annual earned income after adjusting for business expenses. If married, what is your spouse's expected salary?

(Mark <u>one</u> on <u>each</u> line)

	None	Less than $7,000	$7,000 – 9,999	$10,000 – 13,999	$14,000 – 16,999	$17,000 – 19,999	$20,000 – 24,999	$25,000 – 29,999	$30,000 – 34,999	$35,000 – 39,999	$40,000 – 49,999	$50,000 or more	Not married
Your salary	○	○	○	○	○	○	○	○	○	○	○	○	
Spouse's salary	○	○	○	○	○	○	○	○	○	○	○	○	○

33. To what extent do the following statements apply to (A) your current job and (B) your previous job? (Mark <u>all</u> that apply)

	(A) Current job	(B) Previous job
	Very much / Somewhat / Not at all	Very much / Somewhat / Not at all
I am well paid for my work compared with others with the same amount of education	○○○	○○○
I supervise people trained in my field	○○○	○○○
Most of my colleagues are trained in my field	○○○	○○○
I am satisfied with my career progress to date	○○○	○○○
My job offers good future prospects for further advancement	○○○	○○○
My job fits my long-range goals	○○○	○○○
My skills are fully utilized in my job	○○○	○○○
I am working at a professional level	○○○	○○○
I would have liked more training outside of graduate school before I started working	○○○	○○○
I received job training inappropriate for actual requirements of my job	○○○	○○○
I am glad I had the graduate education I did	○○○	○○○
My position required on-the-job training	○○○	○○○

34. How closely related was your graduate training to your current job?

○ Closely related ⟶ Proceed to Question 37
○ Somewhat related ⟍
○ Not related ⟋ ⟶ Continue with Question 35

35. If your current job is only "somewhat" or "not related" to your graduate training, when did you move from your graduate field into this new field? (Write the year in the boxes and mark the corresponding circles)

19 [ ][ ] ⟶ ⓪①②③④⑤⑥⑦⑧⑨
⟶ ⓪①②③④⑤⑥⑦⑧⑨

36. Why are you working in a job only "somewhat" or "not related" to your doctoral study? (Mark all that apply)

○ Never planned to take a closely related job
○ Changed field of science or engineering to one I prefer more
○ Exposed to another field and became interested
○ Prefer current work in a nonscience or nonengineering position
○ First job unrelated to doctoral study; became interested in this work
○ Tried closely related employment, but did not like it
○ Joined family business or firm
○ Found job that offers better chance for career advancement
○ Pay is better where I am
○ No longer in closely related job due to promotion
○ Wanted part-time work, flexible hours
○ Wanted to work at home
○ Science or engineering positions not available
○ Jobs related to doctoral study not available where I live, and
    do not want to move
○ Jobs related to my doctoral field not available
○ Could not get a closely related job, but would prefer one
○ Limited in job selection by situation of spouse, family responsibilities
○ Employment opportunities scarce for people in jobs related to my
    doctoral study
○ Have become technologically obsolete in field of doctoral study
○ In the military
○ Better quality work environment where I am

37. Considering your ability, education, and experience, which of the following statements apply in your current job? (Mark all that apply)

○ I am not underemployed
○ I am underemployed and would prefer a more challenging position
○ I am underemployed but for personal reasons I prefer to remain
    in this or a similar position
○ I am underemployed; my job is not in my field
○ I am underemployed; my job is not commensurate with my
    level of experience
○ I am underemployed; my job is not commensurate with my
    level of training
○ I am underemployed; my job is not commensurate with my
    level of ability
○ I have the skills and knowledge necessary for successful
    performance on my job
○ People with less formal schooling are performing well in jobs
    identical to mine
○ If people with less formal schooling were hired, they could
    do my job as well as I
○ I believe my current job is a nontraditional one for people
    in my PhD field
○ I have held other nontraditional jobs

38. Looking back on your graduate education, please indicate the extent to which it was useful in the following ways: (Mark one on each line)

	Very useful	Somewhat useful	Not useful
Provided a skill that enabled me to get my first job	○	○	○
Increased my chances of finding a good job	○	○	○
Helped me choose my life goals	○	○	○
Gave me knowledge and skills that I use in current job	○	○	○
Graduate degree a factor in being hired by current employer	○	○	○
Graduate degree necessary for promotion	○	○	○

39. To what extent did the following provide knowledge or skills that helped prepare you for your current job? (Mark one on each line)

	Very much	Somewhat	Not at all	Not applicable
Graduate study				
Particular course(s) in major area	○	○	○	○
Courses outside major area	○	○	○	○
Graduate study in general	○	○	○	○
Extracurricular activities while in graduate school	○	○	○	○
Research assistantship	○	○	○	○
Teaching assistantship	○	○	○	○
Other training				
Undergraduate study	○	○	○	○
Formal training program at place of employment	○	○	○	○
Formal training or courses other than programs offered by employer	○	○	○	○
General on-the-job experience	○	○	○	○
Leisure activities	○	○	○	○

40. On the following list, mark each item that applies to A, B, C and D. (Mark all that apply in each column)

(D) Improved significantly in graduate school ⟶
(C) Improved significantly in undergraduate school ⟶
(B) Useful on current job ⟶
(A) Your strong points, compared with those of others with the same education ⟶

	A	B	C	D
General knowledge	Ⓐ	Ⓑ	Ⓒ	Ⓓ
Ability to think clearly	Ⓐ	Ⓑ	Ⓒ	Ⓓ
Leadership ability	Ⓐ	Ⓑ	Ⓒ	Ⓓ
Critical thinking or analytical skills	Ⓐ	Ⓑ	Ⓒ	Ⓓ
Self-confidence	Ⓐ	Ⓑ	Ⓒ	Ⓓ
Self-discipline and ability to follow rules	Ⓐ	Ⓑ	Ⓒ	Ⓓ
Creativity and originality	Ⓐ	Ⓑ	Ⓒ	Ⓓ
Writing ability	Ⓐ	Ⓑ	Ⓒ	Ⓓ
Insight	Ⓐ	Ⓑ	Ⓒ	Ⓓ
Cultural perspective	Ⓐ	Ⓑ	Ⓒ	Ⓓ
Understanding of others	Ⓐ	Ⓑ	Ⓒ	Ⓓ
Political awareness	Ⓐ	Ⓑ	Ⓒ	Ⓓ
Academic ability	Ⓐ	Ⓑ	Ⓒ	Ⓓ
Drive to achieve	Ⓐ	Ⓑ	Ⓒ	Ⓓ
Mathematical ability	Ⓐ	Ⓑ	Ⓒ	Ⓓ
Mechanical ability	Ⓐ	Ⓑ	Ⓒ	Ⓓ
Public speaking ability	Ⓐ	Ⓑ	Ⓒ	Ⓓ
Research skills	Ⓐ	Ⓑ	Ⓒ	Ⓓ

41. Have you changed your career goals since entering graduate school?

- ○ Yes (Continue with Question 42)
- ○ No (Proceed to Question 44)

42. When did you change your career goals? If you have changed your career goals more than once, refer to your most recent decision. (Mark one)

- ○ While in graduate school
- ○ At completion of graduate study
- ○ Within three years after completing graduate study
- ○ Three to nine years after completing graduate study
- ○ Ten or more years after completing graduate study

43. Which of the following influenced your latest change of career goals? (Mark all that apply)

- ○ Available job opportunities in previous field were limited or unattractive
- ○ Decided I did not enjoy first-choice career
- ○ Found more attractive or challenging job opportunities elsewhere
- ○ Changed career aspirations for personal or family reasons
- ○ Became outdated in my first-choice field
- ○ Became interested in different area of study
- ○ Was terminated in a job

44. Were you seeking a job change while on your previous job? (Mark one)

- ○ Yes, actively seeking a job
- ○ Yes, seriously thought of changing jobs for an attractive offer
- ○ No, received an unsolicited offer
- ○ Does not apply

45. Could you have stayed at your previous job? (Mark all that apply)

- ○ Yes, at a better position
- ○ Yes, at the same position
- ○ Yes, at another similar position
- ○ Yes, at a less desirable position
- ○ Uncertain, anticipated tenure being denied
- ○ Uncertain, anticipated termination for other reason
- ○ No, contract not renewed
- ○ No, job terminated
- ○ No, tenure denied
- ○ No, reduction in faculty/staff due to financial exigency
- ○ No, business was bad
- ○ No, cutbacks, layoffs
- ○ No, reached mandatory retirement age

46. How did the monthly starting salary of your current job differ from the salary you would have received if you had stayed on your previous job? (Mark one)

- ○ More than ten percent lower
- ○ One to ten percent lower
- ○ Approximately the same
- ○ One to ten percent higher
- ○ Eleven to twenty-five percent higher
- ○ More than twenty-five percent higher

47. How did your most recent job change affect your other income? (Mark one)

- ○ Substantial increase (eleven or more percent)
- ○ Small increase (one to ten percent)
- ○ No change
- ○ Small decrease (one to ten percent)
- ○ Substantial decrease (eleven or more percent)

48. In securing your current job, which of the following job-search methods/contacts (A) did you use, and (B) were successful? (Mark all that apply)

	(A) Used	(B) Successful
My former professors	○	○
Colleagues in my organization/institution	○	○
Colleagues in other institutions	○	○
College/university placement office	○	○
Public/state employment service	○	○
Private employment agency	○	○
Civil service application	○	○
Recruiting teams from government, industry	○	○
Professional contacts	○	○
Direct personal application to employer	○	○
Professional organizations, meetings	○	○
Newspaper advertisements	○	○
Professional journals, periodicals	○	○
Met new employer through previous job	○	○
Unsolicited offer	○	○
Parents/other relatives	○	○
Friends	○	○
Luck/chance	○	○

49. When you were offered your current position, were you actively seeking employment in the following areas:

(E) Currently seeking position
(D) Received unsolicited offer
(C) Did not seek position
(B) Sought position, but no offer
(A) Sought position and received offer
(Mark all that apply)

Setting	(A)	(B)	(C)	(D)	(E)
University	Ⓐ	Ⓑ	Ⓒ	Ⓓ	Ⓔ
Four-year college	Ⓐ	Ⓑ	Ⓒ	Ⓓ	Ⓔ
Two-year college	Ⓐ	Ⓑ	Ⓒ	Ⓓ	Ⓔ
Elementary/secondary school	Ⓐ	Ⓑ	Ⓒ	Ⓓ	Ⓔ
Federally funded research & development center (e.g., Brookhaven)	Ⓐ	Ⓑ	Ⓒ	Ⓓ	Ⓔ
Federal government	Ⓐ	Ⓑ	Ⓒ	Ⓓ	Ⓔ
State/local government	Ⓐ	Ⓑ	Ⓒ	Ⓓ	Ⓔ
Other nonprofit organization (hospital, research institute)	Ⓐ	Ⓑ	Ⓒ	Ⓓ	Ⓔ
Private business/industrial firm	Ⓐ	Ⓑ	Ⓒ	Ⓓ	Ⓔ
Employment abroad	Ⓐ	Ⓑ	Ⓒ	Ⓓ	Ⓔ
Activity					
Faculty/teacher	Ⓐ	Ⓑ	Ⓒ	Ⓓ	Ⓔ
Administration	Ⓐ	Ⓑ	Ⓒ	Ⓓ	Ⓔ
Nonfaculty/nonadministrative position in academic institution	Ⓐ	Ⓑ	Ⓒ	Ⓓ	Ⓔ
Research/development	Ⓐ	Ⓑ	Ⓒ	Ⓓ	Ⓔ
Sales/marketing/advertising/public relations	Ⓐ	Ⓑ	Ⓒ	Ⓓ	Ⓔ
Accounting/data processing	Ⓐ	Ⓑ	Ⓒ	Ⓓ	Ⓔ
Other	Ⓐ	Ⓑ	Ⓒ	Ⓓ	Ⓔ
Field					
Major field of PhD	Ⓐ	Ⓑ	Ⓒ	Ⓓ	Ⓔ
Other science and engineering field	Ⓐ	Ⓑ	Ⓒ	Ⓓ	Ⓔ
Outside science and engineering	Ⓐ	Ⓑ	Ⓒ	Ⓓ	Ⓔ

50. Indicate the extent to which these statements apply to you.

(Mark one on each line)

Columns: Strongly agree / Somewhat agree / Disagree somewhat / Strongly disagree

I would take a job anywhere as long as there were opportunities to travel. ○○○○

If I were looking for a job now, I would look nationwide ○○○○

There are a limited number of cities in which I would live ○○○○

Climate would be a major factor in my decision to move. ○○○○

I would take a job anywhere for a short period but I have specific preferences for permanent residence ○○○○

I would move anywhere if the salary were attractive enough. ○○○○

I would move anywhere for an extremely satisfying job ○○○○

I will be more mobile when my children are out of school ○○○○

My mobility is limited because my parents are alive. ○○○○

My ideal job location is within 500 miles of the community where I grew up. ○○○○

My occupation severely limits my choice of geographic location ○○○○

My mobility is limited because of spouse's job. ○○○○

My mobility is limited because of spouse's educational plans ○○○○

My mobility is limited because of spouse's preferences about locale ○○○○

If I could begin my career again, I would like to become a college professor ○○○○

I could be equally or more satisfied with a different employer. ○○○○

51. Are you currently engaged in any scholarly or research work that you expect to lead to publication?

○ Yes   ○ No

52. How many of the following have you produced since completing graduate study?

(Mark one on each line)

Columns: None / 1 or 2 / 3 to 5 / 6 to 10 / 11 or more

Scholarly book(s), single authorship. ○○○○○

Scholarly book(s), joint authorship ○○○○○

Scholarly book(s), editor ○○○○○

Other book(s). ○○○○○

Chapters/articles in scholarly books/journals. ○○○○○

Articles in nonscholarly journals. ○○○○○

Book reviews, editorials, abstracts, other published short works ○○○○○

Published reports ○○○○○

Internal reports (unpublished) of article or monograph length ○○○○○

Patentable inventions ○○○○○

53. How much research/publication per year did you accomplish during:

Columns: Great deal / Some / Little / None

First job after completing highest degree ○ ○ ○ ○

Job prior to current position (if different) ○ ○ ○ ○

Current position (if different) ○ ○ ○ ○

54. Overall, how satisfied are you with:

(Mark one on each line)

Columns: Very satisfied / Somewhat satisfied / Not satisfied

Life in general ○ ○ ○

Family life ○ ○ ○

Leisure activities ○ ○ ○

Quality of community cultural life ○ ○ ○

Social life ○ ○ ○

Geographic area in which you live ○ ○ ○

Future prospects ○ ○ ○

55. How many miles away is:

(Mark one on each line)

Columns: In the same place / Under 50 miles / 50 – 99 miles / 100 – 499 miles / 500 – 999 miles / 1,000 – 2,999 miles / 3,000 miles or more

Current or most recent job from hometown (where you attended high school) ○○○○○○○

Current job from institution of highest degree ○○○○○○○

Institution of highest degree from hometown ○○○○○○○

Current job from previous job ○○○○○○○

56. What is your sex?

○ Male
○ Female

57. Year of birth:

19 [ ][ ]   Write the year and mark the circles

○0 ○0
○1 ○1
○2 ○2
○3 ○3
○4 ○4
○5 ○5
○6 ○6
○7 ○7
○8 ○8
○9 ○9

Be sure to answer questions 58—60

58. Are you:

○ American Indian
○ Black/Negro
○ Mexican-American/Chicano
○ Oriental
○ Puerto Rican-American
○ White/Caucasian
○ Other Asian
○ Other

59. What is your marital status?

○ Single (never married)
○ Married
○ Separated, divorced, widowed

60. Number of children:

○ None   ○ Two
○ One   ○ Three or more

61. Are you a member of a professional association?

○ No   ○ Yes.   If yes, which one(s)?

[ ]

62. Are you willing to have: (Mark one)

○ The data from the questionnaire released to the relevant professional association, if your name is not revealed?

○ Your name given to the relevant professional association if the data are not revealed

○ Neither of the above

We would appreciate your name and address; it would be used only if a follow-up study should be planned some years in the future.

Name

Organization

Street Address

City   State   Zip Code

Thank you for your participation in this survey. Please return your questionnaire in the enclosed postage-paid envelope.

SURVEY OF HIGHLY TRAINED PUBLIC SECTOR EMPLOYEES

HIGHER EDUCATION RESEARCH INSTITUTE   ●   4555 WEST 77TH STREET   ●   MINNEAPOLIS, MINNESOTA 55435

DIRECTIONS: Your responses will be read by an optical mark reader. Your careful observance of these few simple rules will be most appreciated.
- Use only a black lead pencil (no. 2½ or less).
- Make heavy black marks that fill the circle.
- Erase cleanly any answer you wish to change.
- Make no stray markings of any kind.
- Where write-in responses are necessary, please confine your writing to the limits of the lines provided.

EXAMPLE: Will marks made with ball-point or felt-tip pen be properly read?   ○ Yes   ● No

4153

PLEASE
DO NOT
WRITE
IN THIS
AREA

NOTE: A postdoctoral appointment should not be classified as a job.

Any reference to "previous job or position" means your most recent former job with a different company or institution.

1. On the following list, please mark (A) all degrees you have earned and (B) the degree(s) for which you are currently working, if any.

	(A) Now hold	(B) Working on
Bachelor's	○	○
Master's	○	○
Doctor of Arts or equivalent	○	○
EdD	○	○
PhD	○	○
Other professional degree (MD, DDS, LLB)	○	○
Other	○	○
None	○	○

2. What were the areas of concentration for (A) your bachelor's and (B) your master's degree? In (C) indicate areas outside your major field of graduate study in which you have taken elective courses as an undergraduate or graduate student. (Mark all that apply)

	(A) Bachelor's	(B) Master's	(C) Elective
Arts & humanities	○	○	○
Social science	○	○	○
Biological science	○	○	○
Physical science	○	○	○
Business	○	○	○
Education	○	○	○
Engineering	○	○	○
Other professional	○	○	○
Other	○	○	○
Same major field as highest degree	○	○	
Do not hold that degree	○	○	

3. **Bachelor's degree-granting institution:** (Please write within the lines)

Name of Institution		City	
		State	

4. **Doctoral degree-granting institution:**

Name of Institution		City	
		State	

5. Mark each of the following (if applicable). (Please write the year in the boxes, and mark the corresponding circle below each box.)

EXAMPLE 19 | 7 0

Year of Bachelor's	Year of Master's	Year completed formal course work for Phd	Year of Doctorate
19	19	19	19

6. As a graduate student, did you receive or attain: (Mark all that apply)
- ○ Woodrow Wilson fellowship
- ○ Other national fellowship based on merit
- ○ University fellowship based on merit
- ○ Academic prize
- ○ Publication of scholarly article
- ○ Completion of dissertation subsequently published as book or monograph

7. When you were in graduate school, how did you rate yourself compared with other students in your academic program?
- ○ Top 20%
- ○ Next 20%
- ○ Average
- ○ Next 20%
- ○ Lowest 20%

8. What was your parents' income level when you were an undergraduate? (If parents were deceased, please respond for the period before their death. If parents were divorced, indicate income of parent with whom you principally resided.)
- ○ Wealthy (among the nation's most affluent 15%)
- ○ Upper middle class (the next 20%)
- ○ Middle class (the middle 30%)
- ○ Lower middle class (the next 20%)
- ○ Poor (among the nation's poorest 15%)

(Please check that your pencil markings are completely darkening the circles. Do not use pen or make ✓'s or ✗'s. THANK YOU)

9a. Listed below are a series of fields.

  (A) Mark the field that <u>most closely</u> represents the major for your highest degree. If your training was interdisciplinary, mark all that apply and then mark "interdisciplinary" under "OTHER" at the end of column. If your field does not appear on the list, mark "OTHER" at the end of the list.

  (B) Mark the field you <u>use most</u> in your current job.

  (C) Mark the specialization you used most in your previous position. If not currently employed, mark only A and C. If you have no previous employer, mark only A and B.

HUMANITIES	SOCIAL SCIENCE	PHYSICAL SCIENCE
Ⓐ Ⓑ Ⓒ English	Ⓐ Ⓑ Ⓒ Anthropology	Ⓐ Ⓑ Ⓒ Chemistry
Ⓐ Ⓑ Ⓒ French	Ⓐ Ⓑ Ⓒ Economics	Ⓐ Ⓑ Ⓒ Mathematics
Ⓐ Ⓑ Ⓒ Spanish	Ⓐ Ⓑ Ⓒ Political Science	Ⓐ Ⓑ Ⓒ Statistics
Ⓐ Ⓑ Ⓒ German	Ⓐ Ⓑ Ⓒ Psychology	Ⓐ Ⓑ Ⓒ Physics
Ⓐ Ⓑ Ⓒ Russian	Ⓐ Ⓑ Ⓒ Sociology	Ⓐ Ⓑ Ⓒ Other
Ⓐ Ⓑ Ⓒ Chinese	Ⓐ Ⓑ Ⓒ Other	**OTHER**
Ⓐ Ⓑ Ⓒ Other Foreign Language		Ⓐ Ⓑ Ⓒ Business
Ⓐ Ⓑ Ⓒ Philosophy	Ⓐ Ⓑ Ⓒ BIOLOGICAL SCIENCE	Ⓐ Ⓑ Ⓒ Education
Ⓐ Ⓑ Ⓒ History		Ⓐ Ⓑ Ⓒ Interdisciplinary
Ⓐ Ⓑ Ⓒ Other	Ⓐ Ⓑ Ⓒ ENGINEERING	Ⓐ Ⓑ Ⓒ Other Field

9b. Please write the principal methodological focus (including time period if applicable) or detailed subspecialty of

A. Your graduate training _____

B. Your present job _____

10. Indicate the extent to which each of the following motivated you to <u>enter</u> a doctoral program. (Mark <u>one</u> response for <u>each</u> line.)

	Very much	Somewhat			Not at all
Graduate study necessary for intended career.	⑤	④	③	②	①
Wanted to become a college teacher.	⑤	④	③	②	①
Improvement in earning potential	⑤	④	③	②	①
Offered financial support (fellowship, assistantship, etc.)	⑤	④	③	②	①
Interest in subject matter of field	⑤	④	③	②	①
Personal satisfaction; felt would enjoy being in graduate school	⑤	④	③	②	①
Encouragement by faculty advisers	⑤	④	③	②	①
Encouragement by friends, family	⑤	④	③	②	①
To postpone the draft.	⑤	④	③	②	①
No attractive employment alternative.	⑤	④	③	②	①
Not admitted to alternative educational program (e.g., law school, medical school)	⑤	④	③	②	①

11. Rate yourself on the following:

	Strong	Adequate	Poor
Foreign language skills	○	○	○
Quantitative skills	○	○	○
Background in science or technology	○	○	○

12. How many full-time jobs with different employers have you held since receiving your highest degree?

○ None   ○ Four-five
○ One   ○ Six-eight
○ Two-three   ○ Nine or more

13. What was the year you most recently changed employers? (Write year in boxes and mark the circles)

19 ⬜ ⬜ → ⓪①②③④⑤⑥⑦⑧⑨
         → ⓪①②③④⑤⑥⑦⑧⑨

14. Were you seeking a job change while on your previous job? (Mark <u>one</u>)

○ Yes, actively seeking a job
○ Yes, seriously thought of changing jobs for an attractive offer
○ No, received an unsolicited offer
○ Does not apply

15. Have you been unemployed and seeking employment for more than one month at any time since receiving your highest degree?

○ No
○ Yes, once
○ Yes, more than once

16. What is the most recent year during which you were unemployed and seeking work for more than one month since receiving your doctorate? (Write year in boxes and mark the circles)

19 ⬜ ⬜ → ⓪①②③④⑤⑥⑦⑧⑨
         → ⓪①②③④⑤⑥⑦⑧⑨

17. Are you presently employed for pay? (Mark <u>one</u>)

○ Yes, employed full-time
○ Yes, employed part-time
○ No, seeking full-time work
○ No, seeking part-time work
○ No, not seeking employment but plan to look within a year
○ No, not seeking employment but plan to look within five years
○ No, not seeking or planning to seek employment

For the next two questions, (A) refers to your current job, (B) refers to your previous job, and (C) refers to your first job after completing the PhD or highest degree. If your present position is your <u>only</u> job since completing your highest degree, mark only A. If you are currently unemployed, mark B and C if applicable. In (D) indicate what activity and employer you would prefer to have.

18. Indicate your primary work activity or occupation in: (Mark <u>one</u> in <u>each</u> column)

(D) Preferred position
(C) First job
(B) Previous job
(A) Present job

	A	B	C	D
Accident prevention	Ⓐ	Ⓑ	Ⓒ	Ⓓ
Accounting	Ⓐ	Ⓑ	Ⓒ	Ⓓ
Administration or management of:				
research & development	Ⓐ	Ⓑ	Ⓒ	Ⓓ
educational institution	Ⓐ	Ⓑ	Ⓒ	Ⓓ
both	Ⓐ	Ⓑ	Ⓒ	Ⓓ
other than research & development and education	Ⓐ	Ⓑ	Ⓒ	Ⓓ
Advertising	Ⓐ	Ⓑ	Ⓒ	Ⓓ
Clerical	Ⓐ	Ⓑ	Ⓒ	Ⓓ
Clinical work	Ⓐ	Ⓑ	Ⓒ	Ⓓ
Consulting/professional services	Ⓐ	Ⓑ	Ⓒ	Ⓓ
Counseling	Ⓐ	Ⓑ	Ⓒ	Ⓓ
Data processing, computer science	Ⓐ	Ⓑ	Ⓒ	Ⓓ
Development	Ⓐ	Ⓑ	Ⓒ	Ⓓ
Engineering	Ⓐ	Ⓑ	Ⓒ	Ⓓ
Environmental protection	Ⓐ	Ⓑ	Ⓒ	Ⓓ
Farming, forestry	Ⓐ	Ⓑ	Ⓒ	Ⓓ
Health services	Ⓐ	Ⓑ	Ⓒ	Ⓓ
Inspection, testing	Ⓐ	Ⓑ	Ⓒ	Ⓓ
Library, museum, archival work	Ⓐ	Ⓑ	Ⓒ	Ⓓ
Mathematical, statistical, actuarial	Ⓐ	Ⓑ	Ⓒ	Ⓓ
Performing, creative arts	Ⓐ	Ⓑ	Ⓒ	Ⓓ
Personnel, employee relations	Ⓐ	Ⓑ	Ⓒ	Ⓓ
Production, quality control	Ⓐ	Ⓑ	Ⓒ	Ⓓ
Program planning, budgeting	Ⓐ	Ⓑ	Ⓒ	Ⓓ
Public relations	Ⓐ	Ⓑ	Ⓒ	Ⓓ
Publications	Ⓐ	Ⓑ	Ⓒ	Ⓓ
Public safety, law enforcement, community service	Ⓐ	Ⓑ	Ⓒ	Ⓓ
Research (applied)	Ⓐ	Ⓑ	Ⓒ	Ⓓ
Research (evaluation)	Ⓐ	Ⓑ	Ⓒ	Ⓓ
Research (laboratory/experimental)	Ⓐ	Ⓑ	Ⓒ	Ⓓ
Research (theoretical/other)	Ⓐ	Ⓑ	Ⓒ	Ⓓ
Sales, marketing, purchasing, merchandising	Ⓐ	Ⓑ	Ⓒ	Ⓓ
Skilled worker	Ⓐ	Ⓑ	Ⓒ	Ⓓ
Speaking to groups, leading discussions	Ⓐ	Ⓑ	Ⓒ	Ⓓ
Teaching	Ⓐ	Ⓑ	Ⓒ	Ⓓ
Technological design, construction	Ⓐ	Ⓑ	Ⓒ	Ⓓ
Technology (other)	Ⓐ	Ⓑ	Ⓒ	Ⓓ
Training	Ⓐ	Ⓑ	Ⓒ	Ⓓ
Unskilled worker	Ⓐ	Ⓑ	Ⓒ	Ⓓ
Writing, editing	Ⓐ	Ⓑ	Ⓒ	Ⓓ
Other	Ⓐ	Ⓑ	Ⓒ	Ⓓ

19. Indicate the type of employer that best describes: (Mark <u>one</u> in <u>each</u> column)

(D) Preferred position
(C) First job
(B) Previous job
(A) Present job

	A	B	C	D
Private, for-profit business corporation	Ⓐ	Ⓑ	Ⓒ	Ⓓ
Four-year college, university, professional school	Ⓐ	Ⓑ	Ⓒ	Ⓓ
Two-year college, technical institute	Ⓐ	Ⓑ	Ⓒ	Ⓓ
Elementary, secondary school	Ⓐ	Ⓑ	Ⓒ	Ⓓ
Federally funded lab	Ⓐ	Ⓑ	Ⓒ	Ⓓ
Library, museum	Ⓐ	Ⓑ	Ⓒ	Ⓓ
Independent research organization	Ⓐ	Ⓑ	Ⓒ	Ⓓ
Human services organization (social welfare, hospital)	Ⓐ	Ⓑ	Ⓒ	Ⓓ
International agency	Ⓐ	Ⓑ	Ⓒ	Ⓓ
Military service, active duty	Ⓐ	Ⓑ	Ⓒ	Ⓓ
U.S. government, civilian employee				
Civil service position	Ⓐ	Ⓑ	Ⓒ	Ⓓ
Other position	Ⓐ	Ⓑ	Ⓒ	Ⓓ
State government	Ⓐ	Ⓑ	Ⓒ	Ⓓ
Local/other government	Ⓐ	Ⓑ	Ⓒ	Ⓓ
Other nonprofit organization	Ⓐ	Ⓑ	Ⓒ	Ⓓ
Other	Ⓐ	Ⓑ	Ⓒ	Ⓓ

20. Indicate the kind of appointment or job security you have/had in:

(B) Previous position
(A) Present position
(Mark <u>one</u> in <u>each</u> column)

	A	B
Tenured	Ⓐ	Ⓑ
No tenure, but on tenure ladder	Ⓐ	Ⓑ
Acting/visiting	Ⓐ	Ⓑ
Seniority rights	Ⓐ	Ⓑ
Civil service tenure	Ⓐ	Ⓑ
Formal security arrangement	Ⓐ	Ⓑ
No formal security or seniority arrangements	Ⓐ	Ⓑ
Fixed-term contract (more than 2 years)	Ⓐ	Ⓑ
Short-term contract (2 years or less)	Ⓐ	Ⓑ
Other	Ⓐ	Ⓑ

21. Indicate the rank or level most closely representing your:

(B) Previous position
(A) Present position
(Mark <u>one</u> in <u>each</u> column)

	A	B
Executive	Ⓐ	Ⓑ
Manager	Ⓐ	Ⓑ
Administrator	Ⓐ	Ⓑ
Professional	Ⓐ	Ⓑ
Research scientist	Ⓐ	Ⓑ
Faculty	Ⓐ	Ⓑ
Technician	Ⓐ	Ⓑ
Supervisor	Ⓐ	Ⓑ
Clerical	Ⓐ	Ⓑ
Teacher (elementary, secondary)	Ⓐ	Ⓑ
Skilled/semi/unskilled worker	Ⓐ	Ⓑ
Other	Ⓐ	Ⓑ

22. What is your job title and the name of your employer for (A) your present <u>primary</u> position, (B) your present <u>secondary</u> position (if applicable), (C) your <u>previous</u> position, and (D) your first full-time job <u>after completing graduate school</u>? If self-employed, write "self" for employer.

(A) <u>Present primary position</u>

Job Title:

Employer:

City/State:

(B) <u>Present secondary position</u>

Job Title:

Employer:

City/State:

(C) <u>Previous primary position</u>

Job Title:

Employer:

City/State:

(D) <u>First full-time job</u>

Job Title:

Employer:

City/State:

23. What proportion of your working time is devoted to your present primary position?

○ Unemployed   ○ 26 – 50%   ○ 76 – 99%
○ 1 – 25%   ○ 51 – 75%   ○ 100%

24. To what extent do you think your doctoral training was appropriate? (If an item is not applicable, do not mark)

	Very much	Somewhat	Not at all
For your first job after advanced graduate study...	⑤ ④ ③ ② ①		
For your present (if not employed, most recent) job	⑤ ④ ③ ② ①		
For your first choice employment	⑤ ④ ③ ② ①		

25. How closely related was your graduate training to your present job?

○ Closely related ——→ Proceed to Question 28
○ Somewhat related ⎤
○ Not related   ⎦ ——→ Continue with Question 26

26. If your present job is only "somewhat" or "not related" to your graduate training, when did you move from your graduate field into this new field? (Write year in boxes and mark the circles)   19 [ ][ ]

⓪⓪ ①① ②② ③③ ④④ ⑤⑤ ⑥⑥ ⑦⑦ ⑧⑧ ⑨⑨

27. Why are you working in a job only "somewhat" or "not related" to your doctoral study? (Mark all that apply)

Never planned to take a closely related job. . . . . ○
Changed field to one I prefer more . . . . ○
Exposed to another field and became interested. . . . . ○
Prefer present work . . . . ○
First job unrelated to doctoral study; became
    interested in this work . . . . ○
Tried closely related employment, but did not like it . . . . . . ○
Joined family business or firm . . . . ○
Found job that offers better chance for career advancement . . ○
Pay is better where I am. . . . . ○
No longer in closely related job due to promotion. . . . . ○
Wanted part-time work, flexible hours . . . . ○
Wanted to work at home . . . . ○
Jobs related to doctoral study not available where I live, and
    do not want to move . . . . ○
Jobs related to my doctoral field not available. . . . . ○
Could not get a closely related job, but would prefer one . . . . ○
Limited in job selection by situation of spouse, family
    responsibilities. . . . . ○
Employment opportunities scarce for people in jobs related
    to my doctoral study . . . . ○
Have become technologically obsolete in field of doctoral study ○
In the military . . . . ○
Better quality work environment where I am . . . . ○

28. How satisfied are you with the following aspects of (A) your present job and (B) your previous job?

	(A) Present job					(B) Previous job				
	Very satisfied	Satisfied	Marginally	Not satisfied	Not applicable	Very satisfied	Satisfied	Marginally	Not satisfied	Not applicable
Overall job satisfaction	○	○	○	○	○	○	○	○	○	○
Salary and fringe benefits	○	○	○	○	○	○	○	○	○	○
Opportunity for scholarly pursuits	○	○	○	○	○	○	○	○	○	○
Opportunity for creativity	○	○	○	○	○	○	○	○	○	○
Opportunity to use training or schooling	○	○	○	○	○	○	○	○	○	○
Resources to get job done	○	○	○	○	○	○	○	○	○	○
Pressure to publish	○	○	○	○	○	○	○	○	○	○
Internal politics	○	○	○	○	○	○	○	○	○	○
Working conditions (hours, location)	○	○	○	○	○	○	○	○	○	○
Status	○	○	○	○	○	○	○	○	○	○
Autonomy and independence	○	○	○	○	○	○	○	○	○	○
Variety in activities	○	○	○	○	○	○	○	○	○	○
Policy-making power	○	○	○	○	○	○	○	○	○	○
Congenial work relationships	○	○	○	○	○	○	○	○	○	○
Competency of colleagues	○	○	○	○	○	○	○	○	○	○
Opportunities for different (better) jobs at this institution/organization	○	○	○	○	○	○	○	○	○	○
Visibility for jobs at other institutions/organizations	○	○	○	○	○	○	○	○	○	○
Challenge	○	○	○	○	○	○	○	○	○	○
Job security	○	○	○	○	○	○	○	○	○	○
Prestige of employer	○	○	○	○	○	○	○	○	○	○

29. What was your basic salary from primary employment, before taxes and deductions, for 1977? If self-employed, indicate your annual earned income after adjusting for business expenses. If married, what was your spouse's salary?

(Mark one on each line)

Categories: None, Less than $7,000, $7,000 – 9,999, $10,000 – 13,999, $14,000 – 16,999, $17,000 – 19,999, $20,000 – 24,999, $25,000 – 29,999, $30,000 – 34,995, $35,000 – 39,999, $40,000 – 49,999, $50,000 or more, Not married

Your salary . . . . ○ ○ ○ ○ ○ ○ ○ ○ ○ ○ ○ ○

Spouse's salary . . . . . ○ ○ ○ ○ ○ ○ ○ ○ ○ ○ ○ ○ ○

30. If you have other family income (e.g., income property, trusts, stocks, bonds), please indicate the range of expected supplemental income for 1977.

○ Less than $1,000
○ $1,000-$4,999
○ $5,000-$9,999
○ $10,000 or over

31. Considering your ability, education, and experience, which of the following statements apply in your current job? (Mark all that apply)

○ I am not underemployed
○ I am underemployed and would prefer a more challenging position
○ I am underemployed but for personal reasons I prefer to remain in this or a similar position
○ I am underemployed; my job is not in my field
○ I am underemployed; my job is not commensurate with my level of experience
○ I am underemployed; my job is not commensurate with my level of training
○ I am underemployed; my job is not commensurate with my level of ability
○ I have the skills and knowledge necessary for successful performance on my job
○ People with less formal schooling are performing well in jobs identical to mine
○ If people with less formal schooling were hired, they could do my job as well as I
○ I believe my present job is a nontraditional one for people in my PhD field
○ I have held other nontraditional jobs
○ I was employed full time for a period of time after receiving my bachelor's and before starting my PhD (or equivalent) program

32a. Did you enter graduate school expecting to become a college or university teacher?
○ Yes
○ No
○ Undecided at that time

b. Have you changed your occupation or career goal since entering graduate school?
○ Yes (Complete c and d.)
○ No (Proceed to Question 33.)

c. When did you change your occupation or career goal?
○ While in graduate school
○ At completion of graduate study
○ Within three years after completing graduate study
○ Three or more years after completing graduate school

d. If you have changed your career goal, indicate which of the following influenced the change. (Mark all that apply.)
○ Available teaching opportunities were limited or unattractive
○ Decided I did not enjoy teaching
○ Available job opportunities in previous field were limited or unattractive
○ Decided I did not enjoy first-choice career
○ Found more attractive or challenging job opportunities elsewhere
○ Changed career aspirations for personal or family reasons
○ Became outdated in my first-choice field
○ Became interested in different area of study
○ Was terminated in a job

33. How many years have you been (were you) employed full- and/or part-time?

(Mark one on each line)

Column headers: None, Less than one year, 1–3 years, 3–6 years, 6–10 years, 10–15 years, 15–20 years, 20–30 years, 30–40 years, More than 40 years

At your current job .... ○○○○○○○○○○
At your previous job .... ○○○○○○○○○○
At your first job after you received your highest degree .... ○○○○○○○○○○
In colleges and universities since you received your highest degree .... ○○○○○○○○○○
Total years employed since you completed your highest degree ...... ○○○○○○○○○○
In state government service..... ○○○○○○○○○○
In federal government service ... ○○○○○○○○○○

34. To what extent do the following statements apply to (A) your present job and (B) your previous job? (Mark all that apply)

	(A) Present job			(B) Previous job		
	Very much	Somewhat	Not at all	Very much	Somewhat	Not at all
I am well paid for my work compared with others with the same amount of education	○	○	○	○	○	○
I supervise people trained in my field	○	○	○	○	○	○
Most of my colleagues are trained in my field.	○	○	○	○	○	○
I am satisfied with my career progress to date.	○	○	○	○	○	○
My job offers good future prospects for further advancement	○	○	○	○	○	○
My job fits my long-range goals	○	○	○	○	○	○
My skills are fully utilized in my job	○	○	○	○	○	○
I am working at a professional level	○	○	○	○	○	○
I would have liked more training outside graduate school before I started working.	○	○	○	○	○	○
I received job training inappropriate for actual requirements of my job	○	○	○	○	○	○
I am glad I had the graduate education I did.	○	○	○	○	○	○
My position required on-the-job training ..	○	○	○	○	○	○

35. Looking back on your graduate education, please indicate the extent to which it was useful in the following ways: (Mark one on each line)

Column headers: Very useful, Somewhat useful, Not useful

Provided a skill that enabled me to get my first job. .... ○ .. ○ .. ○
Increased my chances of finding a good job ..... ○ .. ○ .. ○
Helped me choose my life goals .... ○ .. ○ .. ○
Gave me knowledge and skills that I use in present job .... ○ .. ○ .. ○
Graduate degree a factor in being hired by present employer .... ○ .. ○ .. ○
Graduate degree necessary for promotion ..... ○ .. ○ .. ○

36. To what extent did the following provide knowledge or skills that helped prepare you for your present job?
(Mark <u>one</u> on <u>each</u> line)

Graduate study

Column headers: Very much / Somewhat / Not at all / Not applicable

	Very much	Somewhat	Not at all	Not applicable
Particular course(s) in major area	○	○	○	○
Courses outside major area	○	○	○	○
Graduate study in general	○	○	○	○
Extracurricular activities while in graduate school	○	○	○	○
Research assistantship	○	○	○	○
Teaching assistantship	○	○	○	○

Other training

	Very much	Somewhat	Not at all	Not applicable
Undergraduate study	○	○	○	○
Formal training program at place of employment	○	○	○	○
Formal training or courses other than programs offered by employer	○	○	○	○
General on-the-job experience	○	○	○	○
Leisure activities	○	○	○	○

37. On the following list, mark each item that applies to A, B, C and D.
(Mark <u>all</u> that apply in <u>each</u> column)

(D) Improved significantly in graduate school ———
(C) Improved significantly in undergraduate school ——
(B) Useful in present job ———
(A) Your strong points, compared with those of others with the same education ———

	A	B	C	D
General knowledge	Ⓐ	Ⓑ	Ⓒ	Ⓓ
Ability to think clearly	Ⓐ	Ⓑ	Ⓒ	Ⓓ
Leadership ability	Ⓐ	Ⓑ	Ⓒ	Ⓓ
Critical thinking or analytical skills	Ⓐ	Ⓑ	Ⓒ	Ⓓ
Self-confidence	Ⓐ	Ⓑ	Ⓒ	Ⓓ
Self-discipline and ability to follow rules	Ⓐ	Ⓑ	Ⓒ	Ⓓ
Creativity and originiality	Ⓐ	Ⓑ	Ⓒ	Ⓓ
Writing ability	Ⓐ	Ⓑ	Ⓒ	Ⓓ
Insight	Ⓐ	Ⓑ	Ⓒ	Ⓓ
Cultural perspective	Ⓐ	Ⓑ	Ⓒ	Ⓓ
Understanding of others	Ⓐ	Ⓑ	Ⓒ	Ⓓ
Political awareness	Ⓐ	Ⓑ	Ⓒ	Ⓓ
Academic ability	Ⓐ	Ⓑ	Ⓒ	Ⓓ
Drive to achieve	Ⓐ	Ⓑ	Ⓒ	Ⓓ
Mathematical ability	Ⓐ	Ⓑ	Ⓒ	Ⓓ
Mechanical ability	Ⓐ	Ⓑ	Ⓒ	Ⓓ
Public speaking ability	Ⓐ	Ⓑ	Ⓒ	Ⓓ
Research skills	Ⓐ	Ⓑ	Ⓒ	Ⓓ

38. In light of your work experience, how important do you consider the following in providing better preparation for employment?
(Mark <u>one</u> on <u>each</u> line)

Column headers: Very important / Somewhat important / Not important

	Very important			Somewhat important	Not important
Early career counseling	⑤	④	③	②	①
Career counseling covering broad range of career alternatives	⑤	④	③	②	①
Assistance from graduate faculty in locating a suitable first job	⑤	④	③	②	①
Emphasis on communication skills in graduate courses	⑤	④	③	②	①
Supervised teaching experience while still a graduate student	⑤	④	③	②	①
Training in research skills	⑤	④	③	②	①
Specialized concentration in my subfield	⑤	④	③	②	①
Freedom to take courses outside major department	⑤	④	③	②	①
Personal initiative in selecting a broad range of elective courses	⑤	④	③	②	①
Better information about the future academic job market	⑤	④	③	②	①

39. Since completing graduate study, have you participated in any formal career-oriented programs (e.g., workshops, extension courses, programs outside your doctoral field) for the purpose of making or considering a career change?
○ Yes (Complete a, b, c.)
○ No (Proceed to Question 40.)

a. Indicate the type and duration of program. (If program fits into more than one category, select the category that best describes your motivation for taking the program.)
(Mark <u>not more than one</u> on <u>each</u> line)

Column headers: Less than 1 month / 1 to 6 months / More than 6 months

Program Type	Less than 1 month	1 to 6 months	More than 6 months
Program related to your job	○	○	○
Program related to new career field	○	○	○
Program related to your doctoral field	○	○	○

b. How many programs have you taken?
○ One
○ Two
○ Three
○ Four or more

c. How useful were their programs?

Very useful				Not useful
⑤	④	③	②	①

40. Are you currently engaged in any scholarly or research work that you expect to lead to publication?
○ Yes   ○ No

41. How many of the following have you produced since completing graduate study?
(Mark one on each line)

	None	1 or 2	3 to 5	6 to 10	11 or more
Scholarly book(s), single authorship	○	○	○	○	○
Scholarly book(s), joint authorship	○	○	○	○	○
Scholarly book(s), editor (not copy or production editor)	○	○	○	○	○
Other book(s)	○	○	○	○	○
Chapters/articles in scholarly books/journals	○	○	○	○	○
Articles in nonscholarly journals	○	○	○	○	○
Book reviews, editorials, abstracts, poems, other published short works	○	○	○	○	○
Published reports	○	○	○	○	○
Internal reports (unpublished) or article or monograph	○	○	○	○	○
Patentable inventions	○	○	○	○	○

42. Compared with others in your field and at your degree level, how much research/publication per year did you accomplish during:

	Great deal	Some	Little	None
First job after completing highest degree	○	○	○	○
Job prior to present position (if different)	○	○	○	○
Present position (if different)	○	○	○	○

43. Overall, how satisfied are you with:
(Mark one on each line)

	Very satisfied	Somewhat satisfied	Not satisfied
Life in general	○	○	○
Family life	○	○	○
Leisure activities	○	○	○
Quality of community cultural life	○	○	○
Social life	○	○	○
Geographic area in which you live	○	○	○
Future prospects	○	○	○

44. In securing your present job, which of the following job-search methods/contacts (A) did you use, and (B) were successful?
(Mark all that apply)

	(A) Used	(B) Successful
My former professors	○	○
Colleagues in my organization/institution	○	○
Colleagues in other institutions	○	○
College/university placement office	○	○
Public/state employment service	○	○
Private employment agency	○	○
Civil service application	○	○
Recruiting teams from government, industry	○	○
Professional contacts	○	○
Direct personal application to employer	○	○
Professional organizations, meetings	○	○
Newspaper advertisements	○	○
Professional journals, periodicals	○	○
Met new employer through previous job	○	○
Unsolicited offer	○	○
Parents/other relatives	○	○
Friends	○	○
Luck/chance	○	○

45. When you were offered your present position, were you actively seeking employment in the following areas: (Mark all that apply)

(E) Currently seeking position
(D) Received unsolicited offer
(C) Did not seek position
(B) Sought position, but no offer
(A) Sought position and received offer

Setting

	A	B	C	D	E
University/four-year college	Ⓐ	Ⓑ	Ⓒ	Ⓓ	Ⓔ
Two-year college	Ⓐ	Ⓑ	Ⓒ	Ⓓ	Ⓔ
Elementary/secondary school	Ⓐ	Ⓑ	Ⓒ	Ⓓ	Ⓔ
U.S. government, civilian employee					
Civil service position	Ⓐ	Ⓑ	Ⓒ	Ⓓ	Ⓔ
Other position	Ⓐ	Ⓑ	Ⓒ	Ⓓ	Ⓔ
State government	Ⓐ	Ⓑ	Ⓒ	Ⓓ	Ⓔ
Local/other government	Ⓐ	Ⓑ	Ⓒ	Ⓓ	Ⓔ
Other nonprofit organization (hospital, research institute)	Ⓐ	Ⓑ	Ⓒ	Ⓓ	Ⓔ
Private business/industrial firm	Ⓐ	Ⓑ	Ⓒ	Ⓓ	Ⓔ
Employment abroad	Ⓐ	Ⓑ	Ⓒ	Ⓓ	Ⓔ

Activity

	A	B	C	D	E
Faculty/teacher	Ⓐ	Ⓑ	Ⓒ	Ⓓ	Ⓔ
Administration	Ⓐ	Ⓑ	Ⓒ	Ⓓ	Ⓔ
Nonfaculty/nonadministrative position in academic institution	Ⓐ	Ⓑ	Ⓒ	Ⓓ	Ⓔ
Research/development	Ⓐ	Ⓑ	Ⓒ	Ⓓ	Ⓔ
Library, museum, archival work	Ⓐ	Ⓑ	Ⓒ	Ⓓ	Ⓔ
Sales/marketing/advertising/ public relations	Ⓐ	Ⓑ	Ⓒ	Ⓓ	Ⓔ
Accounting/data processing	Ⓐ	Ⓑ	Ⓒ	Ⓓ	Ⓔ
Other	Ⓐ	Ⓑ	Ⓒ	Ⓓ	Ⓔ

Field

	A	B	C	D	E
Major field of PhD	Ⓐ	Ⓑ	Ⓒ	Ⓓ	Ⓔ
Other field	Ⓐ	Ⓑ	Ⓒ	Ⓓ	Ⓔ

46. How many miles away is:
(Mark one on each line)

	In the same place	Under 50 miles	50 – 99 miles	100 – 499 miles	500 – 999 miles	1,000 – 2,999 miles	3,000 miles or more
Present or most recent job from hometown (where you attended high school)	○	○	○	○	○	○	○
Present job from institution of highest degree	○	○	○	○	○	○	○
Institution of highest degree from hometown	○	○	○	○	○	○	○
Present job from previous job	○	○	○	○	○	○	○

47. What was the highest level of formal education of your parents?

	Mother	Father
Less than 12th grade	○	○
High school graduate	○	○
Some college	○	○
Bachelor's degree	○	○
Master's degree	○	○
Doctorate or equivalent professional degree	○	○

48. Indicate the extent to which these statements apply to you. (Mark one on each line)

Columns: Strongly agree / Somewhat agree / Disagree somewhat / Strongly disagree

Statement	SA	SWA	DS	SD
I would take a job anywhere as long as there were opportunities to travel	○	○	○	○
If I were looking for a job now, I would look nationwide	○	○	○	○
There are a limited number of cities in which I would live	○	○	○	○
Climate would be a major factor in my decision to move.	○	○	○	○
I would take a job anywhere for a short period but I have specific preferences for permanent residence.	○	○	○	○
I would move anywhere if the salary were attractive enough	○	○	○	○
I would move anywhere for an extremely satisfying job	○	○	○	○
I will be more mobile when my children are out of school	○	○	○	○
My mobility is limited because my parents are alive.	○	○	○	○
My ideal job location is within 500 miles of the community where I grew up	○	○	○	○
My occupation severly limits my choice of geographic location	○	○	○	○
My mobility is limited because of spouse's job.	○	○	○	○
My mobility is limited because of spouse's educational plans.	○	○	○	○
My mobility is limited because of spouse's preferences about locale	○	○	○	○
If I could begin my career again, I would like to become a college professor	○	○	○	○
I could be equally or more satisfied with a different employer	○	○	○	○

49. (A) How important were each of the following job characteristics in your decision to choose your current job instead of your next best alternative, and (B) how important would each of these characteristics be in a decision to change jobs now? (Mark one on each line for A and B)

(A) Chosing current job: Very important / Somewhat important / Not important
(B) Changing jobs: Very important / Somewhat important / Not important

Job Characteristics	(A) Very	(A) Somewhat	(A) Not	(B) Very	(B) Somewhat	(B) Not
Congeniality of colleagues	○	○	○	○	○	○
Competency of colleagues	○	○	○	○	○	○
Reputation of employer among scholars	○	○	○	○	○	○
Administration and administrators	○	○	○	○	○	○
Research facilities and opportunities	○	○	○	○	○	○
Salary	○	○	○	○	○	○
Fringe benefits	○	○	○	○	○	○
Rank	○	○	○	○	○	○
Opportunities for outside income	○	○	○	○	○	○
Future salary prospects	○	○	○	○	○	○
Nearness to a graduate school	○	○	○	○	○	○
Nearness to friends and relatives	○	○	○	○	○	○
Climate	○	○	○	○	○	○
Cultural opportunities	○	○	○	○	○	○
Courses taught	○	○	○	○	○	○
Teaching load	○	○	○	○	○	○
Quality of students	○	○	○	○	○	○

50. How much of a salary increase, beyond that finally offered, would have induced you to stay on your previous job?
- ○ Less than $500
- ○ $500 to $999
- ○ $1000 to $1999
- ○ $2000 to $4999
- ○ $5000 to $9999
- ○ $10,000 to $24,999
- ○ $25,000 or more

51. What is your sex?
- ○ Male   ○ Female

52. Year of birth: ⟶ 19 [ ][ ]

53. Are you:
- ○ American Indian
- ○ Black/Negro
- ○ Mexican-American/Chicano
- ○ Oriental
- ○ Puerto Rican-American
- ○ White/Caucasian
- ○ Other Asian

Write year in boxes and mark the circles.

(grid: 0 0 / 1 1 / 2 2 / 3 3 / 4 4 / 5 5 / 6 6 / 7 7 / 8 8 / 9 9)

54. What is your marital status?
- ○ Single (never married)
- ○ Married
- ○ Separated, divorced, widowed

55. Number of children:
- ○ None
- ○ One
- ○ Two
- ○ Three or more

56. We would appreciate your name and address; it would be used only if a follow-up study were planned some years in the future.

Name _____

Organization _____

Street Address _____

City _____

State _____   Zip code _____

Thank you for your participation in this survey. Please return your questionnaire in the enclosed postage-paid envelope.

Appendix B:
A Methodological Note

This appendix is intended for those readers who may be unfamiliar with the tabular presentation of data and with the statistical techniques commonly used in survey research.

The Tables

The tables in the text are cross-tabulations, showing, for the most part, frequency distributions—that is, the proportions of respondents who select a particular alternative or who answer a question in a specified manner. People who failed to respond to a given item are excluded from the base (denominator) used in determining the proportion. For example, suppose a sample was composed of 100 people but only 94 of them answered the question "What is your marital status?" If 7 of those 94 respondents indicated that they were single; 78 indicated that they were married; and 10 indicated that they were widowed, separated, or divorced, then the reported frequencies would be 6.4 percent, 82.9 percent, and 10.6 percent, respectively. This approach avoids ascribing meaning to the fact that 6 people did not answer the question. (Did they inadvertently overlook the item? Did they feel that their marital status was nobody's business? Did they find the question too painful to answer?)

Cross-tabulation tables show responses subdivided by two or more classifying variables. In this report, the three main classifying variables are (1) field of the doctorate (biology, chemistry, physics, mathematics, civil engineering, electrical engineering, mechanical engineering, economics, political science, anthropology, psychology, sociology); (2) employment sector (academe, which is often subdivided into faculty and nonfaculty academics, government, the private sector); and (3) primary work activity (teaching, research, administration, other). In addition, some of the tables dealing with the dynamics of job change (chapter 5) classify respondents by path (type of job change, as defined by the employment sectors both of the previous job and of the current job) and by cohort (the period in which the doctorate was received: prior to 1965, between 1965 and 1970, and after 1970).

A cross-tabulation table shows a set of cells, with the total number of cells equal to the product of the number of categories listed in the stub (the vertical, or left, axis) and the number of categories shown in the column headings (the horizontal, or top, axis). For instance, table 1–7 shows the proportions of respondents indicating that they were very satisfied with their current jobs. The stub lists the twelve fields of the doctorate; the column headings show the three employment sectors, each further subdivided by the four primary work activities, for a total of twelve columns. Thus the total number of cells in the table is 144 (12 × 12). Many cells in this table are, however, blank (—), since a decision was made not to show the percentages for those cells with fewer than ten respondents. For example, fewer than ten respondents with doctorates in mathematics work as researchers in the private sector; thus, the proportion of this group expressing themselves as very satisfied with their current jobs is not shown, since the investigators felt that valid generalizations could not be drawn from so small a sample. The few mathematicians identified by the study as doing research in the private sector may simply be unrepresentative of all mathematicians holding such positions.

Cell-by-cell differences in frequencies can be considered from both a statistical and a conceptual standpoint. Let us suppose that the classifying variable used in a table is sex and that, according to the table, 25 percent of the men and 22 percent of the women are very satisfied with their jobs. Whether the difference of 3 percentage points is statistically significant will depend on the actual number of men and women selecting the ''very satisfied'' option. If the numbers involved are relatively large, then almost all reported differences will be statistically significant. For policymaking purposes, however, not all statistically significant differences can be regarded as conceptually significant. The 3-percentage-point difference in the example is too small to warrant advocating a policy of getting women into different types of jobs so that equal numbers of men and women will be very satisfied; the benefits probably would not be worth the costs. But if 50 percent of the men and only 25 percent of the women are very satisfied with their jobs, then the difference can be viewed as both statistically and substantively significant. In this case, one might be justified in advocating that ways be found to help women get jobs that are more satisfying. Clearly, a value judgment is needed in order to translate statistical differences into policy.

Although most of the tables show only percentages of respondents in various categories, table 1–3 shows absolute numbers of science and engineering Ph.D.'s engaged in different categories of primary work activities for different specific employer types in government and the private sector. In addition, table 1–4 shows the mean or average value for two variables (salary, year of doctorate) and table 5–4 shows the mean for year of the doctorate and for years on the current job.

Method of Analysis

The principal method of analysis used in this study was stepwise multiple regression, a statistical technique that allows the investigator to analyze simultaneously the independent effects of a large number of variables on a given outcome of interest (for example, income, career publication rate). The results of these regression analyses are summarized in the text, although no regression tables are included. (The interested reader may get copies of the regression tables by writing to the Higher Education Research Institute, Suite 835, 924 Westwood Boulevard, Los Angeles, California, 90024.)

To understand how regression analysis works, it is necessary first to understand correlational analysis in general. Measures of correlation reflect the degree of relationship or association between two variables. In other words, they indicate the extent to which the value of one variable changes at the same time that the value of another variable changes.

Variables are either continuous or dichotomous. *Continuous variables* are those that can take on a number of values (for example, income, years since receiving the doctorate); *dichotomous variables,* on the other hand, indicate that a condition either does or does not exist (for example, being male, having a doctorate in biology). Dichotomous variables are usually "scored" so that the existence of the condition is designated "2" and its absence is designated "1."

Two continuous variables are said to be positively correlated if, when one factor (say, years of education) increases, the other factor (say, income) increases as well. This positive correlation means that those people with more years of education tend to earn higher incomes. Two continuous variables are said to be negatively correlated if, when one factor (say, years at the current job) increases, another factor (say, job satisfaction) decreases. This negative correlation means that the longer one has worked at a given job, the less likely one is to be satisfied with that job; or, in other words, the more likely one is to be dissatisfied with the job.

In cases where one of the variables is dichotomous, a correlation is positive when the existence of one condition is associated with the other variable under consideration; the correlation is negative when the absence or nonexistence of the condition (or the existence of the opposite or antithetical condition) is associated with that other variable. Let us suppose that the condition designated "2" is graduation from a private (as opposed to a public) college and that the other variable under consideration is lifetime income. A positive correlation would mean that graduates of private colleges tend to make high lifetime incomes, relative to the lifetime incomes of public-college graduates. A negative correlation would mean that private-college graduates tend to make low lifetime incomes, compared with public-college graduates. Another way to express this negative correlation is to say that the lifetime incomes of public-college graduates tends to be higher than those of private-college graduates.

Cross-tabulation tables like those in this book can give a rough sense of correlation. If such a table shows that in all (or most) fields and across employment sectors, Ph.D.'s whose primary work activity is administration earn higher mean incomes than do Ph.D.'s whose primary work activity is teaching, research, or "other," then one can infer a correlation between administrative work and a relatively high income. Similarly, of cross-tabulations between employment sector and level of job satisfaction show that larger proportions of those working in the private sector than of those working in academe or government report that they are very satisfied with their jobs, then a correlation between private-sector employment and job satisfaction is evident.

A more-direct measure is provided by the zero-order correlation coefficient, designated r. The size of the coefficient can range from -1.00 to $+1.00$. The stronger the positive correlation between two variables, the closer the coefficient will be to $+1.00$; the stronger the negative correlation, the closer it will be to -1.00. When two variables are completely unrelated (for example, blood type and income), the coefficient will be 0.

One point must be emphasized: Correlation does not imply causation. That two variables A and B are correlated does not mean that A causes B. B may be the cause of A; or, more important, a third variable may be the cause of both A and B.

For example, because well-educated people generally make higher incomes than people with less education, it may seem that making a high income is the direct result of having more education or, more simply, that education causes a high income ($E \rightarrow I$). It is also true, however, that people with greater ability (A) tend to get more education than people with less ability ($A \rightarrow E$) and that highly able people, being more productive, tend to earn higher incomes than less-able people, regardless of education ($A \rightarrow I$). From these observations, two hypotheses about causal patterns emerge:

$$A \rightarrow E \rightarrow I; \text{ or} \qquad\qquad (1)$$

$$A \rightarrow E; \text{ and } A \rightarrow I; \qquad\qquad (2)$$

Hence, E is correlated with I because both are caused by A.

In either case, people with either more ability or more education, or both, make higher incomes. But to evaluate the actual effect of education on income, the effect of ability must be taken into account, or controlled for. The question then becomes, What effect does education have on income for two or more people of equal ability? In other words, what is the effect of education, netting out the effect of ability?

To answer such questions, some type of multivariate analysis such as multiple regression is required. In a multiple regression, one variable is designated the "dependent" or "outcome" variable; those variables assumed to have an effect on the outcome are designated the "independent" or "predictor" variables.

In effect, multiple-regression analysis is used to calculate the partial correlation coefficient (so called because the effects of the other independent variables have been partialed out) between each independent variable and the outcome variable. The result is a set of partial correlation coefficients; by comparing their relative sizes, the investigator can then determine the importance of each independent variable as an influence on the outcome under consideration or, in other words, its strength as a predictor of the outcome. For instance, in a regression where income is the dependent variable and ability and education are the independent variables, the partial correlation coefficient on ability indicates the correlation between ability and income when the effect of education is held constant; and the coefficient on education indicates the correlation between education and income when the effect of ability is held constant.

The great advantage of regression analysis is that it allows for more-comprehensive and more-accurate prediction (explanation) of the outcome under consideration than is possible through simple correlational analysis. The investigator can deal with a large number of independent variables simultaneously in order to discover which are indeed significant and which are unrelated to the outcome. Most standard statistical computer programs can take large sample data bases, perform multiple-regression analysis, and print out a set of standard satistical measures. (For a more-comprehensive explanation of regression analysis, and more particularly of how to read regression tables, see Solmon, Ochsner, and Hurwicz 1979, appendix C.)

References

American Council on Education. Staff of the Office of Research. *The American College Freshman: National Norms for 1971*. Washington, D.C.: American Council on Education, 1971.

Astin, A.W.; King, M.R.; and Richardson, G.T. *The American Freshman: National Norms for Fall 1978*. Los Angeles: American Council on Education and University of California at Los Angeles, 1979.

Atelsek, F.J., and Gomberg, I.L. *New Full-Time Faculty 1976–77: Hiring Patterns by Field and Educational Attainment*. Higher Education Panel Report no. 38. Washington, D.C.: American Council on Education, 1978.

Bayer, A.E. *Teaching Faculty in Academe, 1972–73*. ACE Research Reports, vol. 8, no. 2. Washington, D.C.: American Council on Education, 1973.

Becker, G.S. *The Economics of Discrimination*, 2d ed. Chicago: University of Chicago Press, 1971.

Bennett, J.T., and Johnson, M.H. *Demographic Trends in Higher Education: Collective Bargaining and Forced Unionism?* Los Angeles: International Institute for Economic Research, 1979.

Bolles, R. *What Color is Your Parachute? A Practical Manual for Job Hunters and Career Changers*. Berkeley, Calif.: Ten Speed Press, 1972.

Booth, W.C. "An Arrogant Proposal: A New Use for the Dyshumanities." *ADFL Bulletin* 9(1977):5–10.

Bowie, N.E. "Graduate Education and Non-Academic Careers." *Liberal Learning* 63(1977):220–229.

Breneman, D.W. "The Future of the Ph.D. in Language and Literature: An Economist's Perspective." Paper presented at the Modern Language Association Forum, Chicago, December 1977.

Brown, D.G. *The Mobile Professors*. Washington, D.C.: American Council on Education, 1967.

Bureau of Labor Statistics. *Ph.D. Manpower: Employment, Demand, and Supply, 1972–85*. Washington, D.C.: U.S. Government Printing Office, 1975.

Carnegie Commission on Higher Education. *College Graduates and Jobs: Adjusting to a New Labor Market Situation*. New York: McGraw-Hill, 1973.

Cartter, A.M. *Ph.D.'s and the Academic Labor Market*. A Report Prepared for the Carnegie Commission on Higher Education. New York: McGraw-Hill, 1976.

Cartter, A.M., and Solmon, L.C. "Implications for Faculty." *Change* 8(1976): 37–38.

Chemical Marketing Reports. 24 March 1980, p. 2.

Chomsky, N. *Aspects of the Theory of Syntax*. Cambridge, Mass.: MIT Press, 1965.

Cole, J.R., and Cole, S. *Social Stratification in Science*. Chicago: University of Chicago Press, 1973.

Commission of Human Resources. *Doctorate Recipients for U.S. Universities*. Summary Report 1978. Washington, D.C.: National Academy of Sciences, 1979a.

Commission on Human Resources. *Research Excellence Through the Year 2000: The Importance of Maintaining a Flow of New Faculty into Academic Research*. Washington, D.C.: National Academy of Sciences, 1979b.

Committee for Economic Development. *Stimulating Technological Progress*. New York: Committee for Economic Development, 1980.

Cooney, J.E. "The Gypsy Scholors." *Wall Street Journal,* 13 March 1979, pp. 30, 66, 69.

Dresch, S.P. "Educational Saturation: A Demographic-Economic Model." *AAUP Bulletin,* 61(1975):239–247.

Duffey, J. "Federal Government and the Humanities: The Role of the National Endowment." *Liberal Education* 64(1978a):90–93.

———. "Future of the Humanities: A Move Away from Professionalization." *Liberal Education* 64(1978b):182–189.

Frances, C. *College Enrollment Testing the Conventional Wisdom Against the Facts*. Washington, D.C.: American Council on Education, 1980.

Freeman, R.B. *The Market for College-Trained Manpower: A Study in the Economics of Career Choice*. Cambridge, Mass.: Harvard University Press, 1971.

———. *The Over-Educated American*. New York: Academic Press, 1976.

Gardner, E.J. "Ph.D. Degrees in a Changing Scene." In *Graduate Education Today and Tomorrow,* ed. L.J. Kent and G.P. Springer. Alburquerque: University of New Mexico Press, 1972.

Gardner, H. "Faculty in Jeopardy." *Nutshell,* Tenth Anniversary Issue, 1978–1979, pp. 85–92.

Gomberg, W. "Education and leisure: New Curricula." In *Education and Work: Two Worlds or One?* ed. *Change Magazine* New Rochelle, N.Y.: Change Magazine Press, n.d.

Goyne, G.C. "Career Opportunities and the Humanities Major: A Profile of Changing Needs." *College Student Journal* 11(1977):198–203.

Graduate Record Examination Board. *Report on the Council of Graduate Schools, Graduate Record Examinations Board: Survey of Graduate Enrollment 1971–1979*.

Haberly, D.T. "Marketing and Matchmaking: How Departments Can Help Students Find Jobs." *ADFL Bulletin* 9(1977):22–26.

Hernandez, D.J. "Review of Projections of Demand for Ph.D. Scientists and Engineers." In *Research Excellence Through the Year 2000,* ed. Commission on Human Resources.

Hope, Q.M. "The Current Need: More Jobs, Fewer Job Seekers." *ADFL Bulletin* 9(1977):18–21.

Hutchins, R.M. *The Higher Learning in America*. New Haven, Conn.: Yale University Press, 1978. (Originally published 1936.)

Inside R&D 9, 26 March 1980.

Jacobs, R.D. *The Useful Humanists: Alternative Careers for Ph.D.'s in the Humanities*. New York: Rockefeller Foundation, 1977.

Jonathan, R., and Cole, S. *Social Stratification in Science*. Chicago: University of Chicago Press, 1973.

Jones, J. " 'Transvaluing' or 'Value Expansion'? The Case of the Poetic Policemen." *Journal of Higher Education*, 47(1976):711–721.

Keller, P. "Despite Stories, Harvard's 'Core Curriculum' Is No Pedagogical Prop. 13." *Los Angeles Times*, 3 June 1979, part V, p. 3.

Kemerer, F.R., and Baldridge, J.V. *Unions on Campus*. San Francisco: Jossey-Bass, 1975.

Kidd, C.V. "Graduate Education: The New Debate." *Change* 6(1974):43–50.

Klitgaard, R.E. *The Decline of the Best? An Analysis of the Relationship Between Declining Enrollments, Ph.D. Production, and Research,* Discussion Paper Series no. 650. Cambridge, Mass.: John F. Kennedy School of Government, 1979.

Ladefoged, P. *Preliminaries to Linguistic Phonetics*. Chicago: University of Chicago Press, 1971.

Lawrence, B. "The Status and Prospects of the Humanities in Colleges and Universities." *Liberal Education* 64(1978):254–265.

Lee, C.B.T. "New Alliances Between Higher Education and the Non-Collegiate Sector: The Industry Perspective." Paper presented at the Conference on New Alliances Between Higher Education and the Non-Collegiate Sector, Princeton, N.J., January 1979.

Levi, A.W. *The Humanities Today*. Bloomington: Indiana University Press, 1970.

Levitin, T.E.; Quinn, R.P.; and Staines, G.L. "A Woman is 58% of a Man . . ." *Psychology Today* 6(1973):89–91.

Locke, E.A. "The Nature and Causes of Job Satisfaction." In *Handbook of Industrial and Organizational Psychology,* ed. M.D. Dunnette. Chicago: Rand McNally, 1976.

Mayhew, L.B., and Ford, P.J. *Reform in Graduate and Professional Education*. San Francisco: Jossey-Bass, 1974.

Mincer, J. "The Determination of Labor Incomes: A Survey with Special Reference to the Human Capital Approach." *Journal of Economic Literature* 8(1970):1–26.

National Center for Education Statistics. *Projections of Education Statistics to 1985–86*. Washington, D.C.: U.S. Government Printing Office, 1977.

National Center for Education Statistics. *Projections of Education Statistics to 1986–87*. Washington, D.C.: U.S. Government Printing Office, 1978.

National Research Council. *Summary Report 1967–1979 (separate volumes): Doctorate Recipients from United States Universities*. Washington: National Academy of Sciences, 1968–1980.

———. *Science, Engineering, and Humanities Doctorates in the United States: 1977 Profile*. Washington, D.C.: National Academy of Sciences, 1978.

———. *Research Excellence Through the Year 2000*. Washington, D.C.: National Academy of Sciences 1979.

National Science Foundation. *Projections of Science and Engineering Doctorate Supply and Utilization, 1980 and 1985*. Washington, D.C.: U.S. Government Printing Office, 1975.

———. *Detailed Statistical Tables: Manpower Resources for Scientific Activities at Universities and Colleges, January 1977*. NSF 77–321. Washington, D.C.: U.S. Government Printing Office, 1977.

———. *Hiring of Science and Engineering Faculty by Two- and Four-Year Colleges*. Science Resources Studies—Highlights NSF 78–309. Washington, D.C.: U.S. Government Printing Office, 26 June 1978.

———. *Projections of Science and Engineering Doctorate Supply and Utilization: 1982 and 1987*. Washington, D.C.: U.S. Government Printing Office, 1979.

Ochsner, N.L., and Solmon, L.C. *College Education and Employment: The Recent Graduates*. Bethlehem, Penn.: CPC Foundation, 1979a.

———. "Forecasting the Labor Market for Highly Educated Workers." *Review of Higher Education* 2(1979b):34–46.

Price, D. *Little Science, Big Science*. New York: Columbia University Press, 1962.

Reagor, A.S. "State of the Humanities." *Educational Record* 59(1978): 148–155.

Reskin, B.F. "Review of the Literature on the Relationship Between Age and Scientific Productivity." In *Research Excellence Through the Year 2000*, ed. Commission on Human Resources.

Scally, J. "Transvaluing: The Humanities in a Technical-Vocational Curriculum." *Journal of Higher Education* 47(1976):217–226.

Solmon, L.C. "The Definition of College Quality and its Impact on Earnings." *Explorations in Economic Research* 2(1975):537–587.

———. "Attracting Women to Psychology: Effects of University Behavior and the Labor Market." *American Psychologist* 33(1978):990–999.

———. "Ph.D.'s in Nonacademic Careers: Are There Good Jobs?" In *Current Issues in Higher Education: 1979*. Washington, D.C.: American Association for Higher Education, 1979.

Solmon, L.C.; Bisconti, A.S.; and Ochsner, N.L. *College as a Training Ground for Jobs*. New York: Praeger, 1977.

Solmon, L.C., and Ochsner, N.L. "Life After College: Differences Among Graduates." Paper presented at the Annual Meeting of the American Association for Higher Education, Chicago, 3 March 1978.

Solmon, L.C.; Ochsner, N.L.; and Hurwicz, M.L. "Jobs for Humanists." *Change* 10(1978):56–58.

―――. *Alternative Careers for Humanities PhDs: Perspectives of Students and Graduates*. New York: Praeger, 1979.

Stix, H. "San Mateo: Humanists in the Classroom." *Los Angeles Times,* 20 June 1979, part IV, pp. 1, 7, 8.

Sullivan, E.D. "Alternative Careers." *ADFL Bulletin* 9(1977):27–29.

Topf, M.A. "NEH and the Crisis in the Humanities." *College English* 37(1975): 229–242.

U.S. Department of Labor. *Job Satisfaction: Is There a Trend?* Manpower Research Monograph no. 30. Washington, D.C.: U.S. Government Printing Office, 1974.

Veblen, T. *The Higher Learning in America*. New York: Sagamore Press, 1957. (Originally published 1918.)

Wittgenstein, L. *The Blue and Brown Books*. New York: Harper and Row, 1958.

Woodruff, N. "On a Wing and a Prayer." *ADFL Bulletin* 9(1977):30–33.

Young, A.M. *Work Experience of the Population in 1977*. Special Labor Force Report no. 224. Washington, D.C.: Bureau of Labor Statistics, U.S. Department of Labor, 1979.

Zumeta, W. "The State and Doctoral Programs at the University of California: Academic Planning for an Uncertain Future." Ph.D. dissertation, Graduate School of Public Policy, University of California, Berkeley, 1978.

Index

About the Authors

Lewis C. Solmon received the B.Com. in 1964 from the University of Toronto and the Ph.D. in economics in 1968 from the University of Chicago. He is currently a professor in the Graduate School of Education at the University of California at Los Angeles, secretary/treasurer of the Higher Education Research Institute in Los Angeles, and president of the Human Resources Policy Corporation. In October 1978 he was selected by *Change* as one of the 100 young leaders of American higher education.

His books include *Economics; Does College Matter?; Male and Female Graduate Students: The Question of Equal Opportunity; Capital Formation by Expenditures on Formal Education, 1880 and 1890; College as a Training Ground for Jobs; Alternative Careers for Humanities PhDs;* and *The Characteristics and Needs of Adults in Postsecondary Education* (Lexington Books). He has published numerous articles in economics and education and has served on national advisory panels dealing with education and career development.

Laura Kent received the B.A. and the M.A. in English from the University of California at Berkeley, and studied in the Department of Interpretation at Northwestern University. She was an instructor in the Department of Speech at the University of California both at Berkeley and at Santa Barbara, and in the Department of English at Louisiana State University. Between 1965 and 1979, she was a free-lance editor and writer based in Washington, D.C., working for the American Council on Education, the Bureau of Social Science Research, the National Academy of Sciences, and other organizations chiefly concerned with higher-education research. Since 1979, Ms. Kent has been director of communications at the Higher Education Research Institute.

Nancy L. Ochsner received the B.A. in psychology from DePauw University, Indiana, in 1972, and the M.A. in education from the University of California at Riverside in 1975. Between 1975 and 1980, she was a research associate at the Higher Education Research Institute. Since 1980, Ms. Ochsner served as the assistant director in the Office of Planning and Research, New Jersey State Department of Higher Education, and as a research consultant for the American Society of Allied Health Professions, Washington, D.C. She coauthored *College as a Training Ground for Jobs, Alternative Careers for Humanities PhDs,* and several articles on the relationship of undergraduate and graduate education to career development.

Margo-Lea Hurwicz received the A.B. from Bryn Mawr College in 1972, and the M.A. from the University of California at Los Angeles (UCLA) in 1974, both in anthropology. She is currently completing her doctoral work at UCLA. From 1976 to 1979 Ms. Hurwicz was a research associate at the Higher Education

Research Institute where she was involved in several studies of the relationship between education and work, one of which resulted in a book titled *Alternative Careers for Humanities PhDs* which she coauthored. She is currently a research associate at the Neuropsychiatric Institute at UCLA where she is directing a research project on the typology of violent death, sponsored by the National Institute for Mental Health.

DATE DUE